A HISTORI
TO THE NEW TESTAMENT

Robert M. Grant is Professor of New Testament and early Christianity at the University of Chicago Divinity School

338. The Kingdom

ROBERT M. GRANT

A Historical Introduction
to the New Testament

Collins

THE FONTANA LIBRARY
THEOLOGY AND PHILOSOPHY

First published by William Collins Sons & Co Ltd, 1963
First issued in the Fontana Library, 1971
Second Impression November 1974

© Robert M. Grant 1963

Printed in Great Britain
Collins Clear-Type Press
London and Glasgow

PREFACE

Writing this book has taken a good deal of my energy and time since 1959, when it was suggested to me by Eugene Exman and Melvin Arnold. The most difficult part I found to be the expression of the principles of interpretation (Part I) and the attempt to co-ordinate them with what I had already learned about the New Testament. Obviously much remains to be done; I hope that others will do it.

I have argued repeatedly in the book that the New Testament cannot be understood apart from its context in the early Christian Church. This statement, of course, can be reversed. The early Church is incomprehensible unless one reads the New Testament – and I should add that, on a much lower level, the same thing can be said about this book. It is an introduction to the New Testament and is not intended to be a substitute for it.

The omission of practically all references to current literature on the New Testament is intentional. My views concerning modern American study in this field are set forth in an essay to appear under the auspices of the Ford Foundation Project in the Study of the Humanities, and generally speaking I have tried to set forth my own views without too much reference to those of others. Most of the statements about the New Testament which I read are based on presuppositions which usually are not stated. This book at least has the merit of stating the presuppositions, whether or not they are adequately worked out.

It would be wrong to hold my principal New Testament teachers responsible for anything in this book; but conscious and unconscious influences are hard to trace; and I should certainly not refrain from mentioning the debt I owe, for encouraging me in these studies, to my father and to my teachers at the Harvard Divinity School: H. J. Cadbury and A. D. Nock. The quality of their scholarship has inspired me for more than twenty years.

CONTENTS

Contents

Contents

Contents

INTRODUCTION

The purpose of this book is to deal with the New Testament (and other early Christian literature) as reflecting the historical life of the early Christian Church. This literature was produced in this Church, by members of this Church, for the use of this Church. The Church is the primary historical reality which stands behind the literature, and without the 'hypothesis' of the Church the literature does not make sense. The New Testament consists of twenty-seven heterogeneous books which were written at various times and under various circumstances; some of them were accepted and used by Christians almost at once, but as a whole the collection was not universally, or almost universally, accepted until the fourth or fifth century. It was the 'mind of the Church' which finally recognized the significance of all twenty-seven books as setting forth the basic statement of what the earliest Christianity was. No other literature has anything of value to say about Christian origins and the earliest Christian movement. To be sure, there are a few 'traditions' recorded in apocryphal writings or in the works of the Church Fathers, but their historical or theological importance is practically nil. In so far as they can be checked, they have to be checked in relation to the primary documents which the Church recognized.

At the same time, the primary documents are not self-explanatory, as Christians have recognized since very early times. In our present collection we find four gospels, a book of Acts, fourteen letters ascribed (with varying degrees of plausibility) to the apostle Paul, seven general or catholic letters, and a book of Revelation. This scheme of arrangement does little to indicate the meaning and significance of the various writings. In order to understand them, we must look for the history which stands behind the books. This is to say that we are trying to deal historically with the New Testament writings.

The central historical problems in relation to the New Testament can be defined in several ways, but before they can be approached we need to consider the periods into which early Church history can be divided. The question of periodization arose in the second century and has been examined by church historians ever since. Generally speaking, historians have differentiated three periods in the life of the early Church: (1) the period of the Incarnation, or the lifetime of Jesus of Nazareth; (2) the apostolic age, from the resurrection or the ascension to the reign of the emperor Nero; and (3) the sub-apostolic age, from Nero's reign to some later date, not usually defined with any clarity. The real significance of this periodization is to be found not in the periods of time involved but in the characteristics of the Church's life in the various periods and in the key events which mark the transitions from one age to another. In dealing with the characteristics and the events we must recognize that there were continuities and discontinuities; there was sameness and change. We must be on our guard against assuming too readily that either sameness or change was dominant. At the same time, we must remember that the community, usually conscious of its self-identity, was likely to lay more emphasis on continuity than can always be justified by the extant texts. The simple chronological periodization mentioned above may obscure significant changes related to the basic directions which the Christian movement took.

First we should say something about the primary elements which provided continuity. These were to be found in (1) the relation of Christian disciples to the Old Testament with its revelation of God and its proclamation of his future acts; (2) the relation of Christians to Jesus and the community which he brought into existence, and (3) their life of worship and mission in this community. Without these elements there would have been no Church and there would have been no New Testament. But, second, these elements were expressed in different ways because of the different historical circumstances in which Christians lived and in which they carried on the mission. Several of these historical circumstances can easily be identified. (1) The first disciples of Jesus were called in Galilee and accompanied him to Jerusalem; even though there are occasional indications that they moved outside Judæa and Galilee, their primary location was in this area; their mission was addressed to Palestinian Jews; Jesus himself, as Paul said (Rom. 15.8), was 'minister to the circumcision on behalf of God's truth'. It may even be possible, though the evidence is far from clear, to point to differences in emphasis between his proclamation in Galilee and that in Jerusalem. Certainly there are later differences between Galilean and Judaean Christianity. (2) There is also a difference between the life of the early Church in Jerusalem and the life of the gentile communities which gradually came into existence. This difference is reflected in Paul's account of the Jerusalem council (Gal. 2) and in the viewpoints set forth in the materials in Acts which describe events from the standpoints of Jerusalem and of Antioch. The difference is also present even within the Gospel of Matthew, with its two contrasting statements, 'Go not into a way of the gentiles, nor enter a Samaritan city' (10.5) and 'Go, make disciples of all nations' (28.19). (3) There are differences in the ways in which early Christians looked back at the life of Jesus of Nazareth. Not only are there differences between the Gospel of John and the synoptic gospels as a group; there are also differences between each synoptic gospel and the others and between each and John. To some extent these differences can be explained if we attempt to provide historical settings for the various books and relate them to the life of various kinds of community. (4) There is also a difference between the literature which is clearly apostolic and that which is less certainly so. The most obvious example is to be found in II Peter, with its mention of the Christian goal as sharing in the divine nature (1.4) and of entrance into the eternal kingdom of Christ (1.11). In II Peter the earlier idea of the kingdom as inaugurated by Jesus but still to come in power has disappeared. The future coming of Christ has been almost entirely neglected in favour of his past coming (1.16). Another example probably occurs in the Pastoral Epistles as a group. In them the primary emphases of the major Pauline epistles have been, so to speak, domesticated. They reflect the life of churches which live in relation to 'faithful sayings' and are concerned with organizational problems. (5) At the end of the New Testament period come the writings of the Apostolic Fathers, in which we see how the gospel and the life of the Church are being still further interpreted in relation to new environments and new circumstances. There is a difference between these writings and the earlier documents which cannot fully be explained simply in relation to their settings. In the writings of the Apostolic Fathers, as in II Peter and the Pastoral Epistles, the Church has almost become 'established' – not in relation to the State, but in some measure in relation to the various cultures of the Graeco-Roman world. This movement becomes more clearly defined as we move through the Jewish and gentile forms of Christianity in the early second century towards the works of the Apologists.

Our purpose in discussing the history of the New Testament is to see how the Church came into existence, what its life was like, and how it expressed its mission in relation to the various environments in which it lived. Our starting point and our ending point will be the same: the Church as the congregation of believers brought into existence in response to the event of Christ. This event includes his ministry in Galilee and Jerusalem and his crucifixion, but it finds its climax in his resurrection, which can be defined as the creation of the new community. Even though Luke, like the later Gnostics, set an interval between the resurrection and the origin of the Church, such an interval is nowhere reflected in the Pauline epistles, and we may suppose that it is due to an attempt to provide historical periodization at a point where it is not really useful. The Church is the resurrection community; the apostles were apostles of the risen Lord.

Our purpose in dealing with the materials provided by the New Testament and other early Christian literature is not, however, simply to make affirmations or pronouncements about them. It is to deal with these materials in a sober and cautious manner in order to show what is actually known, what is actually not known, and how we can perhaps proceed from the known to the unknown. This is not to suggest that the documents or their contents will somehow miraculously arrange themselves in order to prove our points. There is a kind of dialogue between ourselves and the materials, a dialogue in which we do not lose our own subjectivity although we may hope that it will be modified by what the materials say. We do not necessarily or entirely become 'objective'; but we check our own subjectivity in the light of the subjectivities of those who created and transmitted the materials and (it may be) in the light of others farther back in the chain of tradition. This kind of checking is what one can hope to acquire by means of critical methods.

But before we can turn to the conclusions we hope to reach, we must look at the materials themselves; and before we can look at the materials we must consider the various methods which can be used in looking at them. At this point we therefore turn to the methods used in analysing the New Testament and early Christian literature as a whole, examining these methods in order to make sure that they will bear all the weight that has often been placed on them. To a considerable extent our analysis will seem negative. This negative aspect is certainly present, but it is present for a purpose. We hope that by criticizing criticism we can make it a more useful and effective instrument for proceeding to positive conclusions about the early Christian writings as reflections of the life of the early Church.

THEORY OF INTERPRETATION

Perhaps it may seem odd to begin an introduction to the New Testament with a discussion of the principles to be employed. Are they not either self-evident or so abstruse as to defy explanation? Doesn't everyone employ the historical method, based on enlightened common sense, while some scholars employ it better than others because they are so acute? The answers to these questions must be negative. What characterizes a great deal of modern New Testament study is (1) an inadequate historical method and (2) a rather excessive confidence in those who employ it with sufficient acuteness. These characteristics are no substitute for a carefully-thought-out method which bears a closer relation both to common sense and to historical experience.

The principles will be discussed in the following sequence. (1) We shall deal with the New Testament in the Church in order to determine what the New Testament consists of and how and why it was collected in a canon or authoritative anthology of books. (2) Next we shall consider the transmission of the text of the New Testament and the analytical procedure used in determining (a) the relations of various texts to one another and (b) the textual readings which are probably more original than others. Consideration of the text will lead us to investigate the nature of translations made from the text or texts into other languages. (3) Since understanding a text involves more than a word-by-word translation, we must investigate the ways in which the literary structure of an author's work can be analysed, and try to see what this analysis contributes to our interpretation. (4) In so far as the New Testament documents are related to historical events and historical circumstances, they are subject to historical criticism; but historical criticism deserves much more criticism than it has received in recent New Testament work. (5) Finally, the New Testament writers wrote for a purpose or for purposes which have to be examined by a method which we venture to call both historical and theological.

It is obvious that in setting up this method of analysis we have laid great emphasis on what may perhaps be regarded as a 'phenomenological' approach. We are concerned with what the New Testament authors said, how they said it, and why they said it. This kind of understanding tends to minimize the importance of two other possible approaches. (1) There is what is sometimes called the theological approach, in which the New Testament books are examined for what they have to say, explicitly or implicitly, systematically or unsystematically, to *us*. Our reason for not following this line is that we believe that by undertaking to find out what the New Testament writers said in their own time we may achieve two purposes: (a) we may be able to safeguard our interpretation from an excessive degree of subjectivity and may thereby reach conclusions which can be more generally accepted within the double context of the culture and the Church within which we live and (b) similarly, we may be better able to do justice to the rich complexity which in our opinion characterizes the writings; we shall not be so strongly tempted to search for, or to claim that we have found, a single theological key to all doors, or a single axe to grind. (2) On the other hand, there is what is often regarded as 'the' historical approach, in which the New Testament writings are co-ordinated with what is understood to be their environment

and the result of this co-ordination is used to show the extent
to which the writers were 'historically conditioned'. We are not
emphasizing this approach for two reasons: (*a*) the co-ordination
is highly subjective and to a considerable extent involves the
explanation of the known (the New Testament writings) by the
unknown (their precise environment or environments) and
(*b*) we do not share the view of those who believe that items
which can be correlated with the ancient environment(s) can or
must, for that very reason, be relegated to the dustbin.

Our major emphasis, therefore, will be laid upon the interpretation of the New Testament books themselves, more or less as
they stand, and the method (in theory, at least) primarily
involves literary and historical analysis of them.

I do not claim that there is anything unique about this method.
On the contrary, I have come to believe that it would be
positively wrong to apply a special method of interpretation to
the New Testament. (1) If the New Testament literature is
actually different from other literature, this fact can best be shown
by applying a common method. (2) In so far as the New Testament
literature is literature, it can best be investigated by using a
common method. (3) In so far as the New Testament, theologically and historically considered, reflects the revelation of
God in his incarnate Son, similar observations should be made;
both the divine nature and the human nature (to speak with
fourth-century symbols) can be best approached if we are using
normal literary-historical methods by means of which the
difference between God and man, and the action of man as man,
can be understood. This is to say that in my view a direct and
immediate understanding of the New Testament as either
'spiritual' or 'existential' (in so far as either term is understood
as atemporal) is analogous to the docetic understanding of Christ
as a purely spiritual being. Just as the Incarnation involves
acceptance of the categories of time and space, so the New
Testament is a collection of books created in time and in space,
and it therefore needs to be considered by means of a method
which takes these categories seriously. The uniqueness of the
New Testament, then, becomes clear if, and only if, we use a
method which is not unique.

At the same time, we should probably point out that not

everything in the New Testament is unique. There are words, phrases, forms and ideas which are also to be found in Judaism or in Graeco-Roman culture. Our method must pay some attention to these features of the New Testament; it need not, and indeed must not, neglect them. We have already intimated why this is so. The revelation of God in the New Testament is not confined to the unique items. The Christian claim about Jesus Christ is not that his message was absolutely novel but that it was true. Indeed, the notion that the unique is the revealing was advocated in ancient times not by orthodox Christians but by the dualist New Testament critic Marcion.

We are trying to deal with our subject matter by use of a method at least relatively logical, for in our view such exegesis of the New Testament has suffered from its lack not of theological but of logical method. This is the reason for which we begin with the canon. If we are going to study certain literary phenomena, it is well to have some idea of the basis on which we regard these phenomena as belonging to much the same class. For instance, one might think of the New Testament books as 'Christian classics'; but to classify them as classics would not quite adequately differentiate them from Augustine's *Confessions*, the *Summa Theologica*, or *Concluding Unscientific Postscript*. If we are going to consider something called the New Testament, we need to know what the New Testament is. Now in order to answer this question we can do one of at least two things. We can immediately appeal to authority and say that the New Testament is what the Church, or our particular church, says it is. In the modern world, however, as Hannah Arendt has pointed out, such direct appeals to traditional authority are not as convincing as they once were. People are all too likely to ask why the Church regards these books, and not others, as belonging to the approved list or canon. We are therefore driven, as we so often are, towards a second method – to examine the evidence concerning the canon.

But before we turn to this evidence we should have a few questions in mind. What are we going to look at the evidence for? What do we think we are going to find? Are we going to find that original authentic something which can serve as a norm for our own conclusion, on the view that the earliest is the best? Are we going to say that the history will help us see how the present situation came into existence and therefore, in a way, justify it? Or are we going to examine a process in the course of which the Church reached certain conclusions which, though possessing great weight, are not necessarily infallible? Perhaps we should simply raise these questions without attempting to answer them at this point.

PART I

Prolegomena

I

WHAT THE NEW TESTAMENT CONSISTS OF – THE CANON

The New Testament canon consists of those books which the Church came to regard as definitive expressions of its faith and life as set forth in the earliest period of its existence. The books were written by apostles or by disciples of the apostles, though the question of authorship is not especially significant; the Church itself was the Church of the apostles.

The existence and the nature of the canon thus implies the existence of the Church. This is to say that without the Church there would be no New Testament. Just as the New Testament expresses the response of the apostles and their disciples to Christ, so the Church expresses the same response; but the New Testament is the product of the Church while the Church is not the product of the New Testament. The Church could have proclaimed, and in fact did proclaim, the gospel without possessing the New Testament; but the New Testament could not have come into existence apart from the Church.

Indeed, Helmut Koester has cogently argued that several of the Apostolic Fathers (the earliest Christian writers outside the New Testament) did not even make use of written gospels. Instead, they relied upon oral traditions of the same sort as those recorded by the evangelists. This means that these early Fathers differ from the evangelists in the degree of their closeness to the earliest traditions, not in the kind of relationship to them. The proximity was recognized in the early Church by those who treated the writings of the Apostolic Fathers as scripture or called their authors 'apostolic men' (*apostolici*). Later on, however, it was recognized that the concerns of the Apostolic Fathers were primarily related to the second century, those of canonical writers to the first. On some basis like this the Apostolic Fathers were excluded from the canon. But it is evident that a very sharp dividing line could not and cannot be drawn, except in so far as the New Testament writings reflect the apostolic age as later writings do not.

In dealing with the canon of the New Testament we must begin with some rather negative statements. First, the earliest Christian Bible was not, and did not include, the New Testament. Instead, it was the Old Testament, usually read in Greek, and often interpreted in the light of a number of apocalyptic documents which were not generally recognized as canonical. Thus the Epistle of Jude contains a quotation from the apocalypse of Enoch and an allusion to a strange lost book known as the Assumption of Moses. Until the middle of the third century, Christian writers often regarded these documents as authoritative. The reason for regarding the Old Testament itself as canonical scripture was, of course, that Jesus and his apostles had so regarded it; they had believed that in Jesus the Old Testament, viewed primarily as prophecy, had been fulfilled. Second, no New Testament as such came into existence for several centuries after the beginning of the Christian movement. At an earlier time there were oral traditions, along with books of varying authoritativeness; but there was no New Testament.

It is a little hard to tell just at what point the idea that Christian documents were scriptural arose. If we can make a distinction between documents and their contents, we can say that the contents were always authoritative, though the form in which they were expressed was not quite so important. For instance, Paul clearly regards his own letters as important and expects that what he says will be heeded; but he does not speak of them as scriptural. On the other hand, when the apostolic council at Jerusalem sends out an encyclical letter, this letter is hard to differentiate from its contents; and the decree which it contains begins with the words, 'It seemed good to the Holy Spirit and to us.' Similarly, the Revelation of John is really a revelation of Jesus Christ through his angel to John; it contains a blessing upon those who 'keep' what is written, and a curse upon those who add to or subtract from its contents. Clearly the author of Revelation regards his book as the equivalent of scripture; and the equivalent of scripture is scripture.

If we look for some early Christian writer to whom the Pauline epistles have come to be scripture, we can find him in the author of II Peter. II Peter 3.15–16 says that we are to regard the forbearance of the Lord as salvation – 'as our beloved brother Paul, in accordance with the wisdom given him, wrote to you – as in all the epistles speaking about these matters – epistles in which there are some things hard to understand, which the ignorant and unsteady pervert, as they do the other scriptures, to their own destruction.' The remarkable thing about this sentence is not only its loose syntax but its implicit meaning: (1) the Pauline epistles are regarded as addressed just as generally as II Peter itself is; (2) they have been collected and are regarded as scripture; and (3) among them are the Pastoral Epistles, for the forbearance of the Lord as leading to salvation is mentioned in I Timothy 1.15–16. By this time – whatever the time is – the Pauline epistles have formed at least the nucleus of a New Testament.

Of course we cannot be certain that the 'development' of the canon took place everywhere in the same way at the same time. We do not know enough to say more than that it is possible that (1) within the first century all Christians viewed the gospels and epistles as authoritative; (2) only occasionally did they speak of them as scripture; and (3) the presence or absence of the word 'scripture' is partly due to chance.

If we are willing to limit our inferences in this way, we shall perhaps not find Marcion as striking a figure as church historians have often made him to be. It is true that Marcion, expelled from the Roman church in 144, rejected the authority of the Old Testament and for it substituted three volumes of his own: (1) the *Antitheses* (a collection of Old Testament passages which he found contradicted in the Pauline epistles, in Luke, or – sometimes – even in Matthew); (2) the *Gospel* (that according to Luke, but freed from what he regarded as interpolations; and (3) the *Apostle* (ten relatively non-Jewish letters of Paul). Marcion was impressed by the newness of Christianity and he wanted to cut it loose from its connection with the Old Testament and Judaism. He admired Paul as the one apostle who really understood Jesus, and Luke as the one disciple who really understood Paul's gospel about Jesus. He therefore rejected the other gospels then in circulation, as well as a good deal of Luke, which he viewed on literary grounds – of some sort – as interpolated into the authentic document.

Scholars have sometimes thought that Marcion created the canon of the New Testament. Certainly he gave impetus to the tendency to produce a list of authoritative books from which those without authority were to be excluded. But it is likely that we should give him credit not for the idea of a canon but for the inclusiveness of the canon which the Church did produce. There are second-century analogies to his work and its effect. For instance, before the rise of Valentinian Gnosticism, Christological doctrine was not always carefully formulated; afterwards, Christian authors expressed their ideas more carefully. We should assume that Marcion, then, did not so much formulate a canon as compel more orthodox Christians to use more carefully the authoritative books which they already possessed.

Even before Marcion's time we encounter Christian interest in the origins of New Testament books. Papias of Hierapolis tells us about Mark's intention of preserving all the traditional materials he knew, as well as about Matthew's compilation of 'the dominical oracles', whatever they may have been. It is sometimes suggested that Papias's correlation of Mark with the apostle Peter was due to his reading of I Peter, where Mark is mentioned as Peter's 'son'. We know that Papias knew I Peter. But what we do not know is that in speaking of Mark as Peter's interpreter Papias was restricted to what he could get out of this epistle. Presumably there were a few Christians who could tell what had actually happened. This interest in historical fact may not have been the chief concern of early Christians; it was a real concern, however.

Actually, when we compare Marcion's ideas with those of Papias and other contemporary Christians, it can be said that for the first time we encounter the problem which has constantly recurred in Christian history. On the one hand, there is the rather matter-of-fact Papias with his rather simple notions about the work of the evangelists as recorders or compilers; on the other, there is Marcion, with his view that the work of the evangelist Luke had been interpolated by ingenious advocates of Jewish

Christianity. The true and authentic gospel, in Marcion's view, was to be recovered only by deleting from the Gospel of Luke those passages which the Judaizers had added. Now if one were to ask Marcion, 'How do you know that these passages are interpolations?' he would tell you that the answer is rather complex. First there was the authentic, non-Jewish gospel of Jesus, not written but transmitted – and corrupted – by the Jewish apostles. Then, since this gospel was already being corrupted, there was a reiteration of this gospel in the teaching of the apostle Paul. One might suppose that Paul was not altogether hostile to Judaism; but this idea, Marcion would claim, is due to the form in which the Pauline letters were transmitted. They too were interpolated by Judaizers. Only Marcion had been able to recover that true, authentic gospel of Jesus and Paul which was to be found in his – i.e. Marcion's – writings.

The difference between Marcion and more orthodox Christians was not simply that he was more dualistic than they were; it was that he insisted upon a uniform theological view to be derived from his picture of Jesus and his picture of Paul, while the others were willing to face the difficulties presented by a much more complex picture of both. Around this time such Christian writers as the apologist Justin were speaking of the gospels as 'reminiscences of the apostles' and recognizing four of them – two by apostles, two by disciples of apostles. Justin did nothing to solve the difficulties raised by the existence of various gospels, but at least he was willing to take the risk involved. Similarly, other Christians were accepting not only the Pauline letters which Marcion had recognized but, in addition, four more – to the Hebrews, to Timothy, and to Titus. It is not necessary for us, and as we shall see it was not necessary for early Christians, to maintain that all of these were actually written by Paul. We can now see that when they were included with the other, more genuine Pauline letters, one result was that just as Jesus could not be pin-pointed (since there were four gospels), so Paul could not be pin-pointed either. A Marcion could not say that 'just exactly this and this is what Paul taught' and proceed to construct a dynamic but thoroughly one-sided theology. The inclusiveness of the early Christian canon, as it was coming into existence, meant that Christian theology had to be inclusive too.

To be sure, sometimes the orthodox became alarmed when minority groups made use of one or another of the canonical books, and they were tempted to remove them from the canon. For instance, Montanus, founder of the 'new prophecy' in the middle of the second century, taught that he himself was the Paraclete promised in the Gospel of John. Christian critics then compared John with the synoptics and denied its apostolic origin. Their view, however, was not widely accepted. The Church as a whole resisted the temptation to shrink the canon because of the use being made of some parts of it.

On the other hand, there were limits beyond which inclusiveness could not go. The second century saw the production of apocryphal gospels, acts, epistles and apocalypses, usually written in the names of various apostles and almost always reflecting special points of view. Christians hesitated to reject such works if they were close to books regarded as canonical. In the case of such a treatise as the Gospel of Thomas, recently recovered in a Coptic version, they did not hesitate at all. They could recognize that everything in this gospel, no matter how close it might seem to be to authoritative tradition, had been given a special Gnostic twist.

By the end of the second century there was no longer any question about the core of the New Testament, at least among those writers who in their time and later were regarded as orthodox Christians. There were four gospels, neither more nor less. To be sure, the arguments of Irenaeus (*c.* 180) on this subject are not very convincing. He says there should be four because there are four beasts in the Apocalypse and because there are four corners of the earth. But the very weakness of the argument – to us – may suggest that it was not really necessary to prove the point. Again, in the writings of Irenaeus we encounter the first extensive use of Acts and the Pastoral Epistles. When these books were used, a more balanced picture of Paul and of the early Church could be drawn; it was not necessary to rely solely on Romans and Galatians, and to fall into the jaws of Marcion. Because a more inclusive New Testament was being used, it was possible to produce a more inclusive theology, one which took into account the materials and viewpoints provided in such books as I Peter and I John and Revelation. Irenaeus made considerable use of

Revelation and reported that the visions were seen by John 'practically in our own times, towards the end of Domitian's reign'. In his view, therefore, the New Testament reflected a wide range of Christian insight, even in regard to time, for it included a book written at the very end of the first century. In addition, Irenaeus regarded the *Shepherd* of Hermas (certainly) and I Clement (possibly) as scripture. The fact that he neither mentioned nor alluded to James, Jude and II Peter, then, suggests that he did not know them, for he wanted as wide a range of books as possible, though within the limits of the apostolic faith.

Irenaeus's silence about these books, and his problematic use of Hebrews, brings us to consider the varying views held about Hebrews, the Catholic epistles, and the book of Revelation in the early Church.

HEBREWS

The 'canonical' history of Hebrews is somewhat confused by the fact that while it was used by many early Christian writers, some of them were aware that as it stands it cannot have been written by the apostle Paul (see Chapter XIV). We first encounter clear traces of Hebrews in the letter of Clement to the Corinthians, written at the end of the first century; but Clement does not say what he is quoting from. On the other hand, the teaching of the Roman Hermas (early second century) contradicts that of Hebrews, and Hermas therefore cannot have regarded the letter as absolutely authoritative.

The views of Irenaeus (*c.* 180) are not altogether clear. He certainly alludes to Hebrews (1.3) when he says that the Father created everything 'by the Word of his power' (*Adv. haer.* 2, 30, 9); but this is the only clear allusion in his writings, and he speaks of the Christian 'altar in the heavens' (4, 18, 6) in such a way as to show that he is not relying on what Hebrews has to say on the subject. According to Eusebius (*H. E.* 5, 26) he made use of Hebrews in a book of 'various discourses'; according to Stephen Gobarus (sixth century) he held that Paul did not write the letter. This was also the Roman view: Hebrews is absent from the Muratorian list and was not accepted by Hippolytus, Gaius or Novatian. It was also the African view. Tertullian quoted Hebrews only once and ascribed the quotation to Barnabas (*De pudic.* 20). Indeed, the first Western writer to regard Hebrews as canonical was Hilary of Poitiers (d. 367).

On the other hand, Hebrews was highly valued at Alexandria and elsewhere in the East. Pantaenus (late second century) argued that Paul wrote it anonymously because he was addressing Hebrews who might be suspicious of him. This theory does not explain the stylistic differences between Hebrews and the Pauline epistles, and Clement therefore suggested that Paul wrote the letter in Hebrew while Luke translated it into Greek. Origen further developed this view by maintaining that either Luke or Clement of Rome – both, in Origen's opinion, disciples of Paul – relied on Paul's ideas but expressed them in his own style and provided his own arrangement. Origen was unwilling to reach a definite conclusion. Only God, he said, really knew who wrote Hebrews. This lack of precision is reflected in Origen's writings. In addressing another scholar he criticized those who 'reject the epistle as not written by Paul', but in his own treatises he sometimes ascribed the letter to Paul and sometimes did not. Later Eastern writers regarded the letter as Paul's.

There was considerable confusion in the West at the end of the fourth century. Philastrius of Brescia (d. 397) regarded Hebrews as written by Paul but not canonical; on the other hand, African synods held in 393 and 397 accepted the canonicity of 'thirteen letters of the apostle Paul' and 'of the same, one to the Hebrews', thus maintaining a distinction without a difference. Augustine quoted Hebrews as Paul's in what he wrote before 409, but after that year he cited it simply as 'the Epistle to the Hebrews'. He may have been influenced by Pelagius, who published his commentary on the Pauline epistles about this time and did not include Hebrews among them. Considerations of simplicity seem finally to have carried the day, for a council held at Carthage in 419 spoke of 'fourteen letters of the apostle Paul', and thereafter the question was not discussed.

CATHOLIC EPISTLES

In the earliest period for which we have evidence – the second century – Christian writers made use of only I Peter and I John (though II John was sometimes treated as part of I John). This usage is reflected in the third century by Hippolytus, Novatian and Cyprian, and by Origen, who mentions doubts about other Catholic epistles but not about these (so also Eusebius in the early fourth century). Still later, only these two Catholic epistles were accepted by Diodorus of Tarsus (d. *c*. 394) and Nestorius (d. 451). The Cheltenham list, reflecting North African usage about 360, goes somewhat beyond early practice by including I–II Peter and I–II–III John.

The Muratorian list (*c*. 200) includes Jude and I–II John; it says that 'some among us wish to have the Revelations of John and Peter read', but makes no mention of I Peter. On the other hand, both Clement and Tertullian, writing at about the same time, accept Jude, I Peter, and I–II John.

A much more complete list can be derived from the writings of Origen, who accepted all seven Catholic epistles but expressed his doubts about James, Jude, and II Peter, as did his admirer Eusebius. Most of the Greek writers of the fourth century, however, had no doubts about any of the letters, and their view came to be current in East and West alike, except in Syria.

The Syrian view, a reaction against the growth of the canon, is reflected in the *Doctrine of Addai* and the writings of Aphraates and Ephraem, all in the mid-fourth century. According to it none of the Catholic epistles was acceptable, and the same opinion was expressed in a canon list about 400 and in the writings of Theodore of Mopsuestia (d. 428). Even in the sixth century the Greek traveller Cosmas Indicopleustes shared this view.

A mediating position was held by John Chrysostom, patriarch first of Antioch and later of Constantinople (d. 407) and by Theodore's pupil Theodoret (d. 458): the Catholic letters were James, I Peter, and I John. The same view is reflected in the Syriac version known as the Peshitto and is mentioned by Cosmas.

REVELATION

The Revelation of John was highly regarded by nearly all the second-century writers whom we know, although when the Montanists used it in support of their ideas about the imminent coming of the kingdom, some Christians in Asia Minor and at Rome tried to get it rejected. In the East, Clement of Alexandria and Origen accepted it as canonical; Origen 'demythologized' it by treating it allegorically. His disciple Dionysius found the book hard to deal with, since millennarians were making use of it. He therefore analysed it by means of literary criticism, noting the differences in style, vocabulary and thought between it and the Gospel and 'the Epistle' of John. The literary differences proved that two authors were involved, and since the apostle John wrote the Gospel, Revelation was written by someone else. He was willing to retain Revelation in the canon. He claimed, however, that since its author was not an apostle his work therefore did not possess the apostolic authority of the Gospel of John. Similarly, Dionysius would probably have said that Hebrews was inferior to the Pauline epistles and Mark and Luke to Matthew and John. This kind of distinction means that an 'apostolic' canon is being set up within the New Testament canon. All New Testament books are authoritative, but some are more authoritative than others. Not all Christians were willing to make such subtle analyses. In the fourth century, Revelation was rejected by all Eastern writers outside Alexandria; West Syrian writers did not accept it until the fifth century; East Syrians, as far as I know, never accepted it. Even in the ninth century, many Greek-speaking Christians still had doubts about the book.

OTHER BOOKS

We have thus seen that in the cases of Hebrews, the Catholic epistles, and Revelation, there was a long process of hesitation which preceded acceptance. In other words, for many Christians as late as the fourth and fifth centuries the New Testament was considerably smaller than ours is. On the other hand, especially at Alexandria a good many books were read in the early days which later were not regarded as belonging to the New Testament. Books which we usually classify as among the Apostolic Fathers were especially prominent, usually because they were regarded as written by persons mentioned in the New Testament. Thus Clement regarded the *Didache* or Teaching of the Apostles as scriptural; both he and Origen viewed the author of *I Clement* as the Clement mentioned by Paul in Philippians 4.3 and the author of the *Shepherd* as the Hermas of Romans 16.4. Apocryphal books were also sometimes read in church or otherwise regarded as authoritative. About 190, Serapion of Antioch had some difficulty in displacing the so-called 'Gospel of Peter', and a mysterious fragment recently discovered by Professor Morton Smith shows Clement claiming that at Alexandria there was a 'secret gospel of Mark'. Both Hippolytus and Origen made use of the 'Acts of Paul'.

With the passage of time and the development of some critical sense, most of these documents were kept out of the New Testament. Towards the end of the second century it was recognized that Hermas, for example, lived long after New Testament times, and that the 'Acts of Paul' had been composed not as history but as edifying fiction. One criterion, therefore, was historical authenticity. Another was orthodoxy, not in a rigid sense but in the sense that most of the apocryphal documents had special axes to grind, axes different from those ground in the central New Testament writings. Related to both these criteria was that of apostolicity. In addition, there was the criterion of traditional usage; similarly, this criterion was both historical and theological in nature. It was historical in that it was related to investigations into the books which early Christians had actually employed; it was theological in that it was assumed that these early Christians would not have used unorthodox books.

Perhaps the most important single figure in the history of the New Testament canon was Eusebius, bishop of Caesarea in Palestine early in the fourth century. His basic principle was the same as that of some of his predecessors: church usage implies canonicity. Following a scheme apparently used by Origen, Eusebius classified the books which had any claim to be canonical as (1) 'acknowledged', (2) 'disputed', and (3) 'spurious'. Obviously the first and third categories were more easily settled than the second. The first included the four gospels, and Acts, fourteen epistles of Paul (including Hebrews), I John, I Peter, and Revelation. The third included the Acts of Paul, the Shepherd of Hermas, the Apocalypse of Peter, the Epistle of Barnabas, and the Didache. These writings, though earlier used at Alexandria and elsewhere, were rejected in Eusebius's time. As for the 'disputed' books, they consisted of James, Jude, II Peter, and II–III John.

Eusebius knows that various views are held about the book of Revelation: 'Some reject it, while others reckon it among the "acknowledged" books.' Again, some accepted the Gospel according to the Hebrews (he may be referring to Origen). He himself does not accept it, any more than the gospels ascribed to Peter, Thomas, Matthias, and others, or the Acts of Andrew and John.

Eusebius's difficulties arise in part from his deficient conception of church history; in his view the Church was *semper eadem*, and this theory did not prepare him to deal with the variety found not only among various early Christians but even within the thought of individuals. The fact that at Caesarea Origen's canon was somewhat smaller than it was at Alexandria escaped his notice.

At the same time, he was an important and influential witness to the gradual stabilization of the canon. Though he made no use of Jude, II Peter, or II–III John, he referred to a collection of 'the seven so-called Catholic epistles' and frequently quoted from the letter of James. Though he himself did not regard I Clement as canonical, he knew that some churches so regarded it, and he accepted Hebrews as Pauline in substance, though in his view it was actually written by Clement of Rome.

The books which finally came to be generally regarded as canonical are those which Eusebius treated as 'acknowledged' and 'disputed'. They constitute the New Testament as listed by Athanasius in another influential document, the Easter letter of 367, and even though differing opinions as to the relative importance of the various books have been expressed and continue to be expressed, from the fourth century onward the canon has been fixed – with the exceptions we have noted.

Some questions obviously arise. Athanasius lists the books, but his grounds of judgement were apparently much the same as those of Eusebius, and we do not know that anyone but Eusebius thoroughly investigated the question of early usage. What, then, are we to make of the nature of early usage? No one reading the

Church History of Eusebius can fail to be impressed by the gaps in his information about the early Church. Did he actually have information sufficient to make a judgement as to whether or not the New Testament books were read in the early second century (for example)? This question is probably unanswerable; and because it is probably unanswerable we are driven to seek for some ground of canonicity other than early usage, important though this is. We have already seen that early Christians themselves did not use the criterion of apostolicity in any rigid sense, and certainly those New Testament books which view the apostolic age as past (e.g. Hebrews and Jude), or on other grounds seem to come from a later period (e.g. II Peter), cannot be viewed as precisely apostolic.

Perhaps we must be content with a less exact definition of what the New Testament consists of, and a definition in which historical and theological concerns are blended. What is it of which all the New Testament books speak? Who is it to whom they bear witness? If we ask these questions, involving the intentions and purposes of the New Testament writers, we may be able to say that the New Testament books are those which bear witness to Jesus Christ and to God's act of revelation and redemption in him. Once more, we must go a little beyond such a general definition; we must consider the question of time, of closeness to the event and events of which the authors speak. The New Testament writers are those witnesses to Christ and to these acts of God who stand closest in time to the events. This is not to say that earliness is all-important. Had Pontius Pilate written a report on subversive activities in Palestine, this report would not be part of the New Testament. But it is to say that the New Testament cannot contain writings which are addressed primarily to situations in the second century and later. The sub-apostolic age was obviously a time of much New Testament writing. From it came certainly the Gospels of Mark and Luke and the Epistle to the Hebrews and the book of Revelation – probably a good deal more. But the Christians who preserved the New Testament books and compiled the canon were finally unwilling to include such a letter as *I Clement*, addressed primarily to a situation at the very end of the first century.

These considerations are important in determining what the

canon of the New Testament contains and why its contents were chosen. It must also be stated, once more, that the canon was and is the creation of the Church. If there were no Church there would be no canon, for the canonical books are those which the Church chose to preserve as reflections and representations of its faith, life and work in the earliest period of its life. The New Testament therefore contains testimony not to a 'pre-Christian' Jesus but to the Jesus to whom the Church was the response.

Supplement to Chapter I

THE MURATORIAN FRAGMENT

. . . at which he was present and so he set them down. The third book of the gospel, according to Luke. This Luke was a physician whom, after the ascension of Christ, Paul took with him, since he was a student of the law (?). He wrote in his own name and according to his own view, though he did not himself see the Lord in the flesh and therefore [described events] as far as he was able to ascertain [them]. He began his story from the nativity of John. The fourth of the gospels, of John, one of the disciples. When his fellow disciples and bishops exhorted him, he said, 'Fast today with me for three days, and what will be revealed to any of us, let us tell one another.' The same night it was revealed to Andrew, one of the apostles, that they were all to certify but that John should write everything down under his own name. And therefore, though various beginnings are taught in the several books of the gospels, it makes no difference to the faith of believers, since by one guiding Spirit all things are declared in all of them, concerning the nativity, the passion, the resurrection, the life with his disciples, and his double advent, the first in humility and lowliness, which has taken place, and the second in royal power . . . and glorious, which is to come. Why, then, is it remarkable if John so constantly sets forth each item in his epistles, saying of himself, 'What we have seen with our eyes and heard with our ears and our hands have handled, these things we have written to you'? For thus he professes himself not only an eye-witness and hearer but also a writer of all the miracles of the Lord, in sequence.

And the Acts of all the apostles are written in one book. Luke briefly intimates to 'most excellent Theophilus' that the several events took place in his own presence, as he plainly shows by leaving out the passion of Peter and also the departure of Paul from the city on his journey to Spain.

And the epistles of Paul themselves make plain, to those who wish to understand, what epistles he sent and from what place and for what reason. He wrote first of all to the Corinthians, forbidding schisms and heresies; then to the Galatians, forbidding circumcision; then at greater length to the Romans, setting forth the plan of the scriptures and showing that Christ is their first principle. It is not necessary for us to discuss these individually, since the blessed apostle Paul himself, following the order of his predecessor John, writes by name only to seven churches, in the following order: (1) to the Corinthians, (2) to the Ephesians, (3) to the Philippians, (4) to the Colossians, (5) to the Galatians, (6) to the Thessalonians, and (7) to the Romans. And while for the sake of admonition there is a second to the Corinthians and also to the Thessalonians, yet one Church is recognized as spread throughout the world. For John too, in the Apocalypse, though writing to seven churches yet speaks to all. But to Philemon one and to Titus one and to Timothy two were written down from affection and love, to be in honour with the catholic church for the ordering of ecclesiastical discipline. There are current one to the Laodiceans and one to the Alexandrians, both forged in Paul's name for the heresy of Marcion, as well as many others which cannot be received into the catholic church; for it is not right for gall to be mixed with honey.

Certainly the epistle of Jude and the two bearing John's name are accepted in the Catholic [Church], as well as the Wisdom written by the friends of Solomon in his honour. We also accept the Apocalypses of John and of Peter only, which some of us will not have read in the church. But Hermas wrote the Shepherd very recently, in our own times, in the city of Rome while his brother Pius the bishop was occupying the episcopal chair of the church of the city of Rome; and therefore, while it ought to be read, to the end of the ages it cannot be read publicly in church to the people, either among the prophets (whose ranks are complete) or among the apostles.

II

MATERIALS AND METHODS OF TEXTUAL CRITICISM

In the previous chapter we considered the nature and contents of the New Testament as a whole, in order to see why it was that we were treating together these diverse documents produced within the Christian Church of the first century or even century and a half. Now we must go on to consider the documents not as a collection but as documents. Ordinarily most people read these documents in various English translations, and therefore they may sometimes be tempted to forget that they were originally composed not in English but in Greek. To be sure, some scholars have argued that parts, at least, of some of the books were written not in Greek but in Aramaic, and it may be worth while to state briefly why this view, while it may be interesting, can never be convincing. How does one prove that some text is not originally Greek but was translated from another language? (1) First, one must show that the Greek as it now stands is bad Greek. (If one is dealing with a really good translator, one cannot show that he has translated unless he has said so.) But most of the passages treated as bad Greek for this purpose can be shown to be at least acceptable in the Hellenistic Greek of the time. (2) Second, one must show that the Greek passage does not quite make sense. (3) Finally, one must show that the passage if retranslated into the other language does make sense, and that some very simple error could have resulted in the text we now have. This retranslation is harder to make than might be supposed, and where such efforts can be tested the proportion of successful retranslations is rather low; moreover, experts in Aramaic have a tendency to disagree as to what the original was. For these reasons, and because, after all, we do have the Greek text, it seems fitting to deal with it rather than with something else.

But do we have the Greek text? Or what kind of Greek text do we have?

Some early Christian writers were aware of the importance of old manuscripts for the study of the Bible, and copyists during the Middle Ages, both in the East and in the West, made efforts to find ancient models. It cannot be denied, however, that a much more vigorous concern for ancient writings and manuscripts arose at the time of the Renaissance. As far as Christian writings were involved, this concern was first expressed in regard to the works of the early Fathers. Such editions of the Greek New Testament as those of Erasmus (1516) and Robert Étienne (Stephanus, 1551) were based on the available manuscripts which happened to come from the mediæval Greek Church, and contained a large number of accumulated errors.

In the sixteenth and seventeenth centuries much older manuscripts were discovered. The first of these to be found was the sixth-century Graeco-Latin Codex Bezae, named after the Reformed scholar Theodore Beza, who gave it to the University of Cambridge in 1581. Equally important was the Codex Alexandrinus, now in the British Museum, which in 1628 was sent to the King of England by Cyril Lucar, orthodox patriarch of Constantinople (formerly of Alexandria); he was grateful for English diplomatic assistance against Jesuit intrigues. This fifth-century manuscript contains the whole Bible in Greek, in addition to most of the two letters traditionally ascribed to Clement of Rome. Although the letters were published at Oxford in 1633, the New Testament did not appear until 1786, though scholars earlier made use of the manuscript.

Two more early manuscripts were discovered in the eighteenth and nineteenth centuries. The first of these contains Greek writings of the Syrian Father Ephraem; underneath them can be made out, with considerable difficulty, an incomplete Bible of the fifth century. This manuscript, the Codex Ephraemi Rescriptus ('of Ephraem, written over'), is in the Bibliothèque Nationale at Paris. A later discovery was that of the highly important Codex Vaticanus (fourth century). In Napoleon's time the French removed manuscripts from the Vatican Library and among them was this codex, which their scholars found to contain a text remarkably free from later additions. The manuscript was later returned to Rome, where it now is; it is still one of our most important witnesses to the early text.

Later in the nineteenth century, enthusiasm for antiquities led a German scholar named Constantine Tischendorf to search for manuscripts in the Convent of St. Catherine on Mount Sinai. There, in 1844, he found forty-three leaves of a fourth-century manuscript. Since the monks had been about to throw it away, they were willing to give it to him. Again in 1853, and once more in 1859, he returned to search for the rest of the manuscript, but without success. Just before he left after his last visit, the steward of the convent finally showed him the missing leaves; since they included the long-lost Greek text of the epistle of Barnabas, Tischendorf spent the night copying it. The manuscript finally reached the Imperial Library at St. Petersburg (now Leningrad), after a long series of legal disputes over its ownership. Called Codex Sinaiticus from its place of origin, it was sold in 1933 by the Russian Government to the British Museum for £100,000.

More manuscripts, of course, have been found along the way, but these five are probably the most important. They moved the clock back nearly a thousand years, and showed what the New Testament was like in the fourth and fifth centuries – and even earlier, since they were obviously copied from still older originals.

What of the period before the fourth century? We should not expect to find manuscripts, or fragments, from the first century. First, there were probably very few of them. Second, the originals were probably worn out after repeated reading both private and public. Only in legend were the 'authentic originals' preserved. The case is different for the second and third centuries, however. From the relatively dry rubbish heaps of ancient Egypt have come many fragments of New Testament books – a few from the second century, and a considerable number from the third. Though interest in papyri arose as early as the eighteenth century, it was not until the end of the nineteenth that systematic investigations of sites began, especially at Oxyrhynchus, from which more than twenty volumes of papyri have been published.

The oldest papyrus fragment of any New Testament book is a scrap, about two inches square, which contains verses from the eighteenth chapter of John on both sides. The dates of non-dated papyri can be determined within a margin of about fifty years by comparative study of the styles of writing used in them. This papyrus scrap, now in the John Rylands Library at Manchester, has been assigned to the first half of the second century, perhaps earlier rather than later in the period. By filling in gaps at both ends of the lines, the length of the lines can be calculated; then by filling in gaps between the verses on the front and those on the back we can determine the number of lines to the page; and finally we can estimate the size of the little codex which contained the gospel. Probably the codex contained this book alone; a larger work would have been difficult to handle, given the size of the pages. Thus we see that early in the second century John was valued in Egypt, probably in upper Egypt; indeed, it may have been so highly valued that it was circulated apart from the other gospels.

From the third century come two highly important collections named after the modern Maecenases who purchased them from dealers. The first is the Chester Beatty papyri, containing nearly all of the New Testament except for some Pauline and deutero-Pauline letters and the Catholic epistles. The second is the Bodmer papyri, still in course of publication, including at least the Gospels of Luke and John, as well as I–II Peter and Jude and a number of apocryphal and patristic writings.

In addition to Greek manuscripts, there are other materials which can be used for the reconstruction of early New Testament texts. There are early versions of the New Testament books, especially in Latin, Coptic, Syriac and Armenian; manuscripts of some books in such versions come from as early as the third century. There are also quotations from the New Testament provided by the writers of the early Church, and though the manuscripts of the patristic writings are often late the quotations they give were not often altered by copyists. Sometimes, indeed, we can get back to a very early period in dealing with these quotations. Thus there is a papyrus scrap of the third book of Irenaeus, 'Against Heresies', which contains New Testament quotations. Irenaeus wrote about 180, and the scrap comes from the end of the second century or the beginning of the third. One could hardly get closer.

Finally, there are the lectionaries of various churches, containing excerpts from the New Testament arranged for liturgical reading. Though the lectionaries themselves are late, they sometimes reflect early texts.

What we have endeavoured to show in dealing with the materials is that we do not lack an abundance of manuscripts and other relevant data by means of which we can get back to a period quite early in the history of New Testament transmission. Before the discovery of the Dead Sea Scrolls there was a considerable gap in the transmission of the Old Testament. Such a gap has not existed for some time in New Testament studies. Indeed, a basic difficulty in these studies is not that we have too little, but that we have so much that it is very difficult to control. There are about 4,700 New Testament manuscripts and at least 100,000 patristic quotations or allusions.

The methods employed in dealing with these materials are not free from difficulties. (1) It might be supposed that early manuscripts are naturally better than late manuscripts. Such is not necessarily the case, however, for a manuscript may be late in date but go back to an original text which was very early. Occasionally a group of late manuscripts can be traced back to a hypothetical ancestor, now lost, because of identical errors preserved in them. More often, however, various kinds of readings and 'contaminations' have come into the late manuscripts and ancestry is now impossible to trace. (2) It might be supposed that early versions would provide valuable evidence. Sometimes they do; but often they have been corrected from various kinds of Greek texts and we cannot definitely ascertain what the version's original text was. (3) Patristic quotations are not always absolutely reliable: (*a*) the Church Father may have been quoting not from a text but from memory; (*b*) he may have used more than one manuscript; (*c*) his own works may not have been correctly transmitted; study of their manuscript tradition is required.

Beyond the methods employed in dealing with the manuscripts lie the methods used in relation to the errors they contain. Vaganay has analysed errors as unintentional and intentional. The first group includes (1) additions originating because the scribe wrote the same letter, syllable, word or clause twice (dittography); (2) omissions arising because of the presence of the same elements, sometimes because the scribe's eye skipped a line which ended in the same way as one he had just copied (homoioteleuton); (3) confusions caused by the presence of different vowels or diphthongs which in Greek were pronounced almost identically (e, ē, ei, ai, oi, u; also o and ō); (4) confusions of different letters which in 'uncial' writing (capital letters) looked much the same (E–C, O–Θ, Γ–T); and (5) confusions arising because the earliest manuscripts contained neither word-separation nor punctuation. The second group includes (1) corrections intended to improve spelling, grammar, or style; (2) 'harmonizations' between (a) parallel passages, (b) New Testament citations and Old Testament texts, and (c) New Testament texts and liturgical practice; and (3) exegetical-doctrinal interpolations, suppressions, and tendentious revisions. Exegetical-doctrinal modifications are not very common, but they do exist.

There are a few important passages in the New Testament in which it can be proved conclusively that textual alteration has taken place.

(1) The ending of the Gospel of Mark (16.9–20) is no part of what its author originally wrote: (a) Justin alluded to it and Irenaeus quoted from it; it is included in some important uncial manuscripts, mostly 'Western'. (b) On the other hand, it is absent from the writings of Clement, Origen and Eusebius, and is omitted in Codex Vaticanus and Codex Sinaiticus, as well as in the older Latin and Syriac versions; the Freer manuscript contains a different ending entirely. (c) Therefore, though it was undoubtedly added at an early date, it is not authentic.

(2) The story about a woman 'taken in adultery' and forgiven by Jesus does not belong to the Gospel of John. (a) It occurs in the Byzantine text of the gospel, usually as John 7.53–8.11 but sometimes after John 7.36 or 21.24 (in a small group of manuscripts it is found after Luke 21.38). (b) No manuscript before the end of the fourth century contains it; no Church Father, in the same period, refers to it. (c) Therefore it is not authentic.

(3) A more difficult problem occurs in Luke 22.19b–20: (a) All but a few manuscripts include these verses, which are close to what Paul relates about the Last Supper in I Corinthians 11.24–5. (b) In Codex Bezae and the Old Latin version Jesus

says simply, 'This is my body'; there is no reference to what in the longer version is a second cup at the meal. (*c*) A Eucharist in which the wine preceded the bread seems to be found in the Didache; therefore some scholars have argued that the shorter version of Luke is the authentic one. (*d*) On the other hand, it may be that a scribe found the mention of two cups embarrassing and therefore deleted the second notice.

Other examples occur in the epistles.

(4) According to most of the uncials and the Fathers, the epistle to the Romans ends with a doxology (16.25–7). (*a*) But in the Byzantine text this doxology came at the end of the fourteenth chapter; in the third-century Beatty papyri it occurs after Romans 15.23; in some manuscripts (fifth century and later) it is to be found at the end of both the fourteenth and the sixteenth chapters. (*b*) Marcion omitted it entirely, as did the scribe of one tenth-century uncial – though he left a space at the end of the fourteenth chapter. Marcion, who rejected the Old Testament, may well have deleted the doxology because it refers to 'prophetic scripture'. (*c*) The passage may be an interpolation, though we cannot be absolutely sure.

(5) At the beginning of Ephesians the words 'in Ephesus' present a problem. (*a*) They are to be found in most manuscripts. (*b*) On the other hand, Marcion said that 'Ephesians' was really addressed to the Laodiceans; Origen omitted the words 'in Ephesus'; they do not occur in the Beatty papyri, in Codex Vaticanus, or in Codex Sinaiticus (though in both these codices a corrector added them). (*c*) This evidence suggests that the words are not part of the original letter, though we must not suppose that the addresses of letters always became more specific with the passage of time; Origen omitted a mention of Rome in Romans 1.7 and one Greek manuscript leaves it out both there and in 1.15. Each case must be decided on its own merits.

(6) The text of I John has definitely been interpolated. (*a*) The later manuscripts of the Vulgate read as follows in I John 5.7–8:

There are three which bear witness on earth, the spirit and the water and the blood, and these three are one in Christ Jesus; and there are three who bear witness in heaven, the Father, the Word, and the Spirit, and these three are one.

In these words later Latin theologians found proof that the doctrine of the Trinity, only implicitly present in the New Testament, was actually stated in its text. (*b*) But all early Greek manuscripts, all early Church Fathers (including Jerome and Augustine), all early versions, and the older manuscripts of the Vulgate, read thus:

> There are three which bear witness, the spirit and the water and the blood, and the three are one.

(*c*) The 'heavenly witnesses' are no part of what John wrote.

In cases like these, where the evidence of manuscripts, versions and early quotations is fairly straightforward, it is relatively easy to make decisions about the nature of the original, or more original, text. To be sure, it can still be argued that the additions are valuable for various reasons; but they should not be regarded as part of the earliest New Testament. The statement in I John about the three heavenly witnesses is valuable as an expression of the Church's faith in the fourth century and later, but it does not come from the author of the epistle.

In most cases, however, the evidence is not so straightforward, and it is usually necessary to apply some canons of criticism.

SOME PRINCIPLES OF TEXTUAL CRITICISM

F. C. Grant has listed three basic principles of textual criticism which deserve further analysis. They are these:

1. No one type of text is infallible, or to be preferred by virtue of its generally superior authority.
2. Each reading must be examined on its merits, and preference must be given to those readings which are demonstrably in the style of the author under consideration.
3. Readings which explain other variants, but are not contrariwise to be explained by the others, merit our preference; but this is a very subtle process, involving intangible elements, and liable to subjective judgement on the part of the critic.

All three principles, indeed, contain a large measure of subjectivity. The first is more valuable negatively than positively; it means basically that all manuscripts and all types of manuscripts may contain errors. The second point introduces literary criticism (see the next chapter) into textual study, and makes us raise the question whether an author always writes in what we may call his style. If not, the principle is not altogether persuasive. The third brings us in the direction of historical criticism (see Chapter IV), and since it is admittedly subjective we need say no more than that the meaning of 'explain' is clearer than the means by which the principle is to be employed.

If we try to apply the three principles to a few examples we may be able to see more clearly how they work.

(1) In Mark 1.1 there is a significant variant. Is the 'gospel' that 'of Jesus Christ' or that 'of Jesus Christ the Son of God'? The latter reading is found, sometimes with unimportant variations, in most of the early uncial manuscripts and in most of the quotations in the Fathers. The former reading occurs in the Sinaitic (first hand) and Koridethi uncials and in the writings of Origen. (*a*) The first principle indicates that we cannot immediately decide which reading is correct. (*b*) The second principle leads us to consider the fact that at high points in Mark's gospel he speaks of Jesus as the Son of God (the Transfiguration, the trial before Caiaphas, the Crucifixion). Would Mark's style, then, lead him to employ the expression at the beginning of his book? (*c*) It is hard to tell which of the two readings explains the other. In the earliest manuscripts words were not separated and 'sacred names' were abbreviated. Thus the words 'of Jesus Christ the Son of God' would read something like ΙΥΧΥΥΥΘΥ; confusion would be almost inevitable. But we cannot tell whether the longer or the shorter form is the original one.

(2) In John 1.18 either 'the only-begotten God' or 'the only-begotten Son' revealed God. (*a*) The witnesses to the text disagree, and we cannot give any text type the preference, though in general the earlier ones attest 'God'. (*b*) The parallels in John's own language are hard to assess properly. In John 1.14 we find 'only-begotten' (*monogenēs*) without a noun, while in John 3.14 and 16 we hear of the 'only-begotten Son'. By 'Son' John means 'Son of God', as the rest of his gospel makes

clear. The Logos who became incarnate 'was with God' and 'was God' (1.1); but Jesus is addressed as God only after his ascension (20.28). The author's style, on balance, does not seem to allow us to draw a conclusion. (c) We then ask which reading explains the other. Here we note that the earliest witnesses to 'the only-begotten God' were Gnostics of the second century. Were they responsible for this reading? Or did they make use of a text older than themselves, retaining 'God' though they would perhaps have preferred to read 'only-begotten' alone? Since this question cannot be answered, we finally ask whether 'only-begotten' by itself would not explain the existence of both 'only-begotten God' and 'only-begotten Son'. Both 'God' and 'Son' may have been intended to give exegesis of one difficult term; but such a conclusion is purely conjectural.

(3) An example of a reading even more conjectural is provided in the Revised Standard Version at Jude 5. The manuscripts tell us that the people were saved out of Egypt by 'the Lord' (KC) or by 'God' (ΘC) or by 'Jesus' (IC) or by 'God Christ' (ΘC XC). To make a choice is exceedingly difficult. But by applying the third principle the revisers decided to read '*he who* saved the people', supplying a Greek article (O) in place of any manuscript reading. Decisions will vary on this point; the author very much prefers to read 'Jesus'.

In view of these examples – to which many more could be added – we may wonder whether or not the principles are fully adequate. At the same time, we must recognize that mere antiquity is no adequate indication of the goodness of a particular reading. Early manuscripts may contain multitudes of errors, conscious or unconscious; late manuscripts may preserve readings which seem to be correct.

For this reason, even the discovery of new papyri is not necessarily going to provide a more reliable New Testament text. Perhaps if papyri from the first century should turn up they could be given a considerable measure of confidence. None has turned up, however, and the most important and complete papyri we have come from the third century.

Should we, then, try to do nothing more than trace the history of the varieties of texts from the third century to the tenth or eleventh? This looks like a counsel of despair, and it is not greatly strengthened when it is suggested that the late history of the texts illustrates and illuminates the history of theology. The history of theology is known from the writings of theologians, and New Testament textual variants contribute practically nothing which was not, or could not have been, known independently.

The primary goal of New Testament textual study remains the recovery of what the New Testament writers wrote. We have already suggested that to achieve this goal is wellnigh impossible. Therefore we must be content with what Reinhold Niebuhr and others have called, in other contexts, an 'impossible possibility'. Only a goal of this kind can justify the labours of textual critics and give credit to their achievements and to the distance between what they have achieved and what they have hoped to achieve.

If this, then, is the goal of the textual criticism of the New Testament, we are now able to state what attitude we should take towards the additions in the gospels and the epistles. They are not part of the original text, and they belong to the history of the Church rather than to the New Testament. They have as little, or as much, claim to present the apostolic witness as does such a work as the Gospel of Thomas. The case is not very different when we consider the conjectural emendations intended to go behind disagreements in the manuscripts we possess. Such emendations obviously belong to the history of New Testament study, and emendations were being made as early as Origen's time, not to mention that of Marcion.

On the other hand, if we virtuously claim that we are not making any emendations but are simply following what is written, the question of what *is* written will arise. Are we, so to speak, canonizing a particular manuscript or group of manuscripts? Is there some papyrus or other manuscript which deserves our total allegiance? It would appear that nothing of the sort exists, and that in making decisions about the text, just as in making decisions about the canon, it is still necessary for us to use our minds. Perhaps in consequence of the Fall, human reason has become totally corrupt, but since we are not dogs or cats we must still make use of it.

III

THE NATURE OF TRANSLATION

From ancient times the meaning of translation has been a problem. One of the most vigorous debates of the late fourth century was concerned with the question as to how to translate Origen's treatise *On First Principles* from Greek into Latin. Both sides agreed that a word-for-word translation was useless; one had to translate meanings, not fragments. The question of meaning then had to be faced. In several respects Origen's doctrine differed from that regarded as orthodox by his translators. Should one lay more emphasis on Origen's intention to be orthodox, and then modify his statements in the direction of later orthodoxy? This was the procedure employed by Rufinus. Or should one translate just about what he said, pointing out that at various points his views were heretical? Jerome took this course and accused Rufinus of falsification.

It is obvious that the same kind of problem arises when one translates the New Testament. To be sure, no one expects the New Testament writers to use the terminology of later orthodox theology. But one does expect that they will not absolutely disagree with one another, or with the main thrust of the Old Testament, since they regarded it as inspired and prophetic. If one is translating their meaning rather than their exact words, one inevitably enters the realm of theology; one cannot remain strictly philological – if such a situation is really conceivable.

The question of translation is extremely important in dealing with the New Testament because (1) we are not first-century Greeks (in Palestine or elsewhere) and (2) we all use translations, whether we use those prepared by others or attempt to translate for ourselves. If we use the translations of others, we need some kind of guidance in choosing among them. If we make our own, we need to have in mind some clear principles for translating.

At first glance, it might appear simple enough to make a translation. Assuming that we 'know Greek' or, in other words, have studied its grammar, syntax and vocabulary to such an extent that we do not get lost when confronted with a simple Greek sentence, we may suppose that we can proceed directly to the New Testament – perhaps to the Gospel of John – and then, making use of the rules we have learned and the dictionary we have acquired, 'render' it into English. Sometimes, to be sure, such is almost the case. 'In the beginning was the Word, and the Word was with God, and the Word was God.' If we refrain from asking questions about the meaning of 'beginning', 'Word' and 'God', we may be able to believe that we have an adequate translation. But there is still the difficult word 'and'. What function does it perform in the sentence? And have we translated correctly when we place the three clauses in a straightforward sequence like the one just given? Or should the verse read thus?—

> In the beginning was the Word,
> and the Word was with God,
> and the Word was God.

Apart from these questions, there is of course the problem of the meanings of the words. How do we determine what the words mean? Do we look them up in a simple pocket lexicon which may tell us that '*logos*' means only 'word'? Do we go on to a larger dictionary which will inform us that '*logos*' has a wide range of meanings? And, if we go on, how do we tell which meaning or meanings was or were intended by the author or understood by his readers, early or late?

It seems fairly likely that what the author intended can best be understood by looking at the immediate context of the passage we are translating. If we look at the context of this verse in John, we find that the subject of discussion seems to change from Word through Life to Light, and that nothing more is directly stated about the Word until we reach the sentence which says that 'the Word became flesh and dwelt among us, and we beheld his glory.' But a 'word' which 'became flesh' is not the kind of word which is known in ordinary English usage. How, then, are we to translate '*logos*'? Should we run the risk of ambiguity by simply calling it 'Word' (with a capital letter, since 'the Word of God') – or should we venture into the equally risky area of paraphrase?

Now the sentence with which John begins his gospel is relatively simple when compared with some of the 'hard to understand' (II Pet. 3.16) passages in the Pauline epistles; and in all such instances we are likely to fall into two traps, one on either side of whatever the true path may be. (1) We may take the writings, one by one or all together, and translate them in such a way as to lay emphasis upon the divergent words, phrases and ideas to be found in them. The result of this process will ordinarily be that we shall find the authors contradicting themselves and one another. We shall then be tempted to suppose that various hands in the manuscript have reflected the ideas of various persons; in other words, the documents have been interpolated. (2) On the other hand, we may try to treat the writings so synthetically that we neglect the real differences to be found in them and among them; the result will be that we overlook the genuine diversity to be found not only in style but also in thought and may give the impression that a non-existent uniformity exists.

This is to say that absolutely rigid rules for translating, as for interpreting (in Greek, '*hermeneia*' included both meanings), cannot be laid down. In every case we are dealing with a living author who used grammar and syntax as a means, not as an end in itself. Like Humpty Dumpty in *Alice in Wonderland*, he was the master of his words – though admittedly there may have been occasions on which the words mastered him and he did not clearly or fully express what was in his mind. The point at which to begin, however, is with the grammar and the syntax. For all New Testament writers (see Chapter IV) the sentence and its structure is more immediately comprehensible than are the meanings of words.

But the meanings of words are obviously of supreme importance. First we must determine what effect we wish our translation to give in relation to the meaning of a word. Is it to represent (1) what the word may have meant to the author or (2) what it may have meant to some, at least, of his earliest readers, or (3) what it may have come to mean in later times (the limiting case being a so-called 'inspired mistranslation')? Before we can go any farther we must recognize the ambiguities present in each of these cases. (1) An author may mean several different things by the same word, just as he may use different words to signify the same, or essentially the same, thing. He may use a word in different senses on different occasions, or he may use the word with two senses at the same time (John is fond of this practice). In the case of words which have a long history or, as in the Septuagint, have been used to translate various words in another language – and thus bear diverse connotations – we cannot always be sure which one out of several meanings is dominant in the author's mind as he writes. (2) Similarly, when we speak of the author's 'earliest readers' we must bear in mind (*a*) that we do not often know who his earliest readers were, and (*b*) that often (as at Corinth and Colossae, at least) the earliest readers consisted of at least two groups, both of which claimed to understand what he meant, though they disagreed as to what it was. Such misunderstanding is reflected in I Corinthians 5.9–13, and perhaps in the whole letter. The history of biblical interpretation, in large measure, is the story of disagreements as to the meaning of texts; and these disagreements arose very early. (3) If we speak of what words may have meant in later times, we must ask, 'To whom?' Goethe translated '*logos*' by '*die Tat*'; is he to be taken as a reliable witness? By whom? Is 'the church' to be regarded as the ultimate court of appeal? If so, what is the church? Or does '*logos*' in John 1.1 mean whatever anyone has happened to think it means?

It might appear that the possibility of translating does not really exist; and to some extent such is the case. There can never be an absolutely final translation of the New Testament, for (1) we do not know with mathematical precision what its authors meant or how their readers understood them, and (2) our own language changes from age to age and words acquire and lose meanings.

We should say something about what we do know about the Greek of the New Testament. Obviously it is not classical. What is it? Around the seventeenth century there were those who believed that it was a special language created by the Holy Spirit, but – especially in the late nineteenth century – this view lost favour when a great many letters, business documents and other writings were discovered, preserved in papyrus in the dry climate of the Egyptian desert. The language of these papyri was much the same as that found in the New Testament. Scholars therefore turned to them to find out the meaning of words, grammar and syntax in the Hellenistic period, and in the light of this knowledge to interpret the New Testament. On the other hand, it has proved impossible to pass directly from the papyri to New Testament exegesis, for two reasons. (1) The New Testament writers were saturated in the Greek Old Testament, the Septuagint, and much of their language bears Septuagintal overtones. Some New Testament terms can be understood much better in relation to the Septuagint than in relation to sales contracts. (2) Some of the gospels, and to a certain measure some of the epistles, come from or through men who were bilingual and seem to have thought in two languages at once. One language was Greek; the other was Aramaic or Hebrew. Even though none of the New Testament books was written in Aramaic, the authors of some of them thought in Aramaic, at least at times. And behind the sayings of Jesus in their Greek versions lies a chain of transmission which began in a Semitic language. Obviously this chain cannot be reproduced in a translation. But it has to be taken into account.

Thus far we have been discussing chiefly the problems presented by the materials being translated; but there are also difficulties in our own language and our use of it. The English language has undergone almost constant change since the year 1611, to go back no farther. Words have lost their original, or earlier, meanings and overtones and have acquired other overtones and meanings. Conspicuous examples of such changes can be found by reading Shakespeare, the King James Version, and the Book of Common Prayer – in spite of the fact that alterations have been made in the last two. In a prayer-book collect God is still asked to 'prevent' us, when we are really asking him to lead; the so-called 'comfortable words' are really meant to be encouraging or strengthening. The English of today is also different, generally speaking, in style. King James's translators were trained in a rhetoric rather alien to our own more pedestrian turns of phrase. Where they often favoured long words with Latin derivations we tend to prefer shorter Anglo-Saxon terms.

These differences in vocabulary and style account for many of the variations between the older English versions and the more modern ones.

Sometimes it is suggested that these older translations, hallowed by usage, are the most satisfactory because their archaic language conveys overtones of the antiquity which is actually a feature of the Bible. Such an argument has been advanced by Augustine against Jerome's novel translation of the Old Testament, and by modern opponents of such translations as the Revised Standard Version. There is, of course, something to it. The New Testament writers themselves did not hesitate to make free use of the Septuagint version of the Old Testament, written in a Greek at times very strange and, in their time, a century or so old. In addition, at least some of the New Testament writings were intended for liturgical use, and liturgical language emphasizes the continuity of Christianity by preserving archaic expressions – which are sometimes, though not often, incomprehensible to later generations. Some of the New Testament writings, then, are archaizing in flavour and a purely 'modern' translation does not translate. On the other hand, the narrative portions of Acts and most of the Pauline epistles were written in a style which was not archaizing, and if they are translated archaistically the translation does not convey the authors' intentions. This defence of modernizing, however, cannot be pressed too far, for translations have at least two purposes: (1) private reading for the sake of edification and/or instruction, and (2) liturgical reading. It is possible that a more modern translation may provide more adequate instruction while failing to achieve the goal desired in devotional contemplation or liturgy. At the same time, no 'modern' or 'fresh' translation is likely to remain either modern or fresh, and no archaizing translation can be allowed to remain too far in the past. Translation is a continuing task with a goal never finally attainable.

Then does the New Testament mean whatever anyone may suppose it to mean? Such a conclusion is not valid because, in spite of the severe limits we have tried to place upon 'knowledge falsely so-called', it is still possible to determine something about grammar, syntax, and the meanings of words in the context provided by the authors of the New Testament books.

This is to say that there is a *relative* objectivity in the translation of the New Testament; but there is not, and never will be, a translation which conveys the exact meaning, or range of meanings, found in every passage.

In addition, the presence of ambiguity in the New Testament documents themselves must be recognized. There are quite a few passages in which several translations, often with rather different meanings, are possible. (This fact is made clear especially in the footnotes to the New English Bible.) The possibility of ambiguity arises under various kinds of circumstances. First comes the ambiguity which is to be found in English but not in the original Greek. This situation need not be discussed; it is due to the inadequacy of translation, not to anything in the original text. More important is the ambiguity which actually may exist in Greek. Here the original author may have expressed himself unclearly because of inadequacies either in thought or in expression. The cause of the inadequacy is important. Is it due to the author himself or to the subject matter? If it is due to the author, the translator need do no more than reproduce the inadequacy. If it is due to the subject matter, which may transcend the author's powers of thought or expression, the translator needs to choose words which can convey this impression. Writers who deal with the work of God in history cannot always write with the preciseness of an Aristotle discussing categories or the habits of animals. In translating unclear sentences in which the authors' reach exceeds their grasp because of the 'heavenly' nature of the subject, we must try to let the ambiguity indicate the authors' intentions.

We must also avoid maintaining the notion that there is any one clearly definable key to all the mysteries of the Bible. Martin Luther once wrote these words about the Psalms: 'God be thanked, when I understood the subject matter and knew that "God's righteousness" meant "righteousness through which he justifies us through righteousness freely given in Jesus Christ", then I understood the grammar. Only then did I find the Psalter to my taste.' Certainly justification through grace is a central concern of the New Testament and, to some measure, of the Old. But it is not the only concern, and we must not place New Testament words and thoughts on a Procrustean bed – even Luther's.

IV

LITERARY CRITICISM

Since the New Testament is a collection of books, these books are
subject to literary analysis. Books do not just grow, but are
composed by authors who have certain goals in view and follow
certain methods in arranging and composing their materials.
Presumably their goals can be discovered, to some extent, by
considering the circumstances under which they wrote, but since
(in our opinion) this kind of consideration belongs to historical
criticism we refrain from discussing it at this point. Literary
criticism is properly concerned with analysing the author's
purposes and achievements by means of a detailed examination of
the works themselves. We thus agree with what Allen Tate says
of poets:

> Poets, in their way, are practical men; they are interested in
> results. What is the poem, after it is written? That is the
> question. Not where it came from, or why. The Why and
> Where can never get beyond the guessing stage because, in
> the language of those who think it can, poetry cannot be
> brought to 'laboratory conditions'.

To Tate's What, however, we must add (as he himself would)
the question of How. In attempting to understand a literary work,
we cannot simply read it; we must analyse its structure as a whole
and in relation to the various parts, since the structure is an
indispensable part of the author's achievement.

But we cannot begin with the work as a whole. The whole
cannot be understood – even though its structure can sometimes
be outlined – before the sentence units are analysed. Generally
speaking, the structure of an entire New Testament book is less
easily grasped than the constituent sentences are.

It may be asked why, in our search for units which can be readily understood, we do not begin with individual words. The reason for beginning with sentences lies in our understanding of the nature of New Testament language. In dealing with translations we have already pointed to a number of ways in which the meanings of individual words can be and have been illuminated. But it is our opinion that individual words, no matter how carefully investigated, cannot be understood as exactly or precisely as can the structure of a sentence, especially in an articulated language like Greek. We should claim that the proper approach to a New Testament document, while necessarily involving at least an approximation to the translation of individual words, begins with the diagramming of the sentences in such a way as to bring out the interrelations of words, phrases and clauses. Greek writers did not simply choose to write in a patterned manner; they had to write in a patterned manner because of the nature of their language, and in order to understand them we must understand the structure within which their thought moved.

It is of course possible that by diagramming in this way one may get an over-precise interpretation of thoughts which somehow transcended the limitations of language. But it is surprising how often such writings as the Pauline epistles actually do conform to the rules of Greek sentence-structure.

THE SENTENCE

There are certain features about New Testament sentences which immediately strike the reader's eye, at least the eye which sees them diagrammed. For instance, it is obvious that many of the sayings of Jesus as reported in the synoptic gospels contain *parallelism*, a feature also characteristic of much of the poetic language of the Old Testament. Sometimes this parallelism is *synonymous*. Approximately the same meaning is expressed in two slightly different ways.

> Is it lawful on the Sabbath to do good or to do harm?
> to save a life or to kill? (Mark 3.4)

> If a kingdom be divided against itself,
> that kingdom cannot stand;

and if a house be divided against itself,
   that house cannot stand (Mark 3.24–5).

There is nothing hid
   but that it should be revealed,
nor was anything made secret
   but that it should come to light (Mark 4.22)

Sometimes the parallelism is *antithetical*.

He who has,
   it will be given to him;
and he who has not,
   from him it will be taken away (Mark 4.25).

And sometimes it is *chiastic* (from the Greek letter 'chi', which looks like a cross or X).

You know that
   (*a*) those who are thought to rule over the gentiles
            lord it over them, and
   (*b*) their great men exercise authority over them.

            But it is not so among you. But
   (*b*) whoever wishes to be great among you
            shall be your servant, and
   (*a*) whoever wishes to be first among you
            shall be the slave of all (Mark 10.42–4).

The words 'but it is not so among you' indicate that the parallel is also antithetical.

It is perhaps worth noting at this point that in the synoptic gospels such parallelism occurs only in sayings, not in comments made by the authors themselves. On the other hand, in the Gospel of John it is to be found not only in sayings of Jesus but also in what the evangelist says. Indeed, at some points it is impossible to determine whether it is the evangelist or Jesus who is speaking.

God so loved the world
   that he gave his only Son
            that whoever believes in him should not perish
                        but have eternal life.

For God sent his Son into the world
>not to judge the world
>>but that the world should be saved through him
>>>>>>(John 3.16–17).

Parallelism is also common in the letters of the apostle Paul. From among the many examples we cite only a few.

He who sows sparingly
shall also reap sparingly;

and he who sows bountifully
shall also reap bountifully (II Cor. 9.6).

All things are lawful, but not all things are expedient;
all things are lawful, but not all things edify (I Cor. 10.23).

There are diversities of gifts,
>but the same Spirit;
and there are diversities of ministrations,
>yet the same Lord;
and there are diversities of operations,
>but the same God . . . (I Cor. 12.4–6).

Naturally Paul's style does not consist of parallelisms alone, even though he is very fond of them. In Greek, more than in Hebrew, the structure of a sentence is often controlled by the *prepositions* which indicate the relations between the various nouns and verbs. By considering the sentence-structure in relation to the prepositions, the precise meaning of the sentence often becomes clear.

For us there is one God the Father
>*of* whom are all things and
>*unto* whom are we;
and one Lord Jesus Christ,
>*through* whom are all things and
>*through* whom are we (I Cor. 8.6).

Who is the image of the invisible God, the firstborn of all
>creation; for *in* him were created all things . . .;
>all things were created *through* him and *unto* him;
>and he is *before* all things,
>and all things hold together *in* him (Col. 1.15–17).

Sometimes the precise relationship of the prepositions is not so clear.

> Whom God set forth as an expiation
>> *through* faith
>> *by* his blood
>> *for* the demonstration of his righteousness
>>> *through* the remission of past sins
>>> *in* the forbearance of God;
>> *for* the demonstration of his righteousness
>>> *at* the present time . . . (Rom. 3.25–6).

The words translated 'by his blood' may mean 'in his blood'; in that case, the meaning of the sentence would be somewhat different.

THE PARAGRAPH

After we have looked at individual sentences we are in a position to proceed to the paragraph. Sometimes, indeed often, Paul constructs his paragraphs with great care. For example, when he is giving exact instructions to the Corinthians about eating meat he uses a structure almost legal in form.

(a) *Eat everything* sold in the meat-market,
> *making no distinctions for conscience' sake;*
>> for 'the earth is the Lord's, and the fullness thereof'
>>> (Ps. 24.1).

(b) If any unbeliever invites you (and you wish to go),
> *eat everything* set before you,
> *making no distinctions for conscience' sake.*

(c) But if anyone says to you, 'This has been sacrificed,'
> do not eat,
> for the sake of him who warned you and of conscience
> – I mean not your own but that of your neighbour
>> (I Cor. 10.25–8).

An example of a longer paragraph carefully put together occurs in I Corinthians 12, where a similar arrangement by sense-lines can be provided; but the most famous example is to be found in

I Corinthians 13. Here there is a magnificent combination of repetition and variety. The passage begins with a contrast between various gifts and virtues and the supreme gift of love.

> If I —— and have not love, I have become ——。
> And if I —— and —— and ——,
>   and if I ——, and have not love, I am ——。
> And if I ——,
>   and if I ——, and have not love, I am ——。

The second section is based primarily on verbs which indicate love's nature. First come two positive verbal statements; then a verb with a negative is followed once by the noun love, five times by negative verbal statements. A transition to the positive is made by means of an antithetical parallel, and the section ends with four verbs whose object is 'all things'.

> (*positive*)   Love ——,
>   —— love;
> (*negative*) it does not ——;
>   love does not —— (*six verbs*)
> (*transition*) it does not rejoice over unrighteousness,
>   but it rejoices with the truth;
> (*positive*)   all things it —— (*four times*).

The third section describes the finality of love by means of a series of contrasts which recall the themes of the first section.

> (*contrasts*) Love never fails;
>   if there are ——, they will be ——;
>   if there are ——, they will ——;
>   if there is ——, it will be ——.
> (*transition*) For we —— in part and we —— in part;
>   but when the perfect comes, the partial will be——.
>
> (*an example*) When I was a child,
>   I —— as a child (*three examples*),
>   but when I became a man,
>   I put away the things of a child。

(*eschatological conclusion*) Thus far we see ——,
　　　　　　　　　　　　but then ——.
　　　　　　　　　　　　Thus far I know in part,
　　　　　　　　　　　　but then, ——.

(*summary*) Faith, hope, and love last, these three;
　　　　　　　but the greatest of these is love.

Some of the points can be arranged differently, but it is clear that
a carefully planned arrangement does exist. To discover such
structures in the New Testament writings is the primary task of
exegesis. If we can understand them, we can at least begin to
understand what the writers intended to say.

SPECIAL PARAGRAPH STRUCTURES

In addition to the general problem of understanding sentences
and paragraphs, there is also the question of particular literary
forms which Paul and others may employ. One obvious example
is the *salutation* which we should expect to find in a letter. Less
obvious is the *thanksgiving*, which occurs not only in the Pauline
epistles (except Galatians) but also in other letters of Hellenistic
and Roman times. Such thanksgivings often set forth themes
which are later taken up in the body of the letter itself. (This
subject is fully discussed by Paul Schubert in his *Form and Function
of the Pauline Thanksgivings*, 1939.) In addition, Graeco-Roman
writers were well aware of the possibilities provided by the
ecthesis, or carefully planned digression (I Corinthians 13 is an
example).

Sometimes literary and oral style overlap, as in the instances
where Paul addresses his readers as individuals (e.g. Rom. 2.1 ff.;
cf. also James 2.18 ff.) or quotes from what some of them have
said or written, as in I Corinthians (6.12–13; perhaps 6.18b;
8.1, 4, 8; 10.23). This manner of writing, reflected also in the
question, 'Don't you know that . . . ?', is characteristic of the
diatribe or popular philosophical address developed by Cynics and
Stoics. (Lists of virtues and vices, as well as brief descriptions of
family duties, were also common among Graeco-Roman writers.)

A fascinating example of a special kind of paragraph occurs in
II Corinthians 11.23–33, where Paul is reluctantly 'boasting' to

the Corinthians. As Anton Fridrichsen pointed out, this 'catalogue of crises' finds remarkably close stylistic similarities in the descriptions of the careers of kings and other potentates which were engraved on stone or related in Graeco-Roman biographies. These descriptions, like Paul's, make use of 'many times' and of precise numbers as well; sometimes, like Paul's, they contain brief accounts of significant episodes. The difference, of course, lies in the content. Kings list their achievements; Paul lists examples of his sufferings on behalf of Christ.

Another special kind of paragraph structure which should be mentioned at this point is the *parable*, characteristic of the teaching of Jesus and that of his rabbinical contemporaries. This structure deserves notice especially because of the dogmatic assumptions associated primarily with the work of Adolf Jülicher (*Die Gleichnisreden Jesu*). Jülicher was trying to free the parables of Jesus from the 'over-interpretation' which had frequently been given them in patristic and medieval exegesis. He therefore sharply differentiated allegory from parable. According to his definitions, an allegory was an artificial story intended to convey a variety of meanings; a parable was a realistic story which made one, and only one, point. Unfortunately, while his general idea is correct, not all the parables of Jesus are realistic and not all of them convey only one point. Sometimes, as also among the rabbis, allegory and parable overlap, and we are not in a position to reject those parables which seem to convey more than one meaning or, for that matter, the explanations of the parables which occur in the gospels themselves.

WORDS

We have seen that to understand the New Testament writings we must examine the literary form of sentences and paragraphs. Only after doing so can we turn to the smallest units of expression, the words. But we must remember that the meanings of words depend primarily on the function the words perform within the sentences. One might suppose that the simple connective '*kai*' ordinarily translated 'and', would be easy enough to translate, or that '*kai . . . kai*' could always be rendered as 'both . . . and'. Such is not the case. '*Kai*' obviously means two different things in the following sentence. 'And ("*kai*"), passing by the sea of Galilee, he saw Simon and ("*kai*") Peter' (Mark 1.16). The first refers to a temporal sequence; the second, to the association of two objects of vision. Sometimes the word can bear an adversative sense ('and yet'); sometimes it is 'otiose', conveys practically no meaning, and should not be translated.

When we pass beyond this kind of word to the more difficult terms such as prepositions, we encounter the fact that both in popular Greek and in ordinary English, prepositions are fairly fluid in meaning. The Greek word '*en*' can mean 'in'; it can also mean 'with', 'by', or 'to'. Its precise meaning depends on the context. And when we go on to key words like justification, redemption, salvation, grace (and others) we confront the problem of finding English equivalents (see Chapter III) and, more important, of trying to delimit the range of meanings. We have already seen some of the ways in which scholars have tried to make use of papyri and of the Septuagint, not to mention Hellenistic literature in general. Such dictionaries as those of Walter Bauer and Gerhard Kittel provide indispensable help. But they cannot give us precise definitions of any of these words. They can tell us what meanings the words seem to possess in various writings; we cannot be sure that Paul, for example, always intended to convey any of these meanings in his letters.

Often the best analogies for the meanings of words and the overtones which an author intended to convey are provided in the author's own writings. Thus Bultmann has pointed out that for Paul the verb '*pisteuō*' often bears the meaning 'obey' as well as 'believe'. The author's own usage must be decisive. He was (ordinarily) the master of his own language.

THE QUESTION OF INTERPOLATIONS

Thus far we have been assuming that the documents we possess are the documents the New Testament authors wrote, in spite of the presence of a few textual difficulties. Such cases as Mark 16.9–20 and John 7.33–8.11 are exceptional. But literary critics often attempt to go beyond textual evidence and discover interpolations by using literary criteria alone. We must therefore discuss these criteria and attempt to assess the results of applying them.

Obviously the evidence provided by ancient manuscripts is of primary importance. Passages omitted by early scribes often deserve to have been omitted. On the other hand, if various manuscripts present essentially the same content but with variations in expression we cannot be certain that the passage involved is to be deleted. Probably one or another of the manuscripts has preserved the original version.

After textual criticism comes literary analysis as such. Three questions can be raised. (1) Does the passage in question contain words or phrases alien to the rest of the author's known work? If it does, we may regard it as suspect – though we must remember that vocabularies change and that, even at one time, an author does not use all the words he knows. Closely related to this is the question as to whether or not words in the suspect passage are used in senses different from those in which the author elsewhere employs them – though this question too must be raised with caution, since authors can, after all, use one word to mean several things and several words to convey one meaning. (2) Does the passage in question reflect the style used in other parts of the author's work? If it does not, we may suspect the presence of interpolation. On the other hand, it must be remembered that one author can write in several styles and that in antiquity those who were trained in writing were taught to imitate the styles of various models. Sometimes scholars have listed criteria for finding interpolations by criticizing the style of certain passages. They assume that such an author as John could write well, and therefore interpolations may exist where there are (a) compositional difficulties ('when, then, the Lord knew that the Pharisees had heard that Jesus was making and baptizing more disciples than John,' John 4.1), (b) contradictions ('yet Jesus himself was not baptizing; his disciples were,' 4.2), and (c) obscurities. An excellent example of obscurity occurs in John 4.43–5.

After two days he went forth from there into Galilee. For Jesus himself testified that a prophet has no honour in his own country. When, then, he came into Galilee the Galileans received him, having seen everything that he had done in Jerusalem at the feast; for they themselves had gone to the feast.

What is the sequence of ideas in this passage? Origen found it so difficult that he was sure it was meant allegorically; and he may have been right. The difficulty with these three criteria lies in the assumption that an author (*a*) never has compositional difficulties, (*b*) never contradicts himself, and (*c*) always writes, and intends to write, clearly. This assumption is not necessarily correct.

Literary critics sometimes pass beyond these criteria in the direction of historical criticism. They analyse documents in relation to (1) the presumed author's life and thought, (2) the known course of historical events, and (3) the assumed development of early Christian life and thought. The first of these methods can be regarded as still within the limits of literary criticism. Passages which are inconsistent with what is definitely known about an author's life or thought (as reflected in his writings) may well be regarded as interpolations. In most instances in the New Testament, however, not enough is known about these phenomena for us to be able to say with certainty what is inconsistent with them. The second and third of the methods go well beyond literary criticism. The fact that something seems unhistorical to us does not imply that it seemed unhistorical to a New Testament writer or that, for that matter, he was writing what we should regard as history. For example, it has often been assumed that the description of the last times in Mark 13 was written either before or after the fall of Jerusalem in 70 but, in any event, with closer attention to the book of Daniel than to historical events. On the other hand, the precise reference to the devastation of Jerusalem by a hostile army in Luke 21.20–4 has suggested that Luke is writing after the fall of the city. C. H. Dodd has pointed out, however, that Luke's reference may well be derived from Old Testament passages which speak of the fall of Jerusalem in 586 B.C. Mark, then, is close to Daniel; Luke is close to earlier prophets, and the passage is of no use in dating his book.

As for the third method, it cannot be discussed until we have considered the idea of development as applied to early Christian history (Chapter IV).

QUESTIONS OF AUTHORSHIP

In antiquity, as we have already seen when discussing the canon, questions were raised about the authorship of various New

Testament books. When such questions arose, they were treated primarily in relation to the vocabulary, style and ideas of the authors involved. Thus it was claimed that Paul did not write Hebrews (Origen), that the author of I Peter did not write II Peter (Jerome), and that the author of the Fourth Gospel did not write Revelation (Dionysius of Alexandria). At this point it is enough to say that all these claims are almost certainly correct.

In modern times the range of questioning has widened, and many scholars have held that Paul did not write either Ephesians or the Pastoral Epistles, while none of the Catholic Epistles was written by the author assigned to it. Some have also questioned the authenticity of Colossians and II Thessalonians. In addition, doubts have been vigorously expressed about the authorship of the four gospels, and of the book of Revelation as well. Interestingly enough, if we ask what remains unchallenged we find that it consists of seven Pauline epistles and (probably) of a true tradition behind the gospels. Such a view is almost the same as that advocated by Marcion in the second century. But to suggest that the view is like Marcion's does not relieve us from the responsibility of examining it.

We must therefore consider the criteria for judging authorship. They are much the same as those used in dealing with interpolations, except that the areas of investigation are wider and there is even more use of something like historical criticism. (1) Textual criticism is not especially relevant in so far as the authorship of the document is concerned. More important is the question whether or not old and valuable witnesses contain it. For example, the third-century Beatty papyri are fragmentary at the beginning and the end of the Pauline epistles. From what is missing at the beginning we can calculate the number of pages missing at the end, since the papyrus leaves were simply laid on top of one another and folded. There is not enough space for all the Pastoral Epistles; therefore they were not to be found in this manuscript. But an American scholar noticed that as the scribe got closer to the end of his manuscript his writing became smaller and more cramped. This point suggests that like us he was aware that he had miscalculated the number of pages he needed, and that he may well have intended to include the Pastorals. If his error was too conspicuous, he could have glued on a few additional pages. (2) By means of literary criticism we can compare the vocabulary and style of a questioned document with similar phenomena in unquestioned documents. Thus I Peter has only a hundred words in common with II Peter, while 369 in I Peter are not in II Peter and 230 in II Peter are not in I Peter. This kind of analysis seems fairly conclusive. The two documents were not written by one author. On the other hand, when we consider the relation of the Pastorals and Ephesians to the major Pauline epistles we find an anomalous situation. About a third of the words in the Pastorals do not occur in the other Pauline letters; about a sixth of those in Ephesians are similarly lacking. Admittedly the proportion of 'new' words in the Pastorals seems rather high, especially when compared with that in Ephesians. Two questions arise, however. (*a*) To what extent are we able to judge authenticity on this basis, when we have so few materials with which to deal? It may be that the statistical foundation is absent. (*b*) What proportion of 'new' words is to be regarded as acceptable? In Romans, as compared with earlier Pauline letters, about a quarter of the words are 'new'. Should we say that a quarter is just right, while a third is too much and a sixth is too little? To ask this question is to indicate the absurdity of claiming that this method gives precise results. Stylistic differences may be more significant, though it is difficult to assess their importance exactly. As we have already seen in looking at Paul, he uses different styles on different occasions. Similarly the style of Luke 1.1-4 is very different from that of the two chapters which follow, and in the book of Acts the style becomes more polished as the apostle Paul goes out into the Graeco-Roman world. Presumably the author intended to create this variation. (3) Historical criticism has a special rôle to play in questions of authorship, for these questions would probably not arise were there not ancient traditions which have come to be doubted. Historical and literary criticism thus overlap when the tradition about authorship is being examined. For instance, what Papias tells us about the literary activities of Mark and Matthew has to be considered, as well as what Justin says about the evangelists and the author of Revelation and what Irenaeus relates about the gospels, Acts and the Pauline epistles, and Revelation. Modern scholars have often been highly suspicious of these early Fathers' remarks, and have argued that they reflect inferences from the New Testament books rather than trustworthy traditions. It may be suggested, however, that even if this is the case the Fathers were not necessarily wrong; and it seems hard to deny that they could have possessed reliable information.

We conclude that while some New Testament books may have been ascribed to authors who did not write them, each case has to be considered with great care and caution. Unless highly convincing evidence can be produced against the tradition, there is no reason not to accept it.

SOURCES

Another function of literary criticism is that of determining the sources used by an author in composing his work. Admittedly this function is less important than that of analysing the meaning of the work itself. But it is often useful to note, by comparing the author's work with the source or sources he used, what changes he has made and what he has added or deleted. The discovery of sources is a more difficult process than might be supposed, for in antiquity, as H. J. Cadbury has observed, authors are accustomed not to name the sources they use, and to name sources they do not use.

There are two obvious examples of the use of sources in the New Testament. The first is provided when we find in the second chapter of II Peter a slightly revised version of the Epistle of Jude. Here the stylistic improvements suggest that II Peter is using Jude, not vice versa. The second occurs in Ephesians, much of which is so close to Colossians in content and in vocabulary as to indicate that the author of Ephesians, whether Paul or someone else, was producing a revised version of the earlier epistle. It is likely that Ephesians follows Colossians because the specific situation and specific persons involved in Colossians are lacking.

More significant source-relations are involved in the three synoptic gospels. At many points their wording is so closely similar that we must assume that one or another of the following possibilities is a probability: (1) Mark and Luke followed Matthew; (2) Matthew and Mark followed Luke; (3) Matthew and Luke followed Mark; (4) Matthew followed Mark and Luke; (5) Luke followed Matthew and Mark; or (6) Mark followed Matthew and Luke. All these solutions are possible; we shall later argue that only one of them is probable (Chapter VIII).

In this chapter we have said nothing about the matters, often regarded as belonging to literary criticism, which concern the date and the place of writing of particular documents. In our opinion these matters do not belong to literary criticism. They are concerned with temporal and spatial correlations and therefore belong to historical criticism. Literary criticism is concerned with a document as a document, with the structure of a book rather than with its historical setting or purpose. Obviously we do not intend to exclude historical understanding from our analysis. We claim, however, that literary interpretation comes first.

The primary function of literary criticism, then, is the understanding of the structure of a document and the reflection of the author's purpose as expressed by means of this structure. In the course of performing this primary function a secondary function arises. Do certain passages, or even certain books, reflect the structural procedures of a particular author? It may be necessary to exclude them as interpolations or additions if we are to understand the author's literary purpose. A similar question arises when we deal with his sources, actual and potential. Something of the structure he provides may be due to the necessity for coming to terms with his sources. The secondary function performed by interpolation-theories and source-criticism may therefore assist the critic in achieving his primary goal: the literary understanding of his materials.

HISTORICAL CRITICISM

Textual criticism is concerned with the comparison of various witnesses to the early text of a document and has as its goal the establishment of its earliest form. Literary criticism is concerned with the comparison of various literary forms and materials and has as its goal the literary analysis of a document in order to ascertain the way or ways in which its author expressed his thought. Historical criticism, to which we now turn, is concerned with the time/place setting of a document, its sources, and the events discussed in or implied by the document. Historical criticism builds on textual and literary criticism, and its end product is the writing of history, a narrative which reports events in a sequence roughly chronological. Chronological sequence is the skeleton of history. Without it there can be no historical narrative, and no interpretation of casual relationships; for while what is prior is not necessarily the, or a, cause of what is posterior, that which is posterior can never be the, or a, cause of what is prior. For this reason those who criticize the search for 'what actually happened' as the study of 'mere events' and the results as 'nothing but chronicle' are mistaken. Without chronicle history cannot be written. Even the analysis of the past in relation to social, political, economic, philosophical or theological theory has to be based on a chronological sequence.

Moreover, while it may be held that the record of events provides us with a skeleton and perhaps even a body, but not with a soul or spirit, it must be remembered that a soul or spirit needs the clothing of body if it is to act historically. History is more than the history of ideas. While the sciences of tactics, strategy and logistics are obviously important in interpreting military or naval history, the history of warfare is not just the history of theory. It must be concerned with wars, campaigns and battles in which real men actually made decisions and acted upon them. Similarly, economic and social factors are undoubtedly significant; but historical events cannot be understood solely in relation to them. The Roman empire was the creation not of factors alone but of Julius Caesar and Augustus. Christianity arose not simply because of Jewish apocalypticism and Hellenistic piety but because of the work of Jesus Christ and his apostles.

Before discussing the kinds of materials which the historical critic uses, we should say something about what he can expect to learn from them. He can expect to find out a great deal about significant public events, especially battles, murders and sudden deaths. He can find out about institutions and their organization. What he cannot find out, unless the materials happen to mention it, is any account of what a private person did at a particular time and in a particular place. To obtain this information he must rely upon accounts written by or about such a private person. No amount of inference, however plausible, can lead him to a fact about this person, for this person's motives and actions are unique and cannot be reconstructed hypothetically. It is, of course, possible that the person himself, or a later writer describing him, has misinterpreted his motives or incorrectly described his actions; but existing accounts, whatever their quality, must be given preference over the historian's hypothetical reconstructions. (We shall later consider the problem which arises when the accounts disagree with one another.)

It should also be said that all the materials which the historian uses are modern – that is to say, they exist now. If they did not exist now, he obviously could not use them. Some interpreters of history, or of the writing of history, have therefore argued that the historian's work is strictly contemporary. He uses his materials in order to create a picture which has modern significance and, because he is influenced by his own religious, psychological, social and economic situation – often in ways he does not recognize – he is not, and should not try to be, a discoverer or recoverer of 'what actually happened'. What happened cannot be recovered. No doubt this argument possesses some validity. Absolute 'objectivity' is not an attainable goal. At the same time, a historian who tries to write history rather than propaganda will not be content to impose his own will on the materials with which he deals. He will enter into a conversation with the materials from the past, a conversation in the course of which he will expect to learn something, not simply to engage in a monologue. Such a historian will recognize some of his own limitations as well as the limitations of his method and his materials, and he will try to maintain a scrupulous honesty in the face of data which do not correspond with his preconceptions.

There are various kinds of data with which the historian is concerned. (1) There are archaeological data, some of them non-literary (buildings, artifacts, etc.), others literary (inscriptions, papyri), still others 'mixed' (coins, medals, etc.). Those which are literary or semi-literary in nature must be examined critically. Not every official inscription conveys the whole truth about the events to which it is related; an example is provided by the inscriptions which express the joy of subject populations in celebrating the emperor's birthday. Even a private letter, preserved on papyrus by chance, does not necessarily present a complete account of the events mentioned in it. (2) There are also non-archaeological data, materials which we know because they have been copied and recopied in the course of their transmission. These data usually consist of the literary productions of poets, philosophers, historians, and – for that matter – evangelists. In addition, there are literary or semi-literary documents such as letters; the originals of the Pauline epistles have been lost, but the epistles are known to us from copies of copies.

In dealing with these data there are several distinctions which can be made, and the historian must deal critically not only with the materials but also with the distinctions.

PRIMARY AND SECONDARY

All data have relevance in relation to some situation or other. (1) All data are contemporaneous with the time in which they were written. Thus a letter written in the year 50 is obviously significant for our synthesis of events in that year; in addition, a historical narrative, describing events in the year 10 but written in the year 50, is also significant for 50 because it reflects the interests of that year. For this reason the gospels are important witnesses to the life of the church in the time in which they were written, as well as to the life of Jesus which the evangelists endeavour to describe. The importance of this contemporaneousness should not, however, be exaggerated, since – as we have already argued – historical writers do not simply reflect the concerns of their contemporaries (including themselves), but enter into a dialogue with the past.

(2) Moreover, all data, to a greater or a lesser degree, provide evidence for the time before they were written, since their creators did not create *ex nihilo*. Their language is not their own; many of their ideas are not their own but come from previous generations. In historical writing the historian's testimony is more significant in relation to an earlier time than in relation to his own. Thus, though it is sometimes said that the gospels provide us with evidence from the time when they were written rather than with sources dealing with an earlier period, such a statement can easily mislead the unwary. The evangelists did, indeed, testify to the meaning of Jesus in relation to their own times; but it was Jesus with whose meaning they were concerned. They and their informants were dealing with materials which had been remembered, not invented. To be sure, the locus of remembering is always in the present, but the locus of what is remembered is in the past. The early Church included individuals who not only proclaimed the gospel but also remembered who the Jesus was whose life, death and resurrection were being proclaimed. The apostle Paul was quite capable of differentiating a 'commandment of the Lord' from his own interpretation of it (I Cor. 7.10, 12). The fact that man has a memory means that he is not simply contemporaneous or 'modern'.

At the same time, memory plays tricks. In analysing reports based on memory, therefore, some measure of precedence must be given to accounts written soon after the events and based on the reports of eye-witnesses. (1) The best account is written fairly soon after the event, since at that time the writer has less opportunity to see how he ought to modify the record with a view to preserving his own reputation or that of his friends. Since he cannot usually foresee later consequences he is likely to present an unvarnished account. The farther he gets from the event the more likely he is to fail, voluntarily or involuntarily, to recall and record it correctly. (2) The best account is written by, or based on the reminiscences of, an eye-witness. Such a witness has heard with his own ears and seen with his own eyes; he himself participated in the experience. He is not likely, at least at first, to combine rationalization of the event with his remembrance of it. Yet the measure of precedence the historian gives to early accounts, even by or from eye-witnesses, cannot eliminate other considerations. The eye-witness may have been so much influenced by his expectations of what ought to have taken place that he identified what should have happened with what did happen. He may not have been an accurate observer or an accurate reporter. His memory may have been more reliable than his first-hand testimony was. In other words, there are few, if any, absolutes in the writing of history.

On the other hand, we must remember that as critical analysts we may doubt the accuracy of the witness's record but we cannot substitute our own conjectures for what he has reported. If there are two or more conflicting accounts, we can indicate which of them is to be regarded as the more trustworthy and try to explain how the other or others arose. If there is only one, we cannot invent an alternative account, since historical events are not precisely predictable. All we can do when we have a single, seemingly unreliable narrative, is to indicate why we reject it and admit our ignorance as to what actually happened – if we think anything did happen.

Sometimes a distinction between 'primary' and 'secondary' materials is used in order to make choices between differing accounts of the same, or similar, events. For example, the accounts of Paul's career to be found in his own letter to the Galatians and in the later book of Acts are not altogether in concord. Should we then claim that his letter is a 'primary' source of information, Acts a 'secondary' one? It is most unlikely that history can be analysed so neatly. More probably, Paul writes from one standpoint, the author of Acts from another; neither account deserves absolute confidence to the exclusion of the other. The task of the historian is to compare similarities and differences and to try to construct an inclusive account which will do justice to both points of view. Furthermore, though Paul was obviously an eye-witness and Luke (as far as early events are concerned) was probably not one, it must be recalled that documents later in time (Acts) can be based on materials as early as, or earlier than, documents produced by eye-witnesses. These points mean that no absolute distinction can be drawn between 'primary' and 'secondary', at least without careful critical analysis.

FACT AND INTERPRETATION

Another common distinction is that made between 'fact' and 'interpretation'. Essentially a fact is something which is, or could be, recognizable by all the possible witnesses to an occurrence. Thus it is a fact that Jesus was crucified. An interpretation, on the other hand, is essentially that of an individual or a group; it varies from individual to individual or from group to group. Caiaphas, Judas, Pontius Pilate and the apostles interpreted the crucifixion of Jesus in differing ways. Therefore, it is sometimes held, the historians will deal with the fact after separating the various interpretations from it.

To make such a separation is very difficult, for facts are almost always remembered, and accounts of them are transmitted, because they seemed meaningful both at the time the events occurred and in the period immediately afterwards. In addition, the analyst is trying to deal with the subjective interpretation(s) provided by an ancient author – as well as with the interpretation(s) provided by that author's source(s) – on the basis of his own judgement. Suppose that the analyst can show that the author had a particular axe to grind. It will be hard to show that this axe was different from the axes of earlier witnesses, or that it (or they) necessarily distorted the impression(s) which the original event made on the minds of eye-witnesses at the time. The summaries which Luke gives in the first half of Acts, for example, are his own, but they may accurately reflect the early life of the Jerusalem church.

Only when two or more sources of information are available can the analyst definitely show that a subjective judgement has provided a mistaken interpretation – or when, for example, a summary contradicts or distorts the materials being summarized. Before claiming that contradiction or distortion exists, however, the analyst must be sure that the summary is not based upon materials which the author did not reproduce. If it is based upon such materials, or if it may have been based on them, it is obviously not the product of the author's imagination alone.

If it can be shown that one document, actually in existence, is a source of another existing document (as when Mark is employed by Luke), the analyst can proceed to show how the later writer has modified the materials he employs. Two warnings, however, need to be given at this point. (1) Analysis of Luke's revision of Mark does not justify any conjectures about Mark's possible revision of his other sources. We do not know what those sources were, apart from the preaching and teaching of the apostle Peter (and perhaps others), and we do not know precisely what Mark did with them. (2) The analysis cannot proceed in reverse. It cannot be claimed that the more highly 'developed' of two documents is necessarily the later of the two, for it must first be proved (*a*) that one of the two is later than the other, and (*b*) that the one presumably later makes use of the earlier one. This is to say that apparent literary relationships or cases of 'development' do not provide solid ground for chronology.

THE IDEA OF DEVELOPMENT

Sometimes just such an analysis is used in order to get back to the original form of a tradition or, in other words, to get close to the events or facts by tracing lines of interpretation from the known back into the unknown. Put rather crudely, this use of the theory of development can be expressed geometrically. We assume that we know points D and E on a particular line of tradition; we can assess the distance between D and E and also the direction DE. Then in theory, we can proceed to reconstruct the line (ABC)DE, and even the distances AB, BC, and CD. Unfortunately the course of human events, like that of true love, does not run so smoothly. The idea of development seems to have come from biology, where it is used in reference to the process of evolution from a previous and lower (e.g., embryonic) stage to a later, more complex or more perfect one; this development can involve differentiation into individual organisms and their subsequent histories.[1]

Development involves continuity among the various stages of the organism which develops. It is therefore different from change, in which the phenomenon being considered is distinctly different from what it was. There is also alteration, in which there is a partial change and the identity of the phenomenon is still preserved. It is the notion of development which best combines the elements of sameness and difference – together with an emphasis on the growth of something living.

The basic question, however, is that of the extent to which early Christianity, for example, actually did develop, and the use of a semi-biological term may well confuse the issue by implying that the answer is already known. It may also tend to suggest that there were no radical alterations, or even changes, in the history of the early Church, or that by 'development' is meant a process which from small beginnings (Jesus) brought great things (the Church). Such a notion obviously does not do justice to such revolutionary events as the crucifixion and resurrection of Jesus or the conversion of Paul. Whether or not there was development in the early Church, the idea of development cannot be used as a guide for the reconstruction of its history. It may serve as a hypothesis; it is not an analytical instrument.

CHANGE AND DECAY

What we have said about development should also be applied to theories about an original, authentic, pure Christianity which was later distorted by various secondary factors. Such theories have a long history within, and on the edge of, the Christian Church. Marcion, for example, held that the pure gospel of Jesus was distorted by his disciples who modified it severely when they presented it to Jews; and similar notions are often latent in the work of modern scholars. Since fashions change, the contrasts developed by one generation often differ from those emphasized by the previous one; but it can be shown that underlying a good deal of study supposedly analytical in nature there is a very simple set of antitheses which are supposed to be self-evident. In previous times it was customary to contrast Jesus with Paul, or the Jesus of history with the Christ of faith, or the synoptic gospels with the Fourth Gospel. Alternatively, faith or grace could be contrasted with works, moralism, sacraments, doctrines, and creeds, and the 'New Testament teaching' could be found in Paul but not in James, Matthew, or the synoptic gospels in general. For a time there were those who believed that the essential 'kerygma' could be emphasized at the expense of the less significant 'didache', though the fairly obvious fact that in early Christianity 'gospel' included both preaching and teaching lessens the force of this contrast. More recently it has been fashionable to compare the authentic Hebrew elements in the New Testament with the less satisfactory elements which can be called 'late Jewish' or 'Greek'.

The chief difficulty with these antitheses is that they are not historical. They arise out of the needs of modern writers to pick and choose among the various elements in the New Testament and Christian synthesis, and when they are used as instruments of analysis they become substitutes for thought. They are created by laying emphasis on certain distinctive, or seemingly distinctive, features in the various documents and by neglecting equally important resemblances. A warning can be given if we look at a problem in Old Testament studies. A generation ago it was customary to contrast prophetic with priestly elements. Now the pendulum has swung again, and it is recognized that much prophecy arose out of the priesthood and that priests preserved the writings of prophets. Similarly, the study of Judaism has led to the recognition that there were Greek elements in it, and that a sharp separation of Jewish from Greek ideas is not justifiable. The world in which Christianity arose was not characterized by the contrasts which some scholars have imagined to exist.

CHANGE BUT NO DECAY

A variation on the theme of change is provided by those scholars who insist that by means of historical analysis it can be shown that Christianity was originally a movement of apocalyptic expectation within late Judaism; the prophet Jesus preached that the reign of God was at hand – but he was wrong. Several corollaries can then be deduced from this axiom. Since the movement at first existed within Judaism and only later spread to the Hellenistic world, features which seem Jewish are authentic while those which seem Hellenistic are not (see above). Since it looked only towards the future, features which are concerned with past or present represent revisions of the original message. Since the followers of Jesus regarded him as essentially human, statements about his divine nature or function have been added to the authentic gospel, often by use of ideas derived from 'mystery religions'. Since God's reign was immediately at hand, Jesus could not have established a church or appointed ministers for a long period of time; there were no sacraments in Judaism, therefore references to the Church or its life are not part of the original teaching of Jesus. He preached a purely Jewish gospel. After his death this gospel was changed in the Hellenistic world.

The essential difficulty with this axiom (and these corollaries) is that it rests upon a principle of historical analysis which is not tenable.[1] The gospel materials represent Jesus as teaching that the reign of God is not only future but also somehow present. They represent his followers as considering him both human and more than human, whether as 'Son of God' or as 'Son of Man'. They represent him as appointing apostles (principally, it must be admitted, for an immediate mission) and as binding them to himself and his purpose at his last supper, in which he related his body to the broken bread and his covenant to the outpoured wine. The principle employed in dealing with these materials is that when there is discordant testimony, the evidence to be accepted is that which conflicts with the main lines of later Christian witness. (The principle is therefore analogous with the preference of early textual critics for the 'more difficult reading', whether or not it made sense.) Such a principle assumes that as the genuine, 'difficult' testimony was being modified it passed through the hands of halfhearted forgers who while inserting their own corrections of the tradition somehow felt compelled to retain a few authentic items, presumably for the benefit of modern analysts. The transmitters of tradition were thus 'deceivers, yet true' (II Cor. 6.8). But this assumption is not provable. A more satisfactory assumption, it would appear, is that the authentic gospel of Jesus is to be recovered by considering the various, conflicting items of evidence and by attempting to ascertain what proclamation, perhaps ambiguously expressed, could have been

[1] On this principle in gospel criticism see pages 287–8.

interpreted in divergent ways. (Again, this is like a principle of criticism; we look for the reading which could have resulted in the divergent readings now found in the manuscripts.) The original teaching of Jesus is therefore not to be found by rejecting much of the evidence we possess but by analysing all the evidence and looking for its source.

Another way of viewing the New Testament is that maintained by the 'demythologizers', but since this method is largely theological rather than historical (though it is supposed to have a basis in historical analysis) we shall consider it in our chapter on theological interpretation.

ENVIRONMENTAL STUDY

It is obvious that in speaking of development and change we have come close to the question of the environment or environments of the New Testament writers. The study of this area has occupied a great deal of attention in modern times, before as well as after the discovery of the Dead Sea Scrolls. The purpose of this study has been described as 'setting the church in the village' or, in other words, relating early Christianity to the world in (and in opposition to) which it arose.

The purpose of environmental study is not so obvious. In so far as the early Christian gospel was addressed to Jews and/or gentiles of the first century, it can certainly be understood in a more specific way if we know something about the first-century world; on the other hand, it may be that we shall be tempted to make what was intended generally more specific than it actually was when we relate it too closely to the first century. We may even develop a theory that whatever Jesus said was spoken with a specific reference and that any generalizations are the products of the early Church; such a theory is, of course, unwarranted by the evidence.

We may also try to determine how much of the village has entered the Church and its tradition and, in short, to indicate what elements in early Christianity are shared with (hence, derived from?) its environment and what elements are unique. But unless we start with the presupposition that the unique is the true it is hard to maintain that this kind of analysis can produce meaningful results. Does the gospel of Jesus, for example, consist essentially of what he did not share with his contemporaries? Are ideas which he did share with his contemporaries necessarily wrong? To put the matter a little more precisely, can we speak of an 'ancient world view' and thus dismiss it? To raise these questions is to suggest that environmental study conducted solely for comparative purposes leads nowhere.

On the other hand, useful negative conclusions can be reached from the study of the environment. It is often said that ancient people accepted a 'three-storey universe'; they were wrong and we are right; therefore whatever they say about the universe is to be rejected. Examination of the evidence can indicate that (1) not all of them accepted such a cosmology, and (2) such a cosmology as such has little to do with the teaching of the New Testament. Again, it is held that ancient people accepted miracles while modern ones rightly reject them. Such a generalization is false. In antiquity, as in modern times, some believed in miracles while others did not. Such conclusions, negative in the face of contemporary scholarly clichés, can be reached not by reading modern summaries but by looking at the heterogeneous testimonies given by first-century men. Instead of making statements about 'the ancients' or 'the Jews' or 'the Greeks' we must resolutely face the varieties to be found among individuals, even though the individuals were certainly conditioned (to some extent) by the groups in which they found themselves.

THE HISTORY OF RELIGIONS

Towards the beginning of this century there was great enthusiasm for the comparative study of religions; it was often conducted by scholars who believed that when they had discovered parallels to early Christian expressions, ideas, institutions or rites in other religions they had shown that the Christian phenomena were derived from these other religions and also that their meaning within Christianity was essentially the same as it was within the other religion or religions. In addition, some of them believed that theories based on phenomena in other religions could be applied without alteration to the phenomena of early Christianity. Since some Greek myths were 'aetiological' (composed in order to explain the origins of rites), the story of the Last Supper could be treated as an aetiological myth, intended to explain the origin of the Christian Eucharist – which actually came from the Hellenistic mystery religions. Similarly Paul's idea of dying and rising with Christ, and perhaps the belief in Christ's resurrection itself, came from a prior notion about dying and rising saviour-gods in the Graeco-Roman world. The notion that baptism meant rebirth was viewed as pagan in origin, largely because of the evidence provided by some inscriptions of the fourth century of the Christian era.

The absurdities to which this kind of study led resulted in its being generally discredited, although more recently it seems to be flourishing again in different form. The more modern view is that everything, or almost everything, in early Christianity can be explained as derived either (1) from the kind of Jewish apocalypticism represented by the Dead Sea Scrolls or (2) from the kind of Gnostic thought reflected in the writings criticized by the early Church Fathers or found at Nag-Hammadi in Egypt. Undoubtedly there are affinities between early Christianity and the Qumran community, and less significant ones between early Christianity and Gnosticism. But in each case the differences require as much attention as the resemblances do, and chronological priority, even when it can be established, does not prove the existence of causal connection. *Post hoc* is not the same as *propter hoc*.

Early Christianity certainly deserves to be studied by the historian of religions, and by other students who use his methods. But the methods need to be applied with extreme caution. Is the student studying the history of religion in general or the history of specific religions? More fruitful results will probably be obtained by respecting the individuality of religions as of men – in other words, by emphasizing the word 'history'.

A FINAL PROBLEM

An important aspect of modern New Testament study is the very fact of its modernity or, rather, its supposed modernity. It is obvious that some progress has been made in the course of the last century or so; few scholars today would suppose that New Testament history is significantly illuminated by the use of the erms 'thesis, antithesis, synthesis'. But as we have repeatedly pointed out, other clichés are often employed, no better for their being more recent. It is an open question whether or not genuine progress exists in this area of study. Certainly new evidence has become available, and to the extent that it has been utilized adequately it can be said that some advance has taken place.

It should be said, however, that in each generation an adequate or partially adequate understanding of the New Testament can be achieved only by the abandonment of the 'assured results' of the previous generation and by the fresh creation of openness to the text and to what it may say. The historical method must be employed in dealing with historical critics.

Why, then, should the study be continued if it has not led, and is not likely to lead, to any final results? The answer to this question lies not in any notion of inevitable progress but in the study itself. By means of critical-historical study, properly conducted, each generation comes to know the New Testament – not necessarily more thoroughly than its predecessors knew it, but more thoroughly than at the time it began its own work. Once more, however, we must avoid speaking of 'generations' or groups when we ought to keep the individual in mind. The progress of the individual student can be real though that of his generation may be dubious. Only he can resolutely refine his own method and try to keep himself free from the erroneous generalizations and bad logic which stand in the way of historical understanding.[1]

Above all, the historical analyst must not be ashamed of confessing ignorance – not the easy ignorance due to failure to investigate what can be known, but the hard ignorance due to the real lack of historical records. No amount of speculation supposedly historical can fill in the gaps which exist in our records. No amount of theory can be a substitute for evidence. Moreover, no final explanation can be given, in many instances or perhaps in all, for historical events of which we have some records. The 'explanations' we provide of the life of Paul or the life of Jesus still leave us with mysteries which will never be explained.

THE NECESSITY OF HISTORICAL UNDERSTANDING

Thus far we have concentrated our attention upon negative factors practically to the exclusion of positive ones. We have almost made it appear that historical understanding of the New Testament is an impossibility. In large measure this result has come about because of our phenomenological or, one might say, nominalist approach to the question. It could easily be charged that we have concentrated upon the trees and have lost sight of the forest. As we have been urging that historical understanding goes beyond literary and textual criticism in the direction of subjectivity, we have neglected the objectivity which is given our study by the existence of what we may call the phenomenon behind the phenomena. This phenomenon, more important for historical study than the isolated data which reflect it, is the existence of the early Church. Without awareness of the existence of the Church the isolated data remain isolated. It is the Church in its empirical, historical existence which holds them together and allows us to make sense of them. Without the Church the data might mean almost anything. Indeed, in early Gnostic communities the data did mean almost anything, since the Gnostics were not adherents of the visible Church and were therefore free to interpret New Testament texts in a wholeheartedly subjective way. Only by postulating or, rather, admitting the existence of the Church can we hold the data together and see that they reflect the Church's life and thought.

Of course the existence of the Church can be treated as a merely static hypothesis or fact, and the correlation of the various data can be made on grounds appropriate to such a static situation. Such an analysis, like the atomistic analysis which we have so far advocated, proceeds on non-historical lines to discover eternal truths or absolutes which may do justice to some aspects of the Church's gospel but cannot adequately be related to the variety of outlook present in the New Testament and other early Christian literature.

Because of this inadequacy it would appear that another approach is likely to be more fruitful. This different kind of approach must be one in which the unity and continuity of the Church's life is recognized but, at the same time, the diversity characteristic of any historical process (that is to say, of real events) can be accepted. To say this means that the New Testament must be viewed not only as the Church's book but specifically as the *early* Church's book. It is the book which shows how the good news was brought from Galilee to Jerusalem and to the ends of the Graeco-Roman world. To illustrate the change, or development, which accompanied this movement we may cite two texts:

> Truly, I say to you, there are some standing here who will not taste death before they see the kingdom of God come with power.

> He has granted to us his precious and very great promises, that through these you may escape from the corruption which is in the world because of passion, and become partakers of the divine nature.

The first is from the words of Jesus according to Mark; the second is from II Peter. Between the two lies a process, whether long or short, in the course of which the Christian gospel was redirected in order to become more fully comprehensible to those who lived and thought in the Graeco-Roman world.

The business of historical criticism is to deal with the diverse materials in the New Testament (and in other early Christian literature) and to show (1) their unity in relation to the mission of the Church and (2) the relation of their diversity to the various cultural currents within which the mission was carried on. In other words, historical study should set forth the elements of continuity and discontinuity in the Church's life.

There are, of course, other features of the Church's life, in addition to the question of Hellenization, which deserve attention. First there is the nature of the proclamation of Jesus as the Church remembered it. Was this gospel of the kingdom related (1) exclusively to the future or (2) exclusively to the present or (3) in part to both future and present? Is there any difference between the emphasis found in Galilean preaching and that found at Jerusalem? Second, there is the critical situation in the church of Jerusalem as it confronted, or was confronted by, the mission to gentiles. How was this problem solved – in so far as it was really solved? Third, how did the preaching of Paul to gentiles differ from his preaching to Jews? To what extent was it the same? What held the two kinds of preaching together? Fourth, how did the misunderstandings of his gospel, as reflected in his various letters, come into existence? To what extent did he agree, to what extent disagree, with his opponents of various kinds? Fifth, as members of the Church recorded the common memories of Jesus what did they continue to hold in common and what did they feel free to modify? What (historically) can explain the rather remarkable differences (1) among the synoptic gospels, (2) among all four gospels, and (3) between the synoptics as a group and the Gospel of John? Sixth, what is the difference, if any, between New Testament writings and those of the Apostolic Fathers and the Apologists? Seventh, what factors caused the Church to regard some or all of the New Testament books as 'canonical' while gradually coming to view the writings of the Apostolic Fathers (and other books) as extra-canonical?

Such questions as these require historical answers and lead us beyond the confines of the New Testament as a collection of books to the historical reality of the life of the early Church to which they bear witness. The New Testament points backward to the Old Testament and the old Israel and forward to other early Christian literature and the later Church; still more directly, it points behind or underneath itself to the Christian community in which and for which it was written. It remains incomprehensible unless the existence of this Church is recognized. It is the Church which both historically and theologically holds the New Testament together.

This is to say that the New Testament is the book of the early Church not only in the sense that the New Testament was written for use by the Church but also in the sense that it reflects the life of the Church. The New Testament is a collection of isolated documents and almost random theological statements for anyone who does not recognize the Church reflected and expressed in it. In other words, the New Testament sets forth the beginning, and contains the classical formulation, of the life of the Christian Church; the New Testament documents are the primary documents of church history and of the history of Christian thought. They are classical in the sense that the Church chose them as adequate representations of its beginnings or, to put it more precisely, of its original and thus permanently significant expressions. At the same time, they do not suggest that the Church can be regarded as a static entity. They come out of a historical process, and the dynamism of this process implies that whenever the later Church is true to its origins it too is dynamic.

The purpose, then, of New Testament study is to take the various documents and the insights expressed in the documents and to reconstruct the life out of which the documents and the insights emerged. We have already said more than enough about the necessity for caution in assigning semi-canonical status to our reconstruction. It can never be more than probable; at the same time, it can be rather highly probable, and we should not ask for more. No historical knowledge is more than probable. Of course it is possible to avoid risks by remaining within the circle of what the documents say and simply paraphrasing them. But such paraphrasing contributes nothing to historical knowledge. Such 'exegesis' cannot be related to anything else we know. It stands in splendid isolation, and so does whatever else we may be able to ascertain. Historical knowledge involves the risk of interpretation.

VI

THE NECESSITY OF THEOLOGICAL UNDERSTANDING

Thus far we have considered the collecting of the New Testament books, their copying and translation, and the methods by which one tries to ascertain what their authors were saying and the circumstances under which they wrote. But we seem to have failed to come to grips with the most important question of all. We have considered what they wrote and how they wrote it; we have not considered why they wrote, and this is the ultimate question of New Testament study. Unless we reach this question and make some attempt to solve it, there is no particular reason for us to be studying the New Testament rather than any other collection of ancient documents.

This point should be expressed with appropriate caution. It is not suggested (1) that there is no reason to study other documents, or (2) that the methods of studying the New Testament are necessarily unique to it. It is simply suggested that the New Testament writers had a purpose for writing and that unless this purpose is kept in view the analysis of their writings will be fragmentary and will produce nothing but a collection of fragments.

To some extent the history of New Testament interpretation – or, more accurately, of biblical interpretation – is roughly identical with the history of systematic theology. Most systematic theologians have believed that they were interpreting what the New Testament meant as a whole. To be sure, the use (conscious or unconscious) of the allegorical method often led them to read more into the text than more literal-minded exegetes have been able to find. But even the allegorical method requires that some passages in scripture be taken literally; these passages are usually regarded as the keys to the understanding of the Bible as a whole. In modern times, increasing use of 'the historical method' has led to insistence upon the variety of the outlooks expressed by biblical writers and sometimes to the refusal to lay emphasis upon their common faith. In place of 'biblical theology' or 'New Testament theology' we have varieties of New Testament religion. Such a concern is justifiable in relation to a situation in which differences were obscured and the New Testament was viewed in two dimensions rather than three or four. It is not justifiable if it obscures the ultimate unity of purpose underlying the New Testament books.

Again, the New Testament has sometimes been viewed as historical in the sense that it provides nothing but evidence for the development of early Christianity. The purpose of New Testament study is then regarded as the discovery or uncovering of various layers of tradition which either obscure or rightly draw out the implications of the earliest gospel. Only this earliest gospel is finally to be regarded as authoritative, or else the story of early Christianity, now truly seen, somehow possesses a meaning just because it is seen.

It should be said that such a notion is akin to the theory of Marcion rather than to anything to be found either in the New Testament itself or in the writings of Christian theologians. There is no reason to suppose that only the earliest strata of tradition contain the true gospel; had this been so, we should obviously have no New Testament, and none of the books in it would have been written. What we must look for, instead, is the purpose for which the New Testament authors wrote.

There are several ways in which this purpose has been sought. We have already mentioned the first, called 'biblical theology'. But before turning to it we should mention the preliminary study, popular in antiquity (Origen) and today as well, of the meanings of New Testament words. This study, as we have already argued (Chapter III), does not usually produce absolutely definite results. At the same time, it must be admitted that it is indispensable for our understanding of the texts. Unless we have some idea of the probable ranges of the meanings of words we cannot possibly go beyond what the authors said to why they said it. Literary criticism is a necessary part of theological interpretation. From this kind of literary criticism we then pass on to interpreting whole books and trying to see what their authors were saying, and – to some extent – why they spoke as they did.

But the final questions take us beyond literary criticism into the realm of theology. Why do the various New Testament books exist at all? What impelled their authors to write? Surely it was not that they wanted to achieve literary fame, for few of them were stylists and the Greek which they used is not the same as that of the 'best' writers of their day. Instead, it must be stated that they wrote because of their conviction that what had happened in the life, death and resurrection of Jesus, and in the work of the Spirit in the new community, had given them insight into the plan of God for the salvation of men. The differences among the books and among the individual authors are due to the varying ways in which these authors understood the meaning of the events and the divine plan, and to the varying circumstances in which they wrote. Obviously it is legitimate for us to be concerned with the divergent understandings and the divergent circumstances; but we must constantly bear in mind the fact that the diversity is only an aspect of the more central unity to be found in the common faith – in God, in Christ, and in the Holy Spirit.

The ultimate task of New Testament study, then, is to look for the whole as expressed in the parts. Often this task is rightly regarded as suspect, for students are likely either (1) to force somewhat different statements into a premature or even impossible synthesis, or (2) to treat New Testament, or biblical, doctrines as if they were absolutely normative when taken literally – in other words, to speak as if theology had come to an end with the closing of the canon. The first error may be called the error of rationalism. The only adequate statement, on this view, is the logically consistent one; therefore the New Testament must be made logically consistent. The second error is the error of biblicism; it denies the possibility that some biblical doctrines may have been the product of the first-century mind (if such a thing existed) rather than of the biblical mind (if such a thing existed). It fails to recognize the extent to which the New Testament writings were addressed to specific historical audiences.

On the other hand, there are equally dangerous errors on the other side, as we have already suggested. (1) Students may be content with describing a mass of heterogeneous statements, insisting upon their inconsistencies, and thus losing sight of the ultimate unity of the gospel. (2) They may proceed to a rough and ready job of 'demythologizing', assuming that passages which they do not like are mythological and failing to see that not all such passages were meant literally. They may look for a simple, authentic (i.e., sympathetic) gospel which, freed from all its embarrassing features, may speak directly to them – and support their own views. Both of these errors must be avoided; but no precise rules can be laid down for avoiding them. Probably, however, if a New Testament book seems to be nothing but a collection of contradictions we may suppose that we have misunderstood it; and if it clearly supports our own prejudices we may suppose that we have failed to interpret its message. The temptation to practise exegesis by removing difficult passages, and treating them as scribal errors or the work of stupid editors, should be resisted.

This is to say that in theological exegesis, just as in literary or historical criticism, we must maintain a certain measure of distance between the New Testament and ourselves. It is not so much a question of temporal distance (about 1,900 years) as it is a question of 'emotional distance'. Otherwise the New Testament does not speak to us; we speak for ourselves and use it only as a megaphone.

THE QUESTION OF DEMYTHOLOGIZING

In recent years a favourite method of theological interpretation has been given the name 'demythologizing'. By means of a biblical criticism 'free from compromise' the New Testament materials are first classified into something like primary and secondary. What needs demythologizing is the secondary language in which the primary was expressed, the language which speaks in a 'worldly' way of what is 'unworldly', the language of Jewish apocalyptic mythology or of Hellenistic Gnostic mythology.

Such language, as Rudolf Bultmann once said, is unscientific and cannot be accepted by modern men who use electric light.

According to Bultmann the method, which has affinities with ancient allegorization, builds on what was right in the older Liberal Protestant theology and combines with it the discoveries made in the history of religions. What is primary in the New Testament, freed from mythology, is then to be interpreted in the light of modern existentialism.

One can perhaps suggest that the goal, if less methodically envisaged, is not very different from what Christian theologians have actually sought to achieve in the course of the history of theology. The rigidity of the method seems to arise, at least in part, from a faulty application of historical techniques. (1) Was only the framework of the gospel conditioned while the essence (kerygma?) remained unconditioned? (2) Was there only one ancient world view (or perhaps two – apocalyptic and Gnostic), or did various persons hold various views? The latter conclusion is demonstrated, in my opinion, by my book *Miracle and Natural Law in Graeco-Roman and Early Christian Thought* (Amsterdam, 1952).

Moreover, the demythologizer, like the Liberal Protestant, finds a Jesus who in some ways resembles himself but makes the rise of Christianity incomprehensible. He makes use of classifications supposedly historical and treats central elements as peripheral. Nature miracles, sacraments, death and resurrection are assigned to Hellenistic mythology; exorcisms and prophecies belong to Jewish mythology. What remains is a Jesus who told stories and uttered wise sayings (many of them not authentic because commonplace); he was a teacher, let us say a teacher of theology. Somehow he was crucified, and later he was known to his disciples in an undefinable 'Easter-event'. The retention of the Easter-event keeps the system from losing itself in secular philosophy, though it evidently confuses the secular philosophers to whom it is supposed to be addressed.

But let us leave philosophy to the philosophers and ask one further historical question. Presumably the mythology in which the Christians expressed themselves was intended to convey meaning to prospective converts. But we know that in antiquity there were many who regarded the Christian gospel, with or without myth, as both meaningless and untrue. Can one speak, then, of 'the ancient world view' as that which prevents modern men from recognizing the truth of the gospel?

AN ALTERNATIVE TO DEMYTHOLOGIZING

Of course, it may be argued that since demythologizing, for all its apparatus of scholarship, is highly subjective and, indeed, wilful, we should steer on the opposite tack and simply take the New Testament 'as it stands'. The appearance of objectivity thus given is spurious, however, since the New Testament does not 'stand' in such a manner. Behind and beyond the gospels stands the Jesus whom the evangelists both understand and misunderstand; as for the rest of the New Testament, it is obvious that the apostle Paul is more significant than (for example) Jude or the author of II Peter. Within the New Testament there is a hierarchy of significance; not everything in it is of equal importance. Therefore it is the task of the theological interpreters to discover what that hierarchy is.

THE ROLE OF HISTORICAL ANALYSIS IN THEOLOGY

Historical criticism by itself can never provide a guide to the theological understanding of the New Testament. Historical criticism can only attempt to show what was regarded as important at various historical points. The question then arises whether or not the New Testament is a self-contained unit or, at least, to be interpreted in relation only to itself and to the Old Testament. Here historical criticism is of some value, in that it can suggest that the New Testament books were written in and for a community by men who were members of that community, and that this community, originating in the work of Jesus, has a history which extended beyond his resurrection and, indeed, beyond the apostolic age. In other words, the New Testament writings cannot be understood apart from the life of the apostolic and post-apostolic Church. To be sure, Clement and Ignatius (for example) were as likely to misunderstand the meaning of the gospel as were Matthew and John – or Paul. But the meaning of early Christianity cannot be recovered unless we take into account

D

not only the New Testament but also the post-apostolic writings of the Apostolic Fathers and the Apologists and Irenaeus – to mention no others.

THE THEOLOGICAL SIGNIFICANCE OF GNOSTICISM

When we have mentioned the Apostolic Fathers and others, we immediately confront the question of the limits of early Christianity. It is fairly evident that Simon Magus, for example, is not a good witness for early Christian life; for one thing, he regarded himself as the saviour of mankind, or rather of a small fraction of mankind, the spiritually élite. It is more difficult to assess the evidence provided by Marcion, chiefly because Harnack regarded him as the forerunner of nineteenth-century biblical critics. But it would appear that since Marcion denied that Jesus actually lived as a human being and held that the universe was the product of an inferior god, his testimony to Christian doctrine cannot be accepted. Similarly those apocryphal writings which grind special theological axes must be viewed as belonging to the periphery of Christianity. Jerome suggested that gold might lie in the mud of these documents; but the proportion of mud is remarkably high.

Some early Christian writers, and perhaps even some New Testament writers, were influenced by what seems to us to be Gnostic terminology. But it still remains to be shown that this terminology was always Gnostic and that in Christian writings its overtones were Gnostic. Once more, 'modern' men often find the 'existential'-sounding Gnostic ideas attractive. This is not to say that they (either the men or the ideas) can be regarded as Christian. One of the chief values of the Gnostic movement was that it aided the Church to define its own terms and to reject Gnosticism as such.

HISTORY, TRADITION AND THEOLOGY

Gnosticism ultimately denied the reality of both history and tradition by insisting upon the historical unreality of Jesus. A truly theological interpretation of the New Testament must therefore take its stand upon the ground of historical fact, recognizing that Jesus and his disciples really lived and really taught what the New Testament documents indicate they taught. At the same time, such an interpretation must not deny the reality of modern interpreters and of modern men and their ideas. It must resolutely admit the existence of distance between the New Testament and ourselves. It must not, however, exaggerate the measure of this distance. Modern men often live longer than ancient men did; all men die, and all men are subject to drives which do not vary greatly from one century to another. Their attitudes to death and to these drives will vary, but nothing beyond confusion results if we try to make the New Testament writers share our own attitudes.

The basic question is probably that of theological authority. Is authority within Christianity derived from the Bible alone, or from tradition alone? Or is it a kind of mixed authority in which scripture, tradition and reason all have rôles to play – rôles whose significance can be assessed differently under different circumstances? It would appear – at least, so it appears to the author – that the second option is the only tenable one, given the existence of the Church and the necessity of modifying various aspects of Christian teaching under varying circumstances. This is to say that we read the Bible not with 'eyes of faith' alone but with two eyes which give perspective. With one eye we read the New Testament to see what it may say to us about the gospel and about the early Church which proclaimed the gospel. With the other we look at it more critically to see whether or not what it says to us is historically and theologically true. Both eyes are kept in focus by the use of the glasses provided by tradition, by historical scholarship, and by theological inquiry.

CONCLUSION

What we have been trying to indicate is that the object of New Testament study is the understanding of the New Testament. Such understanding requires us to devote our attention primarily to the New Testament itself and to enter into an encounter with what it says. For this reason we must attempt to devise some kind of method for the encounter – not that the encounter absolutely requires the use of such a method, but that, methods being what they are, it is better to have a more adequate and explicit method than to imagine that we are not using one when we actually do so implicitly.

In dealing with the New Testament, then, the first question to be raised is this: 'What is the New Testament?' Answering this question requires us to investigate the history of the New Testament canon (Chapter I). The next question is, 'What does the New Testament say?' The attempt to deal with this problem leads us into the realm of textual criticism and the study of translations (Chapter II). When we have considered these two 'what' questions, we are ready for the further question, 'How does the New Testament say what it says?' Here we enter the areas of translation and of literary criticism, which is essentially the analysis of the style of the various New Testament writers. Stylistic analysis can lead us towards understanding what the authors intended to say, for style cannot easily be separated from content. The style is the instrument which the author uses for expressing his thought (Chapter IV). Only after these investigations have been made are we ready to investigate the problem of why the authors said what they said. The ultimate 'why' question can be answered in two ways. First, it can be answered historically, in relation to the authors' place within the stream of Christian life and to their various environments in the ancient world (Chapter V). Second, it can (and must) be answered theologically, in relation to the author's purposes in setting forth their basic understanding of the gospel – that is to say, of the ultimate meaning of the revelation of God in Christ (Chapter VI).

The fundamental questions involved, then, are the questions of 'what' (Chapters I and II), of 'what' and 'how' (Chapters III and IV), of 'how' and 'why' (Chapter V), and of 'why' (Chapters V and VI). Naturally there is more overlapping than this schematic statement suggests. We are dealing with real phenomena (the New Testament writings) which cannot be neatly dealt with by having a schematic structure imposed on them. But it can be argued that unless all the steps of this procedure are kept in mind, somehow or other, our interpretation of the New Testament will be unbalanced and/or inadequate.

The final result of this kind of analysis will be historical, we should claim; but it will also be theological in so far as we finally concern ourselves with the basic purpose or purposes which the authors had in view. In this sense, a non-theological interpretation is inadequately historical, and a non-historical interpretation cuts theology (at any rate, Christian theology) loose from its moorings – or, to change the figure, deprives the ship of its rudder.

The same point can be expressed in a different way, if one does not wish to make use of theological language but prefers to remain in the realm of the historical. The historical method, to a very considerable extent, involves placing a document in its historical context and tracing interrelations. The historical context of the New Testament documents is a double one. First, and more generally, there is the context provided by the life and thought of the Graeco-Roman world and, a little more specifically, of Judaism in this world. This context is often regarded as all-important. But there is also the second context which, for the New Testament writers themselves, was the more important of the two. This is the context provided by the life and thought of the early Christian Church. In order to understand this context it is necessary to venture into the areas of biblical and church history and of biblical and Christian theology. By laying emphasis on environmental study at both levels we can cross the bridge between history and theology, provided that we are willing to recognize a considerable measure of continuity between the early Church and the Church today.

Finally, even if we do not recognize the continuity we can at least recognize the significance of the early Church as providing the historical environment for the New Testament. Without the 'hypothesis' of the Church the New Testament documents are like isolated pearls without a string.

PART II

New Testament Literature

VII

THE GOSPELS

Before discussing the individual gospels we should say something about their use in the early Christian Church and about their literary character or characters. We may suggest that two of the evangelists refer to books analogous to their own and that a third almost certainly knows another. (1) At the beginning of the Gospel of Luke we read of 'many' who have undertaken to draw up an account of the matters accomplished among Christians, in accordance with traditions received from eye-witnesses. Among the 'many' is presumably the author of the Gospel of Mark, for as we shall see (Chapter x), Mark was the principal source followed by Luke. Luke's statement implies that Mark was not an eye-witness but received his information from eye-witnesses. (2) At the end of the Gospel of John (20.30) we read that 'Jesus performed many other signs . . . which are not recorded in this book.' This statement may imply the existence of other books in which the 'other signs' were recorded. (3) The principal source followed by the author of Matthew was the Gospel of Mark; Matthew is therefore obviously a witness to Mark's prior existence.

Within the other New Testament writings there seems to be only one reference to a gospel. This occurs in I Timothy 5.18, where quotations from Deuteronomy 25.4 and Luke 10.7 are introduced by the expression, 'the scripture says'. It would appear that the saying of Jesus is to be found in a book and that the book is regarded as scripture.

In the writings of the Apostolic Fathers (see Chapter xvi) there are fairly clear references to written gospels (Matthew in the *Didache* and in *Barnabas*). A certain Papias, bishop (?) of Hierapolis in Phrygia towards the beginning of the second century, discussed at least two of the gospels in his *Exegeses of the Dominical Oracles*, of which only fragments survive. In his preface he stated that he valued oral traditions more highly than books; then he proceeded to discuss books in the light of traditions.

(1) Quoting 'the elder', probably 'the elder John' whom he mentions elsewhere, Papias describes the origin of the Gospel of Mark. It is an accurate account of the Lord's words and deeds, though neither 'in order' nor complete. Mark derived his information from the teaching and preaching of Peter, for whom he had served as 'interpreter'. This statement implies that the order of Mark has been compared with some other order, probably that of John (since the order of Matthew and Luke is much the same as Mark's). It has sometimes been thought that the picture of Mark's relation to Peter is based on I Peter 5.13 ('Mark my son'), since Eusebius says that Papias knew I Peter; but there is no valid reason for supposing that both Papias and I Peter are not reflecting early Roman tradition.

(2) In regard to Matthew, Papias reported that he 'compiled the oracles in the Hebrew language; but each person translated them as he was able.' The statement shows that early in the second century there were several Greek versions of something regarded as Matthew's collection of 'oracles' (Old Testament proof texts?); one of them may have been the apocryphal gospel of the Hebrews, which Eusebius says contained some materials which Papias used. It is conceivable that he regarded both 'Hebrews' and our Gospel of Matthew as translations of an apostolic document. His view may reflect analysis of the Old Testament quotations in Matthew, some of which are much closer to the Hebrew than to the Greek Septuagint.

(3) A so-called 'anti-Marcionite prologue' to the Gospel of John states that John dictated his gospel to Papias himself; but this highly garbled document is not likely to give us any trustworthy information about either Papias or John. Modern study of the prologue places it in the fourth century, or even later.[1]

---

[1] See J. Regul, *Die antimarcionistischen Evangelienprologe* (Vetus Latina: Aus der lateinischen Bibel, 6; Freiburg, 1969).

From Papias, then, we derive some information, possibly correct, about the origin of Mark's gospel and of some of the materials in Matthew. The trouble with this information lies in our own inability to assess it properly. How reliable was Papias? How reliable were his informants? The only way we can tell is to check what he says with the gospels themselves and to see to what extent our analysis confirms his statements. This method means, of course, that our primary sources of evidence lie in the gospels, not in what Papias says about them.

PROBABILITIES ABOUT THE GOSPELS

Before turning directly to the gospels we may well consider a few general factors which are related to the question of their date. We have already looked at what evidence there is within the New Testament which bears on this question. Now we turn to consider some points which have to do with the life of the Christian Church and the apostles.

First of all, it must be admitted that we cannot prove that the gospels were not written at a very early time. The fact that some, if not all, early Christians expected the imminent return of Jesus does not prove that they cannot have written down their memories of his words and deeds. Rabbinic insistence upon not writing down the oral law provides no parallel, since we know that disciples of the rabbis sometimes did write it down; furthermore, apocalyptic literature, though secret, was by definition written, and from the discoveries at Qumran we know that much more was written than might have been supposed. On the other hand, the earlier New Testament documents, such as the Pauline epistles, make no reference to any gospel writings, and in them there is a fairly strong insistence upon the value of oral tradition (I Cor. 11.23; 15.3). Moreover, the synoptic gospels seem to be based, fairly often, directly on oral tradition, especially at points where sayings have been linked by verbal association for the purpose of memorization. Such a procedure is characteristic of oral transmission, not of copying from written documents. These facts suggest that the gospels, while relatively early in date, are likely to come from the second generation of Christians rather than from the first.

What conspicuous historical events may have provided occasions for the writing down of the oral tradition? Two events immediately suggest themselves: (1) the persecution of Roman Christians in the year 64, when some of the leading apostles were probably put to death (we may also mention the death of James the Lord's brother in 62), and (2) the destruction of Jerusalem in the year 70, when the Church came to be more fully conscious of its mission to the gentile world. Of these two the more important was probably the death of some of the apostles. Since the Church's proclamation of the significance of the life, death and resurrection of Jesus was based upon the memories of eye-witnesses to these events (cf. I Cor. 15.5–8; Acts 1.21–2), when those eye-witnesses grew old or died it was obviously necessary to commit their narrative to writing. We do not know how old the apostles were at the time of the crucifixion; perhaps some of them were no more than twenty or so; but by the sixties of the first century the life expectancy of any of them cannot have been great. Given a combination of these factors, we should assume that gospel-writing would begin no later than the time of the persecution under Nero.

Another point, however, must be considered. Our gospels lay almost no emphasis upon eye-witness testimony. Mark and Matthew never do so. Luke mentions eye-witnesses as sources in his prologue but thereafter in his gospel never speaks of them. John refers to eye-witnesses very sporadically (1.14; 19.35; 21.24). The gospels testify primarily to the faith and the memories of the communities out of which they came, not to the historical reliability of their authors. In many respects the synoptic gospels (though not John) resemble folk literature more than the creations of individual artists. What this fact means is either that the evangelists were not interested in historical reliability or that they took it for granted and, in writing their books, proceeded to develop the implications of memories assumed to be trustworthy. The latter conclusion seems to be justified in view of the insistence on historical reliability expressed by Paul, by Luke, and by John. The evangelists made use of historical memories in order to set forth the significance of those memories. As the author of II Peter claims, the apostles did not proclaim the power and presence of their Lord by relying on myths such as those employed by rhetoricians (1.16).[1]

---

[1] See the important discussion, from a somewhat different viewpoint, by D. E. Nineham in *Journal of Theological Studies* 9 (1958), 13–25; 243–52; 11 (1960), 253–64.

The gospels, then, originated fairly soon after the middle of the first century. They were created by and for believers who were concerned with the life, death and resurrection of Jesus and tried to interpret the meaning of this chain of events. It may be that the gospel form did not come into existence before Hellenistic communities (Rome, Antioch, Ephesus) had made Palestinian traditions their own, though the notion that Matthew wrote something in Hebrew may point towards an earlier origin for some, at least, of the traditions found in this gospel. Whether Hebrew or Greek, the gospels originated in relation to (1) the apostolic preaching and teaching, concerned not only with the events of Jesus' life but also with what he taught, (2) the continuing worship of the Christian communities and especially the Lord's Supper, in which his death was proclaimed until he would return (I Cor. 11.26), and (3) the living memories of those who had been with him during his ministry.

These factors are perhaps equally important. Sometimes the liturgical origin of the gospels has been emphasized almost to the exclusion of other considerations, but it must be recalled that while Paul does recall the story of the Last Supper in setting forth regulations for the conduct of the Lord's Supper, he does not state that the story had been recited, or was to be recited, at the Lord's Supper in Corinth; and he does not mention the Supper in any of his letters but I Corinthians. What is clear from his mention of the Last Supper is the fact that the story was told in a context. He reminds the Corinthians of what the Lord Jesus did and said 'on the night when he was betrayed'. This point suggests that well before the year 50 at least the Passion Narrative (Mark 14.15 and parallels) was told as a continuous story. On the other hand, it may be that we should not try to infer too much from what Paul reports. He also possesses a fairly detailed list of resurrection appearances (I Cor. 15), and it is extremely hard to reconcile with the resurrection stories in the gospels.

It has sometimes been argued that the general outline of the synoptic gospels, and especially that of Mark, can be proved historically reliable because of the rough outlines to be found in some of the early Christian sermons in Acts. This point is hard to establish with any degree of certainty because (1) we know that Luke used Mark, and (2) we know that Luke was accustomed to compose speeches (whether he used earlier sources or not) in order to provide discourses he regarded as suitable for various occasions. The second point does not prove that the Marcan outline is unreliable, but it suggests that we are not in a position to say whether it is or not – especially since the outline provided by John is so different. It should be added that one of the few points on which Papias insists is that Mark was not written 'in order'. Since he seems to have known the Gospel of John, he probably means that Mark's chronology seems wrong to him.

Essentially the primary proof of the correctness, or at least the literary adequacy, of Mark's outline lies in the fact that it commended itself, with minor changes, to Matthew and Luke. This point leads us to consider the interrelations of the synoptic gospels, since it is impossible to consider them separately without first trying to see why they are as similar as they are. Several theories in regard to the resemblances and the differences have been set forth. In antiquity, once the tradition that Matthew wrote first had become established, the other two had to be explained in terms of the first. Origen, for example, claimed that the Spirit gave each evangelist a perfect memory; the deviations of Mark and Luke from Matthew were due to theological purposes, often highly subtle in nature. Augustine took another line: according to him, Mark simply abbreviated Matthew. In the nineteenth century, however, it came to be generally held that Mark wrote first and that both Matthew and Luke made use of his book, along with another common source which each of them arranged differently.

The proof of the priority of Mark, often regarded as almost mathematical in nature, is not really mathematical. Briefly stated, it is this. The sequence in which Matthew and Luke write their gospels is never the same unless Mark is in agreement with them; and where Mark is in agreement with them their sequence is always the same. We can put the argument in tabular form:

Matthew	Mark	Luke
A	—	D
B	B	B
C	C	C
D	—	A

It still remains possible, however, that Mark abbreviated Matthew and that Luke changed Matthew's order. Therefore other considerations have to be taken into account. Where Matthew and Luke are parallel to Mark it can be argued that, generally speaking, they differ from Mark in ways (usually different) that suggest that both of them have tried to improve the style or the thought of their common source.

Several examples may serve to illustrate this process.

(1) Mark 10.17–18 is paralleled by Matthew 19.16–17.

Mark 10.17–18	*Matthew 19.16–17*
And as he was setting out on his journey, a man ran up and knelt before him and asked him, Good teacher, what must I do to inherit eternal life? And Jesus said to him, Why do you call me good? No one is good but God alone.	And behold, one came up to him, saying, Teacher, what good deed must I do, to have eternal life? And he said to him, Why do you ask me about what is good? One there is who is good.

(2) In Mark 10.35–45 the sons of Zebedee ask Jesus for the right to sit on his right and left in his 'glory'. In Matthew 20.20–8 their mother makes the request for them, but Jesus replies, exactly as in Mark, 'You do not know what you are asking'; in both instances the 'you' is plural.

(3) The third example shows both Matthew and Luke apparently rewriting Mark:

Matthew 8.16–17	*Mark 1.32–4*	*Luke 4.40–1*
That evening they brought to him	*That evening* at sundown they brought to him all who were sick or	When the sun was setting all those who had any sick *with various diseases* brought them to
many *possessed with demons.*	*possessed with demons.* And the whole city was gathered together about the door.	him.

And he cast out the spirits with a word and *healed* all *who were sick.*	And he *healed* many *who were sick with various diseases* and cast out many *demons,*	And he laid his hands on every one of them and *healed* them. And *demons* also came out of many, crying, You are the Son of God. And he rebuked them, and would not
	and he would not allow the demons *to speak, because they knew* him.	allow them *to speak, because they knew* that he was the Christ.

This was to fulfil what was spoken by the prophet Isaiah . . .

(The words in italic are the same in Greek.)

These examples could be multiplied, but they serve to show that both Matthew and Luke, at least in many instances, modified the materials they took from Mark.[1]

We have just observed a case in which Matthew and Luke seem to have made independent selections from Mark, and there are several others.

Matthew	Mark	Luke
the leprosy was cleansed from him (8.3)	the leprosy departed from him and [he] was cleansed (1.42)	the leprosy departed from him (5.13)
for the sake of my name (19.29)	for the sake of me and the gospel (10.29)	for the sake of the kingdom of God (18.29)
immediately (21.2)	immediately entering (11.2)	entering (19.30)
in this night (24.34)	today in this night (14.30)	today (22.34)

[1] For further discussion cf. B. H. Streeter, *The Four Gospels*, 149–331.

It seems unlikely either that Matthew used Luke or that Luke used Matthew; the only possibilities seem to be that either (1) Mark used both Matthew and Luke (but the cumulative effect of the differences between Mark and the other two gospels suggests that this is not so), or (2) Matthew and Luke used Mark in different ways and for different purposes.

Q FOR QUELLE

Matthew and Luke agree in order at points where they are following Mark. At other points they do not agree in order but have common materials. At such points their agreement is sometimes exact, sometimes a matter of common materials treated somewhat differently. Two explanations of these coincidences have been given. (1) Luke used Matthew but revised his materials. (2) Both Matthew and Luke made use of a common source, usually called Q from the German word 'Quelle', which means 'source'. Sometimes the use of this symbol has led investigators to assume that there was a clearly definable document which could be recovered from Matthew and Luke, but further research has suggested that the limits of Q are much vaguer than had been supposed.

(1) It seems unlikely that Luke used Matthew, for the following reasons. (a) In Matthew many sayings of Jesus have been assembled into a collection called the Sermon on the Mount (Matt. 5–7); in Luke these sayings are scattered over a number of chapters, in different contexts. Would Luke have felt free to treat Matthew in this way? (b) Many sayings of Jesus are connected to one another by verbal association in both Matthew and Luke; but in about seventeen instances the word used for the association by Matthew differs from the word used by Luke. This point proves that both Matthew and Luke drew independently upon a common stock of oral tradition.[1] Other arguments have been advanced to support the independence of Luke from Matthew, but these two (especially the second) are the most convincing.

(2) On the other hand, the notion that there was a single written source to be designated as Q is also untenable, first

[1] Th. Soiron, *Die Logia Jesu* (Münster, 1916); J. Jeremias in *ZNW* 29 (1930), 147–9.

because of the argument just advanced, and second because sometimes the resemblances are very close and at other times they are
rather remote. In the latter case it is uncertain whether a common
source is being used or not. When we speak of Q, then, we are referring to a conglomeration of sources, perhaps partly written (as in the
accounts of the Baptist's preaching and of the baptism and temptation
of Jesus) but more often oral in origin. Perhaps the letter Q should
be dropped; but it is convenient as a designation for non-Marcan
materials common to Matthew and Luke – nothing more.

What do these materials consist of? Various scholars have given
various lists, but a convenient summary, following the order of
Matthew, has been provided by Julius Wellhausen in his *Einleitung
in die drei ersten Evangelien* (1905). He lists the following passages:

M 3.1–12	the mission of John the Baptist	L 3.1–17
M 4.1–11	the baptism and temptation of Jesus	L 4.1–15
	The Sermon on the Mount	
M 5.1–12	the Beatitudes	L 6.20–3
M 5.38–48	counsels of perfection	L 6.27–36
M 6.19–34	heavenly treasure; cares	L 12.22–34
M 7.1–6	judge not	L 6.37–42
M 7.7–11	ask and you will receive	L 11.9–13
M 7.15–27	false prophets; hearing and doing	L 6.43–9
M 8.5–13	the centurion in Capernaum	L 7.1–10
M 10.1 ff.	instructions to the apostles or to the seventy disciples	L 10.1–12; 12.1–12; 12.49–53
M 11.1–19	about John the Baptist	L 7.18–35
M 11.20–4	woes on various cities	L 10.13–15
M 11.25–30	the invitation of Jesus-Wisdom	L 10.21–4
M 12.22–37	the question about Beelzebub	L 11.14–23
M 12.38–42	the sign of Jonah	L 11.29–32
M 12.43–5	the fate of the unclean spirit	L 11.24–6
M 22.1–14	parable of the (wedding) banquet	L 14.16–24
M 23.13–36	woes against Pharisees	L 11.37–52
M 24.1 ff.	apocalyptic predictions	L 17.20–35; 12.35–46
M 25.14–30	parable of the entrusted funds	L 19.11–27

In addition to these fairly extensive passages there are, of course, a good many isolated verses which occur in both Matthew and Luke, but the bulk of the common materials consists of the passages listed above. Perhaps Wellhausen included too much. At several points he has listed not merely verses common to the two gospels but others which seem to continue the thought expressed in one or the other of them.

What kinds of materials are included in this collection? It is rather striking that it contains a beginning – the mission of John the Baptist and the baptism and temptation of Jesus – but no end, unless the apocalyptic predictions could be so regarded. It contains one story of healing and two parables. The rest of it consists of nothing but sayings of Jesus. For this reason it has sometimes been suggested that here we have 'the earliest gospel', a document composed during the lifetime of Jesus. But we have already indicated the reasons which prove that it was not a single document. It generally represents a part of the reservoir of oral tradition from which both Matthew and Luke drew some of their materials, though some of it may well have been available to them in written form.

Can it be determined whether Matthew or Luke reproduced his sources more accurately? Some scholars have believed that they could tell. For example, they regarded Luke 9.60 ('go and proclaim the kingdom of God') as later than Matthew 8.22 ('follow me'), Luke 7.25 as later than Matthew 11.8 because of its better Greek style, and Luke 11.13 as later than Matthew 7.11 because Luke mentions the gift of the Holy Spirit. Such an analysis confuses the idiosyncrasy of an author with the date of his writing. Moreover, in many instances, according to the same scholars, the version of Luke is more 'primitive' than that of Matthew. The upshot of this kind of analysis seems to be that individual cases must be judged on their own merits, and that such judgements will depend on a general view of the development of early Christianity which does not yet exist, if it ever will.

Recently a significant study has been made of the assumptions and the problems involved in postulating the existence of a 'sayings source' such as Q, and of the methods to be followed in proving the hypothesis.[1] (1) The 'Q-hypothesis' cannot be held unless the priority of Mark to Matthew be assumed. (2) In

[1] T. R. Rosché in *JBL* 79 (1960), 210–20.

proceeding towards Q one must first investigate the ways in which Matthew and Luke used their extant source Mark. Such an investigation has four results: (a) Luke reproduced Mark's sayings of Jesus more faithfully than Mark's narrative material; (b) the changes Luke made in Marcan sayings are chiefly grammatical and stylistic; (c) Matthew too remained close to Mark's sayings; (d) he changed their wording primarily for stylistic reasons but often preserved their order. (3) Both Matthew and Luke treated Mark's sayings more respectfully than they did his narrative materials. (4) Since most of the materials found only in Matthew and Luke consist of sayings, it is necessary to see whether or not Matthew and Luke exhibit the same measure of agreement as that found in their treatment of sayings found in Mark. (5) If Matthew and Luke followed the same method in dealing with non-Marcan sayings that they followed in dealing with Marcan sayings, it could be expected that the same degree of agreement would exist in the second case as exists in the first; but it does not exist. (6) The only possible explanations are that (a) Matthew and Luke may not have treated the hypothetical source in the same way, or (b) there is no such source. There are objections to both (a) and (b); the first possibility does not explain why the treatments are different, while the second does not explain the close verbal correspondences in non-Marcan materials common to Matthew and Luke. This objection can be met, however, by reference to carefully memorized oral materials.

If, as seems to be the case in a few of the sayings, a play on Aramaic words underlies our present Greek text, it may be that the original Aramaic should be regarded as closer to the words of Jesus than the words we now possess. But it must be remembered that we do not actually possess such an Aramaic version and that the reconstructions which have been provided must necessarily remain hypothetical.

Our conclusion about Q, then, is that it is no less and no more than a convenient symbol to designate non-Marcan materials common to Matthew and Luke. Since it seems to have been partly written and partly oral, we should not imagine that we are dealing with a written source in any way comparable to Mark. Most of the so-called Q has no greater value than is to be assigned to any of the other materials, oral or written, upon which either Matthew or Luke drew in composing their gospels.

The Gospels

Enthusiasts for sources have rarely found a happier hunting-ground than when they dealt with the synoptic gospels. Unwilling, apparently, to admit the existence or the value of oral tradition, they have sought to reduce the complexity to be found in the interrelations of the synoptic gospels by using various diagrams to show how the later ones developed. In the early years of this century two types of diagrams were especially popular, the first among liberal Protestants, the second among Catholics.

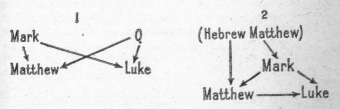

The first diagram had the virtue, if it was a virtue, of simplicity; the second took account of Papias and patristic tradition, as well as of many of the facts to be found by analysing gospel interrelations. (Some scholars simply confused the issue by identifying Q with the 'oracles' compiled by Matthew according to Papias, and saying that Matthew compiled 'sayings of Jesus'; but Papias's word 'logia' is not the same as 'logoi', 'sayings'.) About 1920 further symmetry was given the first diagram by expanding it to include special sources used by Matthew and by Luke.

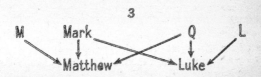

This attractive diagram really conveys no information beyond the fact that both Matthew and Luke used Mark and that, in addition, they have some materials which are common and others which are not common.

Around the same time another theory was devised to explain why, if one removed Marcan materials from Luke, so much remained and why that remainder looked so much like a gospel (the possibility that Luke might have rewritten his sources at some points and not at others was rejected). This theory postulated the existence of something called Proto-Luke, consisting of a document combined out of Q and L (both regarded as written). Proto-Luke, the earliest gospel, was then combined with Mark to make our present Gospel of Luke. The theory carries as much, and as little, conviction as any similar theory essentially based on the removal of part of a book to see what the remainder looks like.

Almost all analysis of this sort ultimately fails because it neglects the extent to which the evangelists were involved in the transmission of the Christian tradition as well as the extent to which they were free to arrange and rewrite their materials in ways which seemed meaningful to them and to the communities of which they were members. It may be that we can create useful hypotheses about the authentic early materials which the evangelists used. What we actually possess consists of the gospels which they wrote.[1]

---

[1] Statistical material in regard to the gospels and other New Testament books are derived primarily from R. Morganthaler, *Statistik des neutestamentlichen Wortschatzes* (Frankfurt, 1958).

VIII

THE GOSPEL OF MARK

The idea that Mark wrote a gospel is attested by Papias, early in the second century; he says that Mark never encountered Jesus but later became the disciple and 'interpreter' of Peter. On the basis of Peter's teaching about the words and deeds of Jesus, he drew up an account which was accurate but not 'in order' (Eusebius, *H.E.* 3, 39, 15). Papias seems to be contrasting Mark's work with a gospel 'in order' and apostolic; probably he has John in mind. A view like that of Papias is expressed by Justin, about 150; he refers to a passage in Mark's gospel as derived from Peter. The Petrine origin of Mark is also attested by Irenaeus and Clement of Alexandria, though Clement adds the statement that Peter neither commended nor disapproved of Mark's work.

Clement's caution may be due to the fact that in the second century Gnostics were especially fond of the gospel. The Carpocratians liked it because of its emphasis on secret teaching; followers of Basilides apparently used it to show that Simon of Cyrene, not Jesus, was crucified (reading Mark 15.21-4 with severe literalism). According to a letter of Clement discovered by Morton Smith, the Carpocratians had their own version of the gospel, while the church of Alexandria used not only the ordinary version but also an esoteric document based upon it.

It is obvious that neither Matthew nor Luke regarded the gospel as fully satisfactory, for while they incorporated most of it in their own writings they did not hesitate to improve its style, its arrangement and its theological ideas. Clement of Alexandria himself quoted from Mark in his lost, early *Hypotyposes* and in his sermon on wealth (of uncertain date), but he made no use of it in his major writings.

The textual problems of the Gospel of Mark occur primarily at the beginning and at the end, although throughout the gospel scribes have made additions in order to bring the book into closer conformity with Matthew and Luke. Indeed, it has been argued that some of these additions point towards the existence of two early editions of Mark's work – one the original version, usually reflected in the Alexandrian text, the other the version used by Matthew and Luke and often reflected in the text of Caesarea. This theory has the advantage of explaining how Matthew and Luke can agree against the Alexandrian text of Mark at points where they are using Mark as a source. The existence of various versions at Alexandria neither supports nor discredits this theory, but it remains only a possibility.

We have discussed the problems related to the beginning and the end in our chapter on textual criticism (Chapter II). Here we should add only that the expression 'beginning of the gospel' has well been compared by A. P. Wikgren[1] with Hebrews 5.12 – 'the elements of the beginning of the oracles of God' – and with a third-century papyrus which speaks of a 'catechumen in the beginning of the gospel'. This comparison suggests that Mark 1.1 is the title of the book, which is a simple treatment of the gospel for converts. In Mark's view the gospel is both what Jesus proclaimed (1.14–15; 8.35; 10.29) and what was proclaimed about him (13.10; 14.9). As for the end, a Greek sentence could be terminated with the word 'for', but a book would hardly conclude in this way – especially since two predictions of resurrection appearances in Galilee (14.28; 16.7) are still unfulfilled. It must be that the original ending is lost; perhaps it underlies Matthew 28.9–10 and 16–20.

The most distinctive feature of Mark's vocabulary, syntax and style is its almost complete lack of distinction. Mark uses 1,270 words and has all but 79 of them in common with other New Testament writers; of these 79 words, 41 also occur in the Septuagint. He is fairly fond of using diminutives and words of Latin origin; both kinds of words are typical of colloquial speech. Similarly, he uses the verb 'to be', especially in the imperfect tense, with a participle, instead of other verbs in the imperfect; his usage thus resembles the English 'he was going' rather than

[1] *Journal of Biblical Literature* 61 (1942), 11–20.

the best Greek. He likes to crowd a sentence with participles, and he enjoys double negatives. Examples of the historical present occur 151 times, seventy-two of them with the verb 'he says' or 'they say'. This usage gives his work a certain vividness, enhanced by twenty-six examples of 'he began to' or 'they began to'. For connecting his sentences he usually contents himself with a simple 'and', although in forty-two instances he uses the word '*euthus*', which can be translated as 'immediately', but may mean little more than 'then'.

Both in his paragraph structure, such as it is, and even within sentences he is accustomed to write parenthetically. This is to say that he combines two thoughts or even narratives simply by placing one within the other.

Some features of his style can be explained as reflections of Aramaic tradition or thinking; in general, however, his manner of writing seems to be due to (1) his intention to report rather than to create, and (2) his training, or lack of it, which results in a style colloquial or 'oral' rather than literary.[1]

Most of the gospel consists of materials, apparently derived from oral tradition, concerning what Jesus did and said. To some extent they are bound together by summaries which reflect the evangelist's own view of these materials. In these summaries we find emphasis laid on preaching by Jesus (1.14–15; 39) and the Twelve (6.12), on the work of healing and exorcism (1.34, 39; 3.10–11; 6.13, 56), and on the general reception of the gospel (1.45; 3.7–8, 11; 7.37). There is also a contrasting emphasis upon secrecy (1.34; 3.12; 4.33–4; 7.36) and on the future death and victory of Jesus (8.31–2; 9.30–1; 10.32–4).

No problem is created by the summaries of the first kind; they seem to be based directly upon the materials which Mark supplies. On the other hand, scholars have often regarded the summaries of the second kind as due either to Mark himself or to the tradition just prior to him. This view seems to be based upon the presupposition that Jesus' work and teaching must have been entirely public; in addition, he cannot have anticipated his death and resurrection.

The motif of secrecy in Mark is a rather complex one. (1) It

[1] An excellent summary in V. Taylor, *The Gospel According to St Mark* (London, 1952).

involves silence on the part of exorcised demons (1.25, 34; 3.12) and of men who have been cured (1.43–5; 5.43; 7.36, 8.26), as well as of the disciples themselves, who are to tell no one about Jesus as Messiah (8.30) or about the transfiguration (9.9) or even about his presence in Tyre (7.24) or his journey through Galilee (9.30). (2) It also involves 'the secret of the kingdom of God' (4.10–12) and secret or 'private' explanations of parables (4.34) and miracles (9.28), as well as revelations of the person of Jesus (9.2) and of things to come (13.3). To a considerable extent the full revelation is given only to the four disciples who were the first to be called (1.16–20, 29; 5.37; 9.2; 13.3; 14.33). Teaching about the passion and resurrection is given only 'on the road' apart from the multitudes (8.27; 9.33; 10.32).

Yet in spite of the fact that the disciples were given secret teaching, they failed to understand the intention of Jesus. They did not understand the parable of the sower (4.13, followed by an allegorical explanation; cf. 7.18); they did not know that Jesus could still a storm (4.40) or walk on the sea (6.49–51). They did not understand about the loaves in the feeding miracles (6.51; 8.14–21). They did not understand the predictions of death and resurrection; indeed, they did not even know what 'resurrection' was (9.10). They could not see how the rich could be saved (10.24, 26). Such ignorance was present not only among the disciples in general but also among the inner circle. Peter did not understand the passion prediction (8.32); James and John mistakenly asked for seats at the right and left of Jesus in his 'glory' (10.35–7).

This combination of revelation and ignorance must mean that, whatever Jesus' disciples did or did not understand, Mark himself now does understand. He knows that they did not fully recognize who Jesus was or what he was doing and teaching. He does not explain how he himself received further illumination; but it seems fairly clear that it was the result of the resurrection. It may be suggested that he can emphasize the ignorance of the apostles only if he assumes that they have later come to understand. His emphasis upon the weakness and ignorance of Peter may be due to what Peter himself later said.

What Mark is trying to say is that the full meaning of Jesus was not understood during his ministry, and that some disciples understood him better than others did. He is also indicating that

ot all of Jesus' teaching was intended for the public. It would be
ash to suppose that Mark's ideas are not in harmony with the
ctual historical situation.

It can hardly be denied, however, that Mark has imposed a
ertain measure of arrangement upon his materials. Our starting
oint for analysing this arrangement must be the central section
f his book, where a singular parallelism exists.

6.33–7.37	8.1–26
five loaves, two fishes (6.38)	seven loaves, a few fishes (8.5–7)
twelve baskets full (6.43)	seven baskets full (8.8)
5,000 fed (6.44)	4,000 fed (8.9)
in a boat to Bethsaida (6.45)	in a boat to 'Dalmanutha' (8.10; the word may mean 'of his own house')
controversy with Pharisees (7.1–23)	controversy with Pharisees (8.11–12)
question of children's bread; exorcism of demon (7.24–30)	question of bread; meaning of feedings (8.13–21)
'through Sidon' (7.32; the words may reflect 'Bethsaida')	to Bethsaida (8.22)
healing of deaf and dumb man by material means (7.32–6)	healing of blind man by material means (8.22–5)
injunction to secrecy (7.36)	injunction to secrecy (8.26)
allusion to Isaiah 35.5–6 (7.37)	(no allusion, but 'blind' is in Is. 35.5)

In view of Mark's explicit reference to the hidden meaning of the two
feedings (8.17–21) we can hardly doubt that his arrangement is
intentional. What does it mean? The two cycles of stories lead up to
Peter's recognition of Jesus as the Christ, and to the story of the
transfiguration which is the divine confirmation of this recognition
(8.27–9.1; 9.2–13; both accounts contain passion motifs). It must be
that in Mark's view the double sequence from feeding to restoration
of hearing/speech and sight was 'fulfilled' in Peter's recognition of
Jesus. But like the blind man Peter did not gain clear vision immediately; he recognized the Christ but not the suffering of the Christ.

Once more, however, we should not maintain that everything about the arrangement is due to Mark's literary work. A similar pattern, almost certainly independent of Mark, occurs in John. There the feeding of the five thousand (6.1–13) is followed by the people's hailing Jesus as prophet and wanting to make him king (6.14–15), and after the discourse on the feeding Peter says, 'We have believed and know that you are the Holy One of God' (6.69). We conclude that the sequence feeding-recognition is traditional but that the careful way in which Mark has developed it is his own.

Mark has a definite tendency to tell similar stories in similar ways; he seems to avoid variation, probably because of the influence of oral tradition and because of the use, in preaching and teaching, of what was transmitted. Two synagogue scenes are practically identical (1.21–7; 6.1–2); the style of some of the exorcism stories is practically uniform (1.23–7; 5.2–20; cf 4.39–41). Preparation for the triumphal entry (11.1–4, 6) is much the same as that for the paschal meal (14.13–14, 16).

Indeed, Austin Farrer has gone so far as to claim that Mark's gospel consists of five 'cycles' in which we find (1) apostolic calling, (2) a healing miracle, (3) private teaching, and (4) public teaching – though sometimes private teaching is replaced by enacted proclamation, or private and public teaching are reversed. The arrangement he recovers is as follows:

I. Mark 1.1–2.12, reiterated in 2.15–3.12   a 'little gospel' foreshadowing the great one;

II. Mark 3.13–6.6, reiterated in 6.7–56   eight healings

III. Mark 7.1–37, reiterated in 8.1–26 (8.27–9.1, an epilogue)   a continuation; three healings

IV. Mark 9.2–10.31, reiterated in 10.32–13.2   the fulfilment of the little gospel;

V. Mark 13.3–14.31, reiterated in 14.32–16.8   three healings

He finds the key to the gospel in the call of the apostles (though this is absent in 7.1). Farrer's theory may be somewhat forced, but it represents an attempt to recognize the fact that as Mark compiled his materials he did not simply transmit them in a random pattern.

It may be, however, in view of the emphasis which Mark lays upon 'secret epiphanies' (Dibelius) or the revelation of the hidden God, that more should be made of the passage which Farrer treats as an epilogue to his third section. This passage (8.27–9.1) begins with a significant parallel to the account of the death of John the Baptist – a story which, whatever its origin may be, is used by Mark as a prefiguration of the death of Jesus (8.27–8; 6.14–16). And it is in this passage that the meaning of Jesus' mission first becomes clear. Peter acknowledges Jesus as the Christ, but the disciples are ordered not to tell anyone; instead, 'he began to teach them that the Son of Man must suffer many things. . . .' This is not precisely an epilogue. Instead, it resembles what Aristotle (*Poetics* 11, 1–10) viewed as essential for the 'middle' of a tragedy. There should be a scene in which recognition of the hero results in the friendship of those destined for good fortune and the enmity of those destined for ill; ideally, there should also be a reversal of the hero's circumstances and the story should go onward to his 'passion' or suffering. Obviously the gospel account does not exactly correspond with Aristotle's analysis, and there is no reason to suppose that Mark had ever seen the *Poetics*. But the literary doctrine had powerfully influenced the popular story-telling of his time, and whether by chance or by intention Mark's outline does combine recognition with reversal, at least as far as the disciples are concerned.

Very generally, we may proceed to use this scene as the fulcrum of the gospel and divide it into four main sections, with some subdivisions.

I. The Gospel of the Kingdom (1.1–4.34)
   A. The proclamation of the gospel (1.1–45)
   B. The reception of the gospel (2.1–3.35)
   C. Teaching about the reception of the gospel (4.1–34)
II. The Inauguration of the Kingdom (4.35–8.26)
   A. The incipient presence of the kingdom (4.35–5.43)
   B. The rejection of the kingdom (6.1–29)
   C. The kingdom anticipated (6.30–7.37; 8.1–26)

III. The Recognition of Jesus as the Christ (8.27–9.13)
IV. Through Death to Victory (9.14–16.8)
  A. The way of the cross (9.14–10.52)
  B. The Christ in Jerusalem (11–13)
  C. The passion (14–15)
  D. The resurrection (16.1–8)

This outline, we should claim, reflects Mark's basic understanding of the mission of Jesus.

We should probably try to say something about the date of Mark's gospel. The oldest clear evidence we possess on this subject comes from Irenaeus (*Adv. haer.* 3, 1, 1): 'after their death [that of Peter aud Paul], Mark, the disciple and interpreter of Peter, transmitted to us in writing what was preached by Peter.' We are probably justified, then, in placing the gospel in the seventh decade of the first century.

IX

THE GOSPEL OF MATTHEW

From the time of Irenaeus (*c.* 180) the Gospel of Matthew has been regarded as the earliest of the four gospels to be written, probably because of a theory of development according to which Jewish elements in the Christian books are regarded as prior to universal-Hellenistic ones. In any event, Matthew is the first gospel for which we have fairly conclusive external evidence. Ignatius, writing about 110, almost certainly alludes to it in one letter (*Philad.* 8, 2) and makes use of the birth story in another (*Eph.* 19, 2–3). II Clement, a Roman document of about 140, refers to Matthew 9.13 as scripture, and Barnabas, about the same time, uses Matthew 22.14 in the same way. If we date the *Didache* early, as we probably should, we find frequent references and allusions to Matthew in it.

It may be that Papias, writing early in the second century, refers to an earlier form of our gospel when he says that 'Matthew compiled the oracles in a Hebrew dialect, and each one interpreted (translated?) them as best he could' (Eusebius, *H.E.* 3, 39, 17). This statement seems to imply the existence of various Greek versions in Papias's time; our gospel would then be one of these. We do not know exactly what 'oracles' means; it usually is used of Old Testament prophecies understood in relation to Jesus, but by extension it may also have included the words of Jesus himself, or the fulfilment of the prophecies. Against Papias, it has been claimed, however, that Matthew cannot be a translation from Hebrew or Aramaic (even though some of the Old Testament quotations seem to have come from the Hebrew Bible), especially since it is written in a clear Greek which reflects an advance over Mark's style and language; there is a play on the Greek words *'kopsontai'* and *'opsontai'* in Matthew 24.30. This claim neglects the wide variety to be found in the work of translators, and the play on Greek words can be balanced by Matthew 1.21: 'you shall call his name Jesus, for it is he who will save his people from their sins' – 'Jesus' and 'save' are related in Hebrew (*yeshuca – yoshica*).

VOCABULARY AND STYLE

Matthew contains a total of 18,300 words and uses a vocabulary of 1,690 words; he is the only New Testament writer to use 112 of these (of which seventy-six occur in the Septuagint). Among his favourite expressions are these: mention of God as 'Father' forty-five times (compared with five in Mark, seventeen in Luke) – including 'our Father', 'your Father', 'the Father in the heavens', 'the heavenly Father' – and of the kingdom as 'the kingdom of the heavens'; 'fulfil' (in regard to prophecy), 'righteousness', 'hypocrite', 'weeping and gnashing of teeth'. In addition, there are some words which are less significant theologically but equally characteristic of his vocabulary: verbs of motion such as 'withdraw' ('*anachōrein*') and 'come to' or 'approach' ('*proserchesthai*'), and favourite connectives like 'then' ('*tote*', ninety times), 'thence' ('*ekeithen*'), and 'just as' ('*hōsper*').

Less significant, but rather striking, is his repetition of 'formulas' such as 'from then he began' (4.17, 16.21), 'do not suppose that I came' (5.17, 10.34), 'sons of the kingdom' (8.12, 13.38), 'to outer darkness' (8.12, 22.13, 25.30), 'the lost sheep of the house of Israel' (10.6, 15.24). Special notice should be given to the formula, 'He who has ears, let him hear' (11.15, 13.9, 43) and the summaries of Jesus' healings (4.23–4, 8.16, 9.35, 14.35). Matthew also likes to end sections of teaching with the expression, 'And it happened when Jesus finished' (these words, or equivalent); it occurs five times (7.28, 11.1, 13.53, 19.1, 26.1), perhaps as a reflection of the five books of Moses.

He arranges his materials rather systematically; thus his gospel begins with a listing of the fourteen generations from Abraham to David, the fourteen generations from David to the Babylonian captivity, and the fourteen generations from the Babylonian captivity to Jesus Christ (1.1–17). The sayings of Jesus are often arranged in groups of threes, fives and sevens.

It is thus all the more surprising when we find more than a dozen sayings of Jesus given twice, as well as four sections of narrative. Since almost all of the sayings are paralleled once in Mark (usually in the same context as in Mark), the most likely explanation is that when Matthew found them not only in Mark but also in some other source – perhaps oral tradition – he used them twice. It is possible that he had already written something like a gospel (Papias's 'compilation of dominical oracles'?) and then revised it completely by incorporating Mark in it.

The theory of Augustine that Mark is nothing but an abbreviation of Matthew is untenable because where the two gospels are parallel the style of Matthew is almost always superior to that of Mark. It is reasonable to suppose that Matthew improved upon Mark's style, not that Mark perverted Matthew's.

It has been claimed that the gospel cannot have been written by an apostle because of its use of Mark; an apostle cannot have relied upon a book written by one who was not an apostle. This claim does not seem very convincing. We cannot tell whether or not an apostle would have followed such a procedure. An apostle might have believed that Mark's outline was largely correct but needed some revision and some supplementation. An apostle who proclaimed the gospel among Jews might have believed that Jewish Christianity, though ultimately only a part of Catholic Christianity, deserved more adequate representation than it found in Mark. But to say what he might or might not have thought is no substitute for examining the gospel itself.

The author of this gospel presents his portrait of Jesus in a manner not unlike that used by the rabbis. He is deeply concerned with the fulfilment of prophecy; indeed, most of what Jesus did he regards as taking place 'that the scripture might be fulfilled'. Thus the virginal conception was foretold in Isaiah 7.14, the birth of Jesus at Bethlehem in Micah 5.2, the 'massacre of the innocents' in Jeremiah 31.15, and Jesus' absence in Egypt in Hosea 11.1. Other events in the life of Jesus are given prophetic antecedents in the same way.

The call of Jesus from Egypt is related to another Old Testament analogy which the author finds significant. For him, Jesus is the new Moses. Just as Pharaoh tried to kill all the sons born to the Hebrews (Exod. 1.22), so Herod slew the little boys of Bethlehem (Matt. 2.16); but both Moses and Jesus escaped (compare Matt. 2.14 with Exod. 2.15). After the king's death both Moses and

Jesus returned to the lands where they were to do God's work (Exod. 2.23; 4.19; Matt. 2.19–20). From a mountain top both Moses and Jesus delivered the law which God has given them (Exod. 19–20; Matt. 5.1). In the sermon on the mount Jesus states that he has come to 'fulfil' the law of Moses, from which no smallest fragment shall pass away until the end of the age (5.17–18).

To a considerable extent Matthew presents Christianity as a reformed and heightened Judaism. Whoever breaks one of the least of the commandments ·will be called least in the kingdom of heaven (5.19; Matthew substitutes 'heaven' for 'God'); what is holy must not be given to dogs, i.e. outsiders (7.6); the disciples' mission is not to gentiles or Samaritans but to the lost sheep of the house of Israel (10.5–6; cf. 15.24). Those who take flight in the last times will be fortunate if the crisis does not come in the winter (as in Mark 13.18) or on a Sabbath (Matthew's addition, 24.20).

Matthew's model is the scribe to whom he refers (13.52), one who brings out of his treasure things new and old – and arranges them systematically.

At the same time, Matthew's interests are not solely rabbinical. He is concerned with Mark's Greek style and often improves it as he copies fom the earlier gospel. He also seems to have some definite theological interests as he sets forth his picture of Jesus and the disciples. For one thing, he omits nine Marcan references to the human indignation, anxiety or compassion of Jesus, and four references to his human inability to do what he wished. He modifies eleven instances of questions which Jesus asked. The best example of this tendency is to be found in Matthew 19.17 (Mark 10.18) – this has already been discussed (see page 111). In addition, Matthew omits some of the passages in which Jesus rebuked his ignorant or faithless disciples. He regards the apostles (a word he uses as Mark did not) more highly than Mark did, and he represents Peter as receiving a special promise (16.17–19) and, like Jesus, walking on water (14.28–31).

Matthew is a Christian who knows that the gospel was intended not only for Jews but also for gentiles – or rather, 'to the Jew first, and also to the Greek' (Rom. 1.16). The original 'sons of the kingdom' will be cast into outer darkness (8.12); the kingdom will be taken away from the Jews and given to a nation which brings forth its fruits (21.43); and at the crucifixion the whole people declares, 'His blood be upon us and upon our children' (27.25). The kingdom is for the Church. Matthew is the only evangelist who uses the word '*ecclesia*', and he does so at two significant points. (1) In Mark, Peter's confession (8.27) is at least partly rejected by Jesus. In Matthew (16.17–19) Jesus blesses Peter because his confession comes from God, not from man; and he declares that on the rock (either of the confession-revelation or of Peter himself) he will build his Church, against which the gates of Hades will not be able to prevail. The Church's decisions will be ratified in heaven. (2) Again, Matthew provides a procedure for the consideration of wrongs done to Christians by Christians. If private consultation proves unsuccessful, the matter is to be brought before the Church; and if the offender refuses to hear the Church, he is to be excommunicated (18.15–18; cf. I Cor. 5.1–6.11). The Church's decision, again, will be confirmed by God, and by Christ (18.19–20; cf. I Cor. 5.4). Because of his concern for the situation of the Church, Matthew expresses the Lord's Prayer (6.9–13) in a form more 'liturgical' than that in Luke (11.2–4). He also modifies Mark's absolute prohibition of divorce (10.9–12) by adding an escape clause, 'except for fornication' (Matt. 19.9; cf. 5.32). His interest in the contemporary situation is also reflected in his report of a contemporary controversy between Jews and Christians about the empty tomb (27.62–6; 28.11–15).

Apparently, as in the example provided by this controversy, he has a tendency to accept legends without much, if any, critical analysis. In this regard he is not very different from most people in his time. For him, more than for the other evangelists, prophetic dreams are significant; examples are provided by the dreams of Joseph (analogous to those of the Old Testament Joseph?) which predict the early events in Jesus' life (1.20–3; 2.13, 19–22), the dream of the Magi (2.12), and the dream of Pilate's wife (27.19), which showed Pilate that Jesus was a 'righteous man' (27.24). A certain field in Jerusalem is called 'the field of blood' because it was bought by the priests with the money which Judas refused to keep (27.3–10). At the time of Jesus' death there was an earthquake (as not in the other gospels) and 'many bodies of the saints who had fallen asleep were raised, and coming forth out of the tombs after his resurrection they entered into the holy city [note the Jewish expression] and appeared to many' (27.52-3). Matthew's story of the coin in the fish's mouth (resembling a tale told by Herodotus 3, 42) is found only in his gospel (17.24-7).

The presence of these legendary elements, however, does not prove that Matthew transmits nothing but legend. It shows only that in some instances he did transmit legends, and that his book was not aimed directly at those who preferred historical testimony (Luke tells none of these stories). It may be that he included them simply to illustrate the universal outreach of the gospel, on which he lays great emphasis at the end of his book. In the last chapter Jesus appears to two women near Jerusalem (28.9), but whereas Luke and John make Jerusalem the centre of the appearances of the risen Lord, Matthew remains faithful to the Marcan tradition that he appeared to his disciples in 'Galilee of the gentiles' (28.10, 16; cf. 4.15). There he commanded them to make disciples of all nations, baptizing them in the name of the Father and the Son and the Holy Spirit and teaching them to keep his commandments; for he would be with them until the end of the age (28.19-20).

Matthew's universalizing concern is also reflected in the great apocalyptic parables which he alone relates. He is deeply interested in the end of the age, when the wicked will finally be separated from the good by the angels (13.47-50), and the nature of the end is illustrated in the parables of the Wise and Foolish Virgins (25.1-12) and of the Sheep and the Goats at the last judgement (25.31-46). He is also interested in the fact that in this present age no such separation takes place.

The special materials of Matthew, then, and his own religious interpretation of the story of Jesus point in the direction of an apocalyptic-minded Christianity emerging from Judaism in the direction of a universalizing Catholicism. Since this gospel was the favourite of the second-century Church, it is not only obvious that Matthew's emphases strongly influenced his successors but also that these successors were in sympathy with the emphases. This conclusion does not imply, however, that the materials and emphases were necessarily selected because of the 'needs of the situation' alone. There was something about the teaching of Jesus which Matthew found meaningful and which he transmitted because of his belief that it not only was meaningful but also came from Jesus himself.

X

THE GOSPEL OF LUKE AND
THE BOOK OF ACTS

Since many have undertaken to draw up an account concerning the events which have taken place among us, as those who from the beginning were eye-witnesses and ministers of the matter delivered (accounts of them) to us, it seemed good also to me, since I followed all of them carefully from the beginning, to write an orderly account for your excellency, Theophilus, so that you might possess accurate knowledge about the matters concerning which you have been informed.

With this preface, characteristic of the writings of Graeco-Roman historians and would-be historians, the author begins the first of his two volumes which deal with the life of Jesus and the continuation of his mission in the spread of the gospel from Jerusalem to Rome. The preface marks a higher level of literary culture than almost anything else in the New Testament (with the exception of the Epistle to the Hebrews, in antiquity sometimes ascribed to the same author). It differs from ordinary prefaces because it does not state who the author is; it resembles them in its statements about (1) the occasion of the work, (2) its reliance on trustworthy materials, and (3) its insistence upon the competence of the author. It is thus evident that the author intends to write a history.

His history, however, is not an ordinary one, since he proceeds from the good Greek style of his preface directly into an account of the miraculous conceptions of John the Baptist and his distant relative Jesus and makes use of a Semitizing style full of reminiscences of the Septuagint. The break is so sharp that scholars have often supposed that he is making use of different sources and not troubling to make them over. Such a conclusion is unwarranted, however, for (1) since Luke writes as a historian he evidently possessed some training in grammar and rhetoric, and therefore had learned to write in various styles, and (2) he varies his own style in accordance with the situation; in Acts his style becomes more 'classical' as the gospel is brought closer to Rome.

Furthermore, it should be stated that he was almost certainly unaware of the modern distinction between 'faith' and 'history'. In his view faith and history worked together, and one way of propagating the faith was to state what the history had been. This is not to say that he was always reliably informed, or that – any more than modern historians – he always presented a severely factual account of events. It does mean that he believed that the events, if represented accurately and in order, at least pointed in the direction of the Christian gospel.

Who was the author? The oldest discussion of this question is also the classical one. Irenaeus (*c.* 180) began, as all critics must begin, with Acts (*Adv. haer.* 3, 14, 1). (1) The author of the 'we-passages' in Acts, presumably from a travel diary, went with Paul to Troas and Macedonia (Acts 16.8–17); he sailed with him back to Troas (20.5–15) and thence to Jerusalem and Rome (21.1–18; 27.1–28.16). (2) Luke alone was with Paul later (II Tim. 4.11); he was a 'beloved physician' in prison with Paul, presumably at Rome (Col. 4.11). (3) Therefore the author of Luke-Acts was Luke. Further identifications were provided later; thus Origen (early third century) thought he was the Lucius of Romans 16.21, while Ephraim Syrus (fourth century) identified him with the Lucius of Cyrene mentioned in Acts 13.1. The reliability of this proof obviously depends on several prior assumptions: (1) Paul must have written Colossians, and from Rome. (2) The tradition reflected in II Timothy must be trustworthy. Others have attempted to support these arguments by claiming that Luke makes use of 'medical language', but H. J. Cadbury has shown that his writings do not reflect the details about ailments and their cures which are found in medical writings, that apart from such details there was no medical language in antiquity, and finally – by a *reductio ad absurdum* – that the arguments used to show that Luke was a physician could prove that he was a veterinary.

On balance we should incline to accept the argument of Irenaeus and to assume that it was intended to confirm a prior belief rather than to introduce a new hypothesis. It should be said, however, that the question of the author's name is not as important as the question of the author's purpose; the latter question can be answered only from his writings.

It has sometimes been claimed that Luke cannot have been a companion of Paul because in neither the gospel nor the Acts is there any trace of the specifically Pauline doctrines to be found in the major epistles. This claim neglects the extent to which it is possible to associate and work with others without necessarily sharing all their concerns; in other words, it fails to do justice either to the variety to be found within the unity of modern Christianity or to that within the early Church.

In the Gospel of Luke there are 19,400 words and, in Acts, 13,380. The vocabulary of the Gospel includes 2,055 words; that of Acts, 2,038. In the Gospel there are 261 words not found elsewhere in the New Testament; in Acts, 413. (Taking the two books together, their vocabulary consists of 2,700 words.)

Among Luke's favourite expressions in the Gospel are the following: the imperfect verb 'egeneto' ('it happened . . .') with 'and' or with a finite verb or with an infinitive. He also employs the preposition 'in' with an article and an infinitive to indicate that something was done or said while something else was going on. Events often take place 'in the presence of' ('enōpion') persons. In this way he demonstrates his concern with historical connections and historical witnesses. In improving the style of Mark he often uses a more 'literary' word for 'immediately' ('parachrēma' for Mark's 'euthus').

The 'formulas' he uses are less striking than those of Matthew, but it is worth noting that he speaks of an 'only' ('monogenēs') son or daughter's being healed, three times (7.12, 8.42, 9.38), and sometimes begins parables with 'what man' (15.4) or 'what woman' (15.8), or 'a certain man' (10.30, 12.16; 14.16, 15.11, 16.1, 19; 19.12).[1]

We can see something of Luke's viewpoint when we consider his use of his principal source, the Gospel of Mark. (Fortunately

---

[1] Parables like these occur only in two instances in Matthew, where they are introduced differently.

we possess this source and therefore are not reduced to pure conjecture.) Luke uses Mark in large blocks, instead of interspersing it with other materials as Matthew's practice was; usually, though not always, he retains the order of Mark. Sometimes he anticipates something which Mark mentions later, and thus it appears that he read large sections of Mark, and perhaps the whole gospel, before writing his own section to correspond to it.

In general his use of Mark can be summarized thus:

Luke 1–2	non-Marcan
3.1–6.19	mostly Mark (1.2–3.19; 6.1–6)
6.20–8.3	non-Marcan
8.4–9.50	Mark (3.31–9.41, omitting 6.17–29; 6.45–8.26)
9.51–18.14	non-Marcan
18.15–24.11	Mark (10.13–16.8)
24.13–53	non-Marcan

He improves Mark's style by omitting repetitious words and clauses; he omits expressions which attribute human emotions to Jesus (so also Matthew); he severely abridges the account of a violent action such as the cleansing of the temple. In the words of Cadbury, 'the conduct of Jesus' disciples and friends towards him in Mark can easily be improved on, and Luke improves it.'

Such observations may point towards an explanation of Luke's omission of Salome's dance in the story of the death of John the Baptist, but they do not indicate why he dropped a whole block of materials from Mark (6.45–8.26). It is most unlikely that Luke began cutting out materials with the story of walking on water because he found it incredible. While ancient standards of credibility were largely personal, the rest of Luke's writings does not suggest that he would have found this story difficult to believe. It has been suggested that the copy of Mark which he used did not contain this section – either because there was an 'original Mark' to which it had not been added as yet, or because somehow some leaves had fallen out of the papyrus codex and Luke either did not notice their absence or did not / could not obtain them. Such theories possess all the fascination of the absolute – in this case, the absolutely hypothetical. We may suggest that Luke, as astute as most modern historians, observed that the materials in Mark 6.45–8.26 add little or nothing to what he could obtain

ither from other passages in Mark or from other materials
vailable to him; he therefore chose to omit them. He could see
hat they were somewhat repetitious (see page 123).

Luke was concerned with writing history. For this reason he
ttached to the public ministry of John and Jesus an elaborate
ynchronism (for which there are parallels in Greek historians
nd Josephus), dating the coming of the word of God to John the
aptist in the fifteenth year of Tiberius Caesar (A.D. 28–9), when
'ontius Pilate was governor of Judaea (26–36), Herod tetrarch of
alilee (4 B.C. – A.D. 39), Philip his brother tetrarch of Iturea
nd Trachonitis (4 B.C. – A.D. 34), Lysanias tetrarch of Abilene
doubtful date), and when Annas and Caiaphas were high
riest (3.1–2). This notice illustrates Luke's desire to set the gospel
arrative in the context of world history; it also reflects a certain
ack of familiarity with Jewish affairs, for only Caiaphas was high
riest at the time (though his father-in-law Annas doubtless
etained the title honorarily). Another difficulty occurs in his story
f the birth of Jesus, which he dates both 'in the days of King
ierod' (1.5, before 4 B.C.) and in relation to a census under
Quirinius, governor of Syria, in A.D. 6 (2.2). Various attempts
ave been made to clear up this apparent contradiction by
ostulating an earlier Roman census in Palestine, but it cannot
e said that they have been entirely successful.

Luke was concerned with the historical setting of the mission of
ohn and Jesus. He is the only evangelist to report John's counsel
o tax-collectors and soldiers (3.12–14). He apparently cannot
gree with Mark that the tetrarch Herod would suppose that
ohn had risen from the dead, so he ascribes this opinion to
thers (9.7–9). He realizes that the beginning of Jesus' mission,
s Mark relates it, is historically incomprehensible, and he
herefore tells how Jesus read from Isaiah in the synagogue at
Nazareth and stated that the prophecy had been fulfilled (4.21).
n his view, Mark's passion narrative did not adequately
mphasize 'non-theological factors', and he therefore lists the
recise charges brought against Jesus: he was overturning the
ation, forbidding the payment of taxes to Caesar, and calling
imself an anointed king (23.2). Since Jesus was a Galilean, he
must have been investigated by Herod (23.6–12). And for the
enturion's recognition of Jesus as 'son of God' (Mark 15.39) he

substitutes his acknowledgment that he was 'an innocent man' (Luke 23.47). It should of course be added that when Luke makes these changes it is easier for us to see that they have been made than to assign definite motives for each change or (and especially) to say whether or not Luke's account is thus more reliable than Mark's. We do not know that he did not possess the reliable information he claims to have had.

Luke emphasizes the concern of Jesus' ministry with rich and poor and with money. In his version of the Beatitudes Jesus blesses the poor (6.20, not the 'poor in spirit' as in Matt. 5.3) and the hungry (6.21, not those who 'hunger and thirst for righteousness' as in Matt. 5.6); Jesus denounces, indeed curses, the rich and those who are now well-fed (6.24–5). There are a good many references to women and their relation to the gospel, even though it is Luke alone who states that 'wives' must be left for sake of discipleship (14.26; 18.29). The range of the mission of Jesus is extended beyond the Jewish people (cf. Mark 7.24–30, which Luke omits) to the despised Samaritans (10.30–7, the Good Samaritan; 17.11–19, the Samaritan leper; a similar interest in Acts 8.5–35). Presumably these Lucan emphases reflect at least one aspect of the ministry of Jesus.

It is clear that as a historian, and as a second-generation Christian, Luke is aware of a certain distance between himself and the earliest disciples. This means that, like the other evangelists, he repeatedly states that the disciples misunderstood Jesus during his ministry; unlike them, he specifically indicates that their eschatological views were wrong. As they approached Jerusalem they 'supposed that the kingdom of God would appear immediately' (19.11), but they were mistaken. Before they knew of the resurrection, some of them could say that 'we hoped that he was the one to redeem Israel' (24.21); even afterwards they could ask, 'Lord, will you restore the kingdom to Israel at this time?' (Acts. 1.6). They did not yet understand that the Christ had to suffer and then enter into his glory (Luke 24.26); they did not know that the Spirit would be given to the Church, which would then witness to Jesus 'to the end of the earth' (Acts 1.8). For this reason Luke reports the saying of Jesus that 'the kingdom of God does not come with watching; people will not say, "Lo here" or "there"; for behold, the kingdom of God is within you' or, in your midst)' (Luke 17.20–1). Luke modifies some of the eschatological material derived from Mark; he agrees that the end will come, but Christians must not follow those who say, 'The time has drawn near' (21.8). It may be that the fall of Jerusalem has come (21.20–4; see p. 69) but, even if it has, the end is not yet.

On the other hand, not all Luke's modifications can be explained in this way. Why does he omit the statement in Mark 10.45, 'the Son of Man came to give his life as a ransom for many'? Why does he substitute the words, 'I am in your midst as one who serves' (Luke 22.27)? He cannot be opposed to mentioning Christ's sacrificial death, for he plainly refers to it in Acts 20.28. Perhaps he believes that the earliest disciples did not understand it as Paul did. This problem leads us to another, the question of the text of Luke 22.19b–20. Some manuscripts state only that at the Last Supper, Jesus took a cup, blessed it, and passed it to his disciples with an oath not to drink wine again until the coming of the kingdom; then he took bread, blessed it, and gave it to them, saying, 'This is my body.' Other manuscripts continue at this point, adding these words:

> given for you; do this in my remembrance. And likewise the cup after supper, saying, This cup is the new covenant in my blood which is poured out for you.

There is a considerable measure of confusion in the order of these words in the various manuscripts, and they are omitted entirely in Codex Bezae and in the Old Latin version, while they are paralleled partly in Mark (14.22–4) and partly in I Corinthians 11.24–5.

It can be argued that (1) the longer version was written by Luke and the confusion is due to the sequence cup-bread-cup, not found in early liturgies and therefore disliked by early copyists, or (2) what Luke wrote was only the shorter version (cup-bread, as in the *Didache*); the confusion is due to the efforts of copyists to apply additional materials.

Here we enter the realm of textual history and can note that there are significant disagreements in other parts of Luke and, above all, in Acts, where Codex Bezae gives us practically a different edition of the book from the one found in other manuscripts. In Luke itself we find such divergences as (1) th ascription of the Magnificat (1.46–55) to Elizabeth rather than t Mary (Irenaeus in the second century, Niceta of Remesiana in th fourth; some Old Latin manuscripts); (2) the appearance of a angel to Jesus in Gethsemane (22.43–4; found in Codex Bezae bu omitted in Alexandrian and Caesarean manuscripts); (3) 'Fathe forgive them, for they do not know what they are doing' (23.3 [cf. Acts 7.60], omitted by many Alexandrian and Caesarea manuscripts, perhaps in opposition to the Jews; contrast Mat 27.25); (4) 'He is not here but has been raised' (24.6; omitted i Codex Bezae and the Old Latin, but found in the parallel, Mar 16.6); (5) Luke 24.12, apparently based on John 20.8–10 an omitted by Codex Bezae, the Old Latin, and Marcion; and (6) th statement about the ascension in Luke 24.51, omitted by the sam witnesses and in one Syriac version.

What does this evidence prove? It proves only that the text Luke has been subject to a good deal of modification – in variou directions. We know that in the second century two tendencie were at work (if not more). On the one hand, Marcion busie himself with deleting what he regarded as interpolations from the gospel; as far as we can tell from later witnesses to his now los work, he rejected Luke 22.43–4 and 24.12 but accepted the othe passages. On the other hand, Tatian prepared his *Diatessaron* i which the four gospels were run together; this process of combina tion tended to result in mixed texts. In consequence of the tw tendencies and inevitable scribal errors, it becomes impossible fo us to say whether the longer text or the shorter in Luke 22.19b–2 is the original one. Marcion himself accepted the longer text removing only the word 'new' from the expression 'new covenant' since he did not believe that there was an old covenant.

While we have indicated that Luke regarded himself as historian, we should bear in mind that his conception of history was to a considerable degree 'rhetorical'. He felt free, as othe ancient historians felt free, to give an arrangement to his material which was not necessarily chronological but brought out thei meaning as he understood it. Thus in Luke 9.51–18.14 we have an account of a journey towards Jerusalem which the evangelis has used to provide an occasion for including materials of variou sorts, mostly without precise indications of time or place.

imilarly the many speeches in Acts are largely in Luke's style
he speech of Stephen in Acts 7 is a partial exception) and reflect
is ideas (or does he reflect theirs?). The tendency towards
niformity in these speeches has been explained as due to the
ommon practice of ancient historians who invented speeches
uited to the occasions they were describing. In this regard,
ecourse is often had to a statement by Thucydides, to the effect
nat when he did not have records of what was actually said he
ied to compose something appropriate. Those who thus appeal
o Thucydides usually neglect the rest of what he said: he stated
nat when he did have reliable reports he used them. Since we
o not know that Luke did not have reliable reports, we cannot
ay that he did more than rewrite his sources, or perhaps write
nem for the first time from oral tradition. It should be added that
Thucydides did not provide the only model known to ancient
istorians, in any event; Polybius, in the second century B.C.,
everely criticized some of his predecessors for inventing speeches
nd said that the historian's business was to record what was
ctually said. And while we know that Luke's contemporary,
osephus, liked to make up appropriate speeches – one of them
vas supposedly delivered in a cave just before all the witnesses
ommitted suicide – we do not know that Luke followed his
xample.

Cadbury's statement about Luke's work is rather enigmatic.
Even though devoid of historical basis in genuine tradition the
peeches in Acts have nevertheless considerable historical value.'[1]
Obviously the speeches have historical value as expressions of
vhat Luke thought the apostles had said; but we do not actually
know that they are devoid of historical basis.

THE ACTS OF THE APOSTLES

The book of Acts, the second of the two volumes written by the
vangelist Luke (probably after his gospel), is first certainly
utilized by Irenaeus of Lyons, towards the end of the second
century. He not only used it but also provided the classical proof
hat it was written by Luke: the detailed information given in the
we-passages' (Acts 16.9–18; 20.5–21.18; 27.1–28.16) proves that

[1] F. J. F. Jackson – K. Lake, *The Beginnings of Christianity*, V (London, 1933), 426.

it was written by a companion of Paul who went with him to Rome; this companion must have been Luke, in prison with Paul at Rome (Col. 4.14) and later (II Tim. 4.11). In the Muratorian fragment the book is described as containing the acts of all the apostles, presumably in order to reject apocryphal books of acts by implication. Thereafter no question was raised about it among orthodox Christians, though it was often neglected in periods when there was little interest in church history.

Even before Irenaeus's time, the book *may* have been known to Clement of Rome and/or Justin Martyr, but the evidence for their use of it is ambiguous.

The text of the book has been transmitted in two quite different forms. (1) Most of the Greek manuscripts, including the old uncials, and most later versions contain the form of Acts which is translated in English New Testaments. (2) On the other hand, in Codex Bezae (sixth century) we find what looks like another edition of the book, full of alterations and additions. Something like this edition was used by the earlier Church Fathers and reflected in the old Latin and Syriac versions.

Two views, with various modifications, have been held concerning the relation of the two kinds of text. (1) The more elaborate version was the original one; later it was revised, perhaps by Luke himself, and the 'standard' version was the result. This theory has been criticized by J. H. Ropes on the following grounds. (*a*) Among the passages omitted in the version supposed to be later are references to the name or the person of (the Lord) Jesus Christ, to the Holy Spirit, and to divine guidance. Did Luke change his mind in this direction? (*b*) In fourteen instances essentially different pictures of events are set forth. Would Luke have rewritten his book in this way? For these reasons Ropes concluded that another solution must be correct. (2) The shorter version was the original one, and during the late first century or early second it was amplified in order to improve the style and add 'religious commonplaces'. These modifications gained widespread acceptance for the book.

A notable example of revision is to be found in the report of the 'apostolic decree' in Acts 15.20 and 29 (also 21.25). Here the original decree was probably concerned with Levitical purity (see page 393). The editor of the expanded version dropped a eference to 'things strangled' and twice added the 'golden rule', thus giving the impression that the decree was concerned with moral requirements.[1]

ACTS – SOURCES

According to an ingenious theory propounded by Harnack, Acts 2–5 is based on two separate sources which describe the same events. The first, from the evangelist Philip and his daughters, he called 'A'; the second, less reliable because more 'theological', he called 'B'. His equations can be summarized in a table.

	A	B
(A miraculous cure)	(3.1–10)	—
Mission preaching of Peter; success	3.11–26; 4.4	2.14–41
The gift of tongues	4.23–31	2.1–13
Sharing of property	4.32, 34–5.16	2.44–5
Arrest and trial of the apostles	4.1–3, 5–22	5.17–42

Harnack recognized that Acts 2.42–3, 46–7 and 4.33 were summaries, and therefore did not include them in either source.

The summaries were further investigated by Cadbury, who argued that they could be isolated and that earlier ones could be differentiated from later. The earlier ones were Acts 2.41–2; 4.32, 34–5; and 5.11–14. Others were added later: 2.43–7, based on the older ones; 4.33, based on 2.47a and 5.42; and 5.15–16. This analysis meant that Harnack's sources were diminished in size, but not necessarily removed from the scene.

The basic question, however, is whether or not the events are really the same. Jeremias has suggested that Peter undoubtedly preached more than once, and that the gift of tongues is not necessarily the same as the shaking of a house (4.31). In addition, he has shown that according to Jewish law a criminal had to be warned before he could be punished. In Acts 4.18 the apostles were warned not to speak, but they were not punished; in Acts 5.28 they were reminded of the warning; and in Acts 5.40 they

---

[1] Ropes claimed that at this point the original decree was correctly reported in the second version, but this claim is inconsistent with his basic theory.

were beaten. The two accounts do not describe the same event.
Therefore the sources 'A' and 'B' did not exist. Acts 2–5 is probably
based primarily on oral tradition, as Luke suggests (Luke 1.2).

As for the materials which follow, it would appear that two
kinds are involved, obviously related to the geography of the early
Christian missions which were based on Jerusalem and Antioch.
These materials reflect two points of view. (1) The viewpoint of
Jerusalem is reflected – as in Acts 2–5 – in Acts 8.5–40 (Philip);
9.31–11.18 (Peter); 12.1–24 (Peter); and 15.1–33 (the Jerusalem
council). (2) The viewpoint of Antioch, and of some Jerusalem
Christians, is reflected in Acts 6.1–8.4 (the story of Stephen
leading on to Saul); 9.1–30 (the story of Saul); 11.19–30 (Saul
and others at Antioch); and 12.25–14.28 (Antioch and its missions).
This Antiochene source, which leads on to what follows the
Jerusalem council, is called by Jeremias 'the only source of Acts
which can be reconstructed with some probability' and 'the oldest
mission history of the Christian Church – the kernel of Acts'.

After this point begins the part of Acts with which Luke as an
eye-witness was directly concerned (unless, as is possible, he is the
Lucius of Acts 13.1), for in Acts 16.10 we find the first of the 'we-
passages', presumably from his diary. The author of the
'we-passages' represents himself as going with Paul to Troas and
then to Macedonia (16.8–11), sailing with him back from
Philippi to Troas (20.5–15) and thence going to Jerusalem
(21.1–18) and Rome (27.1–28.16). The appearance and dis-
appearance of the 'we-passages' has occasioned some criticism.
Their style is the same as that of the rest of Acts, and we may
assume that when Luke wished to emphasize the fact that he had
accompanied Paul on his major journeys he used this means of
doing so. It cannot be determined whether or not he was present
at events described only in the third person, though it would seem
likely that he was. Why did Conrad usually employ the third
person in *The Nigger of the Narcissus* but occasionally speak of 'we'?

The book of Acts, then, is essentially based on (1) oral traditions
about the early church of Jerusalem, (2) other traditions about
the Jerusalem missions, (3) materials about the church of Antioch
for which Luke himself may have been responsible (cf. 13.1), and
(4) an account of the mission of Paul of which to a considerable
extent Luke was an eye-witness. To his narrative he has naturally

added summaries, as well as what have been called 'panels of progress' – which summarize but also indicate the passage of time (2.47; 6.7; 9.31; 12.24; 16.5; 19.20; 28.31). It has been claimed that these passages mark five-year intervals of time, beginning with the year 30 and ending with the year 60. Such a correlation is possible, but we have no reason to suppose that Luke actually regarded five-year periods as significant.

Luke evidently regarded himself as a historian, but many questions can be raised in regard to the reliability of his history, and most of them have been raised in the commentary of Ernst Haenchen (1957; 3rd ed., 1959). In the first fifteen chapters, which deal primarily with the church of Jerusalem, Luke is producing an edifying sketch rather than a history. The speeches and sermons are based on the Septuagint, not on the Hebrew Bible, and therefore reflect Luke's interests, not those of the early community. His 'statistics' are impossible; Peter could not have addressed three thousand hearers without a microphone, and since the population of Jerusalem was about 25–30,000, Christians cannot have numbered five thousand (Acts 4.4). Something is clearly wrong with Luke's chronology, for he has Gamaliel refer to Theudas and Judas in the wrong order, and Theudas actually rebelled about a decade after Gamaliel spoke (5.36–7).

The most important difficulty in the early part of Acts has to do with the conversion of Cornelius, described as a centurion of the Italian cohort (10.1). But during the reign of Herod Agrippa (d. 44), no Roman troops were stationed in his territory. Cornelius is really a stock figure, probably modelled upon the anonymous centurion of Luke 7.1–10. The whole story has been elaborated by Luke in an effort to show that the church of Jerusalem was responsible for the gentile mission. This mission did not involve circumcision (10.45; 11.18). How, then, could the question of circumcision be discussed anew at the 'council of Jerusalem'? How could the Jerusalem Christians have forgotten the story of Cornelius (though Peter alludes to it in Acts 15.7)? In Haenchen's view the apostolic council is 'an imaginative construction and corresponds to no historical reality'.

The parts of Acts which deal primarily with Paul are not much better. Luke constantly reads in notions of his own time, for example in the statement that Paul and Barnabas appointed elders in various churches (14.23) or in the reference to the presbyter-bishops of Ephesus (20.17, 28). Paul's address at Athens reflects Luke's theology, not Paul's; and even if isolated elements in it correspond with isolated elements in Paul's letters, comparisons must be based upon the basic directions present in the theological ideas of both.

Luke makes Paul's relations with Jerusalem much closer than they really were. Paul did not study with Gamaliel, for he was not in Jerusalem in his youth (Gal. 1.22); his exegesis is not essentially rabbinic; and his writings reflect a life-long acquaintance with the Septuagint. Acts 18.22 implies that Luke thought that Paul visited Jerusalem at that point, but he actually did not do so, since Galatians 2.11 shows that there was a complete break between him and the Jerusalem church.

He tries to give an impression of familiarity with Roman officials and their procedures, but Paul's 'trial' is incoherently presented. Why did neither Felix nor Festus give a judgement? Why did Paul not wait for a decision instead of appealing to Caesar? Why did Festus not decide a case of *crimen laesae maiestatis*? When Luke describes Festus's discussion with Agrippa he is doing no more than telling the story 'as he supposed that Roman officials would have told it' (Lake-Cadbury).

Even the story of Paul's final journey to Rome, including the narrative about the shipwreck, is full of theological motives and historical difficulties.

We do not agree that every instance is as unhistorical (in our understanding of the term) as Haenchen claims it is. Historical events are not always historically comprehensible; in their particularity they often resist general or logical classification. But when Haenchen reminds us that in Acts 'we have no photograph of Paul taken by a colleague, but the picture which stood before the eyes of the post-apostolic community – that of a Paul whom the early Catholic Church recognized and revered and until Augustine and Luther was preferred to the Paul of the epistles' (p. 493), we cannot altogether disagree.

This is to say that while the traditions which reached Luke may have been generally, or largely, historical, in some respects they were not, and his own use of them did not often increase their historical value. It is also to say that just as the writings of Greek and Roman historians cannot be accepted at face value by the student of history, so the book of Acts has to be analysed not only internally but also in relation to the Pauline epistles. Its primary value lies in its witness to the picture of the life of the early Church which was developed a decade or so after the fall of Jerusalem and the deaths of the principal apostles.

Why was Acts written at all? Here again Haenchen provides a clear, though disputable, answer (pp. 84–8). In the time it was written two questions were especially important: (1) the time of the coming of the end, and (2) the relation of the gentile mission to the Jewish law. The author could have solved the first problem as John does, by setting what had been future in the present; or he could have done what he actually did, i.e. place the end in the indefinite future. As for the second question, the author clearly minimizes as much as possible the differences between Jews and gentiles in the Church.

It is true that the end is, so to speak, postponed; but we should not agree that it was originally regarded as imminent. Similarly while Luke minimizes Jewish-gentile differences it is possible that in Galatians Paul exaggerates them. The fact that Acts reflects certain purposes on its author's part does not mean that views contrary to those purposes are necessarily authentic, or more authentic.

XI

THE GOSPEL OF JOHN

The earliest evidence for the existence of the Fourth Gospel or, at any rate, of the distinctive ideas of its author, is provided in the letters of Ignatius, bishop of Antioch about 115. The gospel itself was used by the Gnostic teacher Basilides, early in the second century at Alexandria, and from the same period comes a tiny papyrus fragment containing several verses of John 18. Orthodox teachers like Justin made use of the gospel at Rome, and wall paintings in the Roman catacombs (c. 175) portray Johannine themes. The earliest 'commentaries' on John which we know, come from Ptolemaeus and Heracleon, disciples of the Christian Gnostic Valentinus; both of them ascribed the book to John, the disciple of Jesus.

In the late second century a few orthodox writers, reacting against Montanist use of John, denied that he had written the book, but most Christians agreed with Theophilus that it was written by an inspired author and with Irenaeus that this author was John, author of the book of Revelation and teacher of Polycarp of Smyrna. The fact that in Polycarp's extant letter or letters there is only one possible allusion to the gospel does not prove that he did not know the book. It is a question, however, whether or not the gospel and the Apocalypse were written by the same author. Dionysius, bishop of Alexandria (c. 250), argued that considerations of vocabulary, style and thought prove that there were two authors.

After the end of the second century, however, no Christian author doubted that the gospel was written by an apostle; only in modern times has the question been raised again, chiefly because of the differences between John and the synoptic gospels either individually or as a group. We shall consider these differences as we examine Johannine vocabulary, style and thought.

VOCABULARY AND STYLE

The Gospel of John contains 15,240 words, only 1,011 of them different. Of these, 112 do not occur in any other New Testament book. In proportion to its size, the gospel employs the smallest vocabulary in the New Testament; even the book of Revelation reflects a higher proportion of vocabulary to total number of words (9.3 per cent against 6.5 per cent).

Especially characteristic of the gospel's vocabulary are words bearing upon the meaning of Jesus' revelation. There are 120 references to God as 'Father' (only sixty-four in all three synoptics), only three of them qualified by adjectives ('living', 6.57; 'holy', 17.11; 'righteous', 17.25). The Father is often identified as 'he who sent me' (twenty-six times). John usually speaks of 'Jesus', but the terms 'Son' (nineteen times), 'Son of Man' (thirteen times), and 'Son of God' (seven times) also occur. The most common way of indicating the significance of Jesus, however, is in the use of the nominative personal pronoun 'I' (120 times). The most important use of 'I' occurs in the expression 'I am' with a predicate noun.

> I am the bread of life (6.35, 41, 48, 51)
> I am the light of the world (8.12)
> I am the door of the sheep (10.7, 9)
> I am the good shepherd (10.11, 14)
> I am the resurrection and life (11.25)
> I am the way, truth, and life (14.6)
> I am the true vine (15.1, 5)

There are also significant verbs of revealing used with 'I', for example 'I know' (141 times), 'I bear witness' (thirty-three times), 'I speak' (thirty times), 'I glorify' (twenty-one times), and 'I make manifest' (nine times). The response of the believer is indicated especially by 'I believe' (100 times) and 'I behold' (twenty-three times).

The nature of Jesus' revelation is intimated by 'truth' (true, truly, a total of fifty-five times), by 'life' in a special sense (thirty-six times), and by 'light' (twenty-two times). Revelation and response are combined in 'love' (noun and verbs, fifty-seven times), and the response of 'abiding' or 'remaining' is found forty times.

The spiritual environment of the Incarnation is reflected in the word 'world' ('*kosmos*', seventeen times), often co-ordinated with 'the Jews' (sixty-eight times). John mentions a Jewish feast seventeen times, and speaks of 'your law' three times.

There are also favourite words which point towards John's conception of history: 'not yet' ('*oupō*', eight times in a 'theological' sense), two words for 'now' (about thirty times: '*arti*' and '*nun*'). He also employs several words for dealing with spiritual origins: 'whence' ('*pothen*', thirteen times) and 'whither' ('*pou*', about twelve times), 'from above' (five times) and 'from below' (once); similarly, he contrasts heaven with earth.

For the sake of comparison with the synoptics, it may be added that the following words never occur in John, though fairly common in the other gospels: (1) 'Christian' words: apostles, baptism, gospel, repent, repentance, inherit; (2) 'Sociological' words: adultery, demons (exorcisms), divorce, rich, Sadducee, scribe, tax collector. To these should be added words which, though common in the synoptics, are very infrequent in John: (1) cross, crucify, forgive, kingdom, save; (2) blaspheme, blasphemy, marry, marriage, poor, priest, synagogue. Whatever the historical situations of John and the synoptics may be, they are rather different from each other. Perhaps one might say that the synoptic gospels are more concerned with social and historical matters, while John is concerned with theology.

Specialists in Aramaic have often argued that John's gospel was translated from that language. As criteria of proof they have used (1) obscurities which can be explained as misunderstood Aramaic, and (2) bad Greek which may be due to poor translation. Their use of these criteria was undercut in 1931 by E. C. Colwell (*The Greek of the Fourth Gospel*), who showed that the passages were not very obscure and that the Greek was characteristic of the Koiné. Furthermore, different Aramaists retranslate differently. John may have written in Aramaic; but the case has not been proved.

John is fond of varying his Greek words where he intends to convey the same meanings. For example, three different words are used for 'go away' in John 16.5–10, two for 'love' in 21.15–17 (cf. 14.21 and 16.27), and three for 'grieve' in 16.20–2. Two different words for 'ear' are used in John 18.10 and 26, two for 'keep' in 17.12. Lists of 'Johannine synonyms' can easily be constructed. Similarly, when the Johannine Christ says, 'As I told you before,' comparison of what he has previously said with what he says now will reveal that the two sayings are almost never verbally identical. This feature shows John's fondness for variation.

At the same time, John likes to use a single expression with various meanings; sometimes he seems to be indicating that there is not only an obvious or 'surface' meaning but also a deeper significance. This characteristic of his writing occurs not only in the discourses with Nicodemus and the Samaritan woman and in relation to the Feeding of the Five Thousand, but also in conversations with the disciples. John is suggesting that the meaning of Jesus was not exhausted by the interpretations of his person and message which were given by his contemporaries, just as the Darkness did not 'grasp' the Light (1.5). Much of the teaching of Jesus was ambiguous. When he spoke of the temple he really referred to his body (2.19–21). He said that a man must be born 'again' ('from above') of water and the Spirit (3.3–5); and the word '*pneuma*' means both 'spirit' and 'wind' (3.8). To be 'lifted up' (3.14) means both to be exalted (8.28; 12.32–4) and to be crucified (18.32). 'Water' means one thing to the Samaritan woman, another to Jesus (4.7–11). He alone understands the deeper meaning of 'going away' (7.35; 8.21; 13.33–6), of being blind and then seeing (9.39–41), of the sleep of death (11.4, 11–15), and of resurrection (11.23–6). And in this gospel even the high priest delivers an ambiguous prediction (11.50–2; cf. 18.14) and Pilate involuntarily testifies to the significance of Jesus (19.5, 14–15).

Sometimes, on the other hand, John seems to indicate different shades of meaning by the use of different, though related, words. He seems to hint that the verb '*hypagein*' does not mean simply 'to go' but is especially concerned with Christ's going to the Father (7.35; 8.21; 13.33, 36). Similarly the ordinary words '*erchesthai*', 'to come', and '*poreuesthai*', 'to go', are used chiefly of coming from and going to heaven, while the compound verbs meaning 'to come from' and 'to go to' are more frequently related to movement in the world. Special meanings seem to be reserved for '*anabainein*', 'to go up' (to Jerusalem, to the temple, to festivals, to heaven), for '*katabainein*', 'to go down' (to Capernaum for a healing, from heaven), and for '*metabainein*', 'to cross' (from death to life, from the world to the Father; once to Judaea). These words are important because so much of John's thought is related to 'up' and 'down', 'above' and 'below', 'heaven' and 'the world'. The true disciples know where Jesus came from and where he goes; they are 'born from above' and will ascend after him.

It is not certain how far John's use of words is systematic, although Origen may have been right in believing that John regarded Judaea, Jerusalem, the temple and festivals as symbols of heaven, Galilee and Capernaum as symbols of the world. If he regarded them as symbols, he did not mean that they were 'merely' symbols. If they were symbols, they were, so to speak, incarnate symbols.

THOUGHT

If we consider the purpose or purposes of the evangelist in so far as we can infer them from his book itself, we clearly find that he writes in order to inspire and to confirm faith in Jesus as the Christ, the Son of God, so that readers may have true life 'in his name' on the ground of this faith (20.30–1). What he writes consists of 'signs' which Jesus performed in his disciples' presence, and he has made a selection from the many signs of Jesus because he believes that the ones recorded are essential. They include the transformation of water into wine (2.11) and the healing of a royal officer's son (4.54), both at Cana in Galilee; but there are many others, which during Jesus' ministry did not inevitably result in faith (12.37). The picture which John sets forth is thus different from that found in the synoptic gospels, where Jesus denies that any sign will be given to his generation (Mark 8.12) – at any rate, none except 'the sign of Jonah' (Matt. 12.39–40; 16.8; Luke 11.29–30). According to Paul (I Cor. 1.22), 'signs' are sought for by Jews, not by Christians. According to John, even the high priests and the Pharisees recognize that Jesus performed signs (11.47). (Sometimes a deeper meaning for 'sign' is indicated, as in John 6.26.)

The evangelist is concerned with pointing out that John the Baptist 'did no sign' (10.41). Here we encounter one of his most important interests. The Baptist was not the Light but a witness to the Light (1.7). He was not the Christ (1.20; 3.28); he was not the returning Elijah (1.21; contrast Matt. 11.14), nor yet 'the prophet' foretold by Moses (1.21), for this prophet is Jesus (6.14; 7.40). John pointed towards Jesus as really prior to himself (1.15, 27, 30); he recognized him as the Lamb of God (1.29, 36), and he said that as Jesus increased so he himself must diminish (3.30). At least two of his disciples, including Andrew, became disciples of Jesus (1.35–40). Now in Acts 19.1–8 we find evidence for the existence of 'Johannine' Christians, and in the *Clementine Recognitions* (fourth century) we read of disciples of the Baptist who regarded him as the Christ. This outside evidence, scanty though it is, confirms our impression that the evangelist is dealing with the real problem presented by those who revered the Baptist more highly than Jesus. This feature of his gospel suggests that it was written at a relatively early date. The *Clementine Recognitions* are, of course, late; but at many points they make use of early Jewish-Christian traditions, usually heterodox in character.

John is also concerned with the temple and its ritual. The synoptists place the cleansing of the temple just before the passion narrative; John makes it early and insists that the true temple is the body of Jesus (2.13–22). True worship is 'in spirit and truth', not limited to Jerusalem or Samaria (4.20–4). The festivals at Jerusalem are described as 'of the Jews' (5.1; 7.2; 11.55); similarly the law (as law) is assigned to them. Indeed, while in the synoptics Jesus eats the paschal meal with his disciples, in John 18.28 it is made plain that the time for the meal came after his arrest and crucifixion. In some respects John's attitude resembles that of the Dead Sea covenanters. His freedom from the law is balanced by insistence that 'the scripture cannot be broken' (10.35) and the treatment of the Mosaic writings as really written about Jesus (5.46).

Among the most important features of John's thought is his view of Jesus as the incarnate Word of God (1.14), one with the Father (10.30); he who has seen Jesus has seen the Father (14.9). He is the Revealer-Redeemer who comes down from the heavenly Father and returns to him. Along with this concentration upon the person and work of Christ goes a revaluation of eschatology. Emphasis is placed not so much on the return of Christ and the last judgement as on the presence of Christ and the Holy Spirit and on judgement already begun in present life. In regard to Christology and eschatology the point of view of John is somewhat different from that of the synoptic evangelists.

JOHN AND THE SYNOPTICS

We have already referred to many differences between John and the synoptic gospels. The most important of them is probably that of the order in which events are related, especially events located in or near Jerusalem. According to the synoptics, the public ministry of Jesus consisted of journeys about Galilee and one journey to Jerusalem; according to John, he frequently visited the city. According to the synoptics, he cleansed the temple shortly before being crucified; according to John, he did so early in his ministry. The possibilities, historically speaking, are these: (1) either John or the synoptics, or (2) neither John nor the synoptics. If we may assume that the details of the 'triumphal entry' are significant, and that they point towards the Feast of Tabernacles, we may conclude that both John and the synoptic evangelists have transferred an event which originally occurred at Tabernacles to the Feast of Passover – or, more probably, that their predecessors did so. Alternatively, we may assume that the actual feast was not remembered and that those who transmitted the traditional accounts felt free to place the event where they pleased.

There are also many details in which John agrees with the synoptic gospels, and we might suppose that such parallels would clearly indicate John's relative earliness or lateness. Such is not the case. All the evidence is ambiguous, and three possibilities remain open. (1) John did not know either the synoptic traditions or the synoptic gospels, but used independent traditions. (2) John knew some synoptic traditions and used them in his gospel. (3) John knew some or all of the synoptic gospels but consciously rewrote his sources in order to (a) interpret them or (b) supplement them or (c) supplant them. There are no reliable grounds for making a decision.

If we pass back to historical considerations it can be argued that the synoptic gospels fairly reliably reflect the Galilean-Judaean background of Jesus' ministry as well as the exorcisms, parables and message of the kingdom with which he was concerned; all these features are minimized in John. On the other hand, in John we find a thought-world which in some respects resembles that of the Essenes of Qumran (see Chapter XVIII). It can be claimed, then, that the differences are due not to a 'development' from original Jewish ideas to something else but to the reflection of two (or more) different kinds of Judaism. The fact that John speaks in a hostile way about 'the Jews', while the synoptic evangelists pay more attention to smaller groups and to individuals, does not prove that he is not Jewish. The Qumran sectarians similarly criticized the 'orthodox'. Moreover, criticism of 'the Jews' is not necessarily even late. It is found in I Thessalonians 2.15 and in early sermons in Acts (2.23, 3.15, etc.). On specific literary and historical grounds, then, it cannot be proved that John is either earlier or later than the synoptic gospels.

The only grounds on which this point can definitely be 'proved' lie in a general theory of the development of early Christian thought, and the chief support of this theory is provided by the Gospel itself. Since the argument is circular we shall do well to neglect it.

INTERPOLATIONS AND SOURCES

Especially in the twentieth century, scholars have pointed to difficulties in the Gospel of John which suggest that (1) it is not in order as it stands, (2) it has been interpolated by an editor, and (3) either the editor or the author made use of earlier sources which can be detected. It need hardly be said that such theories are not altogether new. Origen was well aware of some of the difficulties, and he used them to support his claim that the evangelist was concerned with spiritual truths rather than with historical events. The modern goal, however, is usually to give a literary-historical explanation of the phenomena.

(1) Proof that the Gospel is not in order is provided quite tellingly by Rudolf Bultmann.[1] (a) According to John 6.1, 'after this Jesus went away to the other side of the sea of Galilee'; but according to the preceding chapter he was in Jerusalem. If

[1] *Die Religion in Geschichte und Gegenwart* (ed. 3, 1959), III, 840-1.

chapter 5 follows chapter 6, everything falls into place. (*b*) Similarly, John 7.15–24 is incomprehensible in its present location; it belongs with the discussion in chapter 5, perhaps at the end; and in this case 7.1–14 goes with 7.25ff. (*c*) John 10.19–21 must be the ending of a longer section dealing with opening the eyes of a blind man; it therefore goes with chapter 9, while 10.1–18 goes with 10.27–9. (*d*) John 12.44–50 has no relation to its context; it too goes with chapter 9. (*e*) Something is wrong with the order of John 13–17, for 14.30–1 leads directly to the passion narrative ('arise, let us go hence') although three chapters of discourses follow. Chapters 15–17 must therefore originally have preceded chapter 14 (or, rather, 13.36–14.31).

If these points be granted – and it is difficult to deny their force – we must admit that the Gospel has been disarranged. The only question that remains is concerned with the extent of the disarrangement.

(2) The question of the activity of an editor is more difficult to decide. What criteria are to be employed? Siegfried Mendner has listed four: (*a*) pedantic dependence on the synoptic gospels, (*b*) unpoetic inadequacy in word or thought, (*c*) unrealistic or unhistorical statements, and (*d*) compositional difficulties and contradictions.[1] Not all of these criteria possess equal force. The original author may have had difficulties, may sometimes have failed to write poetically, and may not have known or been concerned with historical events. As we have already suggested, we do not know whether or not he employed the synoptic traditions or gospels.

Bultmann differentiates late glosses from the work of the editor. He finds that the presence of glosses is often indicated by their being omitted in some manuscripts or versions. These glosses include John 7.53–8.11 (omitted by all ancient witnesses), 5.4 (omitted by most early manuscripts), and the following phrases omitted by some witnesses:

> 6.23 when the Lord gave thanks
> 13.10 except the feet
> 14.30 many things
> 16.16 because I go to the Father.

---

[1] *Zeitschrift für die neutestamentliche Wissenschaft* 47 (1956), 108.

In addition, Bultmann treats as glosses the following expressions which break the continuity of thought or produce confusion in a sentence:

2.15 the sheep and the oxen
4.1 the Lord knew that
4.11 you have no dipper and the well is deep (too obvious)
21.20 following, who also reclined at the supper on his bosom and said, Lord, who is it who betrays you?

After these glosses have been removed, we have the gospel in the shape in which it left the hand of an ecclesiastical editor, late in the first century or early in the second. From this form of the work, then, we must go on to remove items which were added in order to make the gospel conform to late first-century sacramental views or synoptic eschatology or history. The editor had the double purpose of making the work harmonize with church life and with the Church's gospels.

Proof of the existence of this editor is provided first of all by noticing the most obvious additions he has made. The Gospel clearly comes to an end in 20.30–1; we must therefore assume that chapter 21 is an addition. Furthermore, the poetic style of the prologue is interrupted by prosaic verses which refer to John the Baptist (1.6–8, 15; cf. 1.30). Therefore we can go on to discover other additions which break the formal continuity of the book or produce contradictions.

'Synoptic' sayings 1.22–5, 32; 7.20–1; 11.2; perhaps 13.16, 20; also 'John had not yet been imprisoned' (3.24, attempt to correlate with the synoptics)

Contradiction 4.2 'And yet Jesus himself did not baptize, but his disciples did' (contradicts 3.22)

'Mechanical' fulfilment 18.9 'In order that the word . . . might be fulfilled'; also 18.32.

The editor was not concerned with synoptic tradition alone. He was anxious to relate the gospel to the sacramental teaching of the Church and to its eschatology. Therefore he added 6.51b–58 in order to correlate the bread of life with the Eucharist, and 19.34b–35 to show that both baptism and Eucharist were established by the death of Jesus. In addition, he inserted the words 'water and' in a reference to birth from the Spirit (3.5); the parallel in John 3.3 speaks of birth 'from above'. Water is irrelevant. As for eschatology, the true Johannine view involves present realization alone. 'The hour comes and now is' (4.23; 5.25). 'I am the resurrection and the life; he who believes in me, even if he dies, will live, and everyone who lives and believes in me will never die' (11.25–6; cf. also 3.18–19; 9.39). The editor is responsible for additions which speak of resurrection and judgement as future (5.28–9) or of a future gift by the Son of Man (6.27), or refer to 'the last day' (6.39, 40, 44, 54; 12.48). His view is the Jewish eschatological view expressed by Martha in John 11.24 ('I know that he will rise in the resurrection at the last day') and corrected by Jesus.

The points about sacramental teaching and eschatology obviously depend upon a prior assumption that in the evangelist's thought water had nothing to do with birth from above and the bread of life was not related to the Eucharist; similarly his eschatology must have been either futurist or realized. The question, then, must be raised whether or not the evangelist's mind worked as clearly and sharply as does that of a modern literary critic. When Bultmann deletes 'water and' largely on the ground that other critics of the liberal school have done so, his argument is not very convincing.

It should be said, however, that the attempt to disprove Bultmann's claims by pointing to the unity of John's grammar, syntax and vocabulary is not convincing either. An editor who believed that it was important to revise John's work would surely have had some acquaintance with his mode of expression. Moreover, the essence of style, whether ancient or modern, is a certain variety along with some measure of uniformity. No author uses nothing but formulas.

But this variety in thought and word leads us to suspect not only the argument based on Johannine unity but also the argument for the existence of the editor. It remains quite possible that the mysterious editor was also the author of the gospel, although he probably did not leave his work in precisely the form in which we have it. To an editor or to editors we should hesitate to ascribe much more than John 21.24–5, the last verses of the book:

This is the disciple who bears witness of these things, and wrote these things; and we know that his testimony is true. And there are also many other things which Jesus did; if all of them should be written, I suppose that even the world itself could not contain the books that might be written.

SOURCES

It is fairly clear that the opening verses of the Gospel are somewhat different in atmosphere from the rest of the book. This fact has been taken to show that the author was revising an earlier hymn or poem to the creative Word of God, but such an inference is not necessary. He may well have composed the prologue specifically for use in the gospel.

In addition, critics have argued that he made use of a book of 'signs' or significant miracles, and that he reinterpreted the contents of this book for his own purposes. To the 'sign book' Bultmann and others have added special sources consisting of sayings which originally came not from Jesus but from some Gnostic group, perhaps disciples of John the Baptist.

The difficulty with this source analysis lies in the fact that, as Charles Goodwin has pointed out, when John uses a source we can check on – the Old Testament – he does so very allusively. If we did not possess the Old Testament verses to which he alludes we could not reconstruct them. Therefore we cannot reconstruct his other sources, whatever they may have been.[1]

Indeed, unless we have the benefit of a genetic theory of the development of Christian thought, we might even suppose that in his gospel he combined memories of what he had seen and heard with interpretations based on these memories. Presumably revelation, or encounter in general, involves response, and in the absence of photography and tape-recording John was likely to write down what Jesus meant to him rather than to paste together sources which he did not quite understand.

We are left, then, with some very general conclusions which do not greatly assist us in dealing with the gospel. It was written, probably in Greek and not much later than 70, perhaps in Asia

[1] 'How did John treat his Sources?' – *Journal of Biblical Literature*, 73 (1954), 61–75.

Minor. It presents a portrait of Jesus different from the general synoptic picture. According to a tradition certainly in existence by the middle of the second century, its author was John, the disciple of Jesus – perhaps the son of Zebedee. The difficulty with identifying this John with the author of Revelation is that there are conspicuous differences in vocabulary, style and theological ideas. Perhaps there has been some confusion between the two; perhaps both came from the same area and belonged to the same 'school'; but any definite conclusion runs into difficulties.

Was the author a disciple of Jesus? If the synoptics are taken as the norm for the life of Jesus – and the traditions in them seem to underlie later New Testament books as John's do not – we may wonder how a disciple could have written as John does. But it is worth observing that the 'beloved disciple' often identified as John comes on the scene only in or near Jerusalem in this book. Perhaps his 'historical' memories were concerned chiefly with what took place at the end of Jesus' ministry; and in any event it is obvious that he regards remembering as related to the creative work of the Spirit (2.22; 12.16; 14.26). Again, if he is somehow related to the Dead Sea community and its fate after the monastery was destroyed in 68, some of his special emphases can be explained in relation to the audience which he hoped to win for Jesus.

We conclude that the author was probably not the son of Zebedee but a Jerusalem disciple of Jesus who wrote his gospel around the time of the Roman-Jewish war of 66–70 (probably not long after it) in order to present faith in Christ to bewildered and distressed Jewish sectarians. These sectarians lived either in Palestine itself or in the Dispersion.

APPENDIX: BULTMANN'S REARRANGEMENT OF JOHN

Prologue (1.1–18)
   The testimony of John the Baptist (1.19–51)
 1. The Revelation of the Glory before the World (2–12)
   Preliminary revelation (2.1–22)
  A. The Encounter with the Revealer (2.23–4.22)
   1. Jesus and the teachers of Israel
    (2.23–3.21; 3.31–6; 3.22–30)
   2. Jesus in Samaria (4.1–42)

APPENDIX: BULTMANN'S 'SAYINGS-SOURCE'

The Logos 1.1–5, 9–12, 14, 16
Flesh and Spirit 3.6, 8, 11–13, 18, 20–1, 32–6
The Water of Life 7.37–8; 4.13–14
The Bread of Life 6.27, 35, 48, 47, 44–5, 37
Father, Son, and Eternal Life 5.17, 19–21, 24–5; 11.25

The Glory 5.31–2, 39–44; 7.16–18; 8.14, 16, 19; 7.7, 28–9; 8.50, 54–5; 7.33–4; 8.43, 42, 44, 47, 45, 46, 51

The Light of the World 8.12; 12.44–5; 9.39; 12.47–50; 8.23, 28–9; 9.5, 4; 11.9–10; 12.35–6

The Shepherd-Door 10.11–12, 1, 4, 8, 10, 14–15, 27–30, 9

The Coming of the Hour 12.27–8, 23, 31–2

Freedom through Truth 8.31–2, 34–5, 38

The Revelation of Glory 17.1, 4–6, 9–17; 13.31–2

The Vine and the Branches 15.1–2, 4–6, 9–10, 16

Departure of the Revealer / Arrival of the Paraclete 15.18–20, 22, 24, 26; 16.8, 12–14, 16, 20, 22–4, 28; 14.1–7, 9, 14, 16–19, 26–7 (18.37?)

XII

APOCRYPHAL GOSPELS

In addition to the four gospels which alone were accepted by the Church during and after the time of Irenaeus, there were many apocryphal gospels which were favoured by Gnostic and other heretical groups. The most important of these gospels deserve some consideration.

Perhaps the oldest are those named after the groups which employed them: those according to the 'Hebrews', the 'Egyptians', and the 'Ebionites'. Hebrews seems to consist essentially of a modification of the Gospel of Matthew in the direction of Jewish Christianity; its hero is James the Lord's brother, recipient of a special resurrection-appearance (cf. I Cor. 15.17), and head of the Jerusalem church. Egyptians, on the other hand, contained traditions of the sayings of Jesus which portrayed him as having come to 'destroy the works of the female', specifically the work of reproduction. The gospel used by the Ebionites stated that Jesus had come to destroy sacrifices; unless sacrifices were terminated (in the temple at Jerusalem) men would not be saved. These gospels exist today only in fragments from which it is hard to draw definite conclusions. It is probable, however, that none of them was written before the second third of the second century.

In addition to these gospels, scholars have discovered a second-century papyrus which contains episodes in the life of Jesus and some sayings ascribed to him; these materials seem to be based on John and the synoptics, along with some extraneous legends.

Two gospels ascribed to apostles are more important. The first, ascribed to Peter, exists in part in a papyrus fragment which describes the crucifixion and resurrection of Jesus and breaks off when the author says, 'But I, Simon Peter, and Andrew my brother, took our nets and went away to the sea, and with us there was Levi, son of Alphaeus, whom the Lord . . .' This gospel was known to and criticized by Serapion, bishop of Antioch, about 190. The second was discovered in a Coptic version in 1945 but not identified until 1952. This is the famous Gospel of Thomas, a collection of 112 or 114 sayings of Jesus.

THOMAS

This work was discovered in a library of forty-nine Gnostic writings in thirteen leather-bound volumes. Earlier, nothing was known about it except the fact that it was used by several heretical groups such as the Naassenes; some church writers denounced it but did not describe it. Only when Thomas was found could the fragmentary 'sayings of Jesus', published in 1897 and 1903 in *The Oxyrhynchus Papyri*, be assigned to it.

The words of Jesus in the Gospel of Thomas are present as 'secret', i.e. not known in the common tradition of the Church, and it is said that 'whoever finds the interpretation of them will not taste death' (Preface). The idea presented here resembles that found in John 8.52: 'whoever keeps my word will never taste death' – along with the notion that the words of Jesus have a hidden meaning (cf. Mark 4.10–12, 33–4). The true interpreter (saying 1) is he who does not cease from seeking until he finds (cf. Matt. 7.7–8; Luke 11.9–10). No matter how obvious the meaning of various sayings may seem to be, all have a hidden significance, and Jesus spoke all of them after his resurrection.

The literary (or pre-literary) forms in which the various words are cast are strikingly similar to those used in the canonical gospels, especially the synoptics. They include parables, aphorisms, brief dialogues, and pronouncements beginning with 'I'. (The dog in the manger of saying 102 is paralleled in Aesop's fables.) As in some parts of the synoptic gospels, a good many of the sayings seem to be linked by verbal association rather than by similarity of subject matter. In many of Thomas's sayings, too, we encounter reflections of the Semitic parallelism found not only in the synoptics but also in the Old Testament; this feature does not, however, prove the authenticity of any of the sayings, for it could easily be due to imitation.

It is equally important to observe how different the 'Gospel' of Thomas is from the gospel-form employed in the Church. In Thomas there is no attempt at providing a historical framework for the ministry of Jesus (as already noted, the sayings are regarded as spoken after his death); there are no miracles; there is no passion narrative; there is no correlation with the Old Testament. Indeed, there is practically no action of any kind. This means that the final editor of Thomas understood the word 'gospel' in the sense in which it sometimes occurs in Matthew and Mark to refer to the message of Jesus about the kingdom of God. The term is not, however, to be found in the book itself, where we hear of 'secret words' or of the 'mysteries' of Jesus (62) or of 'the word of the Father' (79). Thus while the compilation of Thomas is in form not unlike the collection or collections of sayings of Jesus which may underlie the materials common to Matthew and Luke, there is no reason to suppose that the two are related, or that either was originally known as a gospel. Thomas might also be related to a collection of sayings underlying the Gospel of John, but the existence of such a collection is purely hypothetical (see Chapter XI).

Since Thomas is the first of the early apocryphal gospels to be recovered entire, it is important to assign some date to it. The earliest reference to it which we possess occurs in a homily on Luke which Origen wrote at Alexandria before 231, or else in the *Refutation* of his older contemporary Hippolytus. Since Hippolytus tells us that it was used by the Naassenes, it can be dated no later than the end of the second century. Unfortunately we cannot tell how much older it may have been, since no second-century writer makes use of it or refers to it. The parallels we find in such writers, orthodox and Gnostic alike, are not necessarily derived from this book. It is possible that, as some scholars hold, Thomas was written as early as 140. On the other hand, there seems to be no proof that it was not written a generation or two later.

The theology of Thomas is remarkably similar to that of the Naassenes (cf. Hippolytus, *Ref.* 5, 7–8), though they seem to have used a form of the book somewhat different from the Coptic form; there are significant variations between Hippolytus's quotations and Coptic sayings 4 and 11. But we do not know the precise date or provenance of the Naassenes. They seem to have been an offshoot of the equally mysterious Ophites.

The name Didymus Judas Thomas may point towards Syria, where the Acts of Thomas originated, but the parallels with traditions and apocryphal books known to Clement and Origen suggest Alexandria instead. If this supposition is correct, Thomas sheds some light in the almost total darkness which surrounds Egyptian Christianity in the late second century.

Many of the sayings in the Gospel of Thomas are very much like those found in the four gospels, especially the synoptics. It is a question whether Thomas derived his synoptic-type sayings from the synoptic gospels as written documents or from oral traditions also used by the synoptic evangelists. Similarly, when Thomas makes use of sayings which are also found in such apocryphal gospels as those 'according to the Hebrews' (1, perhaps 12, 104) and 'according to the Egyptians' (22, 37, perhaps 61), we cannot be absolutely sure whether he was using written documents or some of their sources, perhaps including oral traditions. Some of the sayings which he relates are ascribed to oral tradition by the Church Fathers; others are to be found in Gnostic sources which the Fathers quote. If it can be shown that Thomas made use of the synoptic gospels in their present form it becomes fairly likely that he also employed apocryphal gospels in written form. The presence of a good deal of material transmitted orally, however, is not excluded.

It is hard to determine the precise relation of Thomas to oral and written sources because of the fluidity of the situation in second-century Christianity. Perhaps around 125, Papias knew some written gospels but stated his preference for oral traditions; by 150, Justin at Rome reflects a situation where written gospels have superseded most of the oral tradition; but even later at Alexandria oral traditions were still prominent, though tending to be confined to Gnostic groups. Among the Naassenes there was an emphasis on both written and oral materials. A quotation from them given by Hippolytus (*Ref.* 5, 8, 11) shows how by combining written materials they could produce the impression that they were relying on secret tradition. 'Unless you drink my blood and eat my flesh (John 6.53–6), you will not enter into the kingdom of heaven (Matt. 5.20; 18.3); but if you drink the cup which I drink (Mark 10.38), where I go, there you cannot enter (John 8.21; 13.33).' Analogously, the fact that parts of sayings in Thomas can be paralleled in several gospels does not prove that the author used a source earlier than them; it may well indicate simply that he was combining gospel words.

Some of the sayings in Thomas fairly plainly reflect his use of our gospels. Thus in saying 14, Jesus rejects fasting, prayer and almsgiving, and then says, 'if you go into any land and wander in the regions, if they receive you, eat what is set before you, heal the sick among them; for what goes into your mouth will not defile you. . . .' The 'land' and the 'regions' are Thomas's substitute for the 'city' of Luke 10.8, a verse from which receiving and eating what is set before one are derived; 'heal the sick among them' comes from Luke 10.9, though in Thomas it is quite irrelevant to the subject of dietary laws, with which the rest of the saying is concerned (cf. Matt. 15.11). Presumably the first compiler was simply copying from Luke.

Sometimes Thomas separates sayings which in the synoptic gospels were combined. Thus in saying 65 he relates the parable of the vineyard (Mark 12.1–9 and parables; Thomas omits the Old Testament allusions). In the synoptic gospels this parable is concluded with a mention of the cornerstone which the builders rejected (Mark 12.10 and parallels). Thomas turns this conclusion into a separate saying (66), again omitting a reference to the Old Testament.

Another way in which Thomas uses the synoptic tradition or, more probably, the synoptic gospels is by adding materials which make sayings of Jesus look more 'Semitic' because of their parallelism. 'No prophet is acceptable in his village' comes from Luke 4.24; Thomas balances the saying with the false addition, 'no physician heals those who know him' (31). Similarly, in Matt. 5.14 we read that 'a city lying on a mountain cannot be hid.' Thomas expands these words thus: 'a city built on a high mountain and fortified cannot fall and cannot remain hidden' (32). His addition is both confused and false.

The most probable conclusion to draw from passages of this sort is that either Thomas or earlier Gnostic tradition made use of the canonical gospels at points where we find parallels, and that there is no reason to suppose that any passage in Thomas (in spite of interesting textual variants) provides an earlier or a more reliable version of any saying of Jesus.

Some sayings in Thomas suggest that it, or part of it, arose in a Jewish-Christian environment. For example, Jesus tells his disciples that after he departs they will 'go to James the Just, for whose sake heaven and earth came into existence' (12). James the Just is prominent in the Gospel according to the Hebrews, but also among the Naassene Gnostics, who claimed to have traditions derived from him. As a whole, however, Thomas is radically anti-Jewish. If circumcision were 'profitable' (cf. Rom. 3.1), men would be born circumcised (53); fasting, prayer, almsgiving and dietary observances – the cardinal duties enjoined in Jewish piety – are explicitly condemned (6; 14). Jesus will destroy the temple in Jerusalem (71). All external rites are irrelevant; when Jesus speaks of fasting to the world and of keeping the Sabbath as Sabbath (27) he is speaking symbolically.

The goal, and in part the present possession, of the true believer is the Kingdom, also called the Kingdom of Heaven and the Kingdom of the Father. This Kingdom is not in heaven or (for that matter) in the sea; instead, it is within the Gnostic (cf. Luke 17.21) and the Gnostic is within it; he comes to it by knowledge of himself, i.e. of his true nature as a son of the Living Father (3). He enters it again because he has come from it (49), from the Light (50). The Kingdom is already spread out upon the earth, even though most men do not see it (113). In other words, Thomas has removed most of the eschatological element from Christian teaching. The Kingdom can be entered only when sexual distinctions have been overcome or obliterated. 'When you make the two one, and when you make the inner as the outer and the outer as the inner and the upper as the lower, and when you make the male and the female into a single one, so that the male will not be male and the female will not be female . . . then you will enter the Kingdom' (22). Such a process is equivalent to becoming like a child (37; 46); it means that women have to become male in order to enter the Kingdom (114). This notion, perhaps developed from Paul's words in Galatians 3.28 ('in Christ there is . . . neither male nor female'), is also found in apocryphal tradition reflected in II Clement 12.2 and in the Gospel of the Egyptians. Another picture of finding the Kingdom is set forth in terms apparently derived from the Gospel of the Hebrews. 'Let him who seeks not cease seeking until he finds (cf. Matt. 7.7-8), and when he finds he will be troubled, and when he has been troubled he will marvel and will reign over the All' (2; 'trouble' is not mentioned in Hebrews).

The place of Jesus in the system of Thomas is very high. He is, of course, the revealer of these secret sayings (and cf. 28). Simon Peter and Matthew presumably misunderstood him when they call him a 'righteous angel' and a 'philosopher'; Thomas himself should not have called him 'Master' (13; cf. Mark 8.27-9; 10.17). Apparently he was not 'born of woman' (15, contrary to Gal. 4.4); he is either the Father or one with the Father. He is the Son of the Living One (37) and he is himself the Living One (52; 59). More than that, he tells his hearers, 'I am the Light that is above them all, I am the All, the All came forth from me and the All attained to me. Cleave wood, I am there; lift up the stone and you will find me there' (77). Even 'God' is subordinated to Jesus. 'Give what is Caesar's to Caesar, give what is God's to God, and give what is mine to me' (100; cf. Mark 12.17 and parallels). This may be the meaning of saying 30: 'where there are three gods, they are [merely?] gods; where there are two or one, I am with him.'

In Thomas the Jewish and Christian doctrine of election is pushed to its Gnostic extreme. 'I shall choose you, one out of a thousand and two out of ten thousand' (23); the disciples are few in number (73-6; 107); only those who are worthy hear the mysteries or secrets (62). They are hated and persecuted (68-9); in turn, they hate father, mother, brothers, and sisters (55), though at the same time they either truly love their father and mother or else love their true, heavenly father and mother (101). In telling the parable of the dragnet (Matt. 13.47-8) Thomas therefore has to change its point entirely. In the parable, good and bad fish alike are retained until the last judgement; in Thomas, only one good fish is kept (8).

Along with sayings based on the gospels and on known Gnostic traditions, Thomas provides some highly mysterious materials which reflect his theology. One such item is found in saying 7: 'Blessed is the lion which man eats and the lion will become man; and cursed is the man whom the lion eats and the man will become lion.' This may mean that by killing and 'eating' the world the Gnostic overcomes it by assimilating it to himself; if the world eats the Gnostic he is, of course, vanquished. Again, in saying 11, we read that 'on the days when you were eating that which is dead, you were making it as that which lives; when you come into the light, what will you do?' The Gnostic consumes dead matter and makes it live, but when he comes into the light he will have nothing to do with matter. 'Whoever has known the world has known a corpse, and whoever has found a corpse, of him the world is not worthy' (56; cf. 80). The 'corpse' here seems to be the inner, spiritual man who has died to the world, as in Naassene theology.

The principal problems raised by the existence and nature of the apocryphal gospels – especially Thomas – concern the historical and theological value of traditions not preserved in the canonical gospels. *A priori* it is quite possible that 'apocryphal' traditions can be valuable historically. As Jerome suggested, there may be gold in the mud. It may be possible to show, however, that (1) sayings reported in Thomas but not in the canonical gospels reflect special (e.g., Gnostic) tendencies, while (2) sayings reported in Thomas and in the canonical gospels have come from the canonical gospels to Thomas. Admittedly, absolutely convincing proof cannot be provided in all instances. It may be that sometimes Thomas uses written sources, sometimes oral. But it should be added that since the norms for determining authenticity must lie in the canonical gospels, it is hard to see what contribution apocryphal gospels could make even if some of the materials in them should be judged genuine. It should also be said that their theological outlook can be of great assistance in dealing with the history of doctrine, but that since the Church generally rejected them at an early date (see Chapter 1) they illuminate byways or alternatives rather than the main roads of Christian thought.

XIII

THE PAULINE EPISTLES

The earliest explicit references we have to a collection of letters by Paul are to be found in other early Christian letter-collections. II Peter 3.15–16 refers to 'all' Paul's letters, perhaps including the Pastorals (see p. 27). Ignatius of Antioch tells the Ephesians that Paul mentions them in every letter. Polycarp of Smyrna, collector of the letters of Ignatius, refers to those of Paul. Somewhat earlier, Clement of Rome certainly knows I Corinthians, and he probably knows other letters as well. We may assume that soon after Paul's death, or perhaps even in his lifetime, some of his letters were collected. One theory about this collection is that when Acts was published an admirer of Paul who had Colossians and Philemon (Colossae is not mentioned in Acts) visited the areas mentioned in Acts and found various letters which he then assembled, writing Ephesians (based on Colossians and on the other letters in the collection) to accompany them. This theory is ingenious, but it may very well be the case that small collections existed in the principal cities from which Paul wrote, such as Ephesus and Corinth, and that a larger collection was gradually built up out of these. Since Paul dictated his letters, it is perfectly possible that copies were preserved at the points of origin as well as by the recipients.

The order in which the letters stand in most of our manuscripts is not chronological but based on the length of the documents, from longest to shortest – first to communities, second to individuals. Another sequence was provided by Marcion (c. 140), who arranged the letters thus: Galatians, I–II Corinthians, Romans, I–II Thessalonians, Colossians, Philemon, Philippians, 'Laodiceans' (Ephesians). This sequence too is non-chronological; it seems to be based largely on the importance of the letters for

A Historical Introduction to the New Testament

Marcion's theology. Origen attempted to date the letters in relation to Paul's growing consciousness of his own perfection, but this criterion is not dependable.

The only way to give a chronological arrangement to the letters is to correlate them with the events described in Acts. On this basis, the earliest letters are I Thessalonians and II Thessalonians (perhaps addressed to Philippi; see p. 179), written from Corinth about A.D. 50. The next extant letters are I and II Corinthians, the former written from Ephesus between 52 and 55, the latter probably from Macedonia (II Cor. 2.12–13) within the same period. Galatians was probably written shortly after II Corinthians, and Romans from Corinth or Ephesus a few years later.

The dates assigned to Philippians, Colossians, Philemon and Ephesians depend on the place from which Paul, a prisoner, wrote them. Traditionally all four have been regarded as written from Rome, perhaps between 58 and 62. Colossians and Philemon are closely related by the mention of Onesimus, Epaphras, Mark, Aristarchus and Luke in both. The content of Ephesians is strikingly similar to that of Colossians; if genuine, it almost certainly was written at about the same time. Now according to Philemon 22, Paul hopes to be released from prison and to visit Colossae. It has therefore been suggested that the prison is not necessarily at Rome, since Paul was often imprisoned (II Cor. 11.23); Acts describes a lengthy imprisonment at Caesarea, and it has been claimed that he was also a prisoner at Ephesus (II Cor. 1.8–11? I Cor. 15.32?). If he intended to go from Rome to Spain (Rom. 15.24, 28) it is hard to see how he could plan to visit Colossae too; therefore the letters, it is claimed, were not written from Rome. Unfortunately we do not know whether or not Paul's plans to visit Spain remained fixed; he had a way of changing travel plans, as we learn from II Cor. 1.15–2.13; and probably the mention of Mark and Luke (Col. 4.10, 14; Philemon) means that Paul was a prisoner at Rome.

As for Philippians, the mention of the 'praetorium' or 'praetorian guard' in 1.13 and of 'Caesar's household' in 4.22 seems at first glance to point towards Rome, but there were non-Roman praetoria – 'Herod's' at Caesarea is mentioned in Acts 23.35 – and members of Caesar's household (officials and/or slaves) were to be found in various parts of the empire. The retrospective look towards 'the beginning of the gospel' (4.15) does not necessarily mean that a great deal of time has passed. Paul hopes to come to Philippi (1.26–7, 2.24); as we have already said, such a hope does not necessarily mean that Rome is excluded. Our conclusion about the origin of Philippians must be even less certain than about the other imprisonment letters. But if one has to assign a place to it, Rome is as likely as anywhere else.

(For the Pastoral Epistles, see pp. 209 ff.).

Apart from simple curiosity, we may wonder why it is important to try to determine the historical sequence of the Pauline epistles. The main reason for this concern is probably to be found in the desire to reconstruct the life of Paul, thus supplementing the rather meagre data given in Acts and gaining some insight into the development, if any, of his thought. Elaborate attempts have been made to ascertain the nature of this development, especially in relation to a more or less psychological interpretation of Paul's conflicts. It has been thought that if one could trace the development, at least in the major epistles, one could then use the results in order to date the imprisonment epistles and then to trace further development. Probably, however, in view of our ignorance about Paul's early life and the occasional nature of his letters we cannot say much about such a development (see pp. 378 ff.). If we confine our speculations to what can be said with certainty, we know only that Paul wrote to the Thessalonians from Corinth about 50, to the Corinthians from Ephesus about 52, and to the Romans, probably from Corinth, about 55.

On the other hand, consideration of Paul's style and thought can lead us to see a certain development in the ways in which various topics are handled. Subjects may be treated only briefly or incidentally in one letter and receive greater elaboration in a later one, or subjects discussed in full in one letter can be touched on only briefly when they are taken up again. Unfortunately it is often difficult to determine which way the sequence goes, since both kinds of processes are at work. Moreover, the fact that Paul seems to mention a subject for the first time in such-and-such a letter does not mean that he thought of it for the first time as he wrote the letter.

In other words, the question of development in Paul's letters and in his theology must remain a question. We can probably assume that like other human beings he did develop to some extent. But, as in the case of other human beings, the precise extent, and to some degree the direction, of this development escapes us. We can describe what Paul said with some measure of confidence. The same confidence must be lacking when we try to state why he said it.

Therefore in looking at his letters we shall probably do better to try to ascertain (1) what the gospel was which he preached and (2) what the nature of the controversies was in which he was engaged. Each of these points is important. The former is the more important, for the controversies can be understood only on the basis of what Paul allusively says about them. When we try to fill in the other side of the conversation, we have the testimony only of Paul himself, and he is hardly an unprejudiced witness. Indeed, he is not really a witness. He refers to the opinions of his opponents only in order to refute them. The background of his letters in such controversies has often been studied in order to relativize the meaning of what Paul says. He presented his gospel as he did, it is argued, because of the peculiar circumstances in which he wrote. The environment therefore conditioned the response, and we who live in a different environment can now reinterpret the response, setting it free from this conditioning. But in view of our limited understanding of his environment and his opponents it is difficult to apply this principle; furthermore, he did write what he wrote, not something else. For example, he made use of the Graeco-Roman 'diatribe' form in his letters. This fact does not mean that what he wrote in diatribe form is any the less his. The most important question remains, as we have said, what his gospel was and what he believed it meant for his hearers.

In attempting to discover what Paul was saying to his churches, the question of the authenticity of his letters arises. At various times, driven by a yearning for consistency, scholars have doubted the authenticity of nearly every letter, as a whole or in part. One of the principal criteria employed in dealing with this problem has been that of Pauline vocabulary. Though we admit the possibility of using this criterion, we must recognize the severe difficulties involved.

Statistics often look impressive.[1] Thus it may seem significant that the letters of Paul, apart from the Pastorals, contain 29,000

[1] Hebrews is not included in these compilations.

words, of which 2,170 are different (the ratio of vocabulary to
total is thus 7.5 per cent), while the Pastorals contain about
3,500 words, 900 of them different (a ratio of 25.7 per cent). The
difference between the ratios is not so surprising, however, when
one recalls that the longer a document is the lower the ratio will be.

Again, there are very wide variations in Paul's use of words.
His usage depends primarily on his subject matter, not on some
ideal norm. This fact can easily be demonstrated.

Word	Pauline epistles (not Pastorals)	Pastorals	Principal use	Non-use
Agathos (good)	37	10	Romans (21)	I Cor.
Hamartia (sin)	61	3	Romans (48)	II Thess., Phil.
Dikaiosynē (righteousness, justification)	52	5	Romans (33)	I-II Thess., Col.
Thanatos (death)	47	0	Romans (22)	I-II Thess., Gal., Eph.
Kauchasthai (boast)	35	0	II Cor. (20)	I-II Thess., Col.
Nomos (law)	117	2	Romans (72)	I-II Thess., II Cor., Col.
Peritomē (circumcision)	29	1	Romans (14)	I-II Thess., II Cor.
Pistos (faithful)	16	17	—	Rom., Phil.
Sarx (flesh)	90	1	—	I-II Thess.

These examples suggest that word-counting provides no adequate
index to an author's total vocabulary and that this vocabulary depends, as one might expect, on the purpose or purposes for which
he writes. (It might also be observed that Paul could and did write
letters without mentioning sin, flesh, death, the law, and circumcision; one danger in interpreting Paul's thought arises from treating Romans, in which these terms appear, as normative.)

As for Paul's style, we have already discussed several aspects of
it in Chapter III. Perhaps the single most important feature of it is

its personal element. Paul uses the ordinary Greek of the Hellenistic world, with many allusions to and borrowings from the Septuagint; but he makes everything his own. He can vary his words where repetition would produce greater clarity; he can repeat where repetition results in monotony. He can work out studied sentences almost worthy of a rhetorician, or he can pile up clauses and synonyms in a completely unrhetorical way. Sometimes he breaks off the flow of a sentence intentionally; sometimes, it would appear, unintentionally. According to his own testimony, some of his correspondents found his letters 'weighty and powerful' (II Cor. 10.10), but others misunderstood them (I Cor. 5.9–13; cf. II Peter 3.16).

THE THESSALONIAN LETTERS

The two letters which Paul wrote to his converts at Thessalonica about the year 51 are probably the earliest extant Christian documents. Both of them were included by Marcion in his collection of Pauline epistles; their lack of definite attestation in the writings of the Apostolic Fathers and the earlier Apologists can be explained as due to these authors' lack of interest in the subjects discussed in the letters. Irenaeus quotes from both of them, sometimes as if they constituted only one letter (*Adv. haer.* 4, 27, 4), but sometimes clearly recognizing that there are two (3, 7, 2; see also the Muratorian list). No one in antiquity seems to have questioned their canonicity or authenticity, although when Origen laid emphasis on the rôle of Silvanus in their composition he may have been suggesting that the apocalyptic eschatology was not due to Paul.

The style of these letters is characteristic of the Pauline epistles as a whole, as B. Rigaux has shown. Paul is fond of parallelism, often chiastic, and frequently employs antithesis (eighteen times in the two short letters). He makes plays on words. He likes to use long phrases, bound together by participles or prepositions.

Because of the brevity of the letters and the special nature of their subject matter, it is difficult to lay much emphasis on the peculiarities of the vocabulary of the letters.[1] It is worth noting, however, that (as the table on p. 175 has already shown), the

---

[1] I Thessalonians contains 1,472 words and uses a vocabulary of 366 words; II Thessalonians contains 824 words with a vocabulary of 250.

following words are absent from both I and II Thessalonians: *'dikaiosynē'*, *'thanatos'*, *'kauchasthai'*, *'nomos'*, *'peritomē'* and *'sarx'*; *'hamartia'* is also absent from II Thessalonians.

The two letters were addressed by Paul, Silvanus and Timothy to the Christian community at Thessalonica in Macedonia, the second church founded by the apostle after he crossed from Troas on his mission journey after the apostolic council (Acts 17.1–9). I Thessalonians was written after Paul had visited Athens alone (3.1; Acts 17.14–16) and had then been joined at Corinth (Acts 18.5) by Timothy and Silvanus (I Thess. 3.6, Timothy). Paul reminds the Thessalonians of their conversion (1.9–10): 'how you turned to God from idols, to serve a living and true God, and to wait for his Son from heaven, whom he raised from the dead, Jesus who delivers us from the wrath to come.' In these words we find a summary of the apostolic message to gentiles; it corresponds with the fragmentary sermons in Acts 14.15–17 and 17.22–31 (cf. also Rom. 1.18–2.24) and supplements the description of Paul's argument in the synagogue at Thessalonica (Acts 17.3: 'it was necessary for the Christ to suffer and to rise from the dead'; 'this Jesus, whom I proclaim to you, is the Christ').

The community seems to be largely gentile, for Paul tells its members that they have suffered the same things from their own countrymen as the churches in Judaea have suffered from the Jews (2.14). He finds it necessary to remind them to avoid fornication and, instead, to marry (4.3–8); they must not be idle but must work (4.9–12). They must not worry about the fate of believers who die, for when the Lord descends from heaven both the dead and the living will rise to meet him in the air, 'and so we shall always be with the Lord' (4.13–18). The precise time of his coming cannot be predicted, but he will come (5.1–11). 'May the God of peace himself sanctify you wholly; and may your spirit and soul and body be kept sound and blameless at the coming of our Lord Jesus Christ' (5.23).

It is not absolutely certain that all of Paul's counsel is based on what he knows about the Thessalonian church. Generally speaking, he seems well pleased with the Thessalonian Christians (1.2–10; 2.13–20; 3.6–10; 4.1, 9–12; 5.1, 11). And some of the passages which might suggest the presence of problems can be explained as reflections of real problems which Paul was facing not in relation to Thessalonica but in relation to Corinth. It was there that difficulties arose over fornication (I Cor. 6.12–20) and marriage (7.1–7). On the other hand, his urging the Thessalonians to work with their hands (4.11) seems to be related to their preoccupation with eschatological matters (4.13–5.11). This was not, as far as we know, a problem at Corinth.

The central concern of I Thessalonians, then, arises from the acceptance of Paul's proclamation of the imminent coming of the Lord. The Thessalonians were waiting for the coming of Jesus, who delivers us from the wrath to come, and not all of them were devoting enough attention to the matter of their sanctification in the time before his coming (3.13–4.12; 4.5–24).

II Thessalonians deals with a subject closely related to this. The Lord Jesus will be 'revealed from heaven with his mighty angels in flaming fire, inflicting vengeance upon those who do not know God and upon those who do not obey the gospel of our Lord Jesus' (1.7–8); at that time 'the lawless one will be revealed, and the Lord Jesus will slay him with the breath of his mouth and destroy him by his appearing and his coming' (2.8). But these events will not take place in the immediate future. Something (the law and order provided by the Roman empire, according to some patristic commentators) is holding back the eschatological clock; for before the Lord's coming 'the man of lawlessness, the son of perdition' must be revealed and must take his seat in the temple of God, proclaiming himself to be God (2.3–4). If Paul is relying on Jewish apocalyptic ideas, they may have been shaped by events in Palestine a decade earlier, when Caligula's attempt to place his own statue in the temple at Jerusalem was thwarted by the Roman governor of Syria and by other Roman officials.

One problem mentioned in I Thessalonians has become even more acute. Here Paul explicitly points out that Christians ought to imitate his example by hard work. 'Even when we were with you, we gave you this command: If any one will not work, let him not eat' (3.6–13). Once more, the Thessalonians' idleness seems to be related to their misunderstanding of eschatology. They have learned, 'either by spirit or by word, or by letter purporting to be from us', that 'the day of the Lord has already come' (2.2). Perhaps because of the existence of forged letters, Paul concludes the letter in his own handwriting. 'This is the mark in every letter of mine; it is the way I write' (3.17; cf. I Cor. 16.21; Gal. 6.11).

Critics have sometimes argued that II Thessalonians was not written by Paul, chiefly because of the detailed eschatological time-table which is absent from other letters but also because it is difficult to see why Paul was writing two letters, with much the same content, to the same community (perhaps to Jewish members) in approximately the same situation. These difficulties do not seem insuperable. The function of historical analysis is not to show why a document should not be regarded as genuine but to accept it and try to understand its situation. Paul may have wished to reiterate what he had said before; II Thessalonians may have preceded I Thessalonians, in any event. Another possibility, suggested by E. Schweizer, is that II Thessalonians was not originally addressed to the Thessalonians. Polycarp, writing to the Philippians early in the second century, refers to letters (plural) which Paul had written them (*Phil*. 3.2) and, in alluding to this correspondence, seems to quote some words from II Thess. 1.4 (11.3).

THE CORINTHIAN CORRESPONDENCE

In our canon, as in all the ancient manuscripts of the New Testament, there are two letters from Paul to the Corinthian church. I Corinthians is better attested than II Corinthians, presumably because it is the more practical of the two; Clement of Rome refers to it and uses it, while allusions in the letters of Ignatius prove that he knew it. In later times there was no question about either letter; both were in Marcion's collection; allusions to both occur in Theophilus of Antioch, and quotations from both in Irenaeus. Most of Irenaeus's quotations are made in a manner that suggests that he knew the two as one, but this point is not especially significant when we recall that he sometimes treats the Thessalonian letters in the same way. The contemporary Muratorian fragment clearly recognizes two letters.

It is sometimes supposed, however, that the two letters we have are the result of an editing process which produced two letters out of a number considerably larger. The primary grounds for this view are to be found in II Corinthians. (1) II Corinthians 6.14–7.1 has nothing to do with its context (and indeed is close to the thought world of Qumran[1]); it might well come from the 'previous letter' to which reference is made in I Corinthians 5.9. (2) It is psychologically difficult to regard Paul's violent 'boasting' in II Corinthians 10–13 as coming directly after his emphasis on reconciliation and joy in II Corinthians 1–9. (3) It is strange that after speaking about the collection for the saints in II Corinthians 8, Paul should go on to state that he need not mention it to his correspondents (9.1).

For these reasons and other subsidiary ones J. Weiss and others have proposed to split up not only II Corinthians but also I Corinthians into different units. Thus Weiss argued that one letter consisted of II Cor. 6.14–7.1 and I Cor. 9.24–10.22; 6.12–20; 11.2–34; 15; and 16.13–24. Another was made up of I Cor. 1.1–6.11; 7.1–9.23; 10.23–11.1; 12–14; and 16.1–12. Before letting ourselves be overcome by enthusiasm for this kind of procedure, we might recall that in his youth Weiss gave the same kind of treatment to the letter of Barnabas (1888). Among students of the Apostolic Fathers, perhaps less receptive to novelty than New Testament critics, his theory met with no endorsement. Removing inconsistencies by slicing up documents is a fascinating task (see Chapter XI), but it rarely produces convincing results, especially in dealing with an author whose correspondents regarded him as inconsistent. It may be worth noting that an inconsistency remains in Weiss's second letter. In I Corinthians 4.19 Paul says that he is coming to Corinth very soon; in 16.5–9 he is planning to linger at Ephesus. He has taken care of one real difficulty, for in I Corinthians 11, women may pray or prophesy if they wear veils, whereas in 14.33–5 they are not to speak in church at all. But the inconsistency would remain in any case, if the Corinthians took Paul's letters seriously enough to preserve them.

As for the breaking up of II Corinthians, it is fashionable to deride 'psychological explanations' of the transition from 1–9 to 10.13 – as if the rearrangement of these chapters, with 1–9 following 10–13, were not also based on psychological grounds! It seems perfectly reasonable to maintain that there is a break

[1] J. Fitzmyer in *Catholic Biblical Quarterly* (1961).

between the two sections, and that after the receipt of bad news from Corinth the bitter tone of 10–13 is due precisely to reaction from the warmth and friendliness of 1–9.

For these reasons we prefer to treat the letters as they now stand, regarding only II Cor. 6.14–7.1 as a possible interpolation. It is undeniable that these two are only a part of the complete correspondence between Paul and the Corinthian church. First, there was a letter, now lost, from Paul to the Corinthians (I Cor. 5.9); then there was a letter from them to him (7.1); his reply is I Corinthians. In II Corinthians 2.3 and 7.8 we find references to an earlier letter, identical with none of those already mentioned; finally there is II Corinthians itself. (The apocryphal correspondence between Paul and the Corinthians, published in 1958 from a Greek papyrus of the third century, has no claim to authenticity.)

Some interesting conclusions can be drawn from the vocabulary of the Corinthian letters. The conclusions are more negative than positive, for if one takes the words of which Paul is generally fondest and examines instances in which they occur more frequently in the Corinthian letters than anywhere else, it will still be found that in view of the length of these letters they do not occur a disproportionate number of times. There are only four exceptions to this rule: about half the Pauline occurrences of 'hekastos' ('each one'), 'kauchasthai' ('boast'), and 'sōma' ('body') are to be found in I Corinthians, and forty per cent of the examples of 'parakalein' ('exhort') in II Corinthians. It is significant that the word 'agathos' ('good') is absent from I Corinthians, the word 'dikaios' ('just or righteous') from both letters. Related words such as the noun 'dikaiosynē' and the verb 'dikaioun' are very rare in either. Paul could hardly speak much about 'justification by faith' to this congregation. Neither the law nor circumcision is mentioned in II Corinthians.

Four words with which the Corinthians seem to have been especially concerned were apparently picked up by Paul: (1) 'anakrinein' ('discern'), used only in I Corinthians; (2) the adjective 'pneumatikos' ('spiritual'), used fourteen times in I Corinthians, elsewhere in Paul only nine times; (3) 'pneumatikōs' ('spiritually'), only in I Corinthians; and 'syneidēsis' ('conscience'), used eleven times in I-II Corinthians, elsewhere only three times in Romans. He may also have derived the word 'physis' ('nature') from his opponents.

The style of I Corinthians and, to a lesser degree, that of II Corinthians reflects Paul's endeavour to give spiritual direction to an unruly congregation. Nowhere else does he repeat words and phrases so often; nowhere else does he make so much use of the kinds of personal argument characteristic of the Cynic-Stoic moral address. Only in I Corinthians (but cf. Col. 1.15–20) do we find a carefully-worked-out depiction of a theme such as Christian love (see Chapter IV).

The letter begins with a severe criticism of the Corinthians' claim to 'wisdom' and their consequent self-exaltation, which has led to divisions in the community (1–4). The true wisdom, given by God, is to be found only in the crucified Christ; the life of his apostles is marked by service and suffering, not by royal rule in the present age. It would appear that the Corinthians, like some of the Thessalonians, have wrongly supposed that the reign of God is already fully realized.

After this general introduction to the letter, Paul turns to specific problems in the community, dealing with all of them in relation to theological principles, but at the same time giving specific commands to his readers. These problems are related to sexual behaviour (5–7), to dietary regulations (8–10), to Christian worship (11–14), to the question of future resurrection (15), and to practical matters (16).

The 'regulatory' nature of much of the letter can be seen in what Paul explicitly prescribes:

(1) A man who lives with his stepmother is to be excommunicated; no Christian can eat with him (5.1–5, 11).
(2) Disputes among Christians are not to be brought before pagan courts (6.1, 5).
(3) Union with a prostitute is a sin against Christ (6.15–19).
(4) Celibacy is preferable to marriage, but
   a. husband and wife have mutual sexual responsibilities (7.3–5);
   b. if Christian partners separate, neither can remarry (7.10–11);
   c. religious differences are not grounds for divorce (7.12–14);

    d. non-Christians may separate from Christians, but
    Christians must try to preserve the marriage (7.16);

    e. unmarried persons should remain single but can
    marry (7.25–38);

    f. widows should remain single but can marry
    Christians (7.39–40).

(5) Meats offered to idols present a problem.

    a. Eating them in a temple is forbidden (8.10–13);

    b. buying them in a meat-market is permitted (10.25–6);

    c. eating them in a pagan household is permitted
    (10.27), unless the guest is told that they are
    sacrificial (10.28).

(6) Men must not wear head-coverings in church, while
women must do so (11.4–5).

(7) The common meal must be common: all are to eat at
the same time (11.33).

(8) Worship must be orderly.

    a. No more than three persons may speak in tongues, and
    an interpreter must be present (14.27);

    b. no more than three persons may prophesy, and if
    someone else receives a revelation the man who is
    speaking must stop (14.29–30);

    c. women are not to speak in church, even to ask
    questions (14.34–5).

(9) Christians are to set aside money weekly for Jerusalem
(16.1–4).

(10) They are to be subject to such leaders as Stephanas
(16.15–16).

These regulations do not, of course, constitute the whole of the
letter. In chapters 8–10 Paul presents a full discussion of the
relation between freedom and responsibility; in 11 he recalls
what the Lord Jesus did and said at the Last Supper; in 12 he
analyses the relation of the body's members to one another; in 13 he
speaks of the meaning of love; and in 15 he sets forth the meaning
of resurrection. But in order to understand the letter we cannot
neglect the practical elements in favour of the more theoretical.

II Corinthians also arises out of a crisis in Paul's relationship
with the Corinthian community. In I Corinthians 4.19 (modified

by 16.5–9) he had promised to visit Corinth in the near future, but he had been unable to do so. II Corinthians 1–7 (except for 6.14–7.1) therefore deals with the Corinthians' complaint about his lack of reliability and passes on to a full discussion of the Christian ministry as a ministry of reconciliation. Chapters 8 and 9 are concerned with the necessity and indispensability of the collection for the saints. At this point, we may assume, Paul received further bad news from or about Corinth, and he therefore launched into the bitter 'boasting' which marks most of chapters 10–13 (though the bitterness diminishes towards the end). These chapters are more personal than any other passages in the epistles, even such epistles as Galatians and Philippians. They may even corroborate the accusation that 'his letters are weighty and strong, but his bodily presence is weak and his speech contemptible' (10.10).

GALATIANS

This letter was known to, and used by, Ignatius of Antioch, early in the second century. It was included in Marcion's collection and was used by the church writers of the late second century. There has never been any valid question about its genuineness or canonicity; indeed, the opposite problem has been more important, since some theologians like Marcion have treated it with Romans as the key to all of Paul's thought. In some ways it is quite unrepresentative. For instance, the word '*pistis*' ('faith') occurs twenty-two times (forty times in Romans), while in the much longer Corinthian correspondence it is found only fourteen times. The noun '*agapē*' ('love') occurs only three times, and the cognate verb twice. The word '*sōma*' ('body'), used forty-six times in I Corinthians, occurs only once, in reference to Paul's own body. Nowhere else in Paul's letters is an introductory thanksgiving lacking.

In modern times the question of the addressees of the letter has often been discussed, chiefly because scholars have realized that if they could be located in 'south Galatia' the letter could be dated earlier than the other Pauline epistles, and the conference described in Galatians 2.1–10 could be placed before the apostolic council of Acts 15, not identified with it. It should probably be said, however, that parallels between Galatians and both II Corinthians and Romans suggest that the letter belongs with them, not at a point before I-II Thessalonians.

Galatia was a region in central Asia Minor, named after the roving Celts (*Galatai*) who settled there during the Hellenistic period. A Roman province, created in 25 B.C., included both the region around the capital, Ancyra, and various areas to the south, apparently including Lycaonia, Phrygia and Pisidia. Paul visited both areas, first that to the south (Acts 13-14; 16.1-5), later that more towards the north (16.6; 18.23). In his general letter to 'the churches of Galatia' (Gal. 1.2) he says that bodily illness had led to his preaching there – either 'originally' or 'formerly' or 'on the first of two visits' (4.13). Since in Acts we find two visits both to north and to south Galatia, and since (in any event) the word in Galatians probably does *not* imply two visits, Acts does not assist us in locating these churches. It should probably be said, however, that the people addressed as 'Galatians' (3.1) are probably not to be identified with those who, according to Acts 14.11, continued to speak in a local language, Lycaonian. The reference to the work of the Holy Spirit in Acts 16.6 may well be a theological expression of one aspect of Paul's illness. We conclude that the letter was addressed to a group of communities near Ancyra.

These communities were composed of gentiles (4.8; 5.2; 6.12-13). Into them had come men who preached Judaism under the guise of Christianity, urging the Galatians to accept circumcision, though without the observance of the whole Jewish law (6.13; 5.3). They advocated keeping the special days, months, seasons and years of the Jewish calendar (4.10). Apparently they told the Galatians that Paul owed his apostolate to the Jerusalem church (cf. 1.1); they claimed that he himself had encouraged circumcision (5.11; cf. 2.3), and that he modified his message in relation to the circumstances (1.10). They themselves were now presenting the complete gospel (3.3). In consequence, many of the Galatians were 'anxious to be under the law' (4.21) and had begun the programme of 'liturgical enrichment'.

Paul militantly criticizes his opponents' point of view, as well as that of their dupes. Leaving out his customary expression of thanksgiving, he proceeds to deny that either his apostolate or his gospel came through any human agency; both were given him by God the Father and by Jesus Christ. He had hardly any contact with the church of Jerusalem and its 'pillars' (James the Lord's brother, Cephas [Peter] and John) simply recognized the authenticity of his divine commission (1.11–2.10). When Cephas was at Antioch, Paul resisted his attempts to compromise with Judaism (2.11–14). Justification before God comes not from observing the law but from believing in Christ Jesus (2.15–21).

He next proceeds to give arguments based on the Old Testament, on analogies related to it, on personal experience (both theirs and his), and on allegory derived from the Old Testament – all to show that the law cannot justify and that justification comes only from faith (3.1–5.12). Here the figure of Abraham, already significant in Hellenistic Jewish preaching to gentiles, assumes a prominent rôle.

After this he addresses not a group of libertine Gnostics but the whole congregation, reminding them that in spite of their freedom from law they must walk in conformity with the Spirit and bring forth its 'fruits'. There is no reason to suppose that such moral counsel could be given only to antinomians (5.13–6.10).

Paul's conclusion, written in his own hand (the rest of the letter was therefore dictated), recapitulates his earlier statements and reminds the Galatians that 'circumcision is nothing; uncircumcision is nothing; the only thing that counts is new creation' (6.15, NEB).

ROMANS

Romans, a letter written to a congregation which Paul had never visited (though he was now eager to do so), is the longest of the Pauline epistles, though not much longer than I Corinthians (7,100 words against 6,800). It thus constitutes about twenty-five per cent of the total of Paul's letters. None of his favourite words is absent from it. Because of its length, statistics on vocabulary have more validity than they usually do, and we use them to suggest that the emphases of Romans are not entirely characteristic of Paul's thought.[1]

[1] See also table on page 175.

Word	Pauline epistles (not Pastorals)	Romans	Per cent	Non-use
Agathos (good)	37	21	57	I Cor.
Hamartia (sin)	61	48	75	II Thess., Phil.
Dikaios (just)	14	7	50	I–II Cor.
Dikaiosynē (righteousness, justification)	52	33	63	I–II Thess., Col.
Dikaioun (justify)	25	15	60	I–II Thess., II Cor., Phil., Col., Eph.
Dikaiōma (justification)	5	5	100	all epistles
Dikaiōsis (justification)	2	2	100	all epistles
Zōē (life)	29	14	50	I–II Thess.
Nomos (law)	117	72	61	I–II Thess., II Cor., Col.
Peritomē (circumcision)	29	14	50	I–II Thess., II Cor.
Pistis (faith)	109	40	37	no epistles
Sarx (flesh)	90	26	30	I–II Thess.

We can hardly deny that Paul's vocabulary may have been enriched after the time when he wrote to the Thessalonians; but his emphasis on sin, justification, law and circumcision in Romans does not necessarily represent the full range of his thought.

Some indication of the place of Romans in the sequence of Paul's letters is given by (1) his statement that he has long been eager to visit the Roman church (1.10–15), (2) his declaration that he has preached the gospel 'as far round as Illyricum' (east coast of the Adriatic, 15.19), (3) his intention of going to Jerusalem with the contribution made by the churches of Macedonia and Achaea (15.25–6), and (4) his commendation of Phoebe, 'a deaconess of the church at Cenchreae' (one of the ports of Corinth, 16.1). These points would suggest that the letter was written from Greece as Paul was about to set sail for Syria (Acts 20.3). The last of them, however, must be regarded as uncertain because of the textual problem in the last chapter or chapters of the letter.

This problem arises when we consider the doxology with which the letter ends in the oldest uncial manuscripts and in Origen (16.25–7). Origen himself mentions manuscripts in which it was found not at the end of the letter but after 14.23, and there it occurs in the later uncials and minuscules. Codex Alexandrinus and another uncial place it both after 14.23 and at the end of the letter. On the other hand, Marcion left it out entirely, as did the scribe of the ninth-century codex G, while in the third-century Beatty papyrus it is found after 15.33. In other words, it occurs at the end of the fourteenth, fifteenth and sixteenth chapters. In consequence, scholars have sometimes supposed that it should come at the end of the fifteenth chapter (it makes no sense at the end of the fourteenth), and that the sixteenth chapter, consisting largely of greetings and admonitions, really belongs to another letter and was wrongly combined with Romans. The combination can be explained as due to the reference to Phoebe of Cenchreae. Since on other grounds the whole letter seemed to fit the situation described in Acts 20.3, the sixteenth chapter was attached to it because Cenchreae was mentioned. On the other hand, it can be argued that the doxology is a later interpolation – as its wanderings would suggest – and that there is no particular reason to regard the sixteenth chapter as an addition. Indeed, Paul did not have to be at Cenchreae when he recommended Phoebe. The mention of Timothy, Lucius, Sosipatros (Sopater) and Gaius in Romans 16.21–3 suggests that they belong to the group mentioned in Acts 20.4. Jason of Thessalonica is mentioned in Acts 17.5–9; Erastus, in Acts 19.22. According to Acts 19.29, Gaius was a Macedonian who accompanied Paul; Erastus was another helper who was in Macedonia. From these details we should judge it likely that Romans was written not from Greece but from Macedonia, perhaps specifically from Philippi – or perhaps across the Aegean Sea, from Troas (Acts 20.6 – since Lucius is with Paul).

More important than the precise setting of the letter is its content. It was addressed to a community which Paul had never visited, although he was evidently acquainted with many of its members (Rom. 16.3–15). The most obvious purposes of the letter are (1) to set forth the gospel as Paul preached it (1.15–17), especially in regard to the relationship between Jewish and gentile Christians, and (2) to obtain the aid of the Roman church in supporting a missionary journey to Spain (15.24, 28–9). Of these the former is much the more important. Paul is eager to set forth the position he has reached in consequence of his struggles with opponents at Corinth (II Corinthians) and in Galatia. For this reason themes which were treated only partially or allusively in the earlier letters are given a fuller and more careful treatment in Romans. As usual, no doubt, Paul made use of materials which he had employed earlier. For example, the treatment of the just wrath of God in Romans 1.18–2.24 is a development of something only alluded to in I Thessalonians 1.9–10; the discussion of Abraham in Romans 4 is a more elaborate version of Galatians 3.6–16 (compare also Rom. 7.13–25 with Gal. 5.17; Rom. 13.8–10 with Gal. 5.14); and the statement about life in the Church in Romans 12.3–21 summarizes various sections of I Corinthians (6.1–11; 12.4–13.13).

The letter begins with a proclamation of the universal justice of God (1.1–17) in the face of the universality of sin and guilt (1.18–3.20). God has now demonstrated his righteousness through the sacrifice of Christ (3.21–31), in fulfilment of the promise made to Abraham (4) on behalf of sinners, descendants of Adam (5), who die in baptism so that they may be raised with Christ (6). The human situation of inner conflict (7) is changed by God through the gift of life in the Spirit (8). But is God then unjust in regard to the Jewish people as a whole? No, they have trespassed but only temporarily; when all the gentiles have been saved, all Israel will be saved too (9–11). Because of God's gift of the Spirit, men are bound to live together in love, in obedience to the state, and in tolerance of varying opinions (12–15.13). The letter ends with personal notes and admonitions (15.14–16.23).

Sometimes Romans has been viewed as a kind of *Summa* of Paul's theology. Such a view is in part mistaken, since he has in mind the specific problem of the relations between Jews and gentiles (not only in Rom. 9–11 but throughout the letter). It is more largely correct, since Romans gathers up the themes of many earlier letters and presents the mature thought of Paul, concentrated upon a single but crucial problem. The letter has stimulated some of the greatest theologians of the Church towards systematic interpretation of the apostle's insights.

THE IMPRISONMENT EPISTLES

Four of the letters in the Pauline collection were written when Paul was in prison; these are Philippians, Colossians, Philemon, and Ephesians. (1) According to Philippians 1.13, 'it has come to be recognized by the whole Praetorian Guard and by all the others that if I am in fetters it is because of my activities as a Christian' (Beare). The expression 'by the whole Praetorian Guard' is literally 'in the whole praetorium'; the New English Bible gives as alternatives 'to all at headquarters here' or 'to all at the Residency'. There were *praetoria* in places other than Rome – for example, at Jerusalem (Mark 15.16 and parallels) and at Caesarea (Acts 23.35). Some ancient commentators suggested that Paul was referring to Nero's palace on the Palatine hill. By itself, the expression does not show whether Paul was in Rome or in some provincial capital. Again, in Philippians 4.22 Paul speaks of the greetings sent by Christians who belonged to 'Caesar's household'. This phrase is used of 'persons employed in the domestic and administrative establishment of the Emperor' (Beare). Like the mention of the praetorium, this reference does not absolutely prove that Paul was in Rome. Imperial employees were found throughout the Empire. From these two passages it can be concluded that Paul was a prisoner either at Rome or at Caesarea (proof that he was ever a prisoner at Ephesus has not been provided). To be sure, Paul says that he hopes to come to see the Philippians after his release (2.24), whereas according to Romans 15.24, 28, he expected to go from Jerusalem through Rome to Spain. But his hopes expressed in Romans should not be treated as expressions of the decrees of fate or providence. We should hold (with Beare) that there is no reason to reject the second-century tradition (he calls it 'hypothesis') that Philippians was written at Rome.

(2) Colossians too was clearly written from prison (4.3, 10, 18), as was the little letter to Philemon (1, 9, 10, 13, 23). Where was

this prison? Nothing in either letter clearly indicates its location; therefore we must rely upon inferences from what we can find in the letters. First it should be said that the letters are clearly addressed to the same location at the same time; in other words, Philemon was a Colossian Christian. Second, the situation in which Paul writes is the same; in both letters we find mention of Paul's companions Timothy, Aristarchus, Mark, Epaphras, Luke, and Demas – though in Colossians only Aristarchus, and in Philemon only Epaphras, is called a 'fellow-captive' with Paul. The circumstances which caused Paul to write Philemon may shed some light on the situation. Onesimus was a slave belonging to Philemon; he had run away to Paul in prison, and Paul sent him back to his master after converting him to Christianity (cf. Col. 4.9). It has been argued that Paul was more likely to have encountered Onesimus at Ephesus, roughly a hundred miles from Colossae, than at Rome, perhaps ten times as far away. But this kind of argument, based on what may be called 'geophysical probability', is not convincing when one is dealing with the actions of individuals. It might equally well be said that a runaway Colossian slave could much more easily lose himself at Rome than at Ephesus. The fact that in Colossians Paul also refers to correspondence with Laodicea, another town in the Lycus valley of Asia Minor, does not prove that the letters came from nearby Ephesus. Economy of effort is not a good criterion for judging what an early Christian, or a human being, might or might not do.

We know from Acts that Aristarchus was at Ephesus with Paul (19.29), while Timothy was not (19.22). We also know that Aristarchus and the author of the 'we-passages' (whom we take to be Luke) went with Paul to Italy (27.2). We therefore assume that the prison from which Paul wrote was in Rome. Secondary confirmation for this view is provided by the mention of Mark, the cousin of Barnabas (Col. 4.10), and his identification in early tradition with the interpreter of Peter at Rome (Papias; cf. I Pet. 5.13).

(3) A somewhat more difficult problem is posed by Ephesians. Like the other letters we have mentioned, Ephesians was written from prison (3.1; 4.1; 6.19). As we shall see, Ephesians is hard to date and to place. A good deal of its contents is closely parallel

to Colossians, so much so that it has sometimes been regarded as a revised version of that letter. At the same time, it reflects a somewhat different situation and indeed, according to the oldest witnesses to its text, is not addressed to Ephesus. The question whether it was written by Paul or not will be discussed later. Here we need only say that if it was, it came from the same prison as that in which Colossians was written.

In conclusion, we should say only that in our opinion the traditional claim that Philippians, Colossians and Philemon (and perhaps Ephesians) were written at Rome deserves to be accepted.

WAS PAUL EVER IN PRISON AT EPHESUS?

The modern conjecture that Paul was imprisoned for a time at Ephesus deserves some consideration because of its possible bearing on the circumstances of the imprisonment letters. In so far as this conjecture is not based upon the second-century romance called the Acts of Paul, in which Paul meets a friendly and talkative lion in the arena at Ephesus only to be reminded that he had once baptised the beast, it depends on obscure statements in the Corinthian letters and on the fact that not everything Paul did is recorded in Acts.[1]

It may readily be agreed that Acts has many omissions, especially evident when one compares its account with Paul's own list of events in II Corinthians 11.23–5. To say this, however, is not to admit that since Acts does not record an Ephesian imprisonment one therefore existed. In II Corinthians 11.23 Paul says that he has been imprisoned more often than his opponents; but we do not know how often they had been imprisoned. In I Corinthians 15.32 Paul seems to say that *kata anthrōpon* he has fought with wild beasts at Ephesus; the best parallels to this use of *kata anthrōpon* are probably provided in I Corinthians 9.8 and Galatians 3.15, where it indicates that Paul is using metaphorical language. The chief arguments against taking the expression literally are (1) that Roman citizens were not liable to this kind of punishment, and (2) that those who were did not often survive it. On the other hand, Paul does speak of serious trouble which came upon him in Asia (Minor); he felt

[1] C. Schmidt, ΠΡΑΞΕΙΣ ΠΑΥΛΟΥ (Hamburg, 1936), 38–41.

inwardly that he had received a death sentence; but God delivered him from the peril of death (II Cor. 1.8–10). It is clear that he has something extraordinarily serious in view. But it is not clear that he has imprisonment in mind, and had he been condemned 'to the beasts' he would not say that the death sentence was 'in himself' or 'known inwardly'.

We conclude that since so little positive evidence is available for the Ephesian-imprisonment hypothesis it cannot be used in dealing with the Pauline letters.

PHILIPPIANS

This letter was almost certainly known to Polycarp; it was accepted by Marcion; and while only allusions to it occur in Theophilus, explicit quotations are given by Irenaeus and by later writers. Apparently there was never any question as to its canonical authority, and it is found in the Beatty papyri and in later manuscripts.

Philippians contains 1,625 words and employs a vocabulary of 448 words, forty-one of which are not found elsewhere in the New Testament. Only three 'double compounds' occur in the letter: '*apekdechesthai*', 'to expect' (also in I Corinthians, Galatians, and Romans); '*exanastasis*', 'resurrection'; and '*epekteinesthai*', 'to reach out for'. All three are found in the third chapter.

It has sometimes been argued that Philippians is not a unity but consists of two letters (4.10–20; 1.1–3.1, 4.2–9, 21–3), the second of them interpolated (3.2–4.1). Admittedly there is a break between 3.1 and 3.2, and it is possible, as it is in II Corinthians, that the letter we now possess is actually a compilation made from various Pauline materials preserved at Philippi or, less probably, at Rome. If with NEB we translate 3.1b as 'to repeat what I have written to you before is no trouble to me, and it is a safeguard for you', there is some transition between 3.1 and 2, and Paul may well be referring to an earlier letter now lost. It is also argued that since the Philippians' messenger, Epaphroditus, fell sick after delivering their gift to Paul (2.26–8), Paul cannot have waited for him to recover before expressing his thanks to the Philippians; therefore 4.10–20 must have been written earlier than the rest of Philippians. Since

G

Rome was 800 miles from Philippi, and news about Epaphroditus's illness had gone to Philippi and back (2.26), so much time must have elapsed that Paul must have given an earlier 'receipt' (4.18) for the gift. But we do not actually know whether he gave an earlier receipt. Because of our ignorance we prefer to regard the letter as a unity.

In addition, some scholars are persuaded that Philippians 2.6–11 contains a Christological hymn of non- or post-Pauline origin. Certainly some of the key words are not found in the other Pauline epistles ('*harpagmos*', 'plunder'; '*isos*', 'equal' – but 'equality' occurs; and '*morphē*', 'form'); but the key idea is otherwise expressed in II Corinthians 8.9; 'for you he became poor, though he was rich, so that you might be made rich by his poverty', and the notion of Christ as the pre-existent image of God is fairly common in Paul. It has been claimed that Paul's mention of 'death on a cross' in 2.8 shows that he is interpreting someone else's hymn; but it seems equally possible that he is interpreting his own work (cf. I Cor. 12.13b, 14.1).

Philippians is a highly personal letter of gratitude to a church which had repeated to Paul the gift which it had made him 'at the beginning of the gospel' (4.15). The customary thanksgiving recalls their assistance 'from the first day until now' (1.3–11). Then Paul sets forth an interpretation of the meaning of his imprisonment in relation to his correspondents (1.12–30), and calls them to unity and to obedience like that of Christ Jesus (2.1–18). These sections are followed by a statement about the future arrival of Timothy and Epaphroditus at Philippi (2.19–30), a valedictory summary of Paul's career (3.1–4.7), and a valedictory exhortation and expression of gratefulness (4.8–20).

Within each of these sections is an especially personal or exemplary note. Thus Philippians 1.19–26 speaks of Paul's situation ('to live is Christ and to die is gain'); 2.5–11 of the humility and obedience of Christ; 2.22 and 30 of the relation of Timothy and Epaphroditus to Paul; 3.7–14 of Paul's life as a Christian; and 4.11–13 of what Paul has learned from his experience. The tone of the personal sections suggests that the letter as a whole comes from a time late in Paul's mission; the place of 3.7–14 within 3.1–4.7 suggests that the letter as a whole is a unity.

COLOSSIANS

Colossians, probably reflected in the writings of Justin Martyr, was certainly included in Marcion's collection and was later used without question, although in modern times its authenticity has been doubted, largely because of its 'high' Christology and doctrine of the Church. The differences between Paul's views on these subjects in Colossians and those expressed elsewhere can probably be explained, however, as due either to the special problems at Colossae or to the possible development of his thought. With the Thessalonian epistles, Colossians lacks any reference to *dikaiosyne*', '*kauchasthai*', '*logizesthai*' ('account', 'reckon', or 'think'), and '*nomos*'.

The style of Colossians is marked by a fondness for very long sentences (1.3–8, 9–20, 21–3, 24–9; 2.8–15). But the first of these contains a thanksgiving (ordinarily long in Paul's letters), the second a prayer, presumably expressed in semi-liturgical language; the elaborate Christological statement with which it ends can be compared both with the short parallel in I Corinthians 8.6 and with the statement, from a different point of view, in Romans 3.25–6. It should be noted that as the letter continues the sentences become shorter. We should explain this fact as due not to the fatigue of a Paulinist but to the changing mood of Paul himself.

The letter also contains the earliest Christian example of a *Haustafel*, a statement of the mutual responsibilities of members of a household. Such statements are found among Paul's contemporaries, especially Stoics, and it is probable that his example is based in form on theirs, though the content has been given a Christian sanction (compare I Corinthians 7.3–5, where Jewish, Greek and Christian motifs are combined).

The letter to the Colossians is largely concerned with what Paul regards as a false interpretation of the meaning of Christ, combined with an incorrect understanding of the nature of the world. If the Colossians' views could be recovered, the precise meaning of what Paul says would be clearer; but unfortunately his remarks about their views are almost entirely allusive. It is clear, however, that they combined some doctrine about the importance of 'the elemental spirits' with observance of the Jewish calendar, with

asceticism, and with what he calls 'angel-worship' (2.8, 16-1⸱
21). It is not clear whether he or they called their vie⸱
'philosophy' (2.8, only here in the New Testament).

Further inferences can be made from what he says in answer ⸱
them. (1) Christ is the sole agent of universal creation an⸱
reconciliation (1.15-20); this means that while 'the invisibl⸱
orders of thrones, sovereignties, authorities and powers' exist, the⸱
owe their existence to him and are therefore inferior to hi⸱
(1.16); they therefore cannot be worshipped as if they wer⸱
independent. (2) At the crucifixion God or Christ made a publi⸱
spectacle of the authorities and powers and led them captiv⸱
(2.15); in so far as they were in rebellion against God, they hav⸱
been defeated. (3) Through baptism Christians have been burie⸱
and raised again (2.12); they have left the control of the elementa⸱
spirits (2.20); their true life is 'hidden with Christ in Goc⸱
(3.1-3). (4) To be sure, this true life has not yet been fully re⸱
vealed; there are still parts of them which belong to the eart⸱
(3.5); their 'new man' needs constant renewal (3.9-10); but i⸱
principle they are no longer subject to the spirits.

We should infer that some Colossians were uncertain (to say th⸱
least) as to the place of Christ in the heavenly hierarchy and hi⸱
relation to the elemental spirits; that they observed at least par⸱
of the Jewish law, interpreting it in an ascetic direction perhap⸱
because they wanted to keep free from the world – and th⸱
elemental spirits which controlled it. For this reason Paul insist⸱
that Christ is the Head, not only of his body the Church (1.18⸱
but also of every authority and power (2.10), and makes use of ⸱
physiological analogy to show that all the body owes its preserva⸱
tion and growth to the head.

The concept of the Head may well explain some aspects of th⸱
Christological passage (1.15-20). In Hebrew the word for 'head⸱
is 'rosh', while the word for 'beginning' (in Greek, 'archē') i⸱
'reshith'. In Aramaic 'resh' was used for both meanings. It may wel⸱
be that the passage begins with an interpretation of Genesis 1.⸱
('in the beginning,' 'bereshith'), develops it by substituting othe⸱
prepositions for 'in' (Hebrew 'be'), and then goes on to 'head⸱
Perhaps the occasion for this interpretation was provided by th⸱
close association of two Jewish holy days – New Year's Day⸱
('Rosh ha-shanah'), recalling the beginning of creation, and th⸱

ay of Atonement, pointing to reconciliation and peace, not
nly on earth but also in heaven. Paul could have interpreted
e meaning of the days in this way because in his view
ey were 'no more than a shadow of what was to come'
.17, NEB).

Paul also insists upon the unity of God's people; among them
ere is no longer 'Greek or Jew, circumcised or uncircumcised,
arbarian, Scythian, freeman, slave' (3.11; cf. Gal. 3.28); but
Christ is all and in all.' After listing the sins which the Colossians
ust put to death or lay aside (two groups of five, 3.5, 8) and
he garments that suit God's chosen people' (five, 3.12), he
rovides a list of family and household duties like those already in
se among some Stoic teachers (Seneca, *Ep.* 94). The difference
etween Paul's teaching and that of the Stoics lies in the
otivation involved.

It is rather surprising that in this letter the Spirit is mentioned
nly once (1.8, if this is really a reference). Such an omission can
e explained by Paul's concentration upon the Christological
heme. The Colossians were only too ready to believe in
pirits. What they needed was understanding of the cosmic
ole of Christ.

PHILEMON

he shortest book in the New Testament (except for II and III
ohn) is the little letter which from prison Paul wrote with
imothy to Philemon, Apphia, and Archippus, all presumably
embers of the community which met at Philemon's house in
olossae. Though Philemon and Apphia are not mentioned in
olossians, all the other persons named in the note to Philemon
re also named in the longer letter.

The note begins with Paul's characteristic salutation and
anksgiving and goes on to urge Philemon to give kind treatment
 his runaway slave Onesimus, whom Paul has 'begotten' as a
hristian (cf. I Cor. 4.15). Because Paul says that Philemon will
ceive him back 'no longer as a slave but more than a slave'
6) and that he knows that Philemon will do 'even more than I
y' (21), it has sometimes been thought that he is implicitly
ecommending that Onesimus be set free by his master, or even

that Onesimus was the bishop of Ephesus later mentioned b
Ignatius in his letter to the Ephesian Christians. Such a conclusio
would be strengthened if we knew that Paul favoured emancipa
tion, as he does in the RSV translation of I Cor. 7.21; but thi
translation is quite uncertain and the words may mean 'if yo
can gain your freedom, rather make use (of your servitude)'.

The letter, written either from Ephesus or, more probably, fron
Rome, shows a side of Paul quite different from that revealed i
his letters of controversy. It is an intimately personal appeal whicl
resembles much of II Cor. 1–9. In it Paul does not hesitate t
make puns on the name of Onesimus ('useful' or 'beneficial'), a
in verses 11 and 20. Like another non-controversial lettei
Philippians, it contains no direct reference to Paul's apostoli
authority (though such authority is available; see verse 8 an
Phil. 2.12). 'For love's sake I . . . appeal to you' (9).

The external history of the letter to Philemon is interesting
Because of its personal character, we should hardly expect that i
would have survived or would have been included in the canon
Yet, probably because of its close relation to Colossians, Marcio
kept it with his other Pauline letters, and it is mentioned in th
Muratorian list. Theophilus of Antioch alluded to it and Tertullia
mentioned it.

On the other hand, there is apparently no trace of it in th
voluminous writings of Clement of Alexandria and Origen (excep
for one fragment of a rather dubious commentary on Philemon
quoted by Pamphilus in the early fourth century). In Syri
both Ephraem and Aphraates rejected it; so, apparently, di
Apollinarius of Laodicea. Jerome (PL 26, 635–8) noted th
objections of critics who claimed that Paul did not always writ
as an apostle or with Christ speaking in him (II Cor. 13.3)
Others, apparently, argued that the letter was not by Paul – or
even if it was, contained nothing edifying; they added that it ha
been rejected by many ancient writers as merely a letter of recom
mendation. Fortunately traditional usage prevailed against sucl
criticisms.

As far as the text of the letter is concerned, we shall presently se
that it may or may not have been in the Beatty papyri (page 210)
other New Testament manuscripts include it, and it was in th
Old Latin version.

EPHESIANS

The letter to the Ephesians has belonged, as far as one can tell, to the collected Pauline epistles from the earliest times. Clear echoes of it occur in the preface to Ignatius's letter to the Ephesians as well as in Polycarp's letter to the Philippians (1, 3). Marcion knew it and included it in his 'Apostle', although he regarded it as written to the Laodiceans. From his time onward, no question was raised about its canonicity, in spite of the doubt about its addressees; manuscripts known to Origen and others omitted the words 'in Ephesus' in Ephesians 1.3 (see Chapter II).

The letter contains 2,425 words, 529 of them different. The style is somewhat laboured and the thought moves very slowly, with the piling up of subordinate clauses and the use of words in the genitive case which convey the same meaning as the nominatives with which they are connected. To some extent this feature, known as 'pleonasm', is characteristic of the language of prayer; we might expect to find pleonasm in a letter which begins with a two-sentence prayer extending over twenty-one verses.

The theme of the letter is set forth in the opening blessing-thanksgiving. God blessed Christians 'in the heavenly places' by choosing them in Christ before the foundation of the world and by making known the mystery of his will to them. The mystery (a mystery to be revealed to all) was 'a plan for the fullness of time, to unite (or sum up) all things in him (Christ), things in heaven and things on earth' (1.10). God has now made Christ 'the head over all things for the Church, which is his body, the fullness of him who fills all in all' (1.22–3). Christians now dwell 'in the heavenly places in Christ Jesus' (2.6), for 'by grace you have been saved through faith' (2.8).

But whereas in Colossians the uniting of all was viewed chiefly in relation to the cosmos, here it is the union between Jews and gentiles in the Church. The gentiles, once 'far off' (Is. 57.19), had been made 'near' and have become fellow-citizens with the saints, part of the temple of God. Through the Church the manifold wisdom of God is now known even to the principalities and powers in the heavenly places. The unity of the Church is the result of 'growth into the head', by ethical behaviour (especially in family life, since the relation of husband to wife resembles that of Christ to the Church), and by putting on the armour of God in order to contend with hostile spiritual powers.

There is nothing very personal about this letter. Of his readers Paul says that they heard the gospel and believed it (1.13); faith and love are among them (1.15); they were formerly uncircumcised gentiles. Tychicus, the bearer of Colossians (Col. 4.7; cf. Acts 20.4), is taking this letter to its recipients – whom, like the Colossians (Col. 1.4, 9), Paul does not know personally (Eph. 1.15; cf. 3.2–3). Conceivably the letter was a 'general epistle'. The reference to what Paul had written before (3.3) may be to a statement made earlier in this letter itself (e.g., 1.9). Alternatively, it refers to another letter now lost, and Ephesians was written to a specific church – but not at Ephesus.

The letter to the Ephesians has been the occasion of a great deal of controversy between those who have regarded it as Paul's and those who have viewed it as a reinterpretation of Paul's thought by a later disciple. There are excellent grounds for both views, and Professor Cadbury has vigorously and rightly maintained that no valid conclusion can be reached. It may be suggested, however, that just as Romans takes up themes already expressed in the Corinthian letters and Galatians and expresses them somewhat more systematically, so Ephesians recapitulates and further develops themes already present in Colossians. Some scholars have argued that (1) if Ephesians was by Paul, it must have been written immediately after Colossians because so much of it is like Colossians; and on the other hand (2) the changes in the meaning of words show that it was written considerably later; therefore (3) it was not written by Paul. This argument is not conclusive because (1) resemblances to Colossians do not prove anything about the time-sequence, and (2) we do not know either (a) how much later it was written or (b) how long Paul's mind took to change (compare II Corinthians). We shall treat the letter as Paul's while remembering that it may be the creation of someone else.

The most significant difference between Colossians and Ephesians lies in the doctrine of the Church. In Colossians, Christ is the head of the Church (1.18, 24) and 'churches' are mentioned (4.15–16). In Ephesians, however, the Church herself is the Bride of Christ (5.25–32) and is the instrument of God's revelation to the heavenly powers (3.10); the Church holds within herself the fullness of him who himself receives the entire fullness of God' (1.23, NEB). This is to say that in Ephesians, as not in the other Pauline epistles, we find an expression of the cosmic meaning of the Church. It cannot be said that premonitions of these ideas are absent earlier. In I Corinthians 6.17 the Christian is the bride of Christ; in II Corinthians 11.2 (cf. Rom. 7.4) the Church is his bride.

The central arguments against the authenticity of Ephesians are as follows. (1) The key words of Ephesians are more like those used by the Apostolic Fathers than like those in the other Pauline epistles. (2) Stylistically, Ephesians contains unusually long sentences and the thought moves slowly. (3) About three-fifths of Colossians seems to be reflected in Ephesians, though the phrases often bear different meanings. (4) There is no concrete situation reflected in the letter. (5) It comes from a time when the Jewish-gentile controversy is over. (6) The doctrine is new. (a) The Church is universal not local and is the bride of Christ. (b) There is a plea for unity against sectarianism. (c) Apostles and prophets, not Christ, are the foundation of the Church. (d) Christ, not God, reconciles and appoints apostles, prophets, etc. (e) Christ's exaltation replaces his death.

These arguments do not seem conclusive. (1) Out of 618 short phrases in Ephesians, 550 have parallels in the other Pauline epistles (Goodspeed); and the writings of the Apostolic Fathers are neither uniform nor remarkably different from the New Testament. (2) The language of prayer – and of meditation – is different from that employed in, e.g., the diatribe-style often found in other letters. (3) Paul was never a slave to a dictionary. (4) There is no reason for a circular letter like Ephesians to be addressed to a concrete situation. (5) In addressing congregations largely gentile (2.11–13) Paul had no reason to emphasize the importance of Jewish-gentile controversy. (6) The Church is at least potentially universal in I Cor. 15.9, Gal. 1.13 and Phil. 3.6, and is definitely so in I Cor. 10.32, 12.28, and Colossians. Paul pleads for unity in almost all of his epistles, especially in I Corinthians. He does not sharply differentiate the work of God and the work of Christ, nor that of Christ and that of the apostles.

Finally, the saving work of Christ was achieved not only through his death but also through his resurrection (I Cor. 15.12-19 cf. Rom. 6.4, etc.).

A significant question about this letter has been raised by Professor Cadbury in an article entitled 'The Dilemma of Ephesians'. It is this: 'which is more likely – that an imitator of Paul in the first century composed a writing ninety or ninety-five per cent in accordance with Paul's style or that Paul himself wrote a letter diverging five or ten per cent from his usual style?'

The way in which Professor Cadbury phrases his question suggests that another dilemma underlies the one which he discusses. 'Which is more likely,' we might well ask '– that we can determine the authenticity of a letter written ninety or ninety-five per cent in accordance with Paul's style, and his outlook, or that we cannot?' *This* question, it would appear, can be answered. We are not in a position to judge, and since the authenticity of the letter cannot be disproved it should be regarded as genuine.

ADDITIONAL NOTE: GNOSTICISM

The position of Gnosticism in the history of the early Church is very difficult to determine, and in large measure the position given will determine the interpretation of the phenomenon. By placing it here, in relation to the Pauline epistles, we are pointing towards an interpretation of it in relation to Christianity, though various alternatives are possible. Gnosticism is a religion in which emphasis is laid on salvation for the spirit of man, a spirit divine in origin, submerged in evil matter, and rescued by virtue of recognition of its origin and nature. The recognition is the result of the knowledge provided by a redeemer-revealer who comes down from the spirit-world above and returns there. The world of matter in which the spirit is imprisoned is alien to the redeemer-revealer because it was created by a god inferior to him or to his Father, the supreme unknown God.

The major Gnostic systems are known to us from the writings of the Church Fathers, and they came into existence fairly early

---

[1] *New Testament Studies* 5 (1959), 91-102.

n the second century. Historically, it is a question whether or not Gnosticism, or Gnostic systems of any kind, existed either before the end of the first century or in New Testament times. There seems to be no evidence for the existence of a Gnostic redeemer-revealer before the rise of Christianity. It is therefore probable that Christianity was an important factor in producing Gnostic systems. Again, there seems to be no evidence for the existence of Gnostic systems before the end of the first century. It would therefore appear that something in the latter half of the first century caused the crystallization into Gnosticism of the various ingredients which were used.

These ingredients include hostility towards the created world and therefore towards its Creator, often called 'the God of the Jews'; an idea of spirit as separate from matter and superior to it; and a notion of salvation as something essentially already achieved. Most Gnostic systems contain a highly developed angelology related to Jewish apocalyptic thought. In a certain sense, then, Gnosticism can be viewed as a development out of Jewish apocalyptic, a 'heresy' perhaps espoused by those whose apocalyptic hopes had been frustrated. In place of the expectation of God's reign on earth came the idea of escape from the evil world.

In addition, there is the fact that the redeemer-revealer in almost all Gnostic systems is, or is based upon, Jesus. This fact suggests that Gnosticism is not only a Jewish 'heresy' but also a Christian one. Indeed, to put the case quite simply, Gnosticism is based on the rejection of apocalyptic expectations and on the view that salvation has been brought to the elect in the gospel of Jesus. Still more theologically, Gnosticism takes only one side of the Christian emphasis on God's work as Creator and Redeemer; it concentrates upon redemption and, just because of its failure to recognize creation, views redemption as escape.

The primary sources of Gnostic thought, then, can be seen in apocalyptic Judaism and in Christianity. If we wish to combine these two sources we may hold that Gnosticism arose out of Jewish Christianity, but to a considerable extent such a hypothesis only explains one ill-known phenomenon in relation to another.

The importance of Gnosticism in relation to early Christianity lies in the extent to which various parts of the New Testament may be regarded as influenced by it or in conflict with it. In this regard there are three key areas in which questions arise. (1) Who were Paul's opponents at Corinth? (2) Who were his opponents at Colossae? (3) Is the thought-world of the Gospel of John, or of its sources, Gnostic?

'Gnostics' at Corinth

It has often been observed that Paul's opponents at Corinth seem to have understood their own situation in relation to the ideal 'wise man' of Stoic and Cynic thought. He was wise and therefore unique – powerful, well born, and rich. Everything was lawful for him. Like the Cynics, he recognized that the stomach was intended for food and could therefore argue that sexual organs were intended for practical use. He was above ordinary morality, since he was 'spiritual'. He knew that he was 'free', and that sins of the body were not really sins at all.

Since these Corinthians regarded themselves as Christians, we must ask what it was about the Christian gospel which made it possible for them to combine their special notions with it. Obviously Paul's preaching of the Spirit and of freedom in the Spirit contributed something. At many points Paul agreed with the Corinthians, though not in regard to the implications they drew. But why did they believe that they had reached the exalted status which they were claiming to have attained? The answer seems to be hinted at in what Paul says of their claims. They thought that they were already filled, already rich, already kings (I Cor. 4.8). And the idea of being filled and of receiving a kingdom is expressed in the Sermon on the Mount, while that of being rich is implied in various parts of the teaching of Jesus. It would appear that the Corinthians had misunderstood the Christian eschatological message (cf. II Thess. 2.2; II Tim. 2.17), believing that the eschatology had been 'realized'. The kingdom had already arrived.

In addition, from what Paul says about the crucifixion of the Messiah in his opening chapters it seems likely that they laid little emphasis on this fact, just as they could not understand the sufferings of the apostles (4.9–13). In other words, for them Jesus was a redeemer-revealer who had made them aware of their own nature as 'spiritual'.

We should hesitate to believe that the Corinthians were really close to Gnostic ideas, however, were it not that we can point to a real Gnostic system in which notions like theirs are found. Such a system is described by Clement of Alexandria (*Strom.* 3, 27–33), and while it need not be older than the second century some features of it are close to Corinthian thought. (1) Like the Corinthians, these Gnostics (who actually called themselves Gnostics) regarded themselves as 'royal'; they were kings, and they quoted the Greek proverb, 'For a king, law is unwritten'. This is to say that because of their status they were free from the prescriptions of ordinary morality and could live as they pleased. They were superior to 'worldly men' and lived in the world as in an alien land. (2) They also regarded the prescriptions of the Sermon on the Mount as to be fulfilled among themselves or with prospective converts to Gnosticism; thus a Gnostic youth appealed to a Christian virgin with the words 'Give to everyone who asks you' (Matt. 5.42; Luke 6.30). They used other synoptic phrases to describe their own situation, calling themselves 'lords of the Sabbath'. This must mean that they identified themselves with the Son of Man who in Mark 2.28 (and parallels) is called 'lord of the Sabbath'. Clearly their eschatology was 'realized', for they called promiscuous intercourse a 'mystical union' and claimed that it 'lifts them up into the kingdom of God'. (3) Unfortunately we do not know precisely what these Gnostics thought about Jesus. Clement quotes a fragment of their myth, however, in which there is a reference to the generation of 'the Beloved' – presumably the spiritual Christ – from the One. We should probably infer that at a later time 'the Beloved' revealed to Gnostics the way in which he was generated, thus providing them with an archetypal model for their own 'mystical union'. These Gnostics cannot have laid any emphasis upon the crucifixion of Christ.

In view of these parallels, we should incline to say that there were Gnostics at Corinth, and that Gnosticism was essentially a way of viewing the Christian gospel. By treating the eschatology as fully realized the Gnostic necessarily arrived at a notion of his own status as highly exalted. His doctrine was filled out with ideas derived from popular philosophy, but it was primarily Christian in origin. At a later time, and perhaps earlier as well, many ideas were also derived from Jewish apocalyptic thought, but these ideas may have been mediated by Jewish Christianity.

'Gnostics' at Colossae

We have already seen (page 195) that at Colossae there was enthusiasm for what Paul calls 'elemental spirits'; this resulted in 'angel-worship' which was combined with observance of the Jewish calendar and asceticism. It is possible that the Colossian heresy was based on some kind of philosophical view (see Col. 2.8), but we do not know what it was. All we can say about the Colossian situation is that there is nothing which seems to be specifically related to any form of Gnosticism which we know. Some of the terminology was employed by later Gnostics, but this fact proves nothing.

Gnosticism in the Gospel of John

It has often been observed that later Gnostics, especially Valentinians, were fond of the Gospel of John, and it might be supposed that therefore its ideas were especially congenial for them. We must point out, however, that these Gnostics were able to use John for their purposes only by drastically allegorizing it. They took the nouns in the prologue as referring to spiritual 'aeons' and interpreted the persons in the Gospel proper as symbols. This means that as it stood the Gospel was not really suited for their purposes. To be sure, it contains references to a kind of ethical dualism which comes close (in expression) to a metaphysical dualism. This dualism, however, is characteristic of Jewish sectarian thought as found, for example, at Qumran, and the presence of this dualism is not necessarily an indication of Gnostic thought. A real Gnostic would find it difficult to say that God loved the world (John 3.16).

We conclude that within the major New Testament writings the only document which clearly reflects the presence of something like Gnosticism is I Corinthians; and among the Corinthians the

Gnostic ideas are clearly derived from a special interpretation of Paul's preaching to them. The Corinthians needed a context in which to interpret what Paul (and other Christian missionaries) had said. As they provided it they went well beyond what the apostle intended. The result was at least an embryonic form of the later Gnostic systems.

XIV

THE NON-PAULINE EPISTLES

Every classification demands a decision on the part of the classifier, for classifications do not 'just happen'. They are, or should be, intentional; they must result from various kinds of decisions made by the student in relation to his materials. Thus we have already made one kind of decision when we classified Ephesians, in spite of important difficulties, with the Pauline epistles. We are making another kind of decision when we classify the Pastoral Epistles (to Timothy and to Titus) along with Hebrews as non-Pauline. (1) We are not altogether justified in treating the Pastorals and Hebrews together, for the objections to the Pastorals have arisen chiefly in modern times; ancient Christians, who in general knew Greek better than we do, had no difficulty in regarding the Pastorals as authentically Pauline, while they regarded Hebrews as written by someone else. (2) We are not altogether justified in treating any of them as non-Pauline, for the Pastorals explicitly represent themselves as by Paul while Hebrews does so by implication.

In spite of these difficulties, the weight of which we recognize, we are still going to view the Pastorals as probably written by someone other than Paul and Hebrews as certainly written by someone else. This is not to say that the doctrines set forth in these letters are totally non-Pauline, or that the documents must somehow be regarded as inferior to the Pauline epistles. It is simply to say that as far as we can tell they reflect conceptions of Christianity which are not completely identical with Paul's. The situation might be different if with Marcion we held that the only authentic version of Christianity was Paul's; but in our view a doctrine does not have to be Pauline to be either true or Christian.

THE PASTORAL EPISTLES

In the seventeenth century the title 'pastoral' was given to the letters addressed to Timothy and Titus because one of their chief concerns is the duty of pastors in the Church. In this respect they are unlike the other Pauline epistles, which – with the exception of Philemon – are addressed to entire communities (though it should be noted that Philippians is written to the saints 'with the bishops and deacons').

The Pastorals have certainly been regarded as Paul's since the latter half of the second century, for they were so used by Theophilus of Antioch and Irenaeus of Lyons and are to be found in the Muratorian list. Before that time they were open to criticism. From Tertullian we hear that the Gnostics Basilides (*c.* 130) and Marcion (*c.* 140) rejected them, though his statement *may* mean no more than that both did not know them. According to Jerome, Tatian (*c.* 170) accepted only the letter to Titus. Furthermore, though close parallels to them are to be found in the letter of Polycarp (early second century), he does not ascribe such passages to Paul, and it has been suggested (by von Campenhausen) that Polycarp himself wrote the Pastorals. In any event, the parallels do not fully prove that he knew these letters – though we must remember that Christian writers generally are fond of making allusions to New Testament writings instead of quoting them explicitly. The text of the Pastorals has been transmitted along with that of the other Pauline letters except in one instance.

The possible place of the Pastoral Epistles in the third-century Beatty codex of the Pauline letters raises some fascinating problems about ancient books. The codex was made by creating a pile of papyrus leaves and folding it in the middle to create a book. The outside leaves are lost, but since the pages were numbered by the scribe we know how many there were. Papyrus pages were made by gluing together two papyrus leaves; on the front the grain went across; on the back it went vertically. In this codex the front pages (also called the 'recto') are given even numbers, the back pages ('verso'), odd. Therefore the first page was not numbered but either was blank or bore a title. Since seven leaves (fourteen pages) are missing at the beginning, an equal number must be missing at the end.

So much for the missing pages. What does the book contain? It contains Romans, Hebrews, I-II Corinthians, Ephesians, Galatians, Philippians, Colossians, and I Thessalonians (a most unusual sequence). Unfortunately part of the title of the last letter is lost, and we cannot tell whether it read 'To the Thessalonians' or 'To the Thessalonians, I'. What we have of the codex ends with the last verse of I Thessalonians, eight lines down from the top of the page. Since at this point the scribe was writing about thirty-two lines to a page, there was room for a title and about twenty more lines of some letter.

Therefore there was room in the rest of the codex for either 14¾ more pages of Pauline epistles or – if the scribe left the last page blank, like the first – for 13¾ pages. The length of other Pauline epistles in his writing has been calculated, and the following possibilities are available:

		PAGES
II Thessalonians	...	4¾
I Timothy	...	8¼
II Timothy	...	6
Titus	...	3½
Philemon	...	1½

But since, as far as we know, no question was ever raised about II Thessalonians in the ancient church, it must be included. The possibilities are then as follows:

	PAGES
II Thessalonians + I Timothy	13
II Thessalonians + II Timothy + Titus	14¼
II Thessalonians + II Timothy + Philemon	13¾

We may be tempted to leave out Philemon because it is so badly attested in the second century and because debates later arose about its inspiration (see p. 198); but we must finally – after all these calculations – remember that if the scribe wrongly calculated the number of pages for his book he could glue on others at the end. Moreover, it looks as if he did miscalculate; his writing gets smaller as he nears the end, and this process suggests that he was aware that he did not have enough room.

The upshot of this analysis is that while we definitely know that the Pauline epistles were arranged peculiarly in the Beatty codex, we do not know that they did not include the Pastorals.

The style of the letters is exhortatory and rather monotonous. As compared with the other Pauline epistles, the Pastorals contain more abstract formulations and fewer images and metaphors; conjunctions occur less frequently. The thought is not sustained beyond the limit of the individual paragraph. The letters to Timothy begin with the unusual formula of salutation 'grace, mercy, peace', and only II Timothy contains the prayer of thanksgiving with which all the Pauline letters (except Galatians) begin.

As for the vocabulary of the letters, it is 'absolutely homogeneous' (Morgenthaler). The three letters contain 3,482 words and employ a vocabulary of 901 words. This vocabulary includes 306 words not found in the other Pauline epistles (thirty-three per cent, considerably higher than any other letter) and 335 words not found elsewhere in the New Testament, again a high proportion. The 'new' words generally reflect a level of literary culture higher than that found either in the other Pauline epistles or in the rest of the New Testament. In the Pastorals we find a quotation from Epimenides (Tit. 1.12) and possible allusions to Euripides, Pindar, and Menander. (Furthermore, in I Timothy 5.18, Luke 10.7 seems to be regarded as scripture [cf. I Cor. 9.14, however, for an allusion to the same oral tradition]; Luke used Mark, and Mark was written after the death of Paul [see page 126]; but the quotation may not be from Luke.)

The historical situation implied by the letters cannot be reconciled with anything in the other Pauline epistles or in Acts, though there are some parallels. (1) From II Timothy it would appear that Paul is a prisoner in Rome (1.17), where he has already made his 'first defence' (4.16) and now expects to be 'sacrificed' (4.6). He has recently visited Troas (4.13; cf. Acts 20.5) and Miletus (4.20; cf. Acts 20.16–17). Luke is with him; Demas has deserted him; and he asks Timothy to bring Mark (4.10–11; cf. Col. 4.10–14; Acts 15.37–9). He has sent Tychicus to Ephesus (4.12; cf. Eph. 6.21–2; Col. 4.7). Obviously the situation and the parallels can be explained in either of two ways. (*a*) After his 'first defence' at Rome, Paul was released and revisited Asia Minor; the situation resembles that depicted in

Colossians and Ephesians because the two situations actually were similar. (*b*) A forger made use of Colossians and Ephesians in order to create an impression of verisimilitude.

(2) I Timothy depicts Paul as having left Timothy at Ephesus when he himself went to Macedonia (1.3); this situation vaguely resembles what we find in Acts 20.1–6, but is not very close to it. He hopes to visit Ephesus soon (3.14, 4.13).

(3) According to Titus 1.5, Paul has left Titus in Crete (cf. Acts 27.8–11) and now plans to spend the winter at Nicopolis, on the Adriatic coast of Greece; this notice may possibly be related to the mention of Illyricum in Romans 15.19.

It should also be noted that in II Timothy 3.11 Paul reminds Timothy of what befell him at Antioch, at Iconium, and at Lystra. This statement clearly recalls Acts 13–14 and 16.1–2. But if the account in Acts is historically reliable, we should expect such resemblances to exist.

The basic historical difficulty presented by the Pastorals arises in relation to what Paul did after the two years at Rome during which he preached and taught 'openly and unhindered' (Acts 28.30–1). He intended to go on from Rome to Spain (Rom. 12.23–9); according to the probable meaning of I Clement 5.7 he actually did so. Then did he also return to the East? (1) According to Romans 15.23 he no longer had any room for work in that region; did he change his mind? (2) According to Acts 20.25 the elders of Ephesus would see his face no more; apparently he did not expect to return to Asia Minor. Here again we must allow for the possibility that this 'farewell address' was actually followed either by a return or by the expectation of a return. It has often been observed that human events are not absolutely predictable. We should conclude that while the historical situation implied by the Pastorals presents some difficulties, they are not insurmountable.

The Pastorals also reflect a situation in the life of the church which seems to be later than what is found in the major Pauline epistles – though we should beware of assuming that all churches 'developed' in the same way or at the same time. (1) There are semi-Gnostics at Ephesus and in Crete (cf. I Tim. 6.20), chiefly Jewish in outlook (Tit. 1.10); they devote themselves to Jewish myths (Tit. 1.14) to to 'myths and endless genealogies' (I Tim. 1.4,

4.7; Tit. 3.9); they desire to be teachers of the Law (I Tim. .7). They proclaim a kind of 'realized eschatology', saying that he resurrection has already taken place (II Tim. 2.18), and they advocate abstinence from marriage and from meats (I. Tim. 4.4). This picture resembles what we find in the letters of Ignatius. On the other hand, it also resembles certain features of the thought of the opponents of Paul at Corinth and at Colossae, and since we do not know precisely where or when this kind of 'incipient Gnosticism' originated we cannot be certain that Paul did not encounter it. (2) The organization of the churches is somewhat different from that reflected in the major Pauline epistles, where the word 'presbyter' never occurs and 'bishops and deacons' are mentioned only in Philippians 1.1. In the Pastorals there is one bishop in each community (I Tim. 3.1–4; Tit. 1.7) and several deacons (I Tim. 3.8–13). There are also presbyters, in Crete appointed by Titus (1.5); some of them 'preside well' (I Tim. 5.17). They are agents of ordination; Timothy was to govern the Ephesian community because prophecy pointed towards him (I Tim. 5.18), but the gift of ordination was given him 'with the imposition of the hands of the presbytery' (4.14). He himself was to 'lay hands quickly' on no one (5.22); thus he, like the (other?) presbyters, could ordain. The situation seems to be one in which all bishops are presbyters but not all presbyters are bishops. It is thus almost exactly analogous to what we find in Acts 20.17 and 28 and in I Clement. The question, then, is whether or not this situation existed in Paul's lifetime. To answer this question the only evidence we possess lies in the Pastorals themselves.

Our basic difficulty lies in the fact that the word 'bishop', used of a church officer, occurs only four times in the New Testament Acts 20.28, Phil. 1.1, I Tim. 3.2, Tit. 1.7); the word 'presbyter' elder) is used of Christian ministers in Acts ten times and in the Pastorals three times (elsewhere in the New Testament, six times); and the word 'deacon' (servant) is not found in Acts but is used n the major Pauline epistles seven times of Paul, five times of other individuals, twice of Christ, once of Jewish-Christian leaders, and once of local officers as a group (with bishops). It occurs four times in the Pastorals. This evidence may not be adequate for bearing the burden of a picture of the early ministry in which

clear-cut distinctions were always either maintained or ignore
We have Paul's testimony; we have the testimony of t
Apostolic Fathers. It may not be possible for us to work fro
either end in such a way as to reject the evidence given by t
Pastorals, or to date it late.

As for the religious outlook of the author of the Pastorals, it
somewhat different from that of Paul as expressed in the oth
letters. Sound doctrine is important, and it is expressed in th
rather stereotyped 'trustworthy sayings' (I Tim. 1.15, 3.1, 4.9
II Tim. 2.11; Tit. 3.8). In other letters Paul certainly employ
watchwords, but they are not used so formally. In the Pastora
there is an emphasis on 'godliness' or 'religion' ('*eusebeia*', te
times; not elsewhere in Paul; in other New Testament writing
only Acts once and II Peter, four times). At the same time, othe
differences are often exaggerated because some aspects of Paul'
thought are neglected. Could he have said, 'The law is good if on
uses it lawfully' (I Tim. 1.8)? In Romans 7.12 he wrote that 'th
law is holy, and the commandment is holy and just and good
(cf. 8.4, 'the just requirement of the law'). Could he have urge
anyone to 'aim at righteousness, faith, love and peace' (II Tim
2.22) – since these are gifts of God or fruits of the Spirit? But
though God effects the will and the work, Paul instructs Christian
to work out their own salvation in Philippians 2.12–13.

Given the existence of slightly changed circumstances, he coul
have recommended adherence to an orderly way of life, require
not only of church officers but also of Christian women (e.g.,
Tim. 2.9–15), especially of widows, enrolled on the church's lis
(I Tim. 5.9), of slaves (6.1–2), and of the rich (6.17–19). Indeed
'sound doctrine' means especially the observance of mutua
responsibilities (Tit. 2.1–10).

To be sure, in his major epistles he did not speak of 'the sacre
writings which are able to instruct you for salvation through fait
in Christ Jesus' (II Tim. 3.15), nor did he suggest that persever
ance was essential for salvation (I Tim. 4.16), nor did he speal
of baptism as 'the washing of regeneration' (Tit. 3.5). In th
Pastorals the Spirit is hardly ever mentioned, and where it is it i
primarily related to sound doctrine.

It cannot be denied that the tone of the Pastorals is differen
from that of the earlier letters. And yet the tone of the earlie

letters is not uniform. The phrase '*dikaiosyne theou*' ('righteousness' or 'justice' of God) appears eight times in Romans and only once in the other epistles. The verb '*dikaioō*' occurs fifteen times in Romans, eight times in Galatians, twice in I Corinthians, and thereafter, or earlier, only twice – in the Pastoral epistles. Similarly the word '*nomos*' ('law') appears seventy-two times in Romans, thirty-two times in Galatians, nine times in I Corinthians, three times in Colossians, once in Ephesians, but nowhere else in the Pauline epistles – except for two instances in I Timothy. We cite these statistics not as an index of authenticity but simply to recall that Paul's concerns varied and that Romans and Galatians are not the only letters he wrote.

Those who do not believe that Paul can have written the Pastoral Epistles must remember (1) the difficulty of proving non-authenticity by statistics, (2) the genuine gaps in the knowledge we possess about early Christianity in the first century, and (3) the warning possibly provided by a parallel case in classical philology:

> About a hundred years ago the German scholar Otto Ribbeck conjectured that half a dozen of the later satires were not by Juvenal at all but by a forger who copied something of his manner without equalling his spirit. He was right, but the copyist was Juvenal himself, imitating his earlier work after the passion that inspired it had died away.[1]

In reassessing the 'assured results' of older New Testament scholarship, what seemed almost self-evident to it is often to be viewed with some caution.

On the other hand, those who accept these letters as Pauline must consider the real difficulties provided by (1) their style and vocabulary, (2) their historical situation, and (3) their theological outlook. If they were written by Paul, they were almost certainly written by a Paul who was somehow different from (older than?) the author of the major epistles. And if this is so, the theological problem posed by a changing or developing apostle must be faced. The major emphases of the Pastoral Epistles are by no means the same as those expressed in any one of the earlier letters, or in the earlier letters as a group.

[1] Gilbert Highet, *Juvenal the Satirist* (Oxford, 1954), 4–5.

HEBREWS

In Hebrews there are 4,942 words, with a rich vocabulary of 1,038 words.[1] The author's favourite words – in Greek alphabetical order – are 'blood', 'high priest', 'covenant' or 'testament' ('*diathēkē*'), 'promise', 'sacrifice' (noun), 'priest', 'better' ('*kreissōn*') 'offer' (of a sacrifice), and 'tent' or 'tabernacle'. The special subject matter of Hebrews explains its inclusion of 'high priest', 'priest', 'offer', and 'tabernacle', all absent from the Pauline epistles.

The style of Hebrews is literary, almost classical, and is completely different from that of Paul. Greek rhetoricians employed the expressions used in Hebrews to indicate transitions, for example 'about this we have much to say . . .' (5.11), 'now the point in what we are saying is this' (8.1), and 'what more shall I say? Time would fail me' (11.32). There are long periods of a kind lacking in Paul (1.1–4; 6.16–20; 7.1–3; 10.19–25), as well as an interesting tendency, noted by Cadbury, to conclude a clause with the name of Jesus (seven instances). The author seems to pay attention to assonance, rhyming endings, and even to rhythm. Anacoluthon, fairly common in Paul, is absent here, and the formulas for introducing Old Testament citations are quite different from his.

The document can be outlined in various ways, but the best arrangement is that provided by paying attention to the author's own indications, especially his use of rhetorical periods at the beginning or the end of various sections and his employment of connectives. The result is as follows:

I. Revelation through the Son of God (Jesus, not mentioned until 2.9) is superior to revelation through the prophets, as the Son is superior to the angels (1–2, beginning with a period, 1.1–4).

II. Jesus as Son is superior to Moses and Joshua (3.1–4.13, beginning with 'wherefore', 3.1).

III. Jesus is actually the great High Priest who has passed through the heavens (4.14–5.10, beginning with 'having then').

[1] On the place of Hebrews in the canon see Chapter 1.

IV. (exhortation to consider this point, beginning with 'concerning whom', 5.11, and ending with a period, 6.16–20).

V. Jesus is not a Levitical/Aaronic priest but one from the tribe of Judah; he is a priest 'after the order of Melchizedek' (7.1–28, with a period at the beginning, 7.1–3).

VI. Jesus offered his own blood in the true Holy of Holies (8.1–10.18, beginning with 'the chief point', 8.1).

VII. Christians therefore have boldness to enter the holy place by the blood of Jesus (10.19–39, beginning with 'having, then' and a period, 10.19–25).

VIII. The power of faith (11.1–40, beginning with a definition of faith, 11.1, after its mention in 10.39).

IX. Ethical/eschatological implications (12.1–29, beginning with 'consequently', 12.1).

X. Various injunctions (13.1–17, with an abrupt beginning).

XI. Personal remarks, benediction, conclusion (13.18–25).

In form the main part of the document is evidently an address, as some of the transitional expressions clearly show; but in its present state it is a letter or, more properly, a literary epistle: 'I exhort you, brethren, bear with the word of exhortation; for I have written to you in few words' (13.22). As a letter, it concludes with personal notes:

... that I may be restored to you the sooner (13.19)
Our brother Timothy has been released, with whom I shall see you if he comes soon (13.23)
Those from Italy send you greetings (13.24)

Such notes provide a reason for the ascription of Hebrews to Paul in the early Church, but the reason is not altogether convincing. Presumably the author is in prison and is a 'brother' of Timothy, but there is nothing which requires us to identify him with Paul. Early use of the document, at Rome in I Clement and at Alexandria later on, suggests that it was sent to Rome from elsewhere (where there were 'those from Italy') and that the sender was at Alexandria. The close affinities of the author's thought to that of Philo point in the same direction. We should go beyond the evidence were we to ascribe the book precisely to Apollos, 'an Alexandrian by race' who was 'eloquent' and 'mighty in the scriptures' (Acts 18.24); but such an identification remains possible.

As for the date of the document, its references to the temple cult as continuing to exist (9.6–10, 25; 10.1, etc.) and its failure to mention the destruction of the temple – a point which would surely be relevant to its argument – indicate that it was not written after A.D. 70. On the other hand, the statement that salvation was 'declared at first by the Lord and was attested to us by those who heard him' (2.3) points to the sub-apostolic age, presumably not much before the year 60, though possibly earlier.

It is hard to tell whether or not the address 'to Hebrews' is original. If it were original, one might expect to find Hebrews mentioned in the book itself; but such is not the case. On the other hand, the symbolical meaning which E. Käsemann finds in the word is certainly appropriate to the author's message. In the Septuagint version of Genesis 14.13 and I Samuel 13.7 'Hebrews' is rendered as 'wanderers'; Philo gives the same explanation of the word. The document is addressed to 'the wandering people of God', those with whom the author includes himself as having here no lasting city but seeking one which is to come (13.14). This point remains valid whether the author provided the title or some acute early reader added it.

The doctrine set forth in the epistle is not elementary, as the author points out (6.1–2); indeed, it is 'hard to understand' (5.11), for in it various kinds of motifs are combined. Jesus' superiority to the angels is proved by reference to, and reinterpretation of, various Old Testament passages. Moses did not bring the people of Israel into God's 'rest'; even Joshua did not bring them into it, for David, writing at a later time, warns them against hardening their hearts 'today'. Only Jesus can provide the true 'rest', and he did so through his own obedience to God; because of this obedience he was 'named by God a high priest after the order of Melchizedek' (Ps. 110.4). Melchizedek was a priest who had no genealogy (Gen. 14.18) and therefore was an appropriate proto-type of the eternal high priest, Jesus, who 'sat down at the right hand of the Majesty in the heavens' (Ps. 110.1), and is the mediator of a new covenant. The old covenant required annual sacrifices in the Holy of Holies offered by the high priest alone; the new covenant is mediated by the heavenly high priest who offered himself once for all and entered into heaven. He is the author and perfecter of the faith of Christians, the faith which they share with the heroes of the Old Testament, for 'Jesus Christ is the same yesterday and today and for ever'.

This argument can be put even more briefly: the new people of God is on pilgrimage towards a new promised land, but their goal is not an earthly one; they are not moving towards an earthly city with an earthly temple and its sacrifices, but towards a heavenly abode into which Jesus, after offering himself once for all, has entered already.

For what audience is such a document especially appropriate? Surely the first readers of Hebrews must have been deeply concerned with cultic matters and with the relation of Jesus to them. Certainly the author was so concerned, and like Stephen (Acts 7) and the Johannine writings (John 2.19–21; 4.21; Rev. 21.22) he rejected the permanent importance of the temple and its rites. We may be tempted to suppose that the author and his readers may have been related to the priests who, according to Acts 6.7, became converts to Christianity. But the kind of 'spiritualization' of the Old Testament found in Hebrews is closer to Philo than to Jerusalem or to Qumran, and the document can probably best be explained in relation to Alexandrian Jewish Christians who took a great interest in the cosmic meaning of the temple cultus and found this meaning finally expressed in Jesus. They regarded basic Christian doctrines as elementary (among them, teaching about repentance and faith, baptisms and laying on of hands, the resurrection of the dead and eternal judgement, 6.1–2) as compared with the priesthood of Jesus.

THE EPISTLE OF JAMES

This little homily or collection of homilies, in the form of a letter, is addressed by 'James, slave of God and of the Lord Jesus Christ' to 'the twelve tribes which are in the Dispersion'. It thus reflects the Jewish Christianity, centred in Jerusalem, which from later writings we know was deeply concerned with the memory of

James. According to Paul (Gal. 1.19) he was 'the Lord's brother' and was one of the leaders of the Jerusalem church (cf. 2.9, 12); the same impression is given by the book of Acts (15.13–21; 21.18, etc.). According to Jerome, the Gospel according to the Hebrews explained his apostolate by reporting a resurrection-appearance to him (cf. I Cor. 15.6). He is mentioned in the Gospel of Thomas (saying 12) as the one who will rule the disciples after Jesus goes away; for his sake heaven and earth were created.

In view of the prominence of James it is rather surprising that the epistle is used by no Christian writer before Origen, writing at Alexandria early in the third century. No Western writer mentioned it until the fourth century, and at that time it was still rejected by some Syrian churchmen. Both Erasmus and Luther, for different reasons, doubted its apostolic authorship. Today such doubts persist. How could James, the Lord's brother, write such good, rather literary Greek? How could he write without mentioning the name of Jesus more than once in his preface and once (2.1) in the course of his book? The only way to answer such questions is by analysing the treatise itself.

The form of address clearly suggests that we are confronted with a kind of Jewish Christianity, but with one which speaks not only to itself but to its members scattered abroad (cf. I Peter 1.1, 'to the elect who sojourn in the Dispersion'). The notion of twelve tribes is not surprising in view of Jewish Christian ideas expressed in the description of twelve tribes in Revelation 7.4–8 and the mention of them in Matt. 19.28 (Luke 22.30). But the tribes have no relation to the contents of various parts of the letter.

The style of James is marked by a correct, rather simple Greek in which there are practically no Hebraisms. The author employs the Greek Old Testament. He is so much at home in Greek that he can provide plays on Greek words ('*apeirastos*'–'*peirazei*', 1.13; '*aneleos*'–'*eleos*', 2.13) and can indulge in alliteration ('*peirasmois peripesēte poikilois*', 1.3) and in rhyme (1.6, 14; 4.8). These features do not suggest that he was a master of style; they do show that he probably knew Greek well. His vocabulary is close to that employed by Philo and Josephus and in the Greek version of the Testaments of the Twelve Patriarchs. It consists of 560 words, out of a total of 1,740.

Structurally, most of the letter does not hold together. The longest sections which possess any continuity are discourses in Hellenistic diatribe-form. These are on 'respect of persons' (2.1–13), on the necessity of works with faith (2.14–26), on the necessity for teachers and others to bridle their tongues (3.1–18; 4.11–12), and on strife as originating from within (4.1–10). In addition, there are prophetic denunciations of merchants (4.13–17) and of the rich (5.1–6). The beginning (1.2–27) and the ending (5.7–20) of the letter contain rather miscellaneous moral counsels, partly (1.2–8) arranged by verbal association. It should not be supposed, however, that differences in form correspond to differences in thought. Much of what 'James' has to say resembles the teaching of Jesus, especially as compiled in the Sermon on the Mount, and this kind of material is to be found throughout.

James 1.5	Matt. 7.7 (Luke 11.9)
2.5	Luke 6.20 (Matt. 5.3)
3.18	Matt. 5.9
4.4	Matt. 12.39, 16.4
5.1–6	Luke 6.24
5.12	Matt. 5.34–7

The atmosphere of James is close to that of the Old Testament wisdom-literature, and the Hellenistic aspects of the letter are essentially due to the effort to express this atmosphere in good rhetorical language; they are not necessarily based on 'popular philosophy'.

Now if the author was acquainted with rhetoric, as his examples suggest (e.g., in 3.3–6), we must assume that he was capable of providing his work with an arrangement better than the one it possesses. Therefore we probably do not possess it in the form in which he intended it to be. The 'letter' may well consist of a collection of materials which go back to the early days of the Jerusalem church.

The purpose of these materials was severely practical. The author was not interested in speculation or even in such a theological effort as Paul's (as his insistence upon works in 2.14–26 shows – as well as his 'definition' of piety in 1.27). One must not 'judge' the law (4.11); one must do what it says. Yet, for all his

Jewish piety, the author is obviously a Christian. There is a 'royal law': love of neighbour (2.8) – just as Paul insisted (Gal. 5.14; Rom. 13.8–10). And this law is not simply law in the old Jewish sense; it is also the 'law of liberty' (1.25; 2.12).

What we find in James is a representation of primitive Palestinian Christianity (set forth, to be sure, in Greek dress) – a kind of piety which has its roots in the early church of Jerusalem and continued to exist even after the fall of Jerusalem. Not all Jewish Christians became, or came to be regarded as, Ebionites; and there is nothing specifically Ebionite about James. It is true that this letter shows no awareness of the fall of the temple or, for that matter, of such theological developments as those we encounter in John. These omissions do not show whether the letter is early or late.

The fact that it was almost certainly written in Greek proves nothing about its date. Apparently there were Greek-speaking Christians in the Jerusalem church at an early date. Greek literature was studied by Jews in Jerusalem during the first century, even though we cannot be certain that the Hellenists of Acts 6.1 were Greek-speaking Jews. At least by the year 47 James himself was concerned with problems arising out of gentile Christianity. Perhaps he did not possess the rhetorical training implied in parts of this letter; but rulers of churches have been known to use the services of secretaries, or even of ghost writers. The form may come from assistants; there is nothing in the basic attitude which could not come from James.

We conclude, therefore, that the letter is not a letter but a collection of fragments which accurately reflect the Jewish Christian tradition of Jerusalem in the days before the destruction of the temple, and after it as well. It was ascribed to James because he was the ruler of the Jerusalem church and, perhaps, because some of the materials in it were actually derived from him. According to Josephus (*Ant.* 20, 197–203) he was put to death in the year 62. From Paul's letters we know that the expression of the mission to the gentiles was gradually developed; cannot a similar development have taken place at Jerusalem?

What, then, do we learn of the early church in Jerusalem from this little book? We learn that its members lived in expectation of the coming of the Lord, which was close at hand (5.7, 8); the

Lord's coming would presumably inaugurate the kingdom of God, promised to those who, though poor in the world, were rich in faith and loved God (2.5). Indeed, the Christian is already regenerate: 'of his own will he brought us forth by the word of truth that we should be a kind of first fruits of his creatures' (1.18). As in most early Christian writings, the 'indicative' is accompanied by the 'imperative'. James contains a great many moral maxims, though it must be remembered that he has a doctrine of grace as well: God 'yearns jealously over the spirit which he has made to dwell in us' (4.5, from some apocryphal tradition). The meeting place of Christians is called a 'synagogue' (2.2), but the community, governed by presbyters, is a 'church' (5.14). The only rite which James mentions is that of praying over the sick and anointing them with oil; presumably it is also in services of worship that Christians confess their sins to one another and pray for one another (5.14–16).

The community is one which has heard of Paul's preaching of faith as contrasted with works, and doubtless it has learned that Paul appealed to Genesis 15.6, the example of Abraham (2.23; cf. Gal. 3.6; Rom. 4.3). Without rejecting the idea that Abraham was 'our father', James does denounce the implications which, as we learn from Paul's letters themselves, were sometimes drawn from the example. 'Faith apart from works is dead' (2.26). Paul would have expressed this point differently, but he would not have disagreed.

THE EPISTLES OF PETER AND JUDE

One of the most difficult problems in the Catholic Epistles is presented by the interrelations of the letters ascribed to Peter and Jude. The letter which we call I Peter is addressed by the apostle Peter to 'the elect sojourners of the Dispersion in Pontus, Galatia, Cappadocia, Asia and Bithynia' (1.1). Peter writes 'through Silvanus the faithful brother' and sends greetings from 'the elect community in Babylon and Mark my son' (5.12–13). In its present form, then, the letter is an encyclical sent from the Roman church – for 'Babylon' is a common Jewish-Christian designation for Rome – to a group of churches in northern Asia Minor. II Peter definitely styles itself the second letter of Peter

(3.1), but apart from this designation it has practically nothing in common with I Peter and has no particular recipients in view. In this respect it resembles the little letter sent by 'Jude, slave of Jesus Christ and brother of James' to a general Christian audience. And the second chapter of II Peter consists of almost nothing but a slightly revised version of Jude. The author of II Peter thus is aware of the existence of I Peter but is not dependent upon it; he does not mention Jude but uses his work.

Before attempting to discover the situation in which II Peter was written we must consider the nature of the two earlier letters which he knew.

1. *I Peter*

The early existence of I Peter is attested not only by II Peter but also by Papias (according to Eusebius) and by clear allusions in the letters of Polycarp. Towards the end of the second century the letter was used by Theophilus, and it was definitely ascribed to Peter by Irenaeus. While it is not mentioned in the Muratorian list, the omission may be due to textual corruption, since there is no evidence which suggests that the letter's authenticity was questioned except in fourth-century Syria.

There is nothing especially remarkable about either the vocabulary or the style of I Peter. The proportion of vocabulary to words employed (545 to 1,670) is identical with that found in James (560 to 1,740, thirty-two per cent). The author is relatively fond of antithesis (2.14, 23; 3.18; 4.6; 5.2–3), but by no means as fond of it as Paul is. There is no stylistic reason to suppose that the document is composite.

The letter consists of three main divisions. (1) After an epistolary greeting, the author speaks of the new Exodus promised by the prophets (1.3–12) and of the need to progress in the fear of God and in the remembrance of redemption by the blood of Christ (1.13–21). This section has often been regarded as an exhortation to those who are about to be baptized, and it has been suggested that the act of baptism took place at the end of it. (2) There follows a welcome into the redeemed community, with a mention of rebirth (1.22–5); then we hear of baptism, eucharist, sanctification, and priesthood. The initiates are now living stones of a spiritual house; they are a royal priesthood and a holy nation (2.1–10). They are then reminded of the duties of Christian discipleship (2.11–4.11). They learn of life in the various vocations to which they have been called (2.11 – 3.12), and they learn that in all of them they are to suffer in Christ and after his example (3.13–4.6; note the reference to baptism in 3.21). This section ends with a reminder that the last day is at hand; because of this the community must practise mutual love. A doxology follows (4.7–11). (3) The final section consists of various exhortations perhaps expressed in the community's service of worship. Christians are to rejoice in sharing Christ's sufferings (4.12–19); elders-shepherds are to govern the community well, and younger men are to obey them (5.1–5); all are to be humble and sober and watchful, resisting the devil (5.6–10). A doxology follows (5.11), and the treatise ends with an epistolary conclusion (5.12–14); the kiss of love is mentioned here).

Obviously in its present form this is a letter. What kind of materials were used in creating it? The exhortatory sections can evidently be classified as catechetical in nature, and the situation envisaged in the work as a whole seems to be related to baptism, whether or not we accept the hypothesis that baptism takes place between 1.21 and 1.22. Some scholars have gone on to argue that because of the Exodus motifs and because of the emphasis on Christ's sufferings the letter contains a 'paschal liturgy'. In order to prove this point they claim that the fanciful etymology later used for the word '*Pascha*' ('Passover'), which related it to suffering (*paschein*) was already employed by Christians at this time. Certainly Paul refers to Christ as 'our *Pascha*' (I Cor. 5.7), but it is difficult to prove that I Peter knows an etymological theory which we otherwise find only at the end of the second century.

I Peter, then, consists primarily of a homily used in the Roman church in the first century. There are some affinities with Paul's letter to the Romans, but they consist of materials which can be regarded as based on common catechetical ideas. In any event, Romans was known at Rome in Peter's lifetime. There are also affinities with the sermons which in Acts are ascribed to Peter, and as a whole I Peter does not share doctrines which can be regarded as specifically Pauline.

Several objections have been raised to the notion that Peter himself wrote this letter. (1) The Greek style, superior to that of much of the New Testament, suggests that it was not written by Peter, as does the fact that the Old Testament quotations are derived from the Septuagint. On the other hand, the letter presents itself as written through a scribe who had already participated in the writing of I and II Thessalonians. (2) The letter may be composite: (*a*) in the third chapter sufferings are regarded as future (or contingent), while in 5.8 they are present; (*b*) in 2.14 only evildoers are punished, while in 4.14–15 Christians as such are punished. But the possibility that the letter is composite proves nothing about authorship. (3) According to 4.15 it appears that Christians can be punished by the state simply for the 'name'. But from the letter of Pliny, the Roman governor of Bithynia and Pontus (both mentioned in I Peter 1.1), to the emperor Trajan in the year 112 we learn that Pliny was in doubt as to whether punishment should be simply for the name or not. Therefore punishment for the name was first imposed in Asia Minor in the year 112, and I Peter was not written before this date. This objection neglects the extent of (*a*) our ignorance about Roman procedure in the period before 112, and (*b*) Pliny's ignorance about earlier precedents. He writes the emperor because he has not attended earlier investigations of Christians, not because no investigations had taken place. We conclude that, while it is possible that I Peter 4.12–5.14 may have been added at a later date, it is equally possible that it comes from a time of persecution which could well be around the year 64. We do not know that the Neronian persecution extended beyond Rome itself. The Roman Church, or the apostle Peter, may well have supposed that it would do so.

2. Jude

The existence of the little letter of Jude is attested by its use in II Peter, but while it may have been known to Polycarp early in the second century the first mention of it occurs in the Muratorian fragment. Clement of Alexandria certainly regarded it as scripture and wrote exegetical notes on it; Origen too viewed it as scripture, though he once expressed doubt about its universal acceptance. Tertullian claimed that the book of Enoch was inspired because of Jude's testimony to it. As late as the fourth century, however, Eusebius placed Jude among the 'antilegomena'.

It is to be found among the Bodmer papyri, but in a strange anthology (early third century) which consisted of the apocryphal correspondence of Paul with the Corinthians, the (11th) Ode of Solomon, Jude itself, and the two epistles ascribed to Peter. Perhaps the anthologist did not regard it as fully canonical – or else his canon was unusually large.

Jude contains 456 words and employs a vocabulary of 227 words, fifteen unique in the New Testament (three more are shared only with II Peter). Most of these 'unique' words occur in Hellenistic literature but not in the Septuagint; this fact suggests that the writer was fairly well at home in the Greek language of his time, though his style is certainly not literary. His familiarity with apocalyptic literature (reference to the Assumption of Moses in verse 9, to I Enoch in verses 14–15) explains his repeated use of the expression 'these' (8, 10, 12, 16, 19). He is fond of groups of threes, beginning with 'mercy, peace, and love' in verse 2 and continuing throughout the letter. He also likes dramatic effects and seems to strive for them (6, 12–13), once in such a way as to produce obscurity (23).

It is a brief treatise of exhortation, contending for 'the faith once for all delivered to the saints' against those who 'defile the flesh, reject the Lordship [of Christ], and blaspheme the Majesty [of God]'. These persons 'transpose the grace of our God into immorality'; apparently they lay claim to some special kind of knowledge (10), and they may claim to be 'spirituals' (19). They participate in Christian love-feasts but defile them (12). Jude compares them with the great sinners of the Old Testament and recalls that though 'God Christ' (the reading of the Bodmer papyrus) saved the people from Egypt – thus he treats the Exodus as a prefiguration of Christian salvation – he destroyed those who did not believe (5; cf. I Cor. 10.1–11).

The apostles already predicted that such persons would arise in the last times (17–18). Therefore Christians must build themselves up in their 'most holy faith'; as for the others, Christians are to condemn some, save some by snatching them out of fire, and hate their garment stained by the flesh (20–3). Jude thus contends for

orthodoxy in opposition to some kind of proto-Gnosticism not
unlike that of the later Cainites, described by Irenaeus. As he
opposes them he apparently uses some of their terminology: he
speaks of them as 'psychics, not possessing [the] Spirit' (19), and
the 'garment stained by the flesh' is apparently the spiritual
garment they claimed to wear.

In the course of his letter he explicitly refers to I Enoch as
prophecy (14) and also makes use of the apocryphal Assumption
of Moses (9). This usage may suggest that the book is Palestinian
in origin, but we know that these books were used by Jewish
Christians elsewhere, for example in Egypt. It may also indicate
an early date when apocryphal books were freely employed, but
again we know that writers in the second and third centuries were
often not averse to using them.

The author does not claim to be an apostle but identifies himself
as Jude, the brother of James. He is not likely to have been an
apostle, since he refers to early prophecies by the apostles as now
having been fulfilled (17–19). It is also unlikely, in spite of the
assertions of Tertullian and Origen, that he is to be identified with
the 'Judas of James' listed as an apostle in Luke 6.16 and Acts
1.13, since 'of James' probably means 'son of James'. In John
14.22 we hear of a 'Judas, not Iscariot', but the only clearly
identifiable Judas who is brother of James is the Lord's brother
mentioned in Mark 6.3 (Matt. 13.55). Since James became a
convert after the resurrection, it is not impossible that Jude was
also converted (cf. I Cor. 9.5), though no reliable evidence relates
him to the church of Jerusalem.

Because of the lack of early attestation and the post-apostolic
situation, we should be inclined to view this letter as written
towards the end of the first century or even later. Perhaps it was
intended to accompany the letter of James and to warn Greek-
speaking Jewish Christians against novel heresies.

3. *II Peter*

The second epistle of Peter is very poorly attested by early
Christian writers. No one earlier than Origen seems to have
made use of it, and he expressed doubts about its acceptability.
(Eusebius placed it among the 'antilegomena' and said that

according to tradition – that of the Church in the East – it was not canonical.) Didymus of Alexandria (d. 399) wrote that it was a forgery (PG 39, 1774A).

On the other hand, it is to be found among the Bodmer papyri in a little book of the early third century which originally contained both I and II Peter, and in later times it was accepted by all who accepted the Catholic Epistles as a group.

II Peter contains a total of 1,100 words and uses a vocabulary of 400 words, fifty-six of which are unique as far as the New Testament is concerned, while several are very rarely employed by Hellenistic or Graeco-Roman writers. A certain relation between I Peter and II Peter is suggested by the following combinations of words which occur in both: 'grace and peace be multiplied to you' (1, 1.2; 2, 1.2), 'licentiousness, passions' (1, 4.3; cf. 'licentious passions', 2, 2.18), 'without blemish or spot' (1, 1.19, reversed in 2, 3.14), and 'ceased from sin' (1, 4.1; contrast 2, 2.14, 'insatiable for sin' – similar Greek words). But the two epistles cannot come from the same writer. Of the 545 different words in I Peter, 369 do not occur in II Peter, and of the 400 different words in II Peter, 230 are not found in I Peter.

The style of II Peter represents a striving for effect more pronounced than that of I Peter. The author tries to write the periodic sentences characteristic of good Greek, but the result is a combination of obscurity and vagueness. In part, this vagueness is clearly intentional. The author uses the letter of Jude as the foundation of his second chapter, but while Jude regarded I Enoch as scripture, II Peter does not share his view and therefore rewrites the sentence in which Enoch was quoted; similarly he makes obscure the allusion to the Assumption of Moses. We know that II Peter was concerned with the interpretation and the meaning of scripture, for he stated that some persons 'twist' the letters of Paul 'like the rest of the scriptures' (3.16). He may have known written gospels, for his account of the Transfiguration is close to Matthew 17.5 and the prediction of Peter's death may come from John 21.18–19; the parallels, however, do not prove that he was not using oral tradition.

Since he incorporated Jude in his letter and revised it, he clearly did not regard it as scripture.

The letter consists of three parts which correspond to the three chapters into which it is now divided. (1) 'Symeon Peter' wishes to give a farewell discourse to his readers everywhere. What he says is confirmed by his vision of the Lord's greatness, apparently at the time of the Transfiguration. The voice from heaven confirmed the apostles' interpretation of the inspired prophets. Just as prophecy was given by God, so the interpretation of prophetic scriptures is not a matter for private judgement. (2) But as there were false prophets in Israel, so there will be false teachers among you – and here 'Peter' takes over the epistle of Jude in order to describe these teachers and their doctrines. (3) 'This is my second letter to you, to remind you of the words previously spoken by the holy prophets and of the commandment of the Lord and Saviour through your apostles.' The false teachers ask, 'Where is the promise of his coming?' They say that 'since the fathers died everything has remained as it was from the beginning of the creation'. Such persons neglect (a) the fact that there has already been one deluge, and (b) the Old Testament statement that with God 'a thousand years is as a day' (Ps. 90.4); the author states that the converse is also true: 'a day is as a thousand years.' The Lord is patiently awaiting universal repentance, but the day will come like a thief and with fire. Paul too (apparently in I Timothy 1.16) spoke of the 'long-suffering' of the Lord as salvation, though heretics distort his letters like the rest of the scriptures. Therefore avoid error and grow in grace and the knowledge of our Lord and Saviour Jesus Christ.

The lateness of II Peter is evident from several features. (1) No specific group of readers is addressed (1.1), but it is stated that 'this is now the second letter that I have written to you' (3.1). This means that I Peter, written to 'the exiles of the dispersion' in Asia Minor, has now come to be regarded as a general epistle. (2) Similarly the Pauline epistles are treated as general, not specific ('Paul wrote to you,' 3.15), and they are viewed as scripture (3.16). This situation reflects the beginning of the second century or the end of the first.

Is it not only late but also corrupt? Käsemann, for example, claims that it should be excluded from the canon because in it orthodoxy, based on a fictitious Peter, has replaced faith. As in Jude, faith has become adherence to orthodox tradition. The orthodox will enter God's eternal kingdom, while the godless will be destroyed in fire; Christianity is regarded as 'participation in the divine nature' (1.4), and thus (bad) Greek terminology has replaced (good) Hebrew.

This description of II Peter is slightly exaggerated and it does no justice to the historical situation of the Church. On the other hand, it may be admitted that, in part because of this historical situation, II Peter may seem rather less meaningful today than other parts of the New Testament.

THE JOHANNINE EPISTLES

The group of letters traditionally ascribed to John, the author of the Fourth Gospel, contain no mention of their author, except that II and III John are written by someone who calls himself 'the elder'. The first attestation of their authorship is to be found in the writings of Irenaeus, who says that II John was written by 'John the Lord's disciple' (*Adv. haer.* 1, 16, 3) and refers to I and II John as one letter (3, 16, 8).[1] The Muratorian fragment mentions two letters by John, though it is uncertain whether this means I-II John or I/II-III John.

The vocabulary of these epistles is remarkably small. They contain a total of 2,600 words, with a vocabulary of only 302 (11.6 per cent); in this regard, as in the choice of words involved, they closely resemble the Gospel of John (6.5 per cent). Since the third century, at least, it has been recognized that the vocabulary and style of the Gospel and of I John are very closely related, though it is possible, as C. H. Dodd has tried to prove, that the author of I John was a disciple of the evangelist. Because the differences are so slight it seems likely that, as in the case of Ephesians, they should be disregarded.

1. *I John*

From early times the first epistle of John has been well attested

---

[1] This point does not really show that Irenaeus regarded I and II John as one letter; see the sections on the Thessalonian and Corinthian letters.

and almost universally accepted. It was known to Papias, according to Eusebius, and Polycarp too seems to have known it. Irenaeus was the first to state that it was written by the author of the Fourth Gospel, though the resemblances in vocabulary and style are obvious. The main point of the letter is expressed in 3.23: 'and this is his commandment, that we should believe in the name of his Son Jesus Christ, and love one another, as he gave us commandment.' The author is deeply concerned with 'false prophets' (4.1) or 'antichrists' (2.18), who have led nominal Christians out of the Church (2.19). They deny that Jesus is the Christ (2.22); they do not acknowledge that Jesus Christ has come in the flesh (4.2–3); they say that they have no sin (1.8); they say that they know God (2.4). Against them the author insists on love within the community and on the gift of 'chrism from the Holy One' (2.20). He emphasizes that Jesus Christ really came among men 'not by water only but by water and blood' (5.6).

Before we can try to discover who the author's opponents were we must ask whether the document is simple or composite. It has often been noticed that I John is not carefully articulated. There are disconnected thoughts, exhortations, and warnings. Little groups of unrelated maxims are inserted between longer sections. Ideas are frequently repeated in new forms but without any logical development. Because of these features of the letter, scholars have sought to disentangle an original document from a kind of meditation or commentary based upon it. The commentary is to be identified by its use of such expressions as 'we write these things to you' or 'if you know' or 'by this we know'. By means of such an analysis a hypothetical original document has been discovered in I John 1.1–3, 5–10; 2.4–6, 9–11, 15–20, 22–5, 28; 3.11–15, 17–18; 4.1–8, 11–14, 16–5.1; 5.4–10, 12. The rest consists of meditation or commentary.

Unfortunately this analysis is hard to confirm, since it has to be admitted that the style and vocabulary of both the original document and what has been added is the same. It is more profitable to hold that for the purposes of logical analysis the 'original' ideas are the key ones, but that the author was unable or unwilling to write a letter which could be outlined. Logical analysis does not produce results which are directly convertible into the presumed sources of a document.

To identify the author's opponents precisely is a difficult task, but we have a potential candidate in a certain Menander of Antioch, a Gnostic teacher at Antioch towards the end of the first century. He held that he himself was the Saviour or Christ, and that his own special rite of baptism resulted in immediate and permanent immortality. It may be that the author of I John has such teaching in mind when he insists that Jesus is the Christ and came not by the water (of baptism?) alone but by blood (death?) as well. Followers of Menander may well have held that they had no sin and that they knew God.

Some of the author's own expressions have Gnostic parallels. Thus his statement that 'God is light' (1.5) goes beyond the Old Testament or Jewish apocalyptic literature in the direction of Philo and the Hermetic writings. His emphasis on unction with chrism (2.26–7) reminds us of the Naassenes, who held that 'we alone of all men are Christians, who complete the mystery at the third gate and are anointed there with speechless chrism' (Hippolytus, Ref. 5, 9, 22). And the mention of a spiritual 'seed' (3.9) recalls similar Naassene and Valentinian doctrines. At the same time, he is no Gnostic. When he tells us that 'God is love' (4.8, 16) he is speaking of the act of God in sending his Son into the world (John 3.16); he is not providing a definition of God. His use of terminology also found among Gnostics suggests either that he is Christianizing their vocabulary or that both he and they are drawing on a common stock of expressions.

(For a textual problem in I John see p. 47.)

2. II-III John

The situation envisaged in these two little letters is much the same and while we cannot be sure that they were addressed to members of one church at one time, it is at least possible that such was the case. In the first of them 'the elder' or 'the presbyter' addresses an individual community ('the elect lady') and its members, some of whom 'follow the truth', and urges them to love one another by following the commandments of the Father and by acknowledging the coming of Jesus Christ in the flesh. Those who visit the community and do not bring this doctrine are not to be admitted. If the other letter is related to the same situation, it would appear that a certain Diotrephes, 'who likes to put himself first', has refused to allow the first letter to be read in the church, has attacked the author's authority, and has rejected itinerant brothers who have come from him. The letter is addressed to a certain Gaius, who has apparently accepted these brothers; the elder informs Gaius that in this dissension-torn community there is another reliable Christian named Demetrius.

If the two letters belong together, we see an early Christian Church which is being disturbed by both Docetism (the denial that Jesus Christ came 'in the flesh') and the schism-producing jealousy. On the other hand, the circumstances may be different. If this is the case, there are heretics who try to infiltrate one church and power struggles which tear asunder another.

In either case, the elder is evidently someone who has authority in his own community and tries to exercise it in another. It may be that he is not an apostle, for Diotrephes evidently feels free to oppose him; but in view of the opposition faced by the apostle Paul it is impossible to say that apostolic authority was always unquestioned.

XV

THE BOOK OF REVELATION

The most enigmatic book in the New Testament is the book of Revelation, which consists of (1) a brief preface about the revelation which Jesus Christ gave through his angel to John, (2) letters to seven churches in Asia Minor describing aspects of a preliminary vision, (3) the revelation proper, and (4) an epilogue. This book had a tremendous influence on later Christian art and on the minds of Christians who were concerned with details about the future. To theologians, especially in the East, it was often embarrassing, especially since non-theologians tended to find chronology in it rather than symbolism. At an early date it was a favourite of those who expected the imminent coming of God's reign on earth; Papias (early second century) made use of it and supplied other traditions about future miraculous fertility from what (he said) had come from John the Lord's disciple. This point means that soon after the book was written it was ascribed to an apostolic Christian named John – presumably John the son of Zebedee. Such a view was accepted by Justin and Irenaeus in the later second century, although in the third century Dionysius, bishop of Alexandria, attempted to minimize the authority of the book by proving that since John son of Zebedee wrote the gospel ascribed to him, he cannot have written the book of Revelation, since the two writings employ different ideas, styles and vocabularies. His point seems to be well taken. The two books were not written by the same author. But from a perspective perhaps more historical than that of Dionysius we should incline to say that if either book is to be ascribed to the son of Zebedee it is the book of Revelation.

Sometimes it has been claimed that the son of Zebedee cannot have written it, because (1) Irenaeus tells us that the vision was

seen towards the end of the reign of Domitian (*Adv. haer.* 5, 30, 3
perhaps based on Papias) and (2) a late writer quotes Papias
as having said that the sons of Zebedee were put to death by Jews
Since, however, we have no means of telling whether or not John
was put to death at the same time as his brother James (Acts 12.4)
it cannot be proved that John did not live on until the last decade
of the first century. We may suspect that he did not write a book
but suspicions of this sort are not easily confirmed; moreover,
writing in antiquity as in modern times often involved the practice
of dictating.

We should therefore conclude that the book was written or
dictated by an early and significant John, perhaps the son of
Zebedee.

It is not, however, absolutely certain that it was written in the
reign of Domitian. Perhaps we should know more about the date
if we could understand the mystery concealed in the number
assigned the 'beast' in Revelation 13.18, the number 666 or, in
some manuscripts, 616. This number evidently is based on the
practice known as *gematria*, treating the letters in a word or
phrase as numbers and then adding them up. On a wall at
Pompeii someone scribbled, 'I love her whose number is 45' – but
we shall never know who she was. Thus various explanations of
the numbers in Revelation have been given. Irenaeus suggested
'teitan' (Titan) or 'lateinos' (Latin), which in Greek add up to
666. Later guesses have included (1) in Hebrew, '*gsqlgs qsr*'
(Gaius Caligula Caesar) for 616 and '*nron qsr*' (Neron Caesar)
for 666, or (2) in Greek, '*Gaios Kaisar*' for 616 and 'A KAI
ΔΟΜΕΤ ΣΕΒ ΓΕ' (abbreviations sometimes employed for the
emperor Domitian's name and titles) for 666. Of these the most
satisfactory seem to be the ones which refer to Caligula or Nero.
But if any weight be assigned to such guesses, the book of
Revelation, or at least that part of it in which the number occurs,
must go back to a time well before Domitian.

It may be that a reference to the ten diadems on the seven
heads of the beast (13.1) is related to the number of emperors;
by including Galba, Otho, and Vitellius we find Titus, Domitian's
predecessor, to be the tenth. On the other hand, we elsewhere
read (17.10–11) that five kings have fallen (Augustus-Nero), one is
(Galba), another has not yet come (Vitellius). In addition (?), ten

kings have not yet received the kingdom (17.12). There may also be a reference to the idea that Nero was not actually slain (13.3). All we can say is that a situation between 68 and 70 is not excluded.

Revelation contains 9,830 words, with a vocabulary of 916 words; of these, slightly more than a hundred are found nowhere else in the New Testament. Among the author's favourites are such words as the following (listed in Greek alphabetical order): angel, open, number, lamb, star, book, thunder, dragon (snake), seven, animal, beast, throne, horse, smoke, white, great, repent, temple, conquer, like, wear (clothing), blow ('plague'), gate, fire, blow (trumpet), mouth, seal, four, third, vial, voice, thousand, and gold – all of them characteristic of apocalyptic-symbolic writing. He is also fond of stereotyped expressions such as 'a great voice' (twenty times), 'the kings of the earth' (ten times), ' the Lord God, the Almighty' (nine times), the adjective 'true' ('*alēthinos*') with 'faithful', 'holy', or 'righteous' (nine times), 'tribe and language and people and nation' (six times; cf. Dan. 3.4), 'the word of God and the testimony of Jesus' (six times), 'wine of wrath' or 'fierce wine' (five times; cf. Jer. 25.15), and 'the small and the great' (plural, five times).

John's grammar is quite strange. He sometimes uses singular verbs with plural subjects, apparently because he views the subjects as units (8.7, 9.12). At one point he uses an adjective in the nominative case to modify a noun in the dative (1.15); at another, a nominative singular noun (with a collective meaning) is followed by a nominative plural participle, then by one in the accusative plural (7.9). Another feature which can be reproduced in English is the odd doubling of words with approximately the same meaning. (1) 'Behold, I gave before you an opened door, *which* no one can close *it*' (3.8). (2) 'And the woman fled to the desert, *where* she has a place *there*, prepared by God' (12.6).

It has sometimes been argued that these phenomena are due to translation from Hebrew into Greek. The Greek of Revelation contains many grammatical constructions which are normal in Hebrew but – to say the least – unusual in Greek. Ordinarily in Greek, nouns in apposition with other nouns agree with them in case (if accusative, accusative, etc.); not so in Revelation (1.5, 2.13; six other examples). When one writes, 'Grace and peace to you,' one does not continue, 'from he who is and was and is to come' (1.4). Furthermore, there are words which as they stand are practically unintelligible in Greek or to a Greek. 'These things says the Amen' (3.14); 'the "accusing" of our brethren was cast down' (12.10); 'the place called, in Hebrew, Harmagedon' (16.16). 'Abaddon', which means 'destruction', is explained as meaning 'the destroyer' (9.11). What do such passages show?

It is not altogether clear that they show that Revelation was translated from Hebrew into Greek. The expression 'the God Amen' is found in Symmachus's Greek version of Isaiah 65.16; someone like John, then, could have believed that it was adequate Greek among Greek-speaking Jews. 'Abaddon' is used of Sheol or the abyss in several Old Testament passages, and if personified (as sometimes in the New Testament) could be translated as 'the destroyer'. 'Harmagedon' is explicitly described as 'Hebrew', and it is an attempt to transliterate the Hebrew of Zechariah 12.11. As for 'the accusing' (a Greek word used in Hebrew by the rabbis), it points not to a work written in Hebrew but to a Greek work written by someone whose native tongue was probably, indeed almost certainly, Semitic.

We should conclude that as in other New Testament books any evidence which can be adduced to prove that they were written in Hebrew or Aramaic points just as clearly to their having been composed by someone who was imperfectly bilingual. If it be argued that certain passages contain mistranslations of hypothetical Semitic documents which are more comprehensible than the text we possess, it must be answered that we do not know that such documents existed and that exegesis of non-existent documents is hardly the task of the New Testament scholar.

John's style is characterized by pleonasm (unnecessary fullness of expression) both in smaller and in larger units of the book, and by asyndeton (lack of clear connection) in similar fashion. There are also abrupt changes and, indeed, contradictions within the book.

1.10–4.1 John is in the Spirit; 4.2 he is in the Spirit (again);
3.12 there is a temple in heaven; 21.22 there is no temple;
8.7 all the grass is burned; 9.4 the grass is not to be harmed;
16.1 angels are to pour vials on the earth; 16.8 one does so on the sun; 16.17 another does so on the air;
17.3 a woman is sitting on a scarlet beast; 17.15 on waters;

At the same time, he (1) carefully introduces sections which are
to come in his book; Revelation 1.12–20 prepares the reader for
the letters to the churches already mentioned in 1.11; chapters
4 and 5 lead up to chapter 6; and (2) on the other hand, introduces
various matters without explaining them until later (the 'morning
star' of 2.28 is not explained until 22.16; the 'seven thunders' of
10.3 are never explained).

All these features are characteristic of the writing of books of
revelation and do not require explaining by means of theories of
various sources or even of various documents. Above all, like other
apocalyptists, John uses symbols throughout his book and is
especially fond of the hidden significance of numbers. The most
striking example of a hidden meaning is provided by the beast-
worship of Revelation 13.8, to which the following verse refers
with the words, 'Whoever has an ear, let him hear.' The beast,
as we have seen, is given a secret number in Revelation 13.18.

Revelation begins with a brief statement about the nature of
the book: it is a revelation given by God to Christ and indicated
by an angel to God's servant John; and it concerns what is to take
place in the near future (1.1–3). Next come letters dictated by
Christ to John for seven churches in Asia Minor, beginning with
Ephesus and proceeding north through Smyrna to Pergamum,
thence south-east to Thyatira, Sardis, Philadelphia, and Laodicea
(1.4–3.22). They are constructed on a general pattern as follows:

> These things says he who . . .
> I know your works . . .
> But I have this against you . . .
> Repent . . .
> He who has an ear, let him hear what the Spirit
> says to the churches.
> To him who overcomes, to him will I give. . . .

The principal part of the book begins with a statement of what
must take place hereafter – a prophetic vision of perpetual
worship at the throne of God (4). Then John sees, in God's right
hand, a book sealed with seven seals; the opening of the seals, and
the consequent events, are described in 5.1–8.5 (chapter 7 deals
with another sealing, that of 144,000 men out of the twelve tribes
of Israel). After the last seal is opened, there is half an hour's

silence, followed by the sounding of seven trumpets by seven angels (8.6–11.19; chapter 10 is largely concerned with a 'little book' which an angel gives John to eat). The seventh trumpet sounds; then comes war in heaven (12–14; chapter 13 is devoted largely to the beast opposed to God). The war leads to the action of seven angels who pour out seven bowls of the wrath of God (15–16) and to the final destruction of 'Babylon', presumably Rome (17–18). The destruction of this city immediately precedes the final triumph of God (19.1–22.5), beginning with a thousand years' reign of Christ and his true followers (20.1–6), continuing with a brief rebellion by Satan (20.7–10), and concluding with the creation of a new heaven and earth and the descent of the new Jerusalem to be the bride of the Lamb. The book ends with an epilogue (22.6–21).

One of the most important features of the book, apart from the picture of the End which dominates it, is the author's use of hymn-like materials at various points. These hymn-like materials are presumably either identical with or based upon hymns actually used in the Christian worship of his time. Some of them are antiphonal (7.10, 12; 11.15, 17); others build up to powerful climaxes (4.8, 11; 5.9, 12, 13, 9.1–2, 5, 6–8). One is sung by a great voice in heaven (12.10–12). At one point those who have overcome the beast stand by a sea of glass and 'sing the song of Moses the servant of God (Deut. 32) and the song of the Lamb' (15.3–4). The content, and to a considerable extent the form, of these materials resembles the later Anaphora or eucharistic prayer of the Church, and the passages explicitly addressed to the Lamb have reminded scholars that Pliny the Younger, in his letter about the Christians, says that they were accustomed to address a hymn (*carmen*) to Christ. It is no accident that many of these passages were set to music by Handel and Brahms. They inspire such treatment

XVI

THE WRITINGS OF THE
APOSTOLIC FATHERS

In our discussion of the New Testament canon (Chapter 1) we observed that several books now included in it were not included by many Christians before the fourth century, and that some of the writings of the Apostolic Fathers were accepted as canonical, especially at Alexandria, at an earlier date. This fact implies that at least for completeness' sake we should say something about these writings when we deal with New Testament literature. Furthermore, it is likely that three of these writings are as early as many New Testament documents. These three are (1) the Didache, or Teaching of the Twelve Apostles, (2) the letter of Clement of Rome to the Corinthians (I Clement), and (3) the 'epistle' of Barnabas.

The Didache consists of several chapters of moral instruction, followed by a handbook of liturgical and ministerial guidance and concluded by a brief apocalypse. The moral instruction is based on Jewish models; as are the prayers set forth for use at the Eucharist. The church situation is one in which itinerant apostles and prophets are the leaders of the community, though they are being replaced by bishops and deacons. The Didache thus clearly reflects a form of Jewish Christianity, although the date of its composition is a matter of debate. Some (especially J.-P. Audet) have argued that it consists of two parts, of which one refers to the oral gospel, while the other refers to the written Gospel of Matthew; he dates both parts before the year 70. More commonly the document as a whole is placed twenty years later, though it is recognized that it reflects earlier traditions. A few scholars have set it at the end of the second century, viewing it as a pseudo-primitive (perhaps Montanist or anti-Montanist) work. Probably it comes from a time well within the first century.

The letter of Clement is a long treatise which deals with the necessity for humility and obedience to order and lawfully constituted authority. At Corinth there have been schismatic tendencies which have resulted in the deposition of some of the presbyters. Writing in the name of the Roman community, Clement not only uses Old Testament examples, and analogies both Pauline and Stoic, but speaks explicitly of the succession of presbyter-bishops which has come down from the apostles. His work is intended as a description and a defence of ecclesiastical discipline. It probably comes from the last decade of the first century.

The 'letter' of Barnabas is a treatise on the correct exegesis of the Old Testament, which must be understood not in reference to Jews but as pointing towards Christ and Christians. Historical allusions to the rebuilding of the temple may point to a period after 132, although they may indicate earlier events. Use of the Gospel of Matthew as 'scripture' suggests a time not before about 90.

Another work widely accepted as scriptural in early times is the *Shepherd* of Hermas, an allegory in apocalyptic form, containing five visions, twelve commandments, and ten 'parables'. The main occasion of the work is reflected in Hermas's insistence that in the near future one, and only one, more opportunity will be provided for post-baptismal repentance. The agent of revelation, sometimes an angel and sometimes the pre-existent Church, tells Hermas to transmit the content of the visions to two leaders of the Roman church (one named Clement) and to read it himself with 'the elders who preside over the church'. Most of the work suggests a date early in the second century, but the author of the Muratorian fragment (see page 39), in forbidding public reading of the book, states that Hermas wrote it while his brother Pius (mid-second century) was bishop of Rome. Perhaps the document was composed over a period of years.

Other writings of the Apostolic Fathers include the seven letters written about 115 by Ignatius, bishop of Antioch, on his way through Asia Minor to martyrdom at Rome, and the letter or letters of his contemporary Polycarp, bishop of Smyrna, to the Philippians. These documents, clearly related to their second-century circumstances, were apparently never regarded as scripture.

The continuing authority of some of these documents can be seen from the fact that the Codex Sinaiticus contains Barnabas and Hermas, while the Codex Alexandrinus contains the letter of Clement as well as part of a later homily known traditionally as II Clement. For Christian writers after Eusebius, however, it was generally evident that the writings of the Apostolic Fathers belonged to the documents of early church history, not to the New Testament canon. The Didache, out of date as the liturgy and ministry of the Church developed, was rewritten and assimilated into later, larger documents of the same kind (Didascalia, Apostolic Constitutions). The authentic letter of Clement was gradually driven out of circulation by later documents ascribed to him. The 'letter' of Barnabas lost favour because it was too obviously a forgery. Only Hermas continued to be popular, though not among theologians.

As a clear line was drawn between the New Testament and the Apostolic Fathers, the latter were often used as witnesses to early orthodoxy. Unfortunately, the letters of Ignatius gave support to the views of Monophysites and others like them; for this reason the genuine letters were generally supplanted by a new collection of letters interpolated and forged. This collection was soon utilized by the many theologians who found history uninteresting.

Historically, however, the authentic letters are highly significant for the light they shed on gentile Christianity at the beginning of the second century. They reflect the Church's growing concern for unity and doctrinal orthodoxy and, in the case of Ignatius, for the importance of the sacraments. Does this 'development' represent decline or advance? The answer to this question cannot be given on historical grounds but on the basis of a judgement as to the whole sweep of church history.

To a considerable extent the language and thought of Ignatius seems to have been influenced by the Fourth Evangelist, whose disciple (according to later legend) he was. On the other hand, Polycarp, whom tradition also called a disciple of John, betrays only the faintest trace of acquaintance with the Fourth Gospel. He is much closer to the Paul of the Pastoral Epistles; indeed, his (second) letter contains many parallels to the Pastorals. These show either that he knew them well (he is the first witness to their existence) or, as some scholars have speculated, that he himself wrote them. An alternative to this hypothesis would be that the same unknown author wrote both the Pastorals and the 'second' letter to the Philippians.[1]

The writings of the Apostolic Fathers thus reflect many of the difficulties which we have already encountered in dealing with New Testament books. Some ascriptions of authorship are clearly wrong, as in the case of II Clement and Barnabas and, probably, the Didache. Other writings contain interpolations or, at any rate, were circulated both in genuine versions and in versions containing additions. They come from various churches and reflect various points of view. They also come from various periods in the history of the Church. As far as ecclesiastical authority goes, the writings of Clement, Ignatius and Polycarp stand on a level higher than that of the other authors, though admittedly both the Didache and Barnabas were ascribed to apostles. The chief significance of all of them lies in their reflection of the life and thought of the Church in the period soon after the apostolic age.

If those scholars are right to conclude that in the writings of the Apostolic Fathers there are practically no reflections of the synoptic gospels, the Apostolic Fathers stand almost as close to the earliest traditions about Jesus as the synoptic evangelists do. This means that as authorities for his words, if not for his deeds, they are almost as valuable as the canonical writers. The question then arises whether or not historical proximity is as important as canonicity. To answer this question we should have to enter upon the difficult question of the relation of scripture to tradition. Would a saying of Jesus when reported by Clement be tradition, while the same saying found in Matthew or Luke would be scripture? We raise these questions only for the sake of discussion. An attempt to answer them lies beyond the scope of this book.

---

[1] By 'second' letter we mean Polycarp, Phil. 1–12, which almost certainly was written later than Phil. 13–14. This point is worked out by P. N. Harrison, *Polycarp's Two Epistles to the Philippians* (Cambridge, 1936) – a study of permanent value.

PART III

New Testament
History and Theology

CHRISTIAN BEGINNINGS

In the second part of our study, our intention was primarily literary. We endeavoured to examine the various New Testament books and to determine what literary analysis would tell us about them – although, almost inevitably, historical questions kept coming up. The third part will be devoted more specifically to these historical questions; we shall endeavour to find out what the New Testament books have to tell us about Christian origins and early Christian history.

There are, of course, two aspects to early Christian history. (1) The history can be viewed as an 'inner' history, the story of the movement as it was regarded by early Christians themselves, without much correlation with the history of the world outside or, in other words, with the environment (political, social, cultural, etc.). To a considerable extent this way of looking at it results in a 'sacred history' (*Heilsgeschichte*) and often involves little more than simply reading a document such as Luke-Acts. Again, we might take the passages in the Pauline epistles in which we hear about the life and work of Jesus and add to them the passages in which we hear of the life and work of the apostle Paul. This would give us something like Paul's view of the history of early Christianity. (2) The history can also be treated in relation to its background in (*a*) the Graeco-Roman world and, especially, in (*b*) the kinds of Judaism prevalent in Palestine and in the world outside Palestine. By examining this relation we can then create a picture of early Christianity partly *in* its environment and partly *against* its environment. Such an environmental study can be viewed as related to history in general, to the history of ideas, and to the history of religion.

Ideally the first aspect should be studied first, so that we have some idea of what early Christianity was 'in itself' before treating its relations with other phenomena. On the other hand, Christian origins seem to become historically more meaningful when they are treated in relation to their background, and we shall therefore say something about the Graeco-Roman world (Chapter xvii) and Palestine in Graeco-Roman times (Chapter xviii) before turning to the life of Jesus (Chapter xix) and the early Church (Chapter xx).

XVII

THE GRAECO-ROMAN WORLD

It is obvious that in dealing with the Graeco-Roman world at the time when Christianity came into existence our problem is not to obtain sufficient materials for study but to make some kind of selection from these materials. We can discuss only those matters which seem to possess fairly immediate relevance to Christian origins. We shall therefore limit our discussion to those aspects of Graeco-Roman life which bear directly, or almost directly, upon our subject.

THE ROMAN EMPIRE

With the civil wars and the murder of Julius Caesar in 44 B.C., the Roman republic came to an end, and his heir and successor Augustus became the architect of the Roman empire, reigning from 27 B.C. to A.D. 14. For peoples subject to, or allied with, the Roman state, this change in the form of government did not make a great deal of difference, except that in the early years of the empire the power struggles which accompanied the decline of the republic seemed to have come to an end, and tax-collection by private companies, often accompanied by extortion, was replaced by tax-collection by civil servants. Roman control over local affairs remained much the same. The provinces were administered by Roman governors or, in some cases, procurators, whose authority was based on the power of legionary and auxiliary troops. About twenty-four legions were stationed in various trouble spots mostly at the frontiers of the empire.

At the top of the social structure were the members of Roman senatorial families; below them came the equestrian order, followed by free men, freedmen, and slaves. This structure was relatively fluid, since membership in the two highest orders was based chiefly on property qualifications, and in our period many men became rich, partly through politics and partly through trade or ownership of real estate in a time when business was generally good and money was gradually becoming cheaper. Slaves were often able to buy their freedom; non-citizens could purchase Roman citizenship. This citizenship involved such rights as trial before Roman judges, not local ones, and appeal to the imperial court at Rome, as well as exemption from some local taxes. It is not clear how Roman citizenship could be proved; presumably something like a passport was necessary.

Within the empire, and even beyond its confines, a busy commercial life was going on. Trade was primarily responsible for the development of an elaborate network of well built roads and a system of shipping which made full use of the potentialities of the Mediterranean Sea. Bandits had been driven away from most of the overland routes, and piracy had practically been brought to an end. In other words, communications among the various parts of the empire were very good, and the papyrus letters found in Egypt suggest that even though there was no government postal service for private mail it was still possible to send letters without much difficulty.

The distribution of the wealth produced by trade and commerce was extremely uneven, and wage rates for common labourers were low, often a denarius or drachma a day. (Legionary soldiers received little more, but they had opportunities for other gains.) To some extent these low wages were due to the competition provided by slave labour; more significantly, free workmen were rarely organized, and the labour supply tended to exceed demand. The low wage level was balanced, to a considerable extent, by a low price level for necessities and by government subsidy and/or price control. Generally speaking, life for the lower and lowest classes was quite tolerable, especially in the absence of advertising and the invention of new products for mass consumption. The rich were very rich, but their position was often insecure because of demands made upon them by emperors and other officials. They did not have to cope with an income tax, graduated or otherwise, and the inheritance tax was very low (five per cent); at the same time, it was quite possible for them to lose everything by political misadventure.

RELIGION

The religions of the Graeco-Roman world were primarily, and traditionally, civic; this is to say that the gods were the gods who were recognized by the state – either the Roman state or the local city-state. The priesthoods were reserved, in most instances, for the more prominent citizens, and at Rome the emperor himself expressed his religious function in the rôle of *pontifex maximus*. For a considerable time a working relationship between Greek and Roman religion had been effected by means of an identification of Greek and Roman gods; Zeus was Jupiter, Hera Juno, etc. The same kind of identification was made between local gods and Greek gods; when Lycaonians hailed Barnabas as Zeus and Paul as Hermes (Acts 14.12), presumably they had their native deities at least partly in view. This tendency to amalgamate cults and gods was characteristic of the period; though to a considerable extent it was resisted by Jews, there were Jews who used the term 'God most high' in a way which was at least ambiguous. Papyri and inscriptions, along with literary documents, reveal the extent to which various gods and goddesses originally national acquired universality partly by being identified with others. A conspicuous example was the Egyptian goddess Isis.

The gods and goddesses of subject peoples were widely worshipped throughout the empire and often won adherents simply because they were not closely identified with the state. In many instances their worship was conducted by priests who wore vestments of native origin and perpetuated ritual actions of an exotic character. Their rites of initiation, to some extent modelled after the famous and generally acceptable Eleusinian mysteries, were well known, although it is by no means certain that many persons participated in them. The precise meaning of the rites is unclear, and we do not know that in the first century of our era they were regarded as conferring immortality or as involving dying and rising with the god involved. Preliminary purifications were required, and sometimes it was believed that initiation resulted in better moral character. In the rites of the great mother Cybele, legally forbidden to Roman citizens, the initiate castrated himself. Such sacrifices were uncommon.

Following the practice of some oriental and Hellenistic kingdoms, the Roman Senate, after the time of Julius Caesar, was accustomed to vote the deification (*consecratio*) of dead emperors who had served well, and it became a regular custom for some witness to swear that when the dead emperor's pyre was ablaze he had seen the emperor's soul wing heavenward. In the provinces post-mortem deification was sometimes anticipated by enthusiastic loyalists, but in the first century those emperors who during their lifetime claimed to be divine (Caligula, Nero, Domitian) were not so regarded when dead. The first example we possess of compulsory veneration of a living emperor is to be found in Pliny's investigation of the Christians (A.D. 112), and such a practice, not encouraged by Trajan, never became universal. It may, however, be referred to in Revelation 13.15. If so, it probably originated in Asia Minor, a centre of the imperial cult. Popular and provincial reverence for the emperor was usually more pronounced than the attitude at Rome.

EDUCATION

In the Graeco-Roman world considerable emphasis was laid on education, and at the beginning of our era the level of literacy was quite high. Most people could speak, read and write either Greek or Latin, and many could deal with both languages. The common language of the empire was Greek, as we learn from inscriptions and papyri, though in border lands native languages such as Celtic, Punic and Aramaic continued to be employed. A minority of cultivated men (and a few women) went on from grammar to rhetoric, to the 'encyclical studies' which included arithmetic, music and other 'liberal arts', and some ventured into philosophy.

In so far as philosophical theology was studied, it was regarded as a branch of either philosophy or rhetoric. Its relation to philosophy is obvious; not so obvious is the connection with rhetoric. But rhetorical training involved taking various 'theses' and either defending or opposing them, and one such thesis, commonly employed, was 'concerning providence'. A rhetorician's manual lists no fewer than seventeen arguments which could be provided in favour of providence, most of which assume

the existence of God or the gods and proceed to providence by
inference. One example argues for providence from the nature
of the universe.

> The nature of the universe testifies that in accordance with
> providence everything has taken place for the preservation
> of the things in the world: the times of the years receiving
> alteration according to the seasons, the rains and fruits taking
> place in the proper time, and the parts of the body also
> fashioned by nature for their preservation and safety – as
> Xenophon makes clear in his *Memorabilia* (1, 4, 5–8).

The resemblance of this argument to two sermons in Acts (14 and
17) is fairly plain, and it may not be unrelated to Paul's discussion
of the unity of the body in I Corinthians (12).

The doctrine implied and stated in this thesis was widespread
in the Graeco-Roman world, where poets, philosophers and
legislators were regarded, especially by Stoics, as setting forth a
consistent teaching. Only the Sceptics argued in favour of the
relativity of all human opinions, especially in matters of religion.

Combined with the common acceptance of belief in God or the
gods was a strong stress on moral teaching. The manifold variety
of doctrines which could be encountered in early Greek philosophy
and in the early Hellenistic age was abandoned (though to some
extent revived in Gnostic circles), and in its place came a fairly
uniform teaching, largely Stoic in origin, which laid emphasis on
the four virtues of justice, courage, sobriety and understanding,
and was addressed by preachers to individuals. The Stoics and
others compiled lists of virtues and vices; they used short
summaries of the duties of fathers to children and children to
fathers, husbands to wives and vice versa, and masters to slaves
and vice versa. They exhorted the individual to accept social
responsibility; true inner freedom was to be found through and in
this acceptance. In making these exhortations they developed what
is called the 'diatribe', a lively moral address delivered in semi-
conversational style.

Along with belief in the gods and the importance of social
ethics went a widespread faith in the life of the soul after death
and, often, in the celestial spheres. Denial of the innate
immortality of the soul was sometimes expressed (for example,

by Peripatetics), but such denials were unfashionable, especially since the *consecratio* of a dead emperor involved the belief that his soul had been carried into heaven.

As for the heaven or the heavens, the first-century naturalist Pliny expresses views already traditional when he tells us that the universe is spherical and constantly revolves about the earth, which is therefore spherical itself. The learned, therefore, are aware that on the other side of the globe there are men whose feet are opposite ours. The vulgar may ask why these men do not fall off, but in Pliny's view the nature of things keeps this from happening. Not everyone agreed with Pliny.

Between the earth – in the centre of the universe because day and night are equal at the equinox – and the heaven are the seven planets with their different cycles. In the absence of space travel the practical ancients could not see what purpose these planets served, and since it was an axiom of their thought that God or nature does nothing without purpose, the way was open for a widespread acceptance of the principles of astrology. Philosophers might argue for free will against fate, astrological or not, but many men followed the example of the Roman emperors and believed that the stars governed men's lives. Christian writers constantly insisted upon human freedom from astral determinism; indeed, when Paul lists those things which cannot separate us from the love of Christ some of his terms have astrological parallels (Rom. 8.39).

It is obvious that we have severely limited the extent of our discussion of the Graeco-Roman world and have only touched upon three aspects of its life: political-social, religious, and educational. The reason for this limitation has already been indicated in Chapter v. If our basic purpose is to understand the New Testament, some knowledge of its historical environment is essential (and the student will be well advised to add to the meagre materials we have supplied); the study of the environment does not, however, directly illuminate the New Testament writings themselves. For instance, it is important for an archaeologist to find traces of a meat-market in the Agora at Corinth. Such a discovery contributes nothing to our understanding of

I Corinthians 10.25, where such a market is mentioned. The precise nature of an 'appeal to Caesar' is interesting, since according to Acts 25.11 the apostle Paul made such an appeal. It could probably be assumed, however, without reference to the history of Roman law and administration, that such an appeal was made and that the practice was not unheard of.

The function of the study of the New Testament environment seems to be a double one. (1) By correlating the New Testament documents, and the events described within them, with Graeco-Roman records and events, we can see more clearly what in the New Testament was like, what unlike, the world in which the early Church arose. (2) By correlating New Testament studies with the work of modern historians, we associate two kinds of critical investigation and thus make some contribution, however minor it may be, towards holding together a culture seemingly on the verge of disintegration. A theological purpose is also involved. Since the early Church was facing, and at the same time being influenced by, the ancient world, it may be important to know something about what was involved then, in the hope that the situation then may cast some light on the situation now.

For this reason we now turn to the Jewish background of early Christianity.

XVIII

PALESTINE IN GRAECO-ROMAN TIMES

Palestine, situated at the eastern end of the Mediterranean, has always been a buffer area in relation to the powers to the north, the east and the south. After Alexander the Great (d. 323 B.C.) had tried to create a Graeco-Oriental empire, the generals who succeeded him and divided up his empire, and their successors, struggled for generations to control Palestine, since it lay south of the Asia Minor of the Antigonids, south and west of the Syria and Mesopotamia of the Seleucids, and north-east of the Egypt of the Ptolemies. Throughout the third and second centuries B.C., as the kings exhausted themselves and their peoples with incessant warfare, Palestine was a principal arena for their military operations. Only the rise of a new and greater power could have brought peace to the region. Such a power was Rome, and its interventions in the East produced significant changes in the life of Palestine.

A crisis in the second century B.C. was especially important. It began in 168 when the Seleucid king Antiochus Epiphanes was on his way to attack Egypt. Near Pelusium, by the Mediterranean on the Egyptian frontier, he was met by a Roman legate who in the name of the Senate ordered him to withdraw. The king asked for time to consider. 'Decide here', said the Roman, drawing a circle in the sand about him. Doubtless remembering that the Romans had 100,000 men in Asia Minor and Greece, the king withdrew. On his way back to Antioch he decided to make effective a plan which he had formulated for unifying his kingdom. For some time the leaders of the Jewish people had been advocating and implementing the cultural integration of their nation with the Graeco-Oriental monarchy. They had built a

Greek gymnasium in Jerusalem; they had worn Greek hats; and some of them had undergone an operation to efface the effect of their circumcision. The high priest and others had assumed Greek names (Jason, Menelaus) in addition to their ordinary Jewish ones.

These Jewish officials were startled, however, by the intensity with which the king planned to Hellenize. In the temple at Jerusalem another altar was placed over the altar of sacrifice, and on it a pig – unclean in Jewish eyes – was offered to the one god of Greek and Jew alike: Zeus. The response of the Jewish people was instantaneous. Led by a group of brothers known as the Maccabees (probably a nickname from the word for 'hammer'), the people revolted and, after a series of bloody battles, finally recaptured Jerusalem, where in 165 B.C. the temple was cleansed and rededicated. The festival of Hanukkah, observed on the 25th of Kislev (November–December) with the lighting of lamps, still celebrates the memory of this event. It is one of the five great feasts of the Jewish year (see p. 273).

Our information about Maccabean times comes to us from three important documents, in addition to the histories of Josephus and of Graeco-Roman writers.

MACCABEAN WRITINGS

The oldest of these writings is the Old Testament book of Daniel, an apocalypse intended to show that all empires are made to rise and fall by God; it also predicts the destruction of Antiochus Epiphanes. The author did not favour the active revolt of the Maccabees, for in his view God intervenes without human assistance.

He tells how the Persian empire was overcome by Alexander, how his kingdom was then divided among his successors, and how Antiochus Epiphanes persecuted the Jews (8.1–12, cf. 20–6). He predicts that the persecution will last 1,150 days, or nearly three and a half years (8.14) – the years from 168 to 165 B.C. Finally he goes on to predict that after conquering Egypt, Libya and Ethiopia the king will die in his camp between Jerusalem and the Mediterranean (11.40–5). After this event the general resurrection will come (12.1–3).

Since the king actually died early in 164 while fighting the Parthians to the north-east of Palestine, Daniel must have written in 165. The importance of the book lies not in its detailed predictions, which were clearly wrong, but in the theological ideas which it reflects and advocates. It sets forth the apocalyptic hope of Judaism, speaking of 'one like a son of man' who is to come on the clouds of heaven (7.13) and of the bodily resurrection of the dead. Like the prophetic writings it interprets history in relation to the activity of God. God's reign is everlasting, but at various times his intervention in history becomes more clearly manifest. Because of these emphases, and also because later situations seemed to resemble that in which Daniel wrote, his book was influential both among apocalyptic-minded Jews (e.g., Enoch and Sibylline Oracles 3, 388–400) and among many early Christians. It gave hope to those Jews who did not join the Maccabees (and perhaps to those who did) just as in the first Christian century II Esdras and the book of Revelation encouraged Jews and Christians to look for the fall of Rome. Very soon God would take power away from those who had it and would give it to his chosen people. This transfer would mark the inauguration or restoration of God's reign on earth.

Not all Jewish writers shared Daniel's apocalyptic enthusiasm, and in the first book of Maccabees we find a history (originally in Hebrew, now in Greek) written by a more politically-minded author. This writer did not discuss miracles; as far as we can tell, he did not look forward to the resurrection. He expresses his faith in God as the one who helps those who help themselves. His history, based on documents and personal reminiscences, describes events up to the accession of Hyrcanus, high priest in 135.

On the other hand, when a certain Jason of Cyrene wrote five books describing the events up to 161 (our II Maccabees is an abridgement of his work), he emphasized the transcendent power of God. God created the universe out of the non-existent (7.28) and he will bring about the resurrection of the dead (7; 12.43—4). Therefore we are not surprised to find his history full of miracles, even though he may hint that he has put these stories in so that readers will find his work attractive (15.39). In Jason's view the action of God anticipated in Daniel has been realized in Maccabean history.

These three works reflect (1) the significance of the Maccabean crisis and (2) the diversity of theological response to it. Not all Jews were enthusiastic about apocalypses; not all believed that God had intervened in various battles between Antiochus and the Maccabees. All agreed that God ultimately governs the course of events; they disagreed on specific details.

THE RISE OF SECTARIAN GROUPS

Because of the divergent attitudes present within Judaism, various parties or sects came into existence soon after the Maccabees assumed control of the state.

1. *Pharisees*

Much of our information about the Pharisees comes from Josephus, in whose narrative we first encounter them in relation to the reign of Queen Alexandria (*c*. 100 B.C.). If we try to go farther back, it is possible that we find forerunners of the Pharisees in the 'Chasidim', or 'pious', who in the time of Antiochus practised partial pacifism. They observed the Sabbath so scrupulously that they would not defend themselves on that day and were easily overcome by the king's troops. Some survivors were able to join the Maccabees and to reinterpret the Sabbath legislation (I Macc. 2.29–44). But as a party the Pharisees arose later. Their name was probably derived from a word meaning 'separate'. Josephus describes them as 'a party of Jews which seems to be more religious than the others and to explain the laws with more minute care' (*War* 1, 110). In another place he contrasts them with the conservative priestly group known as the Sadducees.

> The Pharisees handed down certain legislation to the people from the tradition of the fathers, legislation which has not been recorded in the laws of Moses; for this reason the party of the Sadducees rejects it, saying that what is written must be considered legislation, but that what comes from the tradition of the fathers need not be observed (*Antiq.* 13, 297).

Certain sociological implications can be drawn from other points which Josephus mentions. The Pharisees were rather urbane and friendly to strangers (*War* 2, 166); they were followed by the masses (*Antiq.* 13, 298); they insisted upon the value of tradition but interpreted the law more freely than the Sadducees did (18, 12). They believed in God's governing of human affairs and believed in life after death; the righteous would rise again, but the souls of the wicked would be punished eternally (18, 2–6). These points suggest that the Pharisees belonged to what we should call a kind of middle class, living chiefly in the cities. They recognized the necessity for making modifications in the law and they used tradition to provide precedents.

With their relatively liberal views, it is not surprising to find various schools existing within Pharisaism itself. For example, at the end of the first century B.C. we meet the famous rabbis Shammai and Hillel, the one representing a more conservative attitude, the other a more liberal view. Thus it was said that a gentile came to Shammai and said to him, 'You may accept me as a proselyte on the condition that you teach me the whole law while I stand on one foot.' Shammai drove him away with a measuring rod. Then he went to Hillel, who received him as a proselyte and said to him, 'What is hateful to you do not do to your fellow: that is the whole law; all the rest is its explanation; go and learn.' (The parallel with Jesus' 'great commandment' is obvious.) Again there was the question of the words to be used at a wedding when dancing before the bride. The school of Hillel said that the formula 'O bride, beautiful and gracious' should be used. The school of Shammai, more scrupulous, disagreed. 'If she is lame or blind, is one to say, "O bride, beautiful and gracious"? Does it not say in the Torah (Exod. 23.7), "Keep thee far from lying"?' The followers of Hillel answered with an analogy from human experience. 'Then, if someone makes a bad purchase in the market, is one to commend it or to run it down? Surely one should commend it.' The schools also disagreed over the question of the grounds for divorce. In Shammai's view the only ground was adultery; Hillel held that there were other grounds resembling the modern 'incompatibility'. Here the teaching of Jesus, as recorded in Matthew, at any rate, sides with Shammai against Hillel.

We should not exaggerate the importance of these divisions. Both Shammai and Hillel stood within the one congregation of Israel. As later tradition relates, 'Israel will be redeemed only when it forms one single band: when all are united, they will receive the presence of the Shekinah. Therefore Hillel said (*Aboth* 2, 5), "Separate not thyself from the community."' And both believed in the importance of the living oral tradition, though it would appear that Hillel had to learn to do so. Before a group of rabbis he once gave learned arguments for the precedence of the Passover over the Sabbath when Passover fell on a Sabbath day. His audience remained unimpressed until he said, 'Thus I heard it from Shemaiah and Abtalion,' his teachers. Then they recognized him as a true Pharisee.

As a group the Pharisees were concerned with modifying the stringencies of the old law so that it could be applied in modern circumstances. Indeed, it was a Pharisaic formula which Jesus expressed when he said that the Sabbath was made for man, not man for the Sabbath (Mark 2.27). We can see these modifications in the criticisms of Matthew 23.16. For instance, the Pharisees said, 'Whosoever shall swear by the temple, it is nothing; but whosoever shall swear by the gold of the temple, he is bound [by his oath].' The purpose of this distinction was to prevent casual oaths from being enforced. Only a deliberate, intentional oath, carefully formulated, was to have binding force. Again, the Pharisees tithed mint and anise and cummin (Matt. 23.23). Here the question involved is that of just what is to be tithed. Surely, if tithing is a matter of law rather than of personal inclination, it is necessary to know what is to be included as taxable. 'Tithe not much by estimation,' said Paul's teacher Gamaliel (*Aboth* 1, 17). In the Gospel of Matthew the Pharisees are criticized not for tithing but for concentrating upon it as the essence of religion. Concentration on minor points is a temptation to be found in every religion.

The Pharisees recognized the positive value of law, which deters men from wrong actions by prescribing penalties and brings them to acknowledge their shortcomings. 'I should never have known sin but for the law' (Rom. 7.7). Since, in their view, the law had been revealed by God, they had to obey its implications as well as its plain statements. They regarded the spirit as binding along with the letter. In order to work out the implications, they developed what we call rabbinic exegesis. G. F. Moore has described it thus:[1]

> To discover, elucidate, and apply what God . . . teaches and enjoins is the task of the scholar as interpreter of scripture. Together with the principle that in God's revelation no word is without significance this conception of scripture leads to an atomistic exegesis, which interprets sentences, clauses, phrases, and even single words, independently of the context of the historical occasion, as divine oracles; combines them with other similarly detached utterances; and makes large use of analogy of expressions, often by purely verbal association.

Moore's criticisms are valid as far as they go. What he himself seems to neglect is the necessity of legal exegesis rather than historical interpretation in dealing with a legal code; and the historical exegesis he admires was practically non-existent in antiquity.

It may be added that to attempt to understand the Pharisees by comparing them with other groups in later times is not an especially rewarding pursuit. Historical understanding must be based on direct contact, not on analogies. Simply to list some of the groups compared with them – Franciscans, New England Puritans, Pietists, Methodists, high churchmen in Anglicanism, and Democrats – is enough to suggest that, in spite of some resemblances, the comparisons add nothing.

2. Sadducees

We know much less about the Sadducees than about their rivals. Judaism became largely Pharisaic after the destruction of the temple in A.D. 70, and the traditions of the Sadducees were not preserved. From the way in which Josephus contrasts them with the Pharisees it is obvious that they represented a priestly aristocracy with rural ties. They were rich and conservative, and they insisted upon a rigid interpretation of the law. According to Josephus they believed that providence was not operative in human affairs, though his statement may mean no more than that they were successful politicians. They did not believe in life

[1] *Judaism* I (Cambridge, Mass., 1927), 319.

after death; according to the book of Acts (23.8) they held that 'there is no resurrection nor angel nor spirit'. If this statement is correct, it would appear that the Sadducees accepted as scripture only the Pentateuch, not the prophets or the other writings. According to Mark 12.18–27 they argued against the possibility of resurrection on the grounds provided by Deuteronomy 25.5–6. The law said that if a man died without offspring his brother was to take the widow and beget children so that the dead man's name might not 'be blotted out in Israel'. Suppose seven brothers in succession had the same wife, the Sadducees suggested; whose wife would she be if there were to be a resurrection?

3. *Essenes*

Before the Dead Sea Scrolls were found, we already knew something about an ascetic sect which flourished in Palestine before the Jewish War of 66–70. This was the sect of the Essenes, described by three ancient authors: the naturalist Pliny the Elder and the Jewish Hellenists Philo and Josephus. Their accounts have to be taken with a few grains of salt, since they were not members of the Essene community, and since they admired it and wanted to describe it in terms which would make their readers admire it too. Probably this explains why they insist that there was no marriage among the Essenes. Asceticism of this kind was popular in the Graeco-Roman world. But the rest of what they say corresponds rather closely with what we know about the Dead Sea community and its satellites.

First of all, Pliny tells us just where most of the Essenes were to be found. He says (*N. H.* 5, 15, 4) that they lived west of the Dead Sea at a point where there is nothing to fear from the sea's exhalations. Surely this suggests a point where the sea would be purified by the fresh water flowing in from the Jordan River – and this is just where Qumran is. Then he tells us what lies to the south of the community. First comes En Geddi (which is actually about sixteen miles south of Qumran); then comes Masada (and this is about ten miles farther on). It seems obvious, and certain, that Pliny is aware that the Essenes were located just where the Qumran community was located; and therefore the Dead Sea people were Essenes.

The places where the Essenes lived are described differently by Philo and Josephus. Philo says once that they lived not in cities but in villages and once that they lived in cities and in villages. Josephus says they lived in various cities. This confusing situation is cleared up by the Zadokite document, which gives one set of rules for those who live in cities, another for those who live in camps. The document's camps are presumably the villages of Philo. The centre of Essene life, then, was at Qumran, but there were other Essenes who observed special rules and lived in cities elsewhere. This variety corresponds in part with what Josephus tells us about two kinds of Essenes. There were those who did not marry but brought up the children of others – thus probably maintaining a kind of orphan asylum as in some mediaeval monasteries. Others did marry and have children. It is not quite clear what the situation at Qumran itself was, since in its burying ground the remains of a few women have been found.

In order to become a member of the community, Josephus says, a 'postulant' had to undergo a year's probation. He was given a shovel for sanitary purposes, a girdle, and a white garment which he wore at meetings of the group. He could not, however, take part in the daily baths of the community or in its noonday meal. Since strangers were admitted to the evening meal, he could participate in this.

At the end of the year he could become a 'candidate'. For two years more he took part in the daily baths, wearing the white garment and entering the water at eleven in the morning. Before sunrise and after sunset he shared in the common prayers; mornings and afternoons were spent in field work or animal husbandry or bee-keeping or work at a craft. He owed strict obedience to the elders of the community and had already turned over his property to the overseer (*epimelētēs*), though presumably he could recover it if he was finally not approved.

After these three years he was ready for initiation. He took solemn oaths that he would observe reverence towards God and justice towards men. He would hate the wicked and help the righteous. He would continue to obey the authorities of the group. If he should become one of the authorities, he would not use his authority for self-aggrandizement. He would love the truth and rebuke liars. He would not conceal his property or his actions. Finally, he would never reveal the teachings of the group to others. He would keep sacred the books of the sect and the secret names of the angels.

All this is to be found almost exactly paralleled in the Dead Sea Manual of Discipline. 'Everyone who wishes to join the community must pledge himself to respect God and man; to live according to the communal rule; ... to love all that God has chosen and to hate all that he has rejected; ... to act truthfully and righteously; ... to love all the children of light ... and to hate all the children of darkness.' Such persons must bring their property into the community of God. They are to take oaths to obey their superiors and to observe the law as the community interprets it. They are to spend a year before being admitted to the state of purity, that is before admission to the baths. Then they are to spend another year of apprenticeship while they work for the community, and only after that year can they be admitted to the common meal. According to Josephus the second period lasted two years; no doubt it was found that one year was not quite long enough a time. We do not know so much about the baths and the common meals from documents, but the remains of the monastery make it plain that the Qumran community did have a common dining hall and an elaborate water supply for purifications. Finally, we know that its members valued the holy books so much that they hid them away in jars, and that in these books there was a great concern for the names of the angels (especially in Enoch).

We must therefore regard the Dead Sea community as an Essene community. It was one of the most important forces in the religious life of Palestine in the first centuries B.C. and A.D. Josephus treats the Essenes as being just as significant as either Pharisees or Sadducees. We get some light on their numerical importance from a couple of ancient statistics. Josephus tells us that there were 6,000 Pharisees in all, and Philo tells us that there were 4,000 Essenes. Of course not all these Essenes lived at Qumran. As far as archaeologists can tell, there was room for not more than two hundred of them there. But there were other Essenes, a third order, so to speak, who lived in the cities and villages of Palestine.

As for the government of the community, Josephus tells us that the most important disciplinary questions had to be settled by a court of at least one hundred members; this is the general council of the Manual of Discipline. According to the Manual, the most severe penalties involved removal from the common meal or expulsion from the community; similarly Josephus says that bad Essenes had no food but had to eat grass. Less important offences resulted in cutting down rations. He also tells us that blasphemy was punished by death, and while in the Manual of Discipline the penalty is excommunication, in the Zadokite Document it is also death.

ESSENE LITERATURE

Some of the literature found in the caves of Qumran deals with the organization and operation of the community. Here should be included the Manual of Discipline, the Zadokite or 'Damascus' Document, and a Formulary of Blessings. Further books contain liturgical materials such as a hymn of initiants found at the end of a copy of the Manual and the hymns or psalms (*hodayoth*) of thanksgiving for redemption. Others contain paraphrases and commentaries related to the Old Testament, such as fragments of the apocryphal books of Enoch and Jubilees and of commentaries on Genesis, Isaiah, Hosea, Micah, Nahum, Habakkuk, and various psalms. (No fragment of Enoch thus far found contains the Similitudes, cc. 37–71, which speak of the coming of a heavenly Son of Man.) In addition, there are military and apocalyptic documents which include the War of the Sons of Light and the Sons of Darkness, a manual of discipline for the time after the war, and fragments on the new covenant and the coming doom.

Other fragments seem to come from highly secret books. These include a Hebrew 'Book of Mysteries', a description of the heavenly Jerusalem, a 'Liturgy of the Three Tongues of Fire', and a treatise with the title 'The Words of the Book that Michael spoke to the Angels'.

The Manual of Discipline begins with the promise which is to be made by those who wish to join the community. They must respect God and man; they must avoid evil and adhere to good;

they must love the children of light and hate the children of darkness. They must turn their property over to the community of God, and they must observe the calendar in force at Qumran, i.e. a year of 364 days. Then they take an oath, confess their sins, and receive a blessing from the priests. The levites pronounce a curse on the children of darkness, and both priests and levites pronounce a curse on hypocrites who join the community. The Manual then goes on to describe an annual review of the children of light. The theological purpose of this review is explained in relation to redemption through knowledge of God's truth and a description of God's having given man the spirits of truth and of perversity. Truth comes from the fountain of light, and the true are ruled by the Prince of Lights; perversity comes from the wellspring of darkness, and the perverse are ruled by the Angel of Darkness. The true will be helped by the God of Israel and the Angel of his truth, and will receive everlasting life, a crown of glory, a robe of honour, and perpetual light. The perverse will be eternally damned, at the time of the final judgement. After this introduction there follow the detailed rules for the life of the community, a community of separation, virtue, holiness and mutual sharing. There is an account of how initiates are to be admitted and how disobedient members are to be punished. There is a description of the government of the community by fifteen 'men of perfect holiness', twelve laymen and three priests. This community is to be the true temple of God, and a true synagogue.

The Zadokite Document contains similar materials but lays more emphasis on the history of Israel as an expression of the principles of the community. It contains two different codes, one for Essenes who live in urban communities, the other for those who live in camps. Finally, there is a supplementary code, most of which deals with oaths and their binding nature.

The Hymns of Thanksgiving are personal in nature but reflect the basic doctrines of Qumran, salvation by knowledge and by membership in the community. Bardtke has suggested that they were not used in formal worship but were intended for private use by members of the group, so that their thoughts would always be directed towards the greatness of the redemption they had received.

Now I am as one
who has entered a stronghold,
taken refuge behind a high wall,
till deliverance come.
For I have stayed myself on thy truth, O God.

The history of creation and redemption, and the hope of eternal security, are blended together in these hymns.

The commentaries are especially interesting because they interpret Old Testament prophecy and psalmody in relation to the history of the community. In the commentary on Micah we read that the prophet's condemnation of Samaria really refers to the wicked priests of Jerusalem, the enemies of God, whom he will punish. Similarly on Nahum we read that 'the abode of the lions' (2, 11) means Jerusalem, where wicked men of the heathen dwell; it will eventually be trodden under. The lion of Nahum 2, 12 may be Demetrius III, in whose time (*c.* 88 B.C.) eight hundred Jews were crucified. In the Habakkuk commentary it is harder to identify the wicked priest who persecuted the Teacher of Righteousness and eventually was punished himself. Gaster may be right when he argues that the case is supposed to be typical; it could be any anti-Essene priest. The significant thing about these commentaries is the evidence they give for the community's interpretation of prophecy in relation to itself. In this way the Essenes were forerunners of the Christian exegetes of the Old Testament.

The War of the Sons of Light with the Sons of Darkness is a plan for the conquest of the world by the Sons of Light; it is the *Mein Kampf* of the Dead Sea generalissimo, who describes the future in a way faintly reminiscent of the entrance of Israel into Canaan but more clearly based on Roman military organization, procedure and strategy. At the end, a form of prayer of thanksgiving for victory is provided.

Finally we have a manual of discipline for the future congregation of Israel, when the war has been won and when a king has been restored to the throne. At that time all Israel will live in the manner of the sons of Zadok. We should note that this common life is to be reserved for those who are Israelites by birth. No gentile mission is contemplated. The gentiles will be dead. And in the fragment which Gaster calls 'The Coming Doom' we read that outsiders do not know what is going to happen, and there is no nation which really hates wrongdoing. Only we know what will take place; only we are going to be saved; for only we truly obey God's will.

The message of the Dead Sea gospel is thus directed to Israelites who wish to know the truth about God, about history, and about themselves. The truth is that God is on their side and is directing history towards a final battle which will involve the triumph of his elect. Who are his elect? *We* are his elect, and we shall eventually rule the world and kill the sons of darkness, who are all men except ourselves. The religion of the Qumran people was characterized by some of the most exclusive sectarianism the world has ever seen, an apocalyptic-eschatological sectarianism which looked for triumph in this world, and soon. This triumph was not achieved.

The resemblances between the life and thought of the Essenes and the life and thought of early Christians are so striking that it may be well to say something about the differences at this point. (1) In spite of resemblances between the 'teacher of righteousness' and Jesus, there seem to be at least two basic differences. (*a*) The Qumran people taught and, indeed, demanded, hatred of enemies. The gospel of Jesus was quite different (Matt. 5.43–7; Luke 6.27–35). (*b*) The Qumran people were greatly concerned with ritual purity; Jesus was not. (2) The mission of Qumran was essentially to itself; the mission of the early Church was to outsiders – first to all Jews, then to gentiles as well. The Church, like Jesus himself, proclaimed the forgiveness of sins. (3) The teacher of righteousness, like Jesus, suffered persecution from his opponents. Jesus was put to death and rose from the dead.

POST-MACCABEAN TIMES

Within a generation after the Maccabean revolt had become a successful revolution, the Jewish state was recognized by the Roman Senate and Rome refused to give sanctuary to political exiles hostile to the leadership of Simon Maccabaeus. By co-operating with various Seleucid kings, the Jewish rulers were able to maintain a relative independence which persisted even after Antiochus Sidetes besieged Jerusalem in 134; the new Jewish king John Hyrcanus (135–105) was able to bring about mutual disarmament. Assuming the office of high priest as well as that of king, he was opposed by the Pharisees – in vain. After a brief interval, his son Alexander Jannaeus ruled from 104 until 78, in spite of popular hostility which resulted in his being pelted with lemons at one feast of Tabernacles, and in turn Alexander's wife Alexandra was queen from 78 to 69, while their son Hyrcanus became high priest. She favoured the Pharisees; the Sadducees sided with her younger son Aristobulus, who led a revolt against his mother and ruled until 63. Hyrcanus retired from office but, with the assistance of Aretas III of Nabataea and his confidant the Idumean Antipater, was able to re-enter Jerusalem in 65. At this point the Roman general Pompey, in the East with his legions, compelled Aretas to evacuate Jerusalem, and two years later various delegates came to Pompey with petitions from Hyrcanus, from Aristobulus, and from 'the Jewish people', who insisted that they preferred Roman to royal rule. In response to this invitation, Pompey proceeded against Jerusalem and captured it on a Sabbath when the Jewish soldiers refused to take up arms. Hyrcanus was confirmed as high priest, while in 46 he received the title of ethnarch. Unable to defend Jerusalem against a Parthian raid, he fled to Rome and was replaced in 43 by Herod, son of Antipater. Roman troops drove the Parthians out, while in 39 B.C. Herod received the title 'king of the Jews'.

From the time of Pompey come the Pharisaic Psalms of Solomon, which emphasize the wickedness of the kings now dethroned and look forward to the rise of a rightly anointed ('messiah') king of Davidic ancestry. This expectation was not fulfilled, for Pompey put Judaea along with the new Roman province of Syria under a governor at Antioch who controlled two legions. Loosely subordinate to him was King Herod.

After Herod's accession he suppressed Galilean 'robbers' (probably revolutionaries) and finally recaptured Jerusalem. During the Roman civil conflicts he first supported Mark Antony, who had momentarily achieved power. At the time of the battle of Actium (31), when Octavian decisively defeated Antony and Cleopatra, Herod had discreetly occupied himself with Arabian affairs; just afterwards, he went to Octavian on the island of

Rhodes and explained that he had urged Antony to kill Cleopatra. He also argued that he had always been faithful to whatever friends he had. Since Octavian needed faithful friends, or welcomed political realists, he confirmed Herod's kingship.

At home, Herod's long rule was marked by innumerable murders and harsh repression; abroad, he contributed lavishly to the monuments which indicated and supported the success of Octavian's reign. When he died in 4 B.C. a legacy of about £2,000,000 to the emperor ensured the preservation of his treasures, while after long disputes and abortive revolts the Senate ratified his will and confirmed the powers of his three sons.

The struggles were severe. In Galilee a certain Judas arose; elsewhere two more revolts broke out, only to be suppressed by a Roman general who crucified two thousand Jews. At Rome itself fifty Jewish delegates asked to have Herod's kingdom placed directly under the governor of Syria. It was decided, however, that half the kingdom, including Judaea, should be ruled by Archelaus; he was to have the title of ethnarch and would later become king if all went well. A quarter, to the north-east, was to go to Herod Philip, and another quarter, consisting of Galilee and Peraea, to Herod Antipas.

All did not go well in Judaea. After ten years of misrule and marital difficulties, Archelaus was removed in A.D. 6 and Judaea was 'temporarily' placed under a Roman procurator named Coponius. A Roman census was undertaken, since for the first time the Roman tax system was being introduced. In Galilee Judas took up arms again, declaring that the Jews had no king but God and that taxes should be paid to the Romans. This time he was killed. The next year, under P. Sulpicius Quirinius, governor of Syria, the census was completed. He made a certain Annas high priest and confirmed Herod Antipas and Philip in their tetrarchies.

Once introduced, the procuratorial system continued in effect. The procurator who stayed longest in Judaea was Pontius Pilatus, sent out from Rome in A.D. 26 at a time when Tiberius's principal adviser was notoriously hostile towards the Jews. Pilate confirmed the high priesthood of Caiaphas, son-in-law of Annas. He had been in office since the year 18, presumably because of his ability to serve Roman interests. Shortly after Pilate's arrival he brought Roman troops into Jerusalem bearing their legionary standards on which images of animals or deities were often carved. This action resulted in rioting which Pilate fiercely suppressed. A little later he expropriated the *corban* trusts held by the temple so that he could build a sixty-mile aqueduct for Jerusalem's water supply. A mob protested against this action but was scattered by soldiers wearing plain clothes and concealed clubs.

The religious impact of Pilate's rule seems to have been felt almost immediately by a certain John, a member of a priestly family who went out to the desert east of the Dead Sea. It is possible that he had been influenced at one time or another by the teaching of the Essenes. In any event, he now began to proclaim the coming wrath of God, stating the necessity of universal repentance; according to Luke 3.10–14 this involved the sharing of possessions, honest tax-collection, and the avoidance of looting by soldiers. A 'baptism of repentance' in the river Jordan was required of all who followed him (see pp. 309ff).

John's preaching created a crisis in Palestine. Great numbers of Jews went out to the desert to see this prophet of doom. His preaching did not last long, however, for he proceeded to denounce Herod Antipas, tetrarch not only of Galilee but also of Peraea, where John was preaching. Like others of the Herodian family this Herod had marital problems. He had become infatuated with Herodias, the wife of his half-brother, and had deserted his own wife to marry her. The situation was dangerous, since his first wife was the daughter of Aretas IV of Nabatea. Therefore when Herod heard that John had denounced the marriage as contrary to Jewish law he suspected the existence of a plot. John was imprisoned in the frontier fortress at Machaerus, near the Dead Sea, and later, at the instigation of Herodias, was beheaded.

It was a time of revolutionary fervour, and when Jesus of Nazareth, once baptized by John, proclaimed in Galilee the imminent reign of God and then came up to Jerusalem, the high priest Caiaphas and a group of Jewish leaders denounced him to Pilate. After a cursory investigation the procurator ordered him crucified along with two 'thieves' who were perhaps revolutionists. His execution probably took place on April 6th, A.D. 30.

The next year, Pilate's influence at Rome was sharply diminished when the anti-Jewish adviser of Tiberius was executed for sedition. A further problem soon arose when he erected Roman votive shields in the old palace of Herod I in Jerusalem. Herod's four sons protested, and Rome sent orders to remove them. Pilate survived in Judaea, however, until the year 36, when a Samaritan prophet gathered a great crowd by promising to show them the authentic sacred vessels which Moses had buried on Mount Gerizim. The procurator hastily sent troops which dispersed the prophet's followers by killing many of them. Samaritan protests to the imperial legate in Syria resulted in Pilate's being dismissed from office and sent to Rome. The fact that he arrived there only after the death of Tiberius early in 37 may have been fortunate for him, but we know nothing more about his life.

Meanwhile further disorders had broken out in Palestine. Aretas of Nabatea had finally moved against his sometime son-in-law, and when the army of Herod Antipas was decisively beaten in the year 36, he appealed to Tiberius for help. Some help arrived, but within three years his enemies accused him of having conspired against Tiberius. They informed the new emperor Gaius that Herod was stock-piling arms in order to join the Parthians against Rome. An investigation revealed that he had acquired enough weapons for seventy thousand troops, and he was thereupon banished to Gaul. A year later unrest arose in Judaea. Gaius, believing firmly in his own deity, ordered a colossal statue of himself to be placed in the temple at Jerusalem. A politic governor of Syria was able to delay transport of the statue to Judaea until Gaius could be murdered by those at Rome who knew he was insane. Jewish delegates sent from Alexandria and elsewhere had been able to combine protestations of loyalty with appeals for the emperor's favour; the assassin's dagger was more effective.

In an attempt to restore order in Palestine, Claudius made Herod Agrippa I, grandson of Herod the Great and, on his mother's side, close to the Roman nobility, king of Judaea in the year 41. Though he was half an Idumean, the grateful Jewish people hailed him as their 'brother' and protector. By implication, at least, he seemed to have restored the kingdom of David, though coins of his last two years bore the Greek word 'Caesar's friend'

Unfortunately Agrippa died in 44 and the rule of the procurators began once more. The first of them, Cuspius Fadus, had to deal with a self-styled 'prophet' named Theudas, who took his followers to the Jordan, assuring them that like Joshua (4.7) he could make the waters divide. For him, as for some of the Essenes, Jerusalem had become a profane city. The procurator sent a detachment of cavalry which defeated Theudas's followers and beheaded him. After Fadus, the next procurator was Tiberius Alexander, nephew of the Jewish philosopher Philo. He had to deal with a severe famine caused by the failure of the Egyptian wheat crop. Apparently revolutionary ideas came to the fore again, for he crucified the sons of the earlier rebel Judas of Galilee.

The next procurator, Ventidius Cumanus (48–52), had to deal with riots in Jerusalem which took place when a Roman soldier ridiculed Passover pilgrims. According to Josephus, twenty thousand men lost their lives in the city. On another occasion a Roman soldier in a village near Jerusalem burned up a scroll containing the Jewish law; this time the procurator, more cautious, had the offender executed. Still later, some Galilean Jews were murdered on their way through Samaria to a festival at Jerusalem. Cumanus, who according to Josephus had been bribed by the Samaritans to remain inactive, did nothing about the incident, and when Jewish zealots took vengeance on the criminals he attacked them. The governor of Syria sent the high priest to Rome, but Cumanus was removed from office.

Antonius Felix, his successor, remained as procurator until about 60, largely by means of vigorous suppression of revolutionary activities. The struggle was becoming acute. In response to Felix there arose a resistance group called the Sicarii (cf. Acts 21.38) because they carried short daggers (*sicae*) in the crowds at festivals and stabbed supporters of the Romans. One victim was the high priest Jonathan. Other Jews, less militant, advocated withdrawal to the desert, where they expected to witness 'signs from heaven'. A famous prophet of this kind was an Egyptian Jew who gathered either four thousand (Acts 21.38) or thirty thousand (Josephus) followers and proposed to go to the Mount of Olives. At his word the walls of Jerusalem would fall as the walls of Jericho had fallen for Joshua. Roman troops arrived before he spoke the word. Since he escaped from the slaughter which followed, a Roman tribune was able to suppose that Paul might be the Egyptian (Acts 21.38).

The result of these movements was that, in Josephus's expression, all Judaea was filled with madness. Procurators after Felix stayed in Judaea no more than two years before being recalled, and open war broke out in 66.

THE TEMPLE

When Jerusalem fell in A.D. 70 the event which most impressed the Jewish people was not the sack of the city but the destruction of the temple by fire. The temple, whose renovation (still incomplete) had been undertaken by Herod in B.C. 20, was the focal point of the Jewish religion. Jerusalem was the 'city of the great king' (Matt. 5.35) because God's house was there. In the temple were conducted the daily sacrifices of animals and produce; the most important of these sacrifices were the people's burnt offering, immolated twice a day. At these ceremonies lamps were lighted and music, both choral and instrumental, was performed. Additional offerings were made on the Sabbath and at the great festivals.

The temple was the centre of the rites of the religious year, which began with the Day of Atonement (Yom Kippur) on the 10th of the month Tishri (September–October). Burnt offerings were sacrificed and the scapegoat was sent away, bearing Israel's sins upon it (Lev. 16.10). The whole fast which followed expressed God's forgiveness of his people. They confessed their sins and he forgave them.

The cycle of festivals began with (1) Tabernacles, from the 15th to the 22nd of Tishri. During this autumn harvest-festival male Israelites lived in booths or 'tabernacles,' in memory of the booths in which they dwelt after the Exodus (Lev. 23.39–43). Josephus calls it, the holiest and greatest of the feasts (*Ant.* 8, 100). In New Testament times it may have had eschatological overtones; perhaps the coming of God's reign could be expected at Tabernacles. The feast is mentioned in John 7.2, and the story of the Transfiguration (Mark 9.2–8) seems to be told in relation to it. (2) The next festival was Hannukah, on the 25th of Kislev (November–December), when the Maccabaean rededication of the temple was commemorated by the lighting of lamps. It was also called 'renewal' (John 10.22) or 'lights' (Josephus, *Antiq.* 12, 235). Other rites which accompanied it resembled those of

Tabernacles (II Macc. 1.9; 10.6). (3) Early in the spring, on the 15th of Adar (February–March), was celebrated the feast of Purim, essentially a *sacre du printemps*; a fourth-century rabbi held that at Purim a man should drink until he could not distinguish 'Cursed be Haman' from 'Blessed be Mordecai'. These two persons are prominent in the book of Esther, included in the Old Testament because it gave instructions for Purim and described the event which was commemorated. (4) Apart from Tabernacles, the greatest feast of the year was Passover, celebrated in the week beginning with the 15th of Nisan (March–April) to commemorate the Exodus from Egypt, God's act of deliverance for his people. Each Israelite family in Jerusalem consumed a roast lamb, killed by the priests in the temple; then followed a week in which only unleavened bread was eaten (Exod. 12.1–28; 13.3–10; Lev. 23.5–8; Deut. 16.1–8). (5) Seven weeks after Passover came the feast of weeks or, from the Greek word for 'fifty', Pentecost (Lev. 23.15–21). In rabbinic times this festival was regarded as commemorating the giving of the law on Sinai.

These festivals, along with the regular sacrifices, cost a great deal of money to maintain. They were supported partly by special gifts from kings and other individuals, partly by an annual tax of half a shekel (about 10s.) from every male Jew over 20 years of age (cf. Matt. 17.24–7), and partly by small free-will offerings (Mark 12.41–4). The funds went to buy animals and other items needed for the sacrifices and to support a community of priests and Levites (temple attendants) perhaps numbering ten thousand.

The temple and its services expressed the faith of Israel in the one God, and the oneness of the temple was often regarded as analogous to the oneness of God himself (for a Christian parallel cf. Eph. 4.4–6). The sacrifices not only expressed the faith but also taught it by means of dramatic action. Further instruction in the content and meaning of the revealed law was necessary, however, and this was provided by means of an institution developed by the Pharisees.

THE SYNAGOGUE

Indeed, the principal institution of Pharisaism was the synagogue. This term (from the Greek word for 'assembly', sometimes used in the Septuagint in relation to the 'congregation' of Israel) referred both to the group involved, consisting of a minimum of ten adult males, and to the building in which it met. The chief purpose of the synagogue was the Sabbath service, consisting of the Shema ('Hear, O Israel, the Lord thy God is one God,' Deut. 6.4–5), the eighteen benedictions, and the benediction of Numbers 6.23–6. Individuals recited psalms; then came the reading of a brief portion of the Old Testament in Hebrew, followed by a *targum* or periphrastic translation into Aramaic or Greek, and a sermon on the lesson for the day. The lesson was apparently fixed by a carefully devised lectionary system. Anyone appointed by the 'head of the synagogue' ('*archisynagogos*') could deliver the sermon (cf. Luke 4.16–27; Acts 17.2). The Fourth Book of Maccabees may represent an expansion of such a homily.

During the week the synagogue was used as a school in which scribes instructed young people in scripture and its exegesis. In these circumstances they learned the two principal exegetical methods, *halacha* and *haggada*. Halachic exegesis involved the interpretation of the law in relation to practical obligations; haggadic exegesis was used for deriving theological and mythological ideas from the Old Testament.

THE AM HA-ARETZ

Most Jews remained outside the circle of the sects we have mentioned. There were very few Sadducees and Essenes. Josephus informs us that there were only six thousand Pharisees. The overwhelming majority of Palestinian Jews belonged to what the Pharisees called the *am ha-aretz*, 'the people of the land'. We know nothing of them from any writings they may have produced; we encounter them in the attacks made upon them by the Pharisees and in the stories about 'tax collectors and sinners' in the gospels. They constituted the 'lost sheep of the house of Israel' (Matt. 10.6; 15.24).

THE DIASPORA OR DISPERSION

Thus far we have considered only the Jews of Palestine. We must not forget, however, that most Jews lived not in Palestine but in the great cities of the Roman empire: Rome, Antioch, Alexandria, Ephesus, and others. There they were the object of considerable hostility from Greeks and Romans who regarded them as superstitious, exclusive, and – in the words of Tacitus – hostile to the human race. Their Sabbath-observance and practice of circumcision were especially criticized. From Egypt one papyrus letter reflects fear of their financial acumen. Above all, however, as emperor-worship became more significant, their refusal to accept the divinity of the Roman emperor was attacked, even though treaties with the Jewish nation exempted them from participating in ruler-cult. (At Jerusalem sacrifices were offered for, not to, the emperor; the cessation of these sacrifices in A.D. 66 marked the beginning of revolt).

One source of difficulty was the existence of Jews who participated in the benefits of Graeco-Roman culture and were citizens of their cities, as well as of the empire, while claiming allegiance to Judaism at the same time. Philo of Alexandria belonged to a wealthy and politically influential family; he was well educated in Greek rhetoric and philosophy; but he stated that as a Jew his native city (*patris*) was Jerusalem. Similarly the apostle Paul was a Jew, a citizen of Tarsus in Cilicia, and a Roman citizen (Acts 21.39; 22.27–8). Roman policy favoured cosmopolitanism; but it had its limits, and turbulence in Palestine did not improve the position of Jews elsewhere.

From the career and the writings of Philo we can see how eager some Jews were to bridge the gap between Judaism and Hellenism. Philo took part in a movement to replace an anti-Jewish governor of Alexandria (*Against Flaccus*) and in an attempt to modify the anti-Jewish attitude of the emperor Gaius (*Embassy to Gaius*). He wrote innumerable volumes containing exegesis of the Jewish law intended to show that it expressed the universal law of nature as well as special laws binding only upon the Jewish people.

THE SOURCE OF PALESTINIAN CONFLICT

The writings of Philo can be viewed as apologetic for Judaism, indicating the hope that mankind would gradually come to recognize the universal aspects of the Jewish law. Philo's attitude was not universally shared, as we have already seen not only in the Dead Sea Scrolls but also in the record of events in first-century Palestine.

In what we may call non-apologetic Judaism there was a long tradition of faith in God's imminent action to take up his power and reign. Israel would be vindicated and restored to power; foreign domination would come to an end. This hope was made up of political and religious motifs which were inextricably combined. The great prophets of exilic times had always concerned themselves with politics. The author of Daniel had stated that 'the kingdom and the dominion, and the greatness of the kingdoms under the whole heaven, shall be given to the people of the saints of the Most High' (7.27). In the time of Pompey the Psalms of Solomon had looked forward to the coming of a Messianic king (17.23). More recently, the Assumption of Moses, written in the time of Archelaus, had anticipated the inauguration of God's reign. No doubt there were many Jews who did not share these hopes, but Palestinian leaders kept them alive among the people.

Scholars have often pointed out that in first-century Judaism there was no one 'doctrine of the Messiah', but this fact means only that Jews differed as to details. Those who were concerned with the coming reign of God could unite on one dogma: foreign oppressors would be driven out and God alone would rule Israel.

This dogma was acutely embarrassing to the pro-Roman aristocracy of priests and Sadducees who governed Palestine in collaboration with the procurators. Their attitude is well expressed in John 19.15: 'We have no king but Caesar.' Indeed, their appeal to Pilate as 'Caesar's friend' (John 19.12) makes use of a term found on coins of Agrippa I. From the official point of view, Jesus was crucified as 'the king of the Jews' (Mark 15.26). One of the principal difficulties in New Testament study, as we shall see in the next chapter, is that of determining the relation of Jesus' mission to the various revolutionary movements.

Why were these movements so strong in first-century Palestine? First of all, we must recall that the Roman empire had only recently come into existence. The peoples subject to it were able to remember times when their own kings had ruled them, and with the passage of time, past misrule tended to be forgotten. Official inscriptions found throughout the empire speak of the glories of Roman rule, but those who erected them did not necessarily speak for all classes of society. Especially towards the borders of the empire there was a great deal of unrest. Second, the burden of Roman taxation was oppressive. It has been calculated that in first-century Palestine the total of Jewish and Roman taxes may have reached a rate of twenty-five per cent; and while in modern times progressive taxation reaches levels far beyond this point, taxation in antiquity was not progressive. Taxes on sales and produce, along with customs and poll taxes, fell evenly, and thus inequitably, on rich and poor alike. Third, the economic situation in Palestine, as elsewhere in the empire, was characterized by extreme inequality.

While this situation was not determinative of the gospel message or its reception, it undoubtedly had something to do with the form in which the gospel was cast.

APPENDIX: THE EIGHTEEN BENEDICTIONS

Current Recension

From the Authorized Daily Prayer Book, tr. S. Singer (1890; 8th ed. 1915), pp. 44–54.

The following prayer (*Amidah*) is to be said standing.

O Lord, open thou my lips,
And my mouth shall declare thy praise.

I

Blessed art thou, O Lord our God and God of our fathers,
God of Abraham, God of Isaac, and God of Jacob,
The great, the mighty, the revered God, the most high God,
Who bestowest lovingkindnesses, and possessest all things;
Who rememberest the pious deeds of the patriarchs,
And in love wilt bring a redeemer to their children's children
    for thy name's sake.
O King, Helper, Saviour, and Shield.
    Blessed art thou, O Lord, the Shield of Abraham.

II

Thou, O Lord, art mighty for ever,
Thou quickenest the dead,
Thou art mighty to save.
Thou sustainest the living with lovingkindness,
Quickenest the dead with great mercy,
Supportest the falling, healest the sick, loosest the bound,
And keepest thy faith with them that sleep in the dust.
Who is like unto thee, Lord of mighty acts,
And who resembleth thee, O King,
Who killest and quickenest,
And causest salvation to spring forth?
Yea, faithful art thou to quicken the dead.
    Blessed art thou, O Lord, who quickenest the dead.

III

Thou art holy,
And thy name is holy,
And holy beings praise thee daily. (Selah.)
    Blessed art thou, O Lord, the holy God.

IV

Thou favourest man with knowledge,
And teachest mortals understanding.
Oh favour us with knowledge, understanding and discernment from thee.
    Blessed art thou, O Lord, gracious Giver of knowledge.

V

Cause us to return, O our Father, unto thy law;
Draw us near, O our King, unto thy service,
And bring us back in perfect repentance unto thy presence.
    Blessed art thou, O Lord, who delightest in repentance.

VI

Forgive us, O our Father, for we have sinned;
Pardon us, O our King, for we have transgressed;
For thou dost pardon and forgive.
    Blessed art thou, O Lord, who art gracious, and dost
    abundantly forgive.

VII

Look upon our affliction and plead our cause,
And redeem us speedily for thy name's sake;
For thou art a mighty Redeemer.
    Blessed art thou, O Lord, the Redeemer of Israel.

VIII

Heal us, O Lord, and we shall be healed;
Save us and we shall be saved;
For thou art our praise.
Vouchsafe a perfect healing to all our wounds;
For thou, almighty King, art a faithful and merciful Physician.
    Blessed art thou, O Lord, who healest the sick of thy people
      Israel.

IX

Bless this year unto us, O Lord our God,
Together with every kind of the produce thereof, for our
    welfare;
Give a blessing upon the face of the earth.
O satisfy us with thy goodness,
And bless our year like other good years.
    Blessed art thou, O Lord, who blessest the years.

X

Sound the great horn for our freedom;
Lift up the ensign to gather our exiles,
And gather us from the four corners of the earth.
    Blessed art thou, O Lord, who gatherest the banished ones
      of thy people Israel.

XI

Restore our judges as at the first,
And our counsellors as at the beginning;
Remove from us grief and suffering;
Reign thou over us, O Lord,
Thou alone, in lovingkindness and tender mercy,
And justify us in judgement.
    Blessed art thou, O Lord, the King who lovest righteousness
      and judgement.

XII

And for slanderers let there be no hope,
And let all wickedness perish as in a moment;
Let all thine enemies be speedily cut off,
And the dominion of arrogance do thou uproot and crush,
Cast down, and humble speedily in our days.
  Blessed art thou, O Lord, who breakest the enemies and
    humblest the arrogant.

XIII

Towards the righteous and the pious,
Towards the elders of thy people the house of Israel,
Towards the remnant of their scribes,
Towards the proselytes of righteousness,
And towards us also may thy tender mercies be stirred,
  O Lord our God;
Grant a good reward unto all who faithfully trust in thy
  name;
Set our portion with them for ever, so that we may not be put
  to shame;
For we have trusted in thee.
  Blessed art thou, O Lord, the stay and trust of the
    righteous.

XIV

And to Jerusalem, thy city, return in mercy,
And dwell therein as thou hast spoken;
Rebuild it soon in our days as an everlasting building,
And speedily set up therein the throne of David.
  Blessed art thou, O Lord, who rebuildest Jerusalem.

XV

Speedily cause the offspring of David, thy servant, to
  flourish,
And let his horn be exalted by thy salvation,
Because we wait for thy salvation all the day.
  Blessed art thou, O Lord, who causest the horn of
    salvation to flourish.

XVI

Hear our voice, O Lord our God;
Spare us and have mercy upon us,
And accept our prayer in mercy and favour;
For thou art a God who hearkenest unto prayers and
supplications:
From thy presence, O our King, turn us not empty away;
For thou hearkenest in mercy to the prayer of thy people Israel.
Blessed art thou, O Lord, who hearkenest unto prayer.

XVII

Accept, O Lord our God, thy people Israel and their prayer;
Restore the service to the oracle of thy house;
Receive in love and favour both the fire-offerings of Israel and
their prayer;
And may the service of thy people Israel be ever acceptable
unto thee.
And let our eyes behold thy return in mercy to Zion.
Blessed art thou, O Lord, who restorest thy divine presence
unto Zion.

XVIII

We give thanks unto thee,
For thou art the Lord our God and the God of our fathers
for ever and ever;
Thou art the Rock of our lives,
The Shield of our salvation through every generation.
We will give thanks unto thee
And declare thy praise for our lives which are committed unto
thy hand,
And for our souls which are in thy charge,
And for thy miracles, which are daily with us,
And for thy wonders and thy benefits, which are wrought
at all times, evening, morn, and noon.
O thou who art all-good, whose mercies fail not;
Thou, merciful Being, whose lovingkindnesses never cease,
We have ever hoped in thee.
For all these things thy name, O our King, shall be
continually blessed and exalted for ever and ever.

And everything that liveth shall give thanks unto thee for
ever,
And shall praise thy name in truth, O God, our salvation and
our help.
Blessed art thou, O Lord, whose name is All-good, and
unto whom it is becoming to give thanks.

XIX

Grant peace, welfare, blessing, grace, lovingkindness and
mercy unto us and unto all Israel, thy people.
Bless us, O our Father, even all of us together, with the light
of thy countenance;
For by the light of thy countenance thou hast given us, O
Lord our God, the Law of life, lovingkindness and
righteousness, blessing, mercy, life and peace;
And may it be good in thy sight to bless thy people Israel at
all times and in every hour with thy peace.
Blessed art thou, O Lord, who blessest thy people Israel
with peace.

Shortened form of the *Amidah*:

First three Benedictions, followed by:

Give us understanding, O Lord our God, to know thy ways;
circumcise our hearts to fear thee, and forgive us so that we
may be redeemed. Keep us far from sorrow; satiate us on the
pastures of thy land, and gather our scattered ones from the
four corners of the earth. Let them that go astray be judged
according to thy will, and wave thy hand over the wicked.
Let the righteous rejoice in the rebuilding of thy city, and
in the establishment of thy temple, and in the flourishing of
the horn of David thy servant, and in the clear-shining light
of the son of Jesse, thine anointed. Even before we call, do
thou answer. Blessed art thou, O Lord, who hearkenest
unto prayer.

Last three Benedictions, and concluding prayers.

XIX

THE PROBLEM OF THE LIFE
OF JESUS

In the nineteenth century there flourished what Albert Schweitzer called 'the quest of the historical Jesus'. It cannot be said that this quest was very successful or that its continuation in the early twentieth century, described by C. C. McCown in his *Search for the Real Jesus*, was especially fruitful. In general the trouble with the nineteenth-century quest was that it overlooked (1) the fact that the gospel materials had been revised as, and before, they were compiled by the evangelists and (2) the crucial importance of the early Christian expectation of the imminent coming of the reign of God. Rather naïvely combining gospel materials as if they were purely factual, many nineteenth-century critics produced a portrait of Jesus which was actually drawn after their own image and likeness. In the first half of the twentieth century this kind of search practically came to a halt because of the rise of form criticism, with its emphasis on the rôle of oral tradition in the creation of the gospels, and the recognition that apocalyptic eschatology had been extremely important in the early Church and (probably) in the teaching of Jesus himself.

To a considerable extent these two factors could have been regarded as mutually exclusive. If the Church controlled the oral tradition to the extent alleged by the form critics, it might have seemed unlikely that early Christians would have preserved the embarrassing (because unfulfilled) predictions of the immediate coming of God's reign which were to be found in the tradition itself. But the two factors were often combined, with the result that one could be sure that (1) Jesus actually predicted the immediate coming of the kingdom, while (2) the Church took pains to adapt his teaching to the various needs produced by situations after his death and resurrection.

At the present time a new concern for the life of Jesus has arisen, partly by way of reaction against the extreme scepticism which flourished a generation ago. This concern, it is claimed, arises out of the theological study of the New Testament and can be justified in relation to it. At this point we have no intention of discussing this kind of problem. We shall simply assume that it is important, in relation to critical historical study of the New Testament, to determine what can be known about the life of Jesus – and equally important to determine what cannot be known. If further justification be needed, we should argue that the existence of a visible community of believers at least tends to imply the existence of a Jesus about whom something more can be said than that he appeared.

Our concern, then, is with what can be known historically about him. But when we use the word 'historically' we are already confronted with difficulties. Traditionally this word has implied the effort to set various data, often divergent in nature, into a context contemporary with them and geographically suitable. In other words, the data are to be located in time and space and, it is assumed, made more fully comprehensible by comparison with other data derived from the same period and area. In addition, the chronological arrangement of the data is expected to point towards the establishment of various causal connections. The discovery or recovery of causal connections is based on a negative premise (what is posterior cannot be a cause of what is prior) and on a positive assumption as well (something which is prior is a cause of what is posterior). Unfortunately – and this point is often overlooked – given the fact that our knowledge of historical phenomena is limited, we are not always in a position to say what data are earlier than others, and because historical phenomena owe their existence to various causes we cannot always determine which causes are the most important.

The difficulties we have already mentioned arise in dealing with all historical phenomena, but in dealing with the life of Jesus we encounter problems which are due to the nature of the sources we use. We have seen that the synoptic gospels present a picture which in general is rather different from the one to be found in John. At first glance, then, we must be cautious; we must not assume too rapidly that either the Johannine or the synoptic outline is the only correct one. On the other hand, since all the gospels agree that Jesus was crucified outside Jerusalem and that prior to this event he taught not only in Jerusalem but also in Galilee, we must admit that there was a certain movement in his ministry, whether it was simply from Galilee to Jerusalem (as in the synoptics) or oscillated between the two areas (as in John).

This conclusion does not amount to much, and because it does not amount to much we have to see what grounds can be used for ascertaining the reliability of more of the gospel materials. At the end of the nineteenth century P. W. Schmiedel pointed to the existence of what he called 'pillar-passages' in the synoptic gospels. These were verses which he thought could not have been invented by the later community or communities because the ideas expressed in them ran counter to the developing theology of the Church. Among them he included Mark 3.21 (the family or friends of Jesus say, 'He is beside himself'), Mark 6.5 ('he was unable to perform any miracle there'), Mark 13.32 ('of that day or hour no one knows, neither the angels in heaven nor the Son'), and others of a similar nature. In other words, the passages Schmiedel accepted were passages which pointed towards either the weakness or the ignorance of Jesus. Since later evangelists or theologians found them difficult to explain, they must have been authentic. There is obviously something to this judgement. It implies that the evangelists were so honest that they were willing to report information which may well have seemed incongruent to them. At the same time, when Matthew 13.58 reads 'he did not perform many miracles there because of their unbelief' we must recognize that essentially this is no different from what we read in Mark 6.5, where Mark's words 'was unable' do not reflect a historical fact but come from the evangelist's judgement as to what took place. And when Matthew 24.36 agrees with Mark 13.32 that the Son does not know the time of the end, both may be making use of a saying revised by the Church in order to counteract enthusiasm for eschatological timetables. Such a conjecture is, of course, not necessary; but it is possible. We mention it only in order to suggest that the solidity of Schmiedel's pillars leaves something to be desired.

Another kind of pillar was erected by Albert Schweitzer himself when he claimed that the gospel of Jesus had as its centre what he called 'thoroughgoing eschatology'. The best passages he could provide came from sections to be found only in the Gospel of Matthew, especially the tenth chapter, where we hear of the imminent coming of the Son of Man. First, the context is rigidly Jewish (hence authentic): 'Do not go to a way of the gentiles, and do not enter a city of the Samaritans; go, instead, to the lost sheep of the house of Israel' (10.6–7). Second, the eschatology is on the verge of realization: 'Truly I say to you, you will not complete the cities of Israel before the Son of Man comes' (10.23). The difficulty with treating these verses as verbatim reports of the sayings of Jesus lies in the fact that they so closely resemble some other expressions in Matthew which clearly present Jesus' ministry as exceedingly close to 'orthodox' Judaism (e.g., 5.18–20) and do not agree with passages in other gospels, and in Matthew itself, which portray his teaching as farther from a literal interpretation of the law. It could, of course, be argued that Mark and Luke, probably writing for gentiles, suppressed such verses. But to make this claim means to hold that whatever in Jesus' teaching is close to Pharisaic-apocalyptic Judaism is genuine, while whatever looks beyond it has been created by the early gentile, or pro-gentile, Church. And we do not know that Pharisaic-apocalyptic Judaism provided the entire framework within which early Christianity arose.

Once more, there is something to this notion. If the gospel had originally been regarded as clearly addressed to all, Jews and gentiles alike, it is difficult to see how a gentile mission could have arisen as gradually as it did (according both to Acts and to Galatians). On the other hand, however, had it contained no seeds of universality the gentile mission could hardly have arisen at all. There must have been a sense in which Jesus addressed himself primarily to the Jewish people (Paul calls him the 'minister of the circumcision', Rom. 15.8); but there must also have been a sense in which he addressed his call to the gentiles as well. The synoptic evangelists reflect such a picture when they mention his encounters with non-Jews in Galilee and its environs. All the evangelists record his controversies over the keeping of the Sabbath.

It could be added that if the mission of Jesus could be defined entirely in relation to ideas already present among the Pharisees or at Qumran he would not have been a historical person, in the sense that there was anything worth recording about his message. To say this is not to assert that his teaching was completely novel, as Marcion urged in the second century. It is merely to insist that had its content not somehow transcended what was ordinarily believed in the Palestine of his day there would have been no reason to preserve it.

A similar observation can be made in regard to his proclamation of the nature and coming of God's reign. The notion that God would soon take up his power and reign for the benefit of those who obeyed and served him was fairly widespread in first-century Palestine. Josephus describes several of the more conspicuous 'prophets' who wrongly anticipated God's action, and the War Scroll from Qumran shows how seriously some Jews took eschatological expectations in which they themselves would participate. Was the prediction of Jesus of the same sort? Did he die in the mistaken belief that God was soon to intervene? It is certainly the case that some of his sayings point in this direction. The comment of Luke that his disciples supposed, as he drew near to Jerusalem, that the reign of God would immediately appear (19.11) seems to reflect a real historical situation; compare Mark 9.1: 'There are some of those standing here who will not taste death before they see the kingdom of God come in power.' Many of the parables of the kingdom point in the same direction.

At the same time, there are passages in which the reign of God is regarded as present at least in nuclear form. The most impressive of these is the saying reported in Luke 11.20 (Matt. 12.28): 'If I by the finger [spirit] of God cast out demons, then the reign of God has already come upon you.' If the reign of God is like a seed or a buried treasure, it would appear that in some sense it already exists. The idea set forth in such passages has been called 'realized eschatology', though in view of the element of expectation which still remains it should probably be called 'inaugurated eschatology' or 'eschatology in the process of realization'. Whatever it may be called, the presence of this element in the teaching of Jesus clearly suggests that he did not simply make predictions about the future. In his teaching there was emphasis on the imminent future; there was also emphasis on the present as an anticipation of the future. The dividing-line between present and future was to some extent blurred.

Again we can pass from mention of specific passages to more general considerations. It is obvious that in the Pauline epistles, or in some Pauline epistles, there is a vigorous emphasis on the nearness of the end and the coming of Jesus from heaven (e.g., I Thess. 4.16–17; Phil. 3.20). Some scholars have claimed that as Paul gets older and the Lord does not return, the emphasis shifts from eschatological expectation to a greater appreciation of the possibilities in the world. With this notion can be combined the fact that in the Gospel of John eschatology is viewed in two ways: it is something already realized in the mission of Jesus (e.g., 11.25); it is also something related to the future (e.g. 5.28–9). The 'hour' often mentioned in John is sometimes future, sometimes both future and present. One conclusion that has been drawn from such data is that both Paul and John have modified the original, purely futurist eschatology of Jesus, chiefly because of the passage of time. Against this conclusion two points can be made: (1) the chronology of the Pauline epistles is not well enough established for us to use it in creating a developmental picture; and, even if it were, we find futurist ideas in epistles often dated late; (2) it is by no means certain that the futurist ideas in the Gospel of John are archaic survivals with which John combines his new ideas; according to Bultmann they are due to ecclesiastical redaction, while on other views they probably represent at least one facet of the evangelist's thought. Moreover the date of the Johannine gospel and the Johannine materials remains open to question. Finally, the rise of Christian Gnosticism at a relatively early period suggests that while the Gnostics undoubtedly made use of only one side of the teaching of Jesus it was apparently there for them to use. Their eschatology, generally speaking, is realized, although in many systems futurist elements remain.

From this overall picture, as well as from the specific passages already mentioned, we conclude that the teaching of Jesus was not a simple futurist eschatology. It had futurist elements, and they were very important. But the eschatology of which he spoke contained aspects both futurist and, in part, present. During the apostolic age some writers emphasized one aspect, some the other.

It was not until the fifth century that the futurist aspects came to be generally neglected. When in II Peter we find a de-emphasizing of the futurist element (3.8) it is still combined with stress on the coming of the Lord; and, in any event, the non-representative character of II Peter is clearly reflected in the failure of most early Christian writers to make use of it.

This conclusion means that one of the cardinal presuppositions of most historical critics of the New Testament is put in jeopardy. If one cannot simply say that unfulfilled apocalyptic predictions are genuine, while passages which regard the kingdom of God as somehow present are late interpretations or misinterpretations, the clear, one-sided picture drawn by Schweitzer and others tends to disappear.

We should not assume, however, that we have now solved all the problems related to the life of Jesus, or even the major ones. Obviously, by insisting upon the double nature of early Christian eschatology we have made it possible to claim that Jesus founded the Church or provided for its existence after his death;[1] we have tried to lay emphasis upon continuity rather than discontinuity in early Christian history. It is equally obvious that this continuity has been challenged and will be challenged.[2] In one sense, at least, the continuity is problematic in so far as the resurrection of Jesus is an event which stands outside the ordinary continuities of history; and it was in, and in consequence of, this event that the Church came into full existence.

JESUS IN NON-CHRISTIAN WRITINGS

Because the Christian movement arose within the Roman empire and spread throughout it, from east to west, we should expect to find some notice taken of it by Greek and Roman writers. They ought to say something about Jesus and his influence. Such an expectation is clearly fulfilled only by four writers of the late first century and the early second; by the time of the anti-Christian writer Celsus (c. 178), nothing authentic about Jesus is preserved in non-Christian sources.

The four writers we have in mind are the Hellenistic Jewish

---

[1] Cf. H. Conzelmann in *Die Religion in Geschichte und Gegenwart* III (ed. 3), 646.
[2] Cf. Conzelmann in *Zeitschrift für Theologie und Kirche* 54 (1957), 277–96.

general and historian Josephus and the Roman officials C. Plinius Secundus (Pliny the Younger), A. Cornelius Tacitus, and C. Tranquillus Suetonius. In dealing with each bit of information we must be just as critical as we should like to be in considering Christian statements. Each of these authors has his own axe or axes to grind; his attitude is not necessarily 'objective' simply because he is not a Christian.

The words of Josephus are especially questionable, since we know that he was militantly opposed to apocalyptic movements which in his view had led to the disastrous war with Rome (66–70); he himself became a devoted supporter of Rome and his work was subsidized by successive emperors. He included three passages bearing on Christian origins in his *Antiquities*, published about the year 93 (significantly, none of them is to be found in parallel passages in his earlier *War*; presumably Christians had become more important in the interval). These three passages deal with (1) John the Baptist, (2) James the brother of Jesus, and (3) Jesus himself.

The passage about John the Baptist (18, 116–19) depicts him as a 'teacher of righteousness' and makes no reference to his eschatological views. His baptism is portrayed as absolutely non-sacramental (see pp. 262–3). The passage about James (20, 197–203) describes his judicial murder by the high priest Ananas in A.D. 62 and refers to him as the brother of 'Jesus, the so-called Christ'. From this passage two inferences can be drawn. (1) James was an important figure in Jerusalem up to the year 62; this confirms the impression we gain from Acts and from the second-century Christian writer Hegesippus. (2) Josephus probably – indeed, almost certainly – had already given some account of the Jesus to whom he referred in this brief notice, though his account was undoubtedly unfavourable.

If we turn to what he does say about Jesus, it is not what we should expect. The passage (18, 63–4) reads as follows:

> At this time lived Jesus, a wise man (if it is right to call him a man), for he was a worker of miracles and a teacher of men who receive the truth with pleasure; as followers he gained many Jews and many of the Hellenic race. He was the Christ, and when by the accusation of the chief men among us

Pilate condemned him to the cross, those who at first had
loved him did not cease from doing so; for he appeared to
them, alive again, on the third day, since the divine prophets
had foretold this as well as countless other marvellous matters
about him. Up to the present day the tribe of Christians,
named after him, has not disappeared.

In this form the description cannot come from Josephus.
(1) It is purely Christian in outlook; indeed, only a Christian
can have written it. (2) Origen, writing about 250, refers
several times to Josephus's testimony to Jesus as contained in
the passage about James; he makes no mention of the fuller
account. Since he had read all the later books of the *Antiquities*,
which he regarded as an excellent historical source, this
passage cannot have been contained in them – or, if it was,
Origen regarded the passage as suspect and therefore refrained
from mentioning it.

Various attempts have been made to improve the text by leaving
out a few words here and there and by reading 'he was *not* the
Christ'; but it is highly unlikely that any authentic original
version can be recovered. We simply do not know the method
which the forger used. All we know is what Origen knew:
Josephus said something about Jesus and spoke of him as the
'so-called Christ'.

Three other testimonies come from a group of Roman officials
hostile to Christianity and other non-Roman religions, which
they regarded as expressions of fanaticism or, as they called them,
'superstition'. Pliny was legate to Bithynia and Pontus and wrote
to the emperor Trajan in January 112; Tacitus, once proconsul
of Asia (where Christians were fairly numerous), wrote his
Annals in 112–13; and Suetonius, formerly an imperial secretary,
published his gossipy *Lives of the Caesars* about 121.

Pliny tells us a good deal about Christians, little about Jesus.
(1) The Christians, he says, were accustomed to sing a hymn 'to
Christ as to a god'. This sentence shows that Pliny knew, or
believed, that Christ should be regarded not as a god but as a
man, one who had actually lived and died as a human being.
(2) Renegade Christians were willing to curse Christ; true
Christians could not be compelled to do so. Pliny was thus aware

of the intensity of Christian devotion to the (human) leader. But his statement (*Ep.* 10, 96) provides no direct data about Jesus himself.

Tacitus describes a great fire at Rome under Nero in the summer of 64, and he mentions the Christians whom the emperor used as scapegoats. As is his custom, he gives a brief summary of background material to explain who the Christians were. We do not know where he got his information. If it comes from police reports, these in turn were probably based on the interrogation of Christians (*Ann.* 15, 44).

> The founder of this sect, Christus, was given the death penalty in the reign of Tiberius by the procurator Pontius Pilate; suppressed for the moment, the detestable superstition broke out again, not only in Judaea where the evil originated, but also in the city [of Rome] to which everything horrible and shameful flows and where it grows.

Again, we learn something about Christianity. Momentarily suppressed at Christ's crucifixion, it 'rose again' in Judaea and spread to Rome (compare the account in Acts). Of Christ himself we learn only that he founded the sect and was executed under Pontius Pilate. This hardly adds much to what the New Testament says; and if Tacitus's ultimate source is Christian, it adds nothing.

Finally, Suetonius mentions the fire at Rome in connection with Christians (*Nero*, 16) and also says that in the reign of Claudius the emperor 'expelled from Rome the Jews who were constantly rioting at the instigation of Chrestus (*impulsore Chresto*)' (*Claudius*, 25). Since Claudius was emperor from 41 to 54, something is obviously wrong with this statement, even though one later Christian writer (Irenaeus) thought that Jesus was crucified during his reign. Probably it is a garbled version of a story about messianic riots in Rome, riots which could have resulted in the expulsion of such Christian Jews as Aquila and Priscilla (Acts 18.2). The passage shows that the name 'Chrestus' (=Christus) was known at Rome during the reign of Claudius. Once more, nothing is added to what we could have inferred from the New Testament.

Our four Graeco-Roman sources, then, contribute nothing to our understanding of the life of Jesus. The Christian interpolator of Josephus undoubtedly thought that he was helping history to confirm faith. All he succeeded in doing was to remove any independent value from the testimony of Josephus.

One might hope for some evidence from rabbinical Jewish sources, but the stories the rabbis tell are late in date and reflect no more than the attitude of the synagogue towards an early heretic.

We are left, then, with Christian testimony. If we wish to recover early non-Christian attitudes towards Jesus we can rely only on what Christian sources are willing to tell us about them. To be sure, we can find that they give us a considerable amount of information. Jesus was frequently accused of violating the Jewish law in regard to Sabbath observances and ritual purity. He was thought to claim divine prerogatives, such as forgiving sins, for himself. His driving out demons was sometimes ascribed to Beelzebul, the prince of demons. The expression 'son of Mary' used of him may perhaps reflect a suggestion (developed in later criticisms) that he was illegitimate. According to Luke, he was accused of leading a revolutionary movement, of forbidding the payment of taxes to the Romans, and of calling himself an anointed king. It is true that in part Christian writers report these accusations in order to contrast them with the true understanding which they themselves possess. But the accusations fit the first-century situation so well that we need not suppose that they were invented. Indeed, if we possessed a report from Pontius Pilate the 'facts' in it could hardly be very different from what the gospels tell us.

Within the Christian testimony, then, we find non-Christian elements. These elements are retained in support of Christian faith in Jesus; but the kind of faith they support is not something unrelated to events. The apostles and the evangelists are giving testimony to events in which, they believe, the work of God was made manifest – though not to all. Because historically the revelation was not received by all, the evangelists are free enough, and honest enough, to record the varying responses which were made to it. These responses, negative as well as positive, were included in the gospel story as they told it.

ORAL TRADITION

It has long been recognized that the gospels as we have them were not written immediately after the events which they describe. There was a period of oral tradition which preceded the writing of gospels, and the existence of this period, and of the traditions, can be proved from the New Testament itself. The earliest New Testament documents – the letters of the apostle Paul – make this point clear.

The first example seems to occur in I Thessalonians 4.15–17, where Paul is encouraging those of his readers who are distressed by the fact that some Christians have died before the coming of the Lord. He therefore makes a statement 'with a word of the Lord'. This word is that

> the Lord himself, at a word of command, at the cry of an archangel and the trumpet of God, will descend from heaven; and the dead in Christ will be raised first, then we who remain alive will be taken up in the clouds to meet the Lord in the air; and thus we shall always be with the Lord.

The closest gospel parallel to this saying is to be found in Matthew 24.30–1:

> they will see the Son of Man coming on the clouds of heaven with power and great glory; and he will send out his angels with a loud trumpet call, and they will gather his elect from the four winds, from one end of heaven to the other.

And in Matthew 24.34 we read that 'this generation will not pass away until all these things take place'. Here is where the problem arises at Thessalonica: some Christians have already passed away. There is another saying in the tradition, however, which allows for the distinction Paul makes; it is found in Matthew 16.27–8. The Son of Man will come with his angels, and there are 'some standing here' who will not taste death until they see him come (cf. Mark 9.1). We conclude that Paul is relying upon a tradition which is also reflected in these sayings in Matthew.

Similarly, when he reminds the Thessalonians that the Day of the Lord comes like a thief in the night (5.2) he has in mind the parable related in Matthew 24.43 (Luke 12.39–40); and his words about the unexpectedness of the Day recall such verses as Matthew 24.39 and Luke 21.34–5. The apocalyptic passage in II Thessalonians 1.7–2.12 is nothing but a further development of the apocalyptic elements in the synoptic gospels. In view of the differences between Paul's words and those reported in the gospels, we infer that he has relied upon oral tradition, however, not written accounts.

In I Corinthians Paul's use of oral tradition becomes even more evident. For instance, when he is giving instructions to married couples he says (7.10–11)

> to the married I give charge, not I but the Lord, that the wife should not separate from her husband (but if she does, let her remain single or else be reconciled to her husband) and that the husband should not divorce his wife.

The whole passage, including the words inserted parenthetically, is close to the words of Jesus as reported in Mark 10.11–12. It may well be that an earlier form of Jesus' saying is to be found in Matthew 19.9, where only divorce by the husband, as in Jewish practice (Deut. 24.1–4) is mentioned; but the extension of the principle is logical, indeed obvious, and is implied by the union of the couple to which Jesus refers (Mark 10.6–9; Gen. 1.27, 2.24).

In this section of I Corinthians it is quite clear that Paul is able to differentiate his own injunctions from those of the Lord. In dealing with mixed marriages he is able to state, 'to the rest I say, not the Lord' (7.12) and he can point out that 'concerning the unmarried I have no command of the Lord' (7.25). At the same time, in dealing with the unmarried he lays emphasis on the principle of being free from worries (7.32–4), and this principle is fully set forth in the tradition underlying Matthew 6.25–34 (Luke 12.22–31).

The payment of ministers is based on a commandment of the Lord (9.14): 'the Lord commanded those who proclaim the gospel to get their living by the gospel' – and this is almost certainly a reflection of the saying addressed to the Twelve in Matthew 10.10 and to the Seventy in Luke 10.7: 'the workman is worthy of his food [or wages].'

When Paul is introducing liturgical reforms at Corinth he reminds his readers of the words and deeds of the Lord Jesus 'on the night in which he was betrayed' (I Cor. 11.23–5). Here he says that he received the tradition 'from the Lord'; he means that the Lord, whether in his earthly ministry or now exalted, is the ultimate source of this account, which is very close to the narratives in the synoptic gospels (Mark 14.22-4 and parallels; especially Luke 22.19-20).

It is not so clear in I Corinthians 14.37 that Paul is referring to words of Jesus. Here he insists that what he is writing is a commandment of the Lord, and he is discussing the necessity for order in Corinthian worship. Perhaps it could be claimed that he is looking back to his injunction to be 'mature' or 'perfect' in thinking (14.20), and this could be based on something like Matthew 5.48 ('be perfect, as your heavenly Father is perfect').

Tradition is evidently reflected in I Corinthians 15.3-7, where Paul sets forth the common account of the death, burial, and resurrection of Jesus and then adds two lists of resurrection appearances; apparently the first comes from the circle of Peter, the second from that of James.

Such traditions are not so apparent in the later letters, though it seems hard to deny that, in setting forth the commandment to love one's neighbour as oneself and treating it as a summary of the law (Gal. 5.14; Rom. 13.8-10), Paul had in mind the fact that Jesus had done the same thing (Mark 12.28-31 and parallels).

From these passages we conclude that Paul was acquainted with collections of traditions which related both the words and the deeds of Jesus. Were they oral or written? From the freedom with which Paul handles them we should incline to think that they were oral. When he refers to writings he seems always to have the Old Testament in mind, and in his letters there is no reference to any gospel materials as recorded in written form ('the scriptures' in I Cor. 15.3-4 are Old Testament prophecies). The only possible exception to this statement occurs in I Timothy 5.18, where 'the scripture' says, 'You shall not muzzle an ox when it is treading out the grain (Deut. 25.4; I Cor. 9.9) and the workman is worthy of his wages (Luke 10.7; cf. I Cor. 9.14).' Here it would appear that the Pastor has referred to a written gospel what in I Corinthians was an allusion to oral tradition. It is most unlikely that the Gospel of Luke was written in Paul's lifetime (see page 211, and, on the Pastoral Epistles, pp. 209ff).

We conclude that Paul was acquainted only with oral traditions about the words and deeds of Jesus. Does this mean that in his time written records did not exist? Such an inference is not justified by what we know about Judaism in the first century, when many apocalypses and other documents were produced by Jewish teachers. Evidence is provided in abundance at Qumran, and the notion that the 'oral law' was entirely oral is not confirmed by students of rabbinic traditions.

At the same time, it seems significant that the tradition of Jesus' sayings, or at any rate of many of them, bears the marks of oral circulation. Many of his sayings have been handed down in an arrangement which reflects not the subject matter involved but a correlation by means of verbal association. Such an arrangement is especially conspicuous in Mark 9.33–50, where the subject changes from 'servant' to 'child' (the same word in Aramaic) to 'my name', then back to 'little ones' and on to 'cause to stumble', 'gehenna', 'fire', and 'salt'. Still more important, at points where Matthew and Luke report the same sayings, often the sayings subsequent to them are different because the verbal associations used as points of departure are different. As one example out of many, Matthew 10.19–21 is bound together by the word 'deliver'; Luke 12.10–12 is based on the phrase 'Holy Spirit'.[1] Such arrangements are characteristic of the transmission of oral materials. They suggest that until a time not long before the composition of the written gospels there was no uniform arrangement of the sayings of Jesus but that the sayings continued to be circulated orally. This is to say that oral traditions not only were characteristic of Paul's day but also continued to be utilized considerably later—at least into the decade between 60 and 70.

Certainly oral tradition continued to exist in much later times; but after written gospels began to be circulated, there was some tendency to favour the written at the expense of the oral, even though defenders of oral tradition like Papias insisted that oral reports of eye-witnesses were more reliable than written documents. 'I supposed that materials taken from books would not assist me as much as those received from a living, surviving oral witness' (Eusebius, *H. E.* 3, 39, 3).

If the tradition underlying the gospels was primarily oral, it is not surprising that efforts have been made to analyse it and to

[1] Cf. J. Jeremias in *ZNW* 29 (1930), 147–9.

attempt to differentiate more authentic materials from less authentic, and to treat the analysis as demonstrating the existence of various layers or levels of tradition.

FORM CRITICISM

Especially since the end of the first World War, scholars have been trying to get behind the written gospels to various stages of the tradition. They seem to have based their method primarily on similar studies of the 'sagas' underlying the patriarchal narratives of the Old Testament and of Germanic folk tradition. Though there is an obvious difference between traditions in circulation over a long period of time and the gospel traditions, crystallized in writing after being transmitted orally for little, if any, more than a generation, these scholars believed that the Christian traditions must have recapitulated in a very short time the processes which in other circles had extended over centuries.

Partly because of the different ways in which the various evangelists connected the single items contained in the traditions, form-critics proceeded to their task by first removing the framework provided by the evangelists. The function of this framework was only that of holding together the small units of tradition, which originally, it was believed, circulated independently. Such a conception of the framework is largely correct. We have already seen the part which verbal association played in combining sayings of Jesus. In addition, many of the links provided in the gospels are not very important. When Mark says 'after some days' or 'again' or 'immediately', it is doubtful that his chronology is very meaningful. When Luke arranges a good deal of material in relation to a journey of Jesus from Galilee to Jerusalem (Luke 9.51–18.14), the connectives he uses ('while on the way', 'after this', 'when he was in a certain place') do not seem very precise. Similarly, the arrangement provided by Matthew seems to exist primarily for the sake of relatively systematic teaching.

After the framework has been removed, we are left with collections of materials of various kinds in which non-literary 'forms' can be detected. (1) One form, especially favoured by Jesus, has already been discussed; this is the *parable.* (See Chapter IV). In addition to parables, there are, of course, other kinds of sayings. These have sometimes been classified as (2) proverbial sayings of the type to be found in Jewish – or for that matter Greek and Egyptian – wisdom literature; (3) prophetic and apocalyptic sayings; (4) legal prescriptions, perhaps formulated within Christian communities; and (5) 'I-sayings', usually of a kind which can be called 'programmatic' ('I came not to ... but to ...'). It is a question whether or not classifications such as this really illuminate the meaning or the transmission of the sayings involved.

There are also stories of various kinds. (1) There are 'apophthegm stories' in which a situation is described so that a setting may be provided for a saying or pronouncement by Jesus. The 'apophthegm' gives the whole story its point. (2) There are miracle stories, usually concerned with healings and exorcisms but sometimes demonstrating Jesus' power over 'inanimate nature'. In them we find (*a*) a description of the situation, (*b*) mention of the word or deed of Jesus, and (*c*) a brief remark about the effect of the miracle. Here too we may wonder whether our understanding of such stories is notably advanced by this classification. In human experience generally, stories are intended to set forth something striking that has been said or done. They begin with a situation and proceed to the word or act which this situation, so to speak, demands.

The basic purpose of form-criticism is not, however, limited to classifying the various units of tradition. Form-critics have generally made use of their classifications to get behind the gospels and look for earlier, purer 'strata of tradition'. For instance, they have held that the explanations of the parables do not belong with the parables, and that the moralizing conclusions often provided are secondary. They have also claimed that some miracle stories can be classified as 'Jewish' (healings and exorcisms) and therefore relatively early and authentic, while others are to be regarded as 'Hellenistic' (the so-called 'nature miracles') and therefore late and unreliable. This analysis is not very satisfactory, for (1) it introduces historical considerations into what was supposed to be literary, or pre-literary, analysis, and (2) as far as the miracle stories are concerned, those classified as 'Hellenistic' have very few Hellenistic parallels. On the other hand, it cannot be denied that those who transmitted the traditions about Jesus may have handled them with some measure of freedom.

The question of the nature of the witnesses to the oral tradition thus becomes important. Did Mark, for example, rely on miscellaneous witnesses when he compiled his materials, or did he make use of the teaching of the apostle Peter? Is the Gospel of Matthew really associated with the apostle whose name it bears?

Some scholars have claimed that the sayings of Jesus were remembered because Jesus taught his disciples to remember them. There seems to be no direct evidence to support this attractive theory, but it can at least be held that the fact that the sayings were remembered suggests that they were spoken in order to be remembered. There is an emphasis upon the words of Jesus in the gospels which seems inexplicable had he not regarded them as worth remembering (see Mark 13.31 and parallels).

It may be that modern analysis of the process of memory will contribute something to our consideration of this problem. In his classical work entitled *Remembering*, F. C. Bartlett has analysed two types of oral transmission. (1) The first he calls 'repeated reproduction'; this takes place when the same person reiterates what he has seen or heard. This kind of transmission presumably existed in the early Church, since not all the apostles died immediately. In repeated reproduction, Bartlett found, stereotypes are likely to arise and literal accuracy is unusual. There is a tendency to introduce rationalizations and even to substitute explanations for what they originally explained. Details are preserved only when they correspond with the transmitter's pre-formed interests and attitudes. The accuracy of the apostles' remembering, then, would depend in large measure on the extent to which they were genuinely dedicated to their mission. We may assume that they were so dedicated, and we may add that, in Bartlett's view, the total effect of repeated reproduction is often close to the original occurrence being remembered. (2) The second kind he calls 'serial remembering'; this takes place when a tradition passes down through a chain of rememberers. Here the situation is less satisfactory. Indeed, 'it looks as if what is said to be reproduced is, far more generally than is commonly admitted, really a construction, serving to justify whatever impression may have been left by the original' (p. 176).

This is to say that Bartlett's experiments confirm what common sense would expect. A record derived from an eye-witness is more reliable than one which has come from a chain of secondary witnesses. In dealing with the gospels, common sense would also suggest that at the time they were written, or may be supposed to have been written, there were eye-witnesses and their testimony was not completely disregarded. This is not to say that everything in the gospels is precisely and literally true. It is to say that in spite of the weaknesses of memory the evangelists' accounts should be given the benefit of the doubt.

The gospels are not simply the product of the Church. (1) Individuals, not communities, write books. (2) The evangelists regarded their function as that of bearing witness to Jesus Christ, not that of composing edifying fiction. There is no reason to suppose – though one form-critic supposed it – that there was ever a special class of 'story-tellers' in the Church. At the same time, the gospels were produced within the Church. They were not produced simply to 'meet the Church's needs' in various historical situations. The evangelists were not trying to 'make the gospel relevant'. They believed that it was relevant because they had accepted the call of Jesus. Though they inevitably wrote what they believed was meaningful to themselves and to others, they were not free to explain the apostolic testimony away.

This means that the gospels must be regarded as largely reliable witnesses to the life, death and resurrection of Jesus, and that the attitudes of the evangelists cannot be completely separated from the materials they are transmitting. For example, Christians had disputes about keeping the Sabbath; they had them because Jesus himself had treated the Sabbath with considerable freedom. They were concerned about divorce because Jesus had been so concerned. The life of the Church was not completely disjoined from the life of Jesus.

THE BIRTH OF JESUS

At a relatively early time, Christians were concerned with asserting that Jesus had not simply 'appeared' among men as if he were an angel or a spirit. He was actually born as a human being; he 'was born of the seed of David according to the flesh' (Rom. 1.3); he 'was born of a woman, born under the law' (Gal. 4.4). 'The

Word became flesh and dwelt among us' (John 1.14). In neither Mark nor John, however, is there any statement about the way in which he was born. In the New Testament such statements are provided only in the gospels of Matthew and Luke, which are in agreement in regard to several points. (1) The mother of Jesus, Mary, was betrothed to Joseph, a descendant of King David, but was a virgin at the time of his birth. (2) The conception of Jesus was due to the Holy Spirit. (3) An angel instructed either Mary or Joseph to name the child Jesus. (4) Jesus was born in Bethlehem during the reign of Herod I. The measure of agreement is obviously significant.

On the other hand, the stories diverge in regard to details. (1) The genealogies of Jesus in both Matthew and Luke are genealogies which (a) disagree with each other and (b) lead from Abraham or Adam to Jesus through Joseph, not Mary. According to Matt. 13.55 a crowd asks, 'Is not this the son of the carpenter?' just as in John 6.42 (cf. Luke 4.22) the Jews ask, 'Is not this Jesus the son of Joseph, whose father and mother we know?' Of course, it can be answered that (a) genealogies can be traced in several ways and that (b) legally, Joseph was the father of Jesus. Crowds are not necessarily reliable authorities. The reference to the brothers and sisters of Jesus (Mark 6.3) is harder to explain, though they may have been children of Joseph.

(2) There are some difficulties in relation to the place of the birth. Mark 6.1 speaks of Nazareth as the *patris* or native city of Jesus. Even though the word *patris* does not necessarily refer to a birthplace (see the reference to Philo, p. 276), Jesus is described as 'from Nazareth' in Acts 10.38 (cf. John 1.45–6). Matthew describes Joseph and Mary as first going to Nazareth after the death of Herod; Luke says that they came from Nazareth to Bethlehem and then returned there. Finally, Matthew 2.5–6 states that the birth in Bethlehem was to fulfil the prophecy of Micah 5.1–3 (cf. John 7.41–2), while Matthew 2.23 relates that Jesus lived in Nazareth because of what was said 'through the prophets': 'he shall be called Nazoraios' (Lev. 21.12? Judges 13.5?). What conclusion should be drawn from these passages?

(3) As we have said, Matthew and Luke agree that Jesus was born in the reign of Herod, in other words not later than 4 B.C. On the other hand, Matthew 2.22 describes the family as coming

to Nazareth while Archelaus was reigning, and Luke 2.1–3 says that Joseph took Mary from Nazareth to Bethlehem at the time of a census which was made for the first time when Quirinius was governor of Syria. The chief difficulty here is that Josephus (*War* 2, 118; *Ant.* 19, 355) describes what seems to be the same census as taking place when Judaea was placed under direct Roman rule in A.D. 6. There is no *direct* historical evidence for an earlier census, though it is possible that one was taken. It is hard to believe, though not inconceivable, that all who claimed Davidic descent were enrolled at Bethlehem rather than at the places where they lived.

Historically, then, there are strong, if not insuperable, difficulties in regard to the story or stories of the conception and birth of Jesus. None of the New Testament evidence shows that the virginal conception was regarded as an indispensable dogma by the earliest Christians.

There are some historical analogies to this idea. The idea that God's work is reflected in the births of patriarchs or heroes is to be found in the Old Testament patriarchal narratives (Gen. 17.19; 18.14; 21.1; 25.21; 29.31; 30.22) and in the accounts of Samson (Judges 13.3) and Samuel (I Sam. 1.19–20) – as well as in the story of John the Baptist (Luke 1.25). In addition, whether the prophecy of Isaiah 7.14 refers to a young woman or to a virgin who would conceive and bear a son Immanuel, among Hellenistic Jews, and doubtless among others, the word was understood to mean 'virgin'. The fact that Greeks, Romans and others told stories about the miraculous conceptions of various 'divine men' suggests how the virginal conception of Jesus may have won ready acceptance in the Graeco-Roman world, but it does not explain the origin of the belief. In other words, analogies to be found either in the Old Testament or in the world outside Judaism are nothing but analogies. They neither substantiate nor demolish the historical nature of the story. Indeed, while some Graeco-Roman writers regarded virginal conceptions as possible, others insisted that they were not.

It has been suggested that the story of the virginal conception reflects an attempt to solve the problem of Christ's nature in relation to his origin. On this view, the picture of the pre-existence and incarnation of the Word in the Gospel of John is the result of a similar attempt with different results. We do not know, however, that the story came into existence for this reason.

If we turn from the main emphases of the stories in Matthew and Luke to their details, we find that Matthew is concerned with relating his version as closely as possible to the Old Testament. He stresses the fulfilment of prophecy and describes Joseph as a dreamer like his Old Testament prototype. Some details have often been questioned. What of the star of Bethlehem and the visit of the Magi? Presumably the star is that predicted in Numbers 24.17, and the Magi are Zoroastrian astrologers who played a significant rôle in the first century. At the court of Archelaus were Chaldaean astrologers and Essenes who interpreted his dreams (Josephus, *War* 2, 112). Magi came to Rome in the year 66 and acknowledged the divine nature of Nero. This is to say that some aspects of the story are historically possible, at least. As for the slaughter of the innocents (Matt. 2.16-18), Matthew regards it as a fulfilment of Jeremiah 31.15. Did he or some predecessor invent the story after finding the prophecy? Is the story intended to explain why Jesus was in Egypt and could be regarded as fulfilling Hosea 11.1? Or was there actually some such massacre in the last years of Herod's bloody reign?

Our judgement on such questions will depend upon the view we take of Matthew's writing as a whole. The entire second chapter of his gospel is tied together by means of a series of 'prophecies' regarded as fulfilled in the early life of Jesus. (1) There is an allusion to the star and rising sceptre of Numbers; then (2) comes an explicit quotation from Micah 5.2 (Bethlehem). (3) The journey to and return from Egypt fulfils Hosea 11.1, treated as prophecy because in Hebrew the perfect tense can refer either to past or to future. At the end of the chapter come (4) the quotation from Jeremiah and (5) the statement about the Nazoraios to which we have already referred. What are we to make of this collection of prophecies, and of the stories related to them? Some scholars have spoken of Matthew as a writer of haggadic legends, based on Old Testament texts and imaginatively expanding them. This theory might well explain the choice of all the Old Testament passages but one, Jeremiah 31.15, and Matthew or some earlier Christian may have been meditating upon the general resemblances between the early life of Jesus and such messianic texts as those discovered at Qumran. The fact that Matthew's narrative is historically possible does not prove that the events occurred just as he describes them, and it is very hard to reconcile with the account given in Luke 2.8–40.

The ultimate difficulty with the whole narrative of the conception, birth and infancy of Jesus lies in the modern (and ancient, too) belief in the general regularity of natural processes. In early Jewish Christianity there were those who held that Jesus was the son of Joseph and Mary, though we do not know why they maintained this view. Theological ideas have varied in relation to this subject. Most Christians have insisted that if Jesus was the Son of God he must not have had a human father. Others have argued that if he was fully human as well as fully divine he must have had two human parents. The more traditional view is based on a definition of human and divine nature in terms of essences, natures or origins. The less traditional view is primarily concerned with Jesus in terms of the response of faith to him, though the question of 'nature' is not necessarily overlooked.

The story of the virginal conception is not central to the New Testament picture of the life, death, and resurrection of Jesus. Without such an event as the resurrection or, at least, the visions of the first Easter, the existence of the Church is inexplicable (cf. I Cor. 15.14-18), though obviously the theological significance of the event is not limited to its 'happenedness' or to the explanations given by the earliest witnesses. Such a story as that of the virginal conception is less important. It has no place in the apostolic preaching to Jews or to gentiles; there is not even an allusion to it except in the two or to gentiles; there is not even an allusion to it except in the two narratives in Matthew and Luke; even where Paul and others point towards esoteric teaching they are not pointing in the direction of this story. What it must represent is an attempt to state a way in which God's creative activity, reflected in the resurrection and in the ministry of Jesus, was manifest in the way in which he was generated. In Matthew the virginal conception takes place in order to show that Jesus' origin was due to the Holy Spirit. He is, in the words of the prophet Isaiah, Emmanuel, 'God with us'. Similarly in Luke's account Mary is to conceive because the Holy Spirit will come upon her and the power of the

Most High will overshadow her; her son will be called the Son of God. The environment of both stories is to be found in Jewish Christianity, but it is a kind of Jewish Christianity concerned with making the meaning of Jesus comprehensible to gentiles. And it is at this point that we can probably understand the tendency of Ebionite Jewish Christianity to speak of Jesus as the son of Joseph and Mary. Not only did the Ebionites often retain archaic traditions; they had no mission to the gentile world except in the sense that they wanted gentiles to become Jews and accept Jewish customs.

The kind of Jewish Christianity in which the story of the virginal conception makes historical sense is one which, like that of Philo, looks outward to the gentile world and has a mission to it. And this is obviously the kind of Jewish Christianity reflected in both Matthew and Luke. In Matthew, Jesus first sends his disciples only to the empirical Israel, but after his resurrection he sends them out to all the world; a similar picture is set forth in Luke; after the resurrection the disciples are told to remain in Jerusalem until they have received power from on high and then to preach to all nations.

The story of the virginal conception, then, is likely to be an explanation of the significance of Jesus in terms of origins and in the light of the resurrection and the consequent gentile mission. It is analogous to Paul's interpretation of Jesus as the pre-existent Wisdom of God, the instrument not only of redemption but also of creation, and to John's picture of the pre-existent word of God who became incarnate. Symbolically it is important because it reflects an insistence upon God's freedom to act and to create novelty. God's freedom is not limited by his creatures. But at the same time, as some of the early Fathers recognized, the Jesus who was son of Mary was not a creature in the sense that God created him absolutely *de novo*. Because he was son of Mary he was a human being. He really lived, really grew up (as Luke makes clear), and really died.

It is always difficult, if not dangerous, to try to separate events from their significance, or vice versa. But there are examples in the Old Testament of 'events' which, while not historical in the ordinary sense, convey important theological insights. The most obvious example is the story of creation and the life of Adam in paradise. And it may well be the case that not everything in the New Testament should be regarded as historically true. Probably it would be right to say that everything is historically true in the sense that it reflects the life and thought of the early Church, but not in the sense that it is literally true.

If one attempts to by-pass theological questions by an 'appeal to history' it must be admitted that the historical method as such can provide little guidance on this problem. Two evangelists describe the virginal conception and the birth of Jesus in rather different ways. If they were in complete agreement, it might be suspected that they had relied on a previously invented story. Suspicion arises in relation to the differences which now exist. How many differences would be required in order for us to regard their narratives as absolutely authentic and reliable? To ask this question suggests that it cannot be answered.

JESUS IN THE TEMPLE

The apocryphal gospels tell us stories of the early years of Jesus. He made clay pigeons which would actually fly; he restored to life a playmate whom he had accidentally pushed off a rooftop; he amazed a teacher who wanted him to express the second letter of the alphabet by asking him the real meaning of the first letter. The legendary character of such accounts is self-evident.

In three of our gospels we hear nothing of Jesus' early years. Luke, however, describes two episodes from this period, both related to the temple in Jerusalem. The first story deals with the purification of Mary after childbirth, in accordance with the law of Leviticus 12.4–8. Since her means were inadequate for the purchase of a lamb, she bought two sacrificial birds, as the law allowed. Luke's emphasis, however, is not on the mother but on the child. The visit of the family to Jerusalem took place so that Jesus could be presented to God in the temple, in accordance with Exodus 13.2, 'Sanctify unto me all the first-born.' It was the occasion of prophecies delivered by the aged Symeon and Anna, both of whom were awaiting the deliverance of Israel. They found prophecies fulfilled in the presence of Jesus. The second story is concerned with a visit of Jesus to the temple at the age of twelve, when he was probably first regarded as old enough to participate n the Passover celebration there. His parents left him behind when they began their homeward journey, and when they returned to Jerusalem they found him in the temple raising questions with the 'teachers' there. Naturally they were surprised at his situation; they were even more surprised when he told them that he had to be in his Father's house. This view of the temple suggests that the story comes from early Jewish Christianity such as that reflected in Acts 3.1, where Peter and John are described as going up to the temple to pray.

The source of these stories is clearly described by Luke (2.51) as the mother of Jesus. Their atmosphere is clearly quite different from that of the apocryphal gospels, and it may possibly be the case that Mary did remember them and transmit them to others. According to Acts 1.14 she was a member of the early Church in Jerusalem.

JOHN THE BAPTIST

By the time Jesus was 'about thirty years old' (Luke 3.23), a prophet had arisen in the region near the Jordan River and not far from Qumran. Luke dates the coming of God's word to this person, John the Baptist, as taking place in the fifteenth year of Tiberius Caesar (3.1); by this year he means either A.D. 26 or A.D. 27.

In order to understand the rise of John we must bear in mind the expectations of the Essenes. They looked forward to the time when God would act to destroy evil and evil men, and would reward those who had become members of the holy congregation. There would be a final war, a final victory, and a final judgement. But when? The Habakkuk Commentary says that 'the final moment may be protracted beyond anything the prophets have foretold.' The War Scroll seems to suggest that unpredictable comets will indicate the coming of the final struggle. And a fragment on the new covenant says that God will choose a people in the time of his good pleasure; in other words, one cannot tell when he will do so.

At that time, there was to come a prophet, the one foretold by Moses, and two Messiahs, one a layman, the other a priest. Sometimes the prophet is not mentioned and we hear simply of the coming of a 'faithful shepherd' like Moses himself. At the hour of judgement, says one of the hymns of thanksgiving, rivers like fire will pour forth, consuming everything in their way.

Now if we bear these expectations in mind we can understand the sudden appearance of John the Baptist. John was an ascetic. He wore camel's hair clothing and a leather girdle; he ate locusts and wild honey (mentioned in the Zadokite Document). And he preached a 'baptism of repentance for the remission of sins'. To his hearers he repeated the words of the prophet Isaiah, 'The voice of one crying in the wilderness, "Make ready the way of the Lord, make his paths straight"' (Is. 40.3). Here we must wonder whether our evangelists have quoted John correctly, for we now know that in the Manual of Discipline men were told to go into the wilderness to prepare the way – reading Isaiah not as 'a voice in the wilderness' but 'in the wilderness make ready a way'. This is what those who followed John did; they went into the 'wilderness' to be baptized by him.

To those who went out he said, 'You offspring of vipers, who warned you to flee from the wrath to come?' Then he launched into an attack on those who thought that they would be saved simply because of their Jewish descent. 'Do not say in yourselves, "We have Abraham for our father," for God can raise up children for Abraham from these stones.'

> Right now the axe is laid at the root of the trees; every tree that does not bring forth good fruit will be cut down and cast into the fire.

This is the same sharp distinction between good and evil which we have already seen in the Dead Sea community and its message. And John's prescription for goodness is the same as that of the Essenes. 'He who has two coats is to give to him who has none, and he who has food is to do likewise.' All were to share their property.

But then who was John? Was he himself the expected Messiah? No, he says,

> I indeed baptize you with water; but after me
> there comes one greater than I am, whose sandal's thong

I am not worthy to loosen; he will baptize you
in spirit and fire:
his winnowing-fan is in his hand, and he will thoroughly
cleanse his threshing-floor,
and gather the wheat into his barn;
but the chaff he will burn up with unquenchable fire.

John himself was the 'prophet' of the coming Messiah, not the
Messiah himself; and he predicted the sprinkling of the Spirit
by the Messiah, and the cosmic fire, which the Dead Sea people
foretold.

Here we must turn aside to look at a different account of
John's work which is given by the historian Josephus; and we
must remember that Josephus is always anxious to show how
politically harmless the leaders of Jewish religion were, and how
little they predicted coming disasters. Josephus can be expected
to leave out whatever was distinctive about John's message. In
any event this is what Josephus says of John:

> This good man told the Jews to practise justice towards one
> another and piety towards God, and then to come to
> baptism. For the washing would then be acceptable to God,
> not as a begging-off for certain sins but as a purification of
> the body; the soul was already purified by justice.

Two points deserve notice. (1) It has often been supposed that the
contrast between body and soul is Josephus's own contribution,
based on Greek ideas. We now know, however, that the Essenes
of Qumran also contrasted body with soul. Moreover, while
'justice' and 'piety' are clearly Greek terms (Josephus was writing
in Greek), he uses the same ones when he describes the initiation
oath of the Essenes. (2) The Qumran Manual of Discipline
agrees exactly with what Josephus says when it states that 'no
one is to go into water to attain the purity of holy men; for men
cannot be purified unless they repent their evil.' In other words,
Josephus describes John in language which reveals how close
John was to the Essenes. He gives no reason for John's proclamation and omits any reference to God's wrath or to one who
would come later, since he wants to divorce 'this good man' from
apocalyptic hopes.

The preaching of John thus closely resembles that of the Dead Sea community, near which his baptism was performed. But the two kinds of baptism were not identical. At Qumran baptism was not only a rite of initiation but also a rite frequently repeated. It was only for members of the monastic community. For John, baptism took place once only, and he offered it to any who would come.

It is possible that John had once been a member of the Qumran community. He differed from it, however, in two respects: (1) God would express his wrath without the military assistance of the Essene army, and (2) God's blessings were to be offered to the Jewish people as a whole, not just to the sect's members. In this way, it might be supposed, he modified the teaching of the Dead Sea group much as the apostle Paul modified that of earlier Jewish Christianity. And just as the old Jewish Christianity gradually disappeared while gentile Christianity flourished, so the Qumran group was finally destroyed while in John and Jesus its message, completely reinterpreted, lived on. Neither Jewish Christianity nor the Dead Sea group was able to last for long after the fall of Jerusalem.

John's relation to the Essenes is important; much more important is the relation between him and Jesus. Here we have to deal with the gospels with considerable care. The evangelists are very anxious to make two points clear. First, they want to remind their readers that John was not the Messiah; this point is stressed in the gospels of Luke (3.15) and John (1.20; 3.28). They say plainly that he is not the Messiah; and this view seems to be historically sound, at least in the sense that he makes no claim for himself, even though in the second century there was a Jewish sect which made the claim for him (*Clem. Rec.* 1, 60). Second, the evangelists want to indicate that John recognized Jesus as the Coming One whom he preceded.

At this point their evidence is somewhat ambiguous. It is undoubtedly a fact that Jesus was baptized by John. The evangelist Matthew finds the story so embarrassing that he has John say that he would prefer to be baptized by Jesus (3.14). But both Matthew (11.3) and Luke (7.19) tell us that when John was in prison he sent disciples to ask Jesus, 'Are you the Coming One, or do we expect someone else?' This question suggests that by having John recognize Jesus at his baptism the evangelists are making explicit a relationship which was not quite so clear. Before his death, John may have decided that Jesus was the one whose coming he had foretold; probably he did not recognize him in the crowds who came to the Jordan. In the Gospel of John, Jesus' earliest disciples come from those of the Baptist. This idea may well be historically correct, and it helps explain the Gospel of John itself, as we shall later see.

It is significant that Jesus was baptized by John. This means that he, like others who took part in this baptism, believed that John was right in predicting the coming fire and cosmic conflict; that he too believed that the end was at hand. It means that he believed that God was going to act as judge, and that those who lived in accordance with God's will would be judged favourably.

Once more, just as John's message was not precisely that of the Essenes, so the message of Jesus was not that of either the Essenes or John. For the Essenes, the way of the future was the way of battle and victory. For John it was escape from the coming disaster. For Jesus it was whole hearted acceptance of what God might bring, in obedience to his will.

THE BAPTISM OF JESUS

The synoptic gospels agree that Jesus was baptized by John, and that as he came up from the water he saw the Spirit of God descending as a dove upon him. Luke adds that he was praying and that the Spirit descended 'in bodily form like a dove'. John says that it was John the Baptist who saw the Spirit descend. Apparently both evangelists are trying to make the experience less subjective.

A similar tendency is evident when Matthew rewrites Mark. In Mark there is a voice from heaven (like the *bath qol* mentioned by the rabbis) which says, 'You are my beloved Son; with you I am well pleased' (Psalm 2.7; Is. 42.1). In Matthew the voice says, 'This is my beloved Son. . . .' Thus testimony is given to the witnesses present rather than to Jesus. A few manuscripts of Luke modify the statement still more by making it a direct quotation of Psalm 2.7, but this reading is hardly original.

THE TEMPTATION OF JESUS

According to the three synoptic gospels, Jesus was tempted or tested by Satan in the desert immediately after his baptism. John makes no mention of this occurrence, probably because in his view the incarnate Word was not subject to temptation. The accounts in the synoptics are rather divergent. According to Mark, the Spirit (received at the baptism) drove him into the desert, where for forty days he was tempted by Satan. There he was with wild animals, and angels served him – presumably with food, as in the story of Elijah (I Kings 19.5–8). Angelic guardians and the danger of wild beasts are also found in Psalm 91.11–13. Matthew and Luke, evidently following a common written source at this point, describe Jesus as fasting for forty days and nights (as Moses did, Exod. 34.28), and then being tempted by the devil. The first temptation was therefore 'if you are the Son of God' to convert stones into bread. To this suggestion Jesus replied by quoting Deuteronomy 8.3: 'Man will not live by bread alone, but by every word which proceeds from the mouth of God.' Matthew and Luke present the other two temptations in different sequences. According to Matthew, the second took place when the devil took Jesus to the 'wing' of the temple and said to him, 'If you are the Son of God, cast yourself down.' Psalm 91.11–12 contained a promise that angels would protect the godly man. Jesus replied by quoting Deuteronomy again: 'you shall not test the Lord your God' (6.16; cf. Isaiah 7.12). Finally the devil took him to a high mountain and showed him all the kingdoms of the world; these would be his if he would worship him. Once more a verse from Deuteronomy provided the answer: 'you shall worship the Lord your God . . .' (6.13).

The point conveyed by this story may be that, though Jesus as Son of God possessed the powers ascribed to him by the devil, he was unwilling to use them for Satan's purposes. But since this point is not brought out in the third temptation, it is more likely that the basic purpose of the narrative is the same as that in Mark. It depicts a struggle between Jesus and Satan which resembles the testing of Adam and Eve in the garden of Eden. Adam and Eve yielded to Satan's wiles; Jesus resisted them and remained obedient to God. The details of the story can hardly be taken literally. As Origen pointed out, there are no mountains from which all the kingdoms of the world can be seen. Presumably the account was not intended literally. It is a portrayal of an inner struggle, not one which can be located geographically.

Some of the Church Fathers thought that the devil did not know who Jesus was; he was trying to find out by means of his suggestions. This interpretation is improbable since the devil's ignorance is intimated, in the New Testament, only in I Corinthians 2.8, and in the synoptics as a whole, demonic powers are depicted as recognizing Jesus without difficulty.

It has also been held that in this story Jesus is rejecting the use of miraculous powers altogether. Such a notion finds a parallel in Mark 8.12, where Jesus tells the Pharisees that 'no sign will be given to this generation'. It is evident, however, that none of the synoptic evangelists can have understood it in this way. All three of them describe the multiplication of loaves and fishes and the stilling of a storm; Matthew and Mark report that Jesus walked on the Lake of Galilee. It is hard to find a non-miraculous kernel of the gospel.

After the temptation, the public ministry of Jesus begins.

THE GOSPEL IN GALILEE

Though the baptism of Jesus took place in the Jordan, probably near the point where it enters the Dead Sea, and the temptation was in some desert region perhaps in the same vicinity, Jesus began his ministry in Galilee, the region in which he had been brought up. The gospels disagree as to the way in which this beginning was made.

Mark (1.14–21) gives the following sequence of events: (1) the arrest of John the Baptist, (2) Jesus' entrance into Galilee, (3) his call of the first four disciples, and (4) his teaching in the synagogue at Capernaum. Matthew and Luke agree that Jesus entered Galilee after John's arrest, though the Fourth Evangelist explicitly states that John had not yet been imprisoned (3.24). Both Matthew and Luke place the call of the disciples after Jesus' teaching in Capernaum. Matthew emphasizes the importance of Capernaum by saying that the preaching there fulfilled the prophecy of Isaiah 9.1–2; but he does not describe Jesus' activities as Mark does. Luke has the ministry begin at Nazareth (4.16–30), though he alludes to events which previously took place at Capernaum (4.23); Jesus then goes to Capernaum, now identified as 'a city of Galilee' (4.31). Oddly enough, though John gives a completely different account of the beginning of the ministry, he does state that from Cana in Galilee Jesus went down to Capernaum with his mother, his brothers and his disciples; but he adds that they stayed there 'not many days' (2.12). For John the 'holy city' of Galilee is Cana, not Capernaum.

In the gospels only two indications of the occasion of Jesus' first preaching can be found. (1) The quotation of Isaiah in Matthew points towards 'Galilee of the gentiles' as a land of messianic expectation. 'The people that walked in darkness have seen a great light: they that dwelt in the land of the shadow of death, upon them has the light shined.' It was in Galilee that the revolutionist Judas had proclaimed that God alone should be king. Though no other evangelist uses the prophecy in this way (cf. Luke 1.79), Jesus may have chosen Galilee not only because he was familiar with it but also because it was a land of 'darkness'. Certainly Judaeans were not enthusiastic about it. 'Can any good thing come out of Nazareth?' (John 1.46) 'Search, and see that no prophet arises out of Galilee' (7.52). (2) The synoptists' mention of the arrest of John the Baptist may provide an occasion for Jesus' proclamation. Having been baptized by John, he could recognize in his arrest a beginning of God's wrathful judgement. Such an explanation, however, seems suspect in view of the explicit statement in the Gospel of John that the Baptist had not yet been put in prison. More probably, both Jesus and John were working at the same time, at least for some months.

What Jesus proclaimed is briefly set forth by Mark in these words: 'the time has been completed and the kingdom of God has drawn near; repent and believe in the gospel.' (Luke 4.16–27 is an expansion of this theme and contains typically Lucan allusions to gentiles.) Like other allusive reports of mission preaching (e.g., I Thess. 1.9–10), this one is not fully comprehensible unless it is expanded. (1) What is the 'time' which has been completed? Presumably the background of this word lies in Jewish apocalyptic literature like the book of Daniel, in which we read that 'the ancient of days came, and judgement was given o the saints of the Most High, and the time came that the saints possessed the kingdom' (7.22). (2) The 'kingdom of God' is his everlasting dominion which he will give to 'the people of the saints of the Most High' (Dan. 7.27). (3) The 'gospel' is the message that the kingdom of God is at hand, though it could be expanded by statements about God's demands upon men such as we find in the synoptics.

If men sought evidence that the reign of God was being inaugurated, they could find it in the power of Jesus over demons and diseases, as we learn elsewhere in the gospels.

THE CALL OF THE FIRST DISCIPLES

Jesus was not content to proclaim the coming of the reign of God; he also called disciples to assist him in his mission. This call (and consequently the picture of the mission) is presented in different ways by the various evangelists. (1) In Mark 1.16–20 Jesus is walking along the lake of Galilee when he sees two brothers, Simon and Andrew, casting their nets. He says to them, 'Follow me and I will make you fishers for men.' They follow; soon afterwards, they encounter two more brothers, James and John, who join the group. In the Old Testament the image of fishing for men is used of God's judgement. The fishermen are representatives of God's wrath; they take the fish from the water and harm them with nets or hooks (Amos 4.2; Hab. 1.15; Jer. 16.16). The same figure is to be found in the Dead Sea Psalms of Thanksgiving (col. 5, 7–8). The meaning of the word of Jesus is presumably analogous. Those who follow him will be proclaiming the coming wrath of God, though they must also be telling men how this wrath is to be avoided by repentance (cf. Mark 1.15). (2) The same story is told in Matthew 4.18–22, but in Matthew 13.47–50 the significance of the net is modified in relation to the Church. In the kingdom of heaven there are both good and bad fish; they will be separated by angels at the end of the world. (3) Luke (5.1–10) changes the story by placing it in a context of a miraculous catch of fish. He makes no reference to any possible eschatological meaning. Instead, Simon, James and John are astounded by their catch and because of their astonishment are ready to follow Jesus. (4) In the Gospel of John (1.35–51) the saying about fishing for men disappears entirely. John the Baptist tells Andrew and someone else that Jesus is the Lamb of God. After the two visit Jesus, Andrew brings his brother Simon to him. The next day, Jesus calls Philip simply by saying, 'Follow me,' and Philip informs Nathanael that Jesus is the one predicted in the law and the prophets. Nathanael, impressed by Jesus' recognition of him before his call, hails him as the Son of God and the king of Israel. The whole account has been set in a different key.

If we assume, as we probably should, that both Matthew and Luke represent versions secondary to that in Mark, we are left with a choice between Mark and John. Both narratives treat Simon and Andrew as among the earliest disciples, though in John, Simon is the third disciple to follow Jesus, not the first (cf. John 20.2–8; 21.7, 15–23). The call itself is delivered in different ways. In Mark it consists of the saying about fishers for men, while in John it is based on a word of John the Baptist and Jesus' own command to come and follow him. In John, as in the rest of his gospel (except 21.2), there is no mention of the sons of Zebedee. How can these differences be explained? Presumably the most satisfactory conclusion is to admit that both are right and that some disciples followed Jesus for one reason, others for another. Some of his disciples may well have come to him from John the Baptist; others probably did not. The notion that Simon Peter was called only indirectly may be due to a special concern of the Fourth Evangelist, but we cannot tell whether this concern was based on fact or not. Mark's notion of Peter's chronological primacy may be due to Peter's own view of the matter.

These human factors must be borne in mind rather than any *a priori* theory as to how early Christianity developed.

APOSTLES

According to Mark 3.14–16 there was a special group among the disciples of Jesus. Mark says that 'he made twelve to be with him and to send them to preach and to have authority to cast out demons.' Then he repeats his first words: 'and he made the twelve.' There follows a list of twelve names. In Mark 6.7 we read that he sent out the twelve, two by two; when they return, Mark (6.30) speaks of them as 'the apostles'. Matthew (10.1–2) identifies the twelve disciples as the twelve apostles; so does Luke.

It is fairly evident that at a very early time it was recognized that Jesus was accompanied by a group of disciples called 'the twelve'; this title occurs in all four gospels, as well as in I Corinthians 15.5. In Luke 22.30 Jesus tells his disciples that they will 'sit on thrones judging the twelve tribes of Israel'; Matthew (19.28) probably does no more than make explicit what was already implied when he refers to 'twelve thrones'.

Difficulties arise when we try to determine (1) who the Twelve were and (2) whether Jesus called them apostles or not. In the synoptic gospels and Acts we find four lists of the twelve.

Mark 3.16–19

(1) Simon Peter
(2) James s. Zebedee
(3) John s. Zebedee
(4) Andrew
(5) Philip
(6) Bartholomew
(7) Matthew
(8) Thomas
(9) James s. Alphaeus
(10) Thaddaeus
(11) Simon Cananaeus
(12) Judas Iscariot

Apart from minor differences in order, the lists all agree as to the first eight names, though some manuscripts of Matthew substitute 'Lebbaeus' for Thomas (No. 8, in seventh position); others combine Lebbaeus with Thomas; and the Old Latin version substitutes 'Judas the Zealot'. In Luke–Acts the description of Simon as Cananaeus is interpreted by calling him 'Simon the Zealot', and 'Judas son of James' is substituted for Thaddaeus. Only half of these names are mentioned in the Gospel of John, but the evangelist mentions 'the Twelve' three times. From these facts we should conclude that the names of most of the Twelve were fairly well known, but that some of them were not especially significant in relation to the story of Jesus.

Did Jesus call them 'apostles'? Only Luke (6.13) says that he did so, and it seems more likely that the name developed from later recognition of the mission which they performed. In the non-technical sense ('one sent') the word occurs in John 13.16 (compare Matt. 10.24, where 'disciple' is used), and it may also be non-technical in Mark 6.30. Such a picture may be confirmed by I Corinthians 15.5–7, where the Twelve are differentiated from 'all the apostles'.

What we discover in the New Testament record, then, is that Jesus called twelve disciples to accompany him and to proclaim his gospel; at the coming of the kingdom they were to act as judges of the twelve tribes. That they expected such honour is suggested by the story about the request made by James and John, the sons of Zebedee (Mark 10.35–45), who asked Jesus for positions on his right and on his left. It should be added that an element of judgement was already present in their preaching mission. Those who accepted the gospel would enter into the kingdom; those who rejected it had judged themselves already. If men did not receive them, they were to shake off the dust under their feet as a testimony to them (Mark 6.11; cf. Matt. 10.14–15; Luke 10.10–12). There is no record of their going into gentile territory or of conducting any mission to gentiles. As Matthew (10.5–6) reports, they were to go to the lost sheep of the house of Israel – primarily to those Jews who owed no allegiance to the parties of the Pharisees or the Sadducees or, for that matter, the Essenes.

The Twelve, then, had a present function and a future office. Apparently it was after the death and resurrection of Jesus that they came to be called apostles and that, indeed, the conception of apostles as the leaders of the community arose. This question will be discussed in Chapter XXI.

MIRACLES

For modern readers of the gospels it is often something of an embarrassment that so much of the ministry of Jesus is characterized by works of power, by 'paradoxical events', by 'works', and by 'marvels' – in short, by miracles. Sometimes refuge is sought in the meaning of the word especially favoured by John, a 'sign' which points beyond the outward and visible 'work' to its inner meaning for faith. This solution is not very happy, for John not only lays stress on signs but also insists upon the reality of the works. Other ways of avoiding miracle have been found by means of a kind of historical criticism. Exorcisms were characteristic of first-century Palestine, and Jesus therefore performed them. Stories which describe miracles which we find more incredible can be assigned to the Graeco-Roman world. Such criticism, while in matters of detail perhaps correct, does not touch the real problem: the ministry of Jesus is full of miracles and the expectation of more miracles; his resurrection is the miraculous culmination of his ministry. Sometimes it is supposed that miracles are the result of 'projections' backwards into the ministry from the resurrection. It seems more accurate, however, to suggest that the disciples would not have believed in the resurrection had they not been prepared to accept its reality on the ground of something that had happened earlier.

It may be added that objection to miracles is not a modern phenomenon. In antiquity there were those who did not accept the truth of stories about them. Indeed, the so-called Gospel of Thomas can be regarded as an anti-miraculous document. Jesus was so spiritual that he cannot have bothered to deal with the natural world. (Of course this is not the only ground on which miracles were or are rejected.)

In dealing with miracle-stories we may make a distinction, for convenience, between (1) exorcisms and healings and (2) what we call nature-miracles, though we must bear in mind that the early tradition did not draw such a line. Jesus addressed a demon and a storm at sea in the same way (Mark 1.25; 4.39) and he once cursed a fig tree (11.14).

Yet he himself clearly regarded exorcisms and healings as of primary importance. 'If I by the finger of God cast out demons,' he said, 'then the reign of God has come upon you' (Luke 11.20; cf. Matt. 12.28). The expulsion of these invisible powers, responsible for sin and disease, was the chief sign of the coming of God's kingdom. Thus Mark tells of an unclean spirit who recognizes Jesus as the Holy One of God and comes out of a man at his command (1.23–6). According to Mark's summaries Jesus cured many demoniacs (1.34; 2.11), though the evangelist gives only three other examples, all special cases (the Gerasene demoniac, 5.2–20; the Greek woman's daughter, 7.25–30; and the man whom the disciples could not cure, 9.14–29). It is plain that Jesus was well known as an exorcist, for it was said that others used his name in order to expel demons (9.38–9), and the 'scribes from Jerusalem' argued that he possessed the demon Beelzebub and therefore was casting out demons by their chief. Jesus pointed out the absurdity of their claim. How could Satan cast out Satan? Such inconsistent conduct would bring his reign to an end (3.22–6).

In ancient belief it was necessary for demons, since they were discarnate spirits, to find some other abode once they had left their victims. For this reason the 'legion' possessing the Gerasene demoniac went into two thousand swine and may have drowned with them in the sea. Sometimes, as Jesus observes, an unclean spirit returns, along with others more wicked than himself, and with their aid makes the victim's final situation worse than it was originally (Luke 11.24–6; Matt. 12.43–5). The power of the exorcist is shown by the numbers expelled, as in the case of the seven driven out of Mary Magdalene (Luke 8.2).

The presence of demons was detected by abnormal actions such as shouting (Mark 1.23), living in tombs while shouting and cutting oneself with stones (5.5), foaming at the mouth, gnashing teeth, and fainting, as well as jumping into fire (9.18, 20). Inability to speak could also be caused by a demon (Luke 11.14; Matt. 9.32). Clearly such cases resemble those of psychological ailments common enough today. Jesus cured them with a word of command (Mark 1.25; 5.8; 9.25), following a preliminary question of concern and recognition by the demon (1.24; 5.7) or a statement of faith by a relative of the patient (9.24). The result was a loud cry of crisis (1.26; 9.26) and an immediate cure, with subsequent health (7.30).

Closely related to these illnesses which we should call mental are the cases of physical illness. Jesus regarded his cures of these as important, for he sent word about them to John in prison (Luke 7.22–3; Matt. 11.4–6). He cured Peter's mother-in-law of a fever by raising her by the hand; 'the fever left her and she served them' (Mark 1.29–31). Jesus touched and spoke to a leper, and the leprosy left him at once (1.40–2; ultimately it makes little difference whether or not ancient and modern leprosy are the same). When he stated that a paralytic's sins were forgiven and told him to get up, lift up his bed, and walk, he was immediately cured (2.3–12). He restored a withered hand with a word (3.1–5). Jairus's daughter was actually dead when Jesus held her by the hand and said, 'Girl, get up'; she got up, walked, and ate (5.22–3, 35–43). A woman whom doctors could not cure touched Jesus' garment in a crowd and was healed at once. Jesus felt that power had gone out from him and looked for her, telling her that her faith had healed her (5.25–34).

Sometimes the technique of healing is more fully described. In order to cure a deaf-mute he put his fingers in his ears and touched his tongue with spittle; with a groan he looked up to heaven and said, 'Be opened' (Mark 7.32–5). Again, to cure a blind man he spat on his eyes and laid his hands on him, producing a partial cure which was completed only by a second imposition of hands (8.22–5). Both examples are omitted by the later evangelists; both resemble the 'sympathetic magic' employed by other healers in the ancient world. Neither is discussed in any extant writings of ante-Nicene commentators, perhaps because both were regarded as too much like other instances of thaumaturgy. But there is no reason to suppose that our standards, or those of some early Christians, as to what is edifying can serve as historical criteria. From the complaints of critics as recorded in the gospels we should suppose that Jesus was not concerned with the question of technique. He could use whatever technique seemed suitable at the moment. In the last healing in Mark, that of blind Bartimaeus, Jesus simply says, 'Your faith has healed you' (10.52; cf. 7.34).

Thus far we have discussed only the stories in Mark. Those reported by the other synoptic evangelists are not essentially different, though there is a slight tendency to heighten the difficulty of the miracles. Luke gives five additional instances. The slave of a centurion in Capernaum is about to die when, because of the centurion's faith, Jesus heals him without seeing or touching him; and the only son of a widow at Nain is about to be buried when Jesus takes pity on the mother, touches the bier, and says, 'Young man, be raised.' He sits up and speaks (7.1–16). A woman had a 'spirit of sickness' for eighteen years and could not stand erect; she was healed by a word of 'release' and the laying on of hands (13.11–13). A man had dropsy and was cured (14.2–4). Ten lepers – among whom the only grateful one was a Samaritan – were cured (17.12–19). Matthew's stories are essentially the same, except that he twice tells a story, based on that about Bartimaeus, about two blind men (9.27–31; 20.30–4).

In all three synoptics the stories about exorcisms and healings are told only in relation to Galilee or its surroundings. Only in Matthew (21.14) do we read that 'the blind and the lame came to him in the temple and he healed them' – but he knows no miracle story related to Jerusalem.

From these stories it is evident that Jesus was known to his contemporaries as one who could drive out demons or perform the analogous function of healing diseases. He was not what today is called a 'faith healer'. Sometimes faith is mentioned in the stories; sometimes it is not. The tradition is concerned with one thing only, to show that the power of God was present in him. That this power existed is also plain from the criticisms made by his opponents. They did not question his power; they only argued that it was demonic rather than divine. That others had it as well, and that Jesus believed that they did, is also clear. 'By whom do your sons cast them out?' (Matt. 12.27; Luke 11.19). We conclude that the existence of a power to exorcise and to heal was not open to question in Galilee in Jesus' time. What differentiated his work from that of others? We must assume that the context was what was important. Jesus did not exorcise and heal 'for the works' sake' but because these activities were united with his proclamation of the coming kingdom, already potentially present in the miracles.

The exorcisms are absent from the Gospel of John, perhaps because the evangelist or his readers did not find them edifying. The charge that Jesus was possessed by a demon is set forth, but it is understood as meaning that he was crazy (8.48; 10.20). Some of the healings are described; they have become great signs of Jesus' heavenly glory manifest on earth. Four healing stories are told. The centurion's slave (Luke) or boy (Matthew) has become a royal officer's son, and as in Matthew he is healed just at the hour when Jesus speaks to his (here) father (4.46–53). A man has been paralysed for thirty-eight years and Jesus tells him to take up his bed and walk, and to sin no more (5.8–9, 14). This story resembles the version in Mark (2.3–12), and like it is related to Sabbath observance. A third healing is that of a man born blind; it is effected by putting a mixture of mud and spittle on his eyes (cf. Mark 8.23) and by ordering him to wash in the pool of Siloam (9.6–7). The fourth is the most striking of all: the raising of Lazarus, dead for four days (11.1–44). Nothing quite like it is found in the synoptic tradition, even though there too we find raisings from the dead. The uniqueness of John's story lies in his insistence that Jesus rejoiced because he had not been with the sick Lazarus; therefore Lazarus could die and rise. The miracle is performed not so much for the sake of Lazarus as to manifest the glory of God. Here John expresses a meaning which is less explicit in the synoptic tradition.

It is undoubtedly significant that exorcisms of demons occur in the synoptic gospels (but only in relation to events in Galilee) and that they are absent from the Gospel of John and are not mentioned in the Pauline epistles (or in any of the epistles except, by implication, James). The only exorcisms to be found in Acts are mentioned in a brief summary (Acts 19.11–12) describing the effects of contact with Paul's handkerchiefs or aprons, and in the subsequent verses which describe the activities of 'seven sons of a Jewish high priest named Sceva' (19.14); but demons are not mentioned.

This means that exorcism, while characteristic of the Galilean period of the church's life, was not characteristic of the gentile mission, at least until the time of the Apologists, when mention of it recurs.

Exorcisms, healings and raisings thus make up the bulk of the gospel accounts of the miracles of Jesus. We now turn to the other stories which illustrate the power of Jesus, and of his disciples, over 'nature' – remembering once more that the distinction we draw is our own, not theirs. This power is clearly set forth in the word of Jesus, 'Whoever says to this mountain, Be lifted up and be cast into the sea, and does not doubt in his heart but believes that what he says is taking place, for him it will take place' (Mark 11.23; cf. Matt. 21.21). A similar saying is preserved in different contexts in both Matthew (17.20) and Luke (17.6) and is referred to by

Paul (I Cor. 13.2). We shall later discuss what seems to be the probable original context (see page 351). Here it is enough to say that the saying illustrates the faith of Jesus and of his disciples in a God who works 'mighty acts' and can make his power available for believers. 'All things are possible for him who believes' (Mark 9.23). 'I can do all things through him who strengthens me' (Phil. 4.13).

The miracles are closely related to the belief of Christians that in Jesus God has decisively acted; and this faith was shared by Jesus himself. Thus the nature miràcles do not really differ in kind from the others which we have already discussed. The most important of them is the story of the feeding of the five thousand, related by all four evangelists and handed down by three of them in connection with Jesus' walking on the lake of Galilee. (Mark and Matthew give the story twice, once as the feeding of five thousand, once as that of four thousand.)

In Mark the story is set after the Galilean mission of the disciples (6.30–3, 34–44). The weary missioners are to come to a desert place and 'rest a little', but a crowd follows, eager to satisfy its curiosity. The hour becomes late and Jesus tells the disciples to feed the crowd. Among them, however, they have only five loaves of bread and two fish. Jesus then commands the crowd to recline in groups of fifty and a hundred; taking the bread and fish he blesses it, breaks it, and gives it to the disciples to distribute. 'All of them ate and were filled.' The leftovers fill twelve wicker baskets (characteristic of Jews, says the Roman poet Juvenal).

There are several ways of looking at this story. The most common view in Western Christendom has been that it provides an example, and can be used as a proof, of Jesus' power over nature. This view, doubtless given credence by the following miracle of walking on water, leads to almost insuperable difficulties when the details are pressed. Hilary of Poitiers (fourth century) was embarrassed by such questions as these: where did the bread multiply? In the hands of Jesus? in the hands of the disciples? in the mouths of those who ate? Naturally an equally literalistic explanation was advanced by rationalists. Even a tiny amount of bread and fish (1/5000 of 7 loaves + 2 fish) seemed a considerable amount to men under the spell of Jesus. Alternatively, those in the crowd had bread and fish of their own and suddenly began to share at this point.

More modern students have attempted to explain the story in relation to various motifs which can be found by considering parallels. (1) There is a somewhat similar story about Elisha in II Kings 4.42–4, where the man of God, through his servant, feeds a hundred men with only twenty barley loaves (the barley loaves recur in John's version, 6.9, 13). If Elijah had come as a forerunner of Jesus (Mark 9.13), it was conceivable that the work of his successor Elisha, who had received a 'double portion of Elijah's spirit' (II Kings 2.9–14), should be surpassed by Jesus. (2) A second motif is eucharistic. As Mark tells the story, it is remarkably similar to his account of the Last Supper, where Jesus took bread, blessed it, broke it, and distributed it to the disciples. All his disciples (and the crowd) eat of the loaves and fish as they all ate and drank at the Last Supper. (3) A third motif is eschatological. The feeding of the five thousand corresponds to God's miraculous feeding of the children of Israel in the desert on their way to the promised land. This feeding was regarded by Jews and Christians alike as a prefiguration of the 'messianic banquet' in the kingdom of God. The rabbis give various picturesque details – thus the marine monsters will finally serve God's purpose when they are eaten in the kingdom. No such details are given in the gospels, but the expectation of such a banquet is there; Jesus swears that he will not drink wine again until he drinks it (a)new in the kingdom of God (Mark 14.25). The reclining of the crowd by fifties and hundreds points closely to the eschatological idea. It was Moses in the Exodus who instructed the children of Israel to assemble in groups of thousands, hundreds and fifties; and this command was reiterated among the covenanters by the Dead Sea. As one greater than Moses, Jesus prepares his disciples and the crowd for their march into the new land of promise, the kingdom of God.

As Schweitzer puts it, Jesus 'consecrates them as partakers in the coming Messianic feast, and gives them the guarantee that they, who had shared his table in the time of his obscurity, would also share it in the time of his glory'.

The baskets of leftovers may be related to the mention of leftovers in the story of Elisha or else to the Exodus story of the double supply of manna which was provided on the day before the Sabbath (Exodus 16.22–7). The numbers of the baskets (twelve after the feeding of the five thousand, seven after four thousand) may be symbolical, but the twelve is easier to explain (apostles, tribes) than the seven is.

These motifs certainly illuminate the meanings which early Christians may have found, and indeed almost certainly did find, in the story. They do not indicate either that the event took place or that it did not. A decision on this point must be reached on grounds extraneous to the New Testament itself. The same kind of decision must be made in regard to the story of walking on water. Some critics have suggested that the story is simply a heightened account of the parallel, or somewhat parallel, story of the stilling of the storm (Mark 4.35–41). In both instances Jesus and his disciples wish to cross the lake of Galilee; it is evening, and a strong wind troubles the disciples, who are afraid. At a word of Jesus the sea goes down and the disciples either fear even more or are astonished. There are differences, however. In the first storm story Jesus is calmly asleep in the boat and the disciples criticize his lack of concern (4.38), while in the second he comes to them by walking on the sea, just as in Job it is God who, poetically speaking, walks on the waves (9.8; 38.16) and in Sirach it is Wisdom who does so (24.5). Again, in the first story Jesus rebukes the wind as if it were a demonic power (cf. Mark 11.14, 23), while in the second the wind goes down after he announces, 'It is I, do not fear', and gets into the boat. Finally, the points made by the two stories are different. In the first the emphasis is laid on stilling the storm; in the second, on walking on water. Both stories may reflect the Old Testament motif of Yahweh's victory over chaos.

The conclusion in regard to Jesus, no matter how different the stories may be, is the same. 'Who is this,' the disciples ask (4.41), 'that wind and sea obey him?' The power of Jesus over water, an unpredictable element of nature, is such that he can still it or walk on it as he chooses. We cannot get rid of these stories by ascribing them to an 'ancient world view'. The ancients were well aware that bodies heavier than water sink in it. The conclusion that Christians drew from these stories was that Jesus was different from other human beings. Indeed, in Mark 6.49 the disciples suppose that he must be a ghost or phantom. Who was he? He was one in whom the creative power of God was at work. Job had said that it is God alone 'who speaks to the sun and it does not rise . . . who walks on the sea as on dry land' (9.7–8). Yet God's power could be given, according to the Old Testament, to his holy ones. When Moses stretched forth his hand, God made part of the sea like dry land (Exod. 14.21); the priests carrying the ark crossed the Jordan, along with all Israel, on dry ground (Josh. 3.17); Elisha too divided the waters of the Jordan (II Kings 2.14). It may be, then, that in the story of walking on water we meet the Exodus motif once more – a motif also found in the 'messianic expectations' of Jesus' day (see page 272).

The same questions arise, of course, in regard to this story as in regard to the feeding miracles. Do the stories reflect reminiscences of what happened or were they created in order to set forth in symbolic fashion the ways in which the ministry of Jesus constituted a new Exodus? Historically, we are not in a position to answer such questions. In the later gospels we can see some tendencies to develop the stories, but the later existence of such developments proves nothing about the origins of that from which the developments took place. Theologically, we can weigh various considerations such as the nature of the Incarnation if related to such stories treated as fact, and can argue that to treat the stories as factual would mean denying the reality of Christ's human nature. But such arguments are often inconclusive, and in any case the precise historical nature of an occurrence (or non-occurrence) should not be determined by our feeling that it was, or was not, 'fitting'.

The most important retelling of the story of the feeding is that provided by John, who clearly recognizes its triple significance. (1) It points backward towards its Old Testament antecedents; John mentions barley loaves, probably because of the story of Elisha, and he devotes a long discourse to the relation of the feeding to the gift of manna at the Exodus. (2) It points forward towards the eucharist. This point is made explicit in the long discourse, and is also implied by John's omission of any account of the institution at the Last Supper. (3) It also has historical consequences. Those who saw the 'sign' said, 'Truly this is the prophet who is to come into the world' (6.14) – presumably the prophet 'like Moses' who was to succeed him (Deut. 18.15). Jesus, 'knowing that they were going to come and seize him to make him king', fled from them to a mountain (6.15). John may be giving authentic historical information. The Galilean mission resulted in enthusiasm, but this enthusiasm was misguided. Those who shared it thought that Jesus was a political leader. They took the miracle to some extent as Schweitzer takes it.

John certainly believed in the miraculous. He did not, however, believe in miracle for miracle's sake. In the 'sign' with which he has Jesus' public ministry begin, the changing of water into wine at Cana, there is no effect on a crowd. The servants at the wedding banquet know that water has been transformed (water once more!), but the glory of Jesus thus manifested results in belief only for his disciples (2.11). Sometimes it has been urged that John has Christianized a popular tale, for example about the god Dionysus, who annually transformed water into wine at his festival. (It should be added that many ancient writers were unconvinced of the reality of the Dionysiacs' miracle.) Once more, however, the story may well reflect the conception of the eschatological banquet, often regarded as a wedding feast, at which wine, given by God, would flow freely. Taken literally, the story presents difficulties. Chrysostom, writing in the fourth century, mentions non-Christian critics who suggested that the guests at the wedding were unable to distinguish wine from water. And as early as the second century, when Marcosian Gnostics attempted to repeat the miracle in their eucharists, use was made of some kind of powder to produce the desired effect. Excavations of a well in Gerasa, where the miracle was reproduced in the fourth century, suggest that one pipe line brought water, another wine. The dangers of literalism are obvious, though it must be admitted that to treat this miracle, like others, as purely 'spiritual' can be equally unconvincing. If we do treat it as symbolic, we must recognize that those early Christians who did so did not ordinarily separate the outward and visible sign from the inward and spiritual grace. Whether we do or do not keep them together, we must recognize historically that early Christians did so and that historical analysis as such cannot tell us what actually happened. Even if we believe that the stories do not record what happened, we are in no position to say what did.

It should be added, however, that the fact that early Christians, or some early Christians, do not differentiate outward experience from inward experience, or nature from history, does not prohibit the historian from making an attempt to do so. The apostle Paul is quite willing to tell the Corinthians that among them 'the signs of a true apostle were performed ... in all patience, with signs and wonders and mighty works' (II Cor. 12.12). But he hesitates when he is describing 'a man in Christ' who was caught up to the third heaven and into paradise. Twice he uses the expression 'whether in the body or out of the body I do not know, God knows' (12.2–3). If his description involves cosmological concerns, we must go beyond what he says and insist that such a journey was not one which can be charted. Again, when he says that 'if I have all faith, so as to remove mountains, but have not love, I am nothing' (I Cor. 13.2) there are two points which should be made. First, he seems to have freed the saying of Jesus in Mark 11.23 from its precise eschatological relation to the Mount of Olives (as in Zechariah 14.4); the saying has become a general word about faith. Second, he rigorously subordinates wonder-working faith to love. This is to say that in the early Church miracles were important because they pointed towards the creative activity of God, not because of anything they were in themselves; and also that the creative activity of God is better expressed in works of love than in signs and wonders.

WHAT JESUS TAUGHT

To discover what Jesus taught and, perhaps, why he taught it is just as difficult as to consider the historical meaning of miracle stories. We must be constantly on guard against the natural tendency to assume that because we agree (or because we disagree) with the content of a particular saying it is therefore authentic. Kirsopp Lake has been quoted as making this statement: 'The genuineness of a saying attributed to Jesus can be judged only by men free if necessary to say without emotion that, so far as they can see, Jesus did teach in the way under discussion, but that on this point they disagree with Jesus.' Probably Lake's emotion-free men do not exist, but a measure of this attitude is required in the study of the gospels. It can be called a sense of the 'distance' between the viewer and the object viewed. Christians may find that to achieve this distance is difficult, but in all historical study it is a necessity, if only for a moment. Perspective can be gained only from some degree of distance.[1]

There are, of course, some obstacles which stand in the way of recovering what Jesus taught. At first his sayings were handed down either separately or in little clusters. These sayings were translated from Aramaic into Greek and edited by the evangelists and their predecessors – who did not aim at completeness (cf. John 20.30, 21.25). The process of transmission lasted a minimum of thirty years. But the time involved is not as important as the motivations of the transmitters. There is every likelihood that they intended to remain faithful to the teaching they were handing down; at the same time, it is probable that they could not help modifying it, consciously or unconsciously, in relation to their own attitudes and to the circumstances in which they, and the churches of which they were leaders, found themselves. One obvious example is found in the reports of Jesus' teaching on divorce and remarriage. Under Jewish law, in the circumstances under which Jesus taught, a man could divorce his wife but she could not divorce him. It is therefore likely that when Mark 10.12 refers to a wife's divorcing her husband the tradition known to the evangelist has modified the original saying in order to widen its range. Other examples can be found in the brief moralizing and generalizing conclusions which the various evangelists append to the parables.

(It should be added that such modifications do not necessarily diminish the religious or theological relevance of the sayings as they now stand, since those who transmitted the sayings may have correctly interpreted them for their environment or environments, and the situation of the transmitters may not be very different from our own. But such considerations cannot be taken into account when we try to determine what Jesus himself taught.)

What Jesus was concerned with proclaiming was the kingdom of God, and especially the requirements laid by God the king on those who took upon themselves the 'yoke of the kingdom'. He used various forms of speech in order to make his proclamation

---

[1] It may be added that a man may be anxious to affirm the authenticity of a saying in order to justify his personal rejection of Christianity.

(parables, sayings, etc.), but these are not as important as what the proclamation contained. In the gospels we find one summary of his message, and it is based on two passages in the Old Testament. A scribe in Jerusalem asked him which was the primary commandment of the law, and he replied (Mark 12.28–30):

> The first is, Hear, O Israel: the Lord our God, the Lord is one; and you shall love the Lord your God with all your heart and all your soul and all your understanding and all your strength (Deut. 6.4–5). The second is this: You shall love your neighbour as yourself (Lev. 19.18).

This saying too is an illustration of expansion and interpretation; the words 'with all your understanding' are absent from the Old Testament, since the Hebrew man thought with his heart; they have been added in Greek Christian circles in order to point up the completeness of response required of man.

The primary commandment, then, requires love of God and love of neighbour. Jewish teachers in the time of Jesus were also concerned with providing such summaries (as we have seen, page 258). None of them, however, seems to have chosen these two passages from the Old Testament; the parallel often cited from the Testaments of the Twelve Patriarchs is from a book which in its present form is Christian.

To love God means to imitate him. 'You shall be perfect as your heavenly Father is perfect' (Matt. 5.48). The term 'perfect' probably means to be holy as God is holy, as in a parallel command in Leviticus 19.2; it probably also involves the 'merciful' character of God, as in the analogous command in Luke 6.36. In other words, the command looks both Godward and manward. To love God means also to trust him, not to worry about food or clothing, after which 'the gentiles' seek (Matt. 6.32). He feeds the birds and clothes flowers with beauty; *a fortiori* he will feed and clothe men (Matt. 6.26–30). If men first seek for God's reign and his righteousness, he will give them all they need (6.33; 7.7–11). If men forgive, God will forgive them (6.14–15). His forgiveness has no limits if men repent, for he is the Father of the prodigal son (Luke 15.11–32). At the same time, his forgiveness is accompanied by his wrath. If men do not forgive, their heavenly Father will not forgive them (Matt. 6.15). God can destroy both soul and body in hell (Matt. 10.28). And at the final judgement rejection will be the fate of those who have rejected God's reign.

It may be asked what is particularly different about the teaching of Jesus when it is compared with the Old Testament. First, of course, it must be stated that it cannot be, and never is, compared with the whole of the Old Testament; some process of selection is involved. The teaching of Jesus resembles most closely that of the prophets. Second, we should not expect to find a sharp contrast between the prophets and Jesus, since in his view his God was theirs – and that of the patriarchs as well (Mark 12.26). In agreement with some Jewish teachers of his time, he often spoke to his disciples of God as their Father; but he went beyond them in emphasizing that God was *his* Father. He pointed towards a closeness of relationship in which Christians soon found intimations of what became the doctrine of the Trinity.

The emphasis in Jesus' teaching, however, lies not so much on love of God as on love of neighbour. This love is to be all-inclusive; men are not to be loved because they are members of the community but also, and especially, when they are outsiders. Such a kind of love is not only repeatedly expressed in the gospel records but is also set forth in the Holiness Code in Leviticus. 'The stranger who sojourns with you shall be as the home-born among you, and you shall love him as yourself; for you were strangers in the land of Egypt; I am the Lord your God' (Lev. 19.34). In the gospels it is dramatically portrayed in the parable of the Good Samaritan (Luke 10.30-7) and systematically defined by Matthew in the first half of the Sermon on the Mount, where sayings are collected and related to the appropriate commandments of the decalogue and other parts of Old Testament law.

In this Sermon Jesus defines the righteousness of his disciples as one which must surpass that of the scribes and the Pharisees. The old law said, 'You shall not commit murder' (Exod. 20.13). Jesus tells his disciples that to be angry with one's brother (some manuscripts limit the range of his words by adding 'without cause') or to speak abusively to him is equivalent to murder. A gift cannot be offered to the temple by one who has not been reconciled with his brother (Matt. 5.21-4).

Again, the old law said, 'You shall not commit adultery'

(Exod. 20.14). Jesus tells his disciples that to look at a woman with lust for her is equivalent to adultery. If one's eye or hand lead one to offend, it would be better to lack these members than to be cast into Gehenna, where the wicked dead are punished in fire (5.28–30). The old law forbade false oaths (Lev. 19.12). Jesus forbids oaths of any kind. The disciple is simply to say Yes or No; anything further is from the 'evil one', presumably because it implies the possibility of falsehood (5.34–7). The old law said, 'An eye for an eye and a tooth for a tooth' (Exod. 21.24–5), thus limiting revenge by justice. Jesus tells his disciples not to seek revenge at all. 'Whoever strikes you on one cheek, turn the other to him' (5.38–42). The old law said, 'Love your neighbour' and (at least among the Dead Sea sectarians) 'hate your enemy.' Jesus tells his disciples to love their enemies and pray for their persecutors, for their love, like God's, must be all-inclusive (5.44–7). He tells them to forgive a repentant brother's sins seven times a day (Luke 17.3–4), and when Peter asks if seven is the limit, he replies that seventy-seven times (at least) are possible, and indeed necessary (Matt. 18.21–2). God will not condemn one who has not condemned; he will forgive him who has forgiven (Matt. 6.12–15; Luke 6.37–8). The man who does not forgive is compared to a merciless lender who forgets his own debts (Matt. 18.23–35).

Because of Jesus' insistence upon genuine love of neighbour, a good deal of his teaching is directed against insincerity in the name of religion. Prayer and almsgiving should not be done for show (Matt. 6.1–8), even for inward 'peace of mind' (Luke 18.10–14), nor should fasting be ostentatious (Matt. 6.16–18). (The semi-Gnostic Gospel of Thomas misrepresents his teaching by claiming that he opposed prayer, fasting and almsgiving.) The true disciple cannot judge others but must judge himself (Matt. 7.1–5); he must bring forth good fruits (7.16–20); he must humble himself (Luke 14.7–11). He cannot lay up treasures on earth; he cannot serve God and money (Matt. 6.19–21, 24). To save his life, he must lose it (Mark 8.35). He must become a 'eunuch' for the kingdom's sake (Matt. 19.12); he must leave everything to follow Jesus (Mark 10.21). 'No one who has put his hand to the plough and then looks back is fit for the kingdom of God' (Luke 9.62). Only one thing (discipleship) is necessary (10.42).

It has sometimes been argued that (1) Jesus gave no binding commandments applicable to every conceivable situation; indeed, in the tradition some commandments are in contradiction with others (contrast Mark 10.9 with Luke 14.26; Mark 10.21 with Luke 19.8), and that, therefore, (2) only 'following Jesus' can be called for (e.g. Mark 1.17, 2.14, 10.21); this way is the way of the cross (Mark 8.34–5). The purpose of this interpretation is to free Christians from the concrete historical nature of the call of Jesus and to view it more in the manner of John 14.6, where we read that Jesus himself is 'the Way, the Truth, and the Life' (an Aramaic original of this could mean 'true and living Way'). Its modern theological value, however, is probably greater than its approximation to what Jesus actually taught and to what his disciples understood him as teaching.

Perhaps the question as to what they understood can be approached by asking why they became disciples. There seem to be five main reasons for this action. (1) They were doubtless impressed by Jesus' power over demons and diseases; they were convinced that something greater than Solomon or Jonah was present among them and in their leader. (2) They probably recognized that the moral teaching of the prophets and their call to repentance were being set forth anew – and in a manner like that used by the prophets, in poetic and symbolic form and with the performance of symbolic actions. The tone of authority with which Jesus spoke was also like that of the prophets. (3) Jesus also appealed to men as intelligent, observant persons. He argued from the ubiquity of sunshine and rainfall to the inclusiveness of God's love (Matt. 5.45; Luke 6.35). A man should not swear by his head, for he cannot make one hair white or black (Matt. 5.36). A man should not lay up treasures on earth, since moth and rust destroy them and thieves dig through and steal (6.20). Birds and flowers provide examples of God's care for his creation (6.26, 28), and by worrying no one can add a few feet to his stature (6.27). A father does not give his son a stone for bread or a snake for fish (7.9–10). A good tree does not produce bad fruit (7.17). All these are analogies. If such is the case on earth, how much more is it so with God? Indeed, all the parables are based on the same kind of analogical reasoning, proceeding from the creation to the Creator, from the area ruled to the Ruler. It is probably Luke who is responsible for the formulation of the question, 'Why do you not judge from yourselves what is right?' (12.57), but the question is true to the spirit of Jesus. (4) The hearer of Jesus might well be one who, influenced by apocalyptic expectations, was waiting for the imminent coming of God's kingdom. Many apocalypses were in circulation, and many (not only at Qumran) interpreted the prophets as guides to the immediate future. Roman-Herodian oppression seemed to be a sign of its coming. (5) Jesus promised rewards for those who would follow him and punishments for those who did not. Like the prophets, he used such promises as moral levers, and appealed to the rewards as providing a motive for repentance.

These rewards included acquittal in the coming judgement, entrance into the kingdom, and the inheritance of life with all its treasures. The penalties were suffering in Gehenna and exclusion from the life of the kingdom. Generally speaking, the poor, unimpeded by possessions, were expected to receive the rewards; the rich, who could not leave their wealth to serve God, found it difficult to follow Jesus. 'It is easier for a camel to pass through the eye of a needle [i.e., impossible], than for a rich man to enter the kingdom of God' (Mark 10.25). Luke tells many parables which illustrate the condition of the rich; Matthew too is aware of their condition.

It is not certain, however, that Jesus was speaking sociologically when he described conditions for entrance into the kingdom or the rewards which would ensue. We may suspect that his teaching was not altogether 'spiritual', especially when we recall that for pious Jews 'heaven' was often a word substituted for 'God', and that as the gospel left Jewish soil this use of 'heaven' could easily be misunderstood so that the this-worldly became other-worldly. When Peter claims that the disciples have left everything to follow Jesus, his master tells him that 'there is no one who has left home or brothers or sisters or mother or father or children or fields, for my sake and the gospel's, who will not receive a hundredfold now in this time, houses and brothers and sisters and mothers and children and fields – with persecutions – and in the coming age, eternal life' (Mark 10.29–30). When we compare the Lucan version of this sentence (18.29) we seem to see difficulties being added and taken away. Luke adds 'wife' to the relatives to be abandoned; he omits any reference to the future receipt of fields. Considerably later, Origen argued that the prediction must be taken allegorically since the brothers, sisters, mothers and children must be symbolical. This means that the concreteness of the expectation has vanished. But how concrete was it? To answer this question we also have to consider the problem raised by eschatological predictions in general in the gospels. Was the kingdom present? Was it being inaugurated? Was it purely future? Or did Jesus explicitly say what he believed about it?

Before turning to the nature of the kingdom of God we should tentatively suggest that the question about its being this-worldly or otherworldly and its being present or future is analogous to one more question, that concerning Jesus' view of himself as Messiah or Son of Man (see pp. 342ff.). On all these questions various scholars have assumed varying positions, usually emphasizing one or the other horn of the dilemmas and arguing that inconvenient texts are not genuine. They thus have used literary criticism (1) in a highly subjective way and (2) in order to solve a problem historical in nature. A more adequate solution can undoubtedly be reached by trying to discover what attitude assumed and expressed by Jesus could have led to the varying interpretations, each of which has something to commend it. (It should be noted that we are *not* advocating some kind of synthesis of opposing views; what we should like to discover is a prior condition, attested by evidence, which can explain the existence of later circumstances, divergent but related to their source.)

The two extremes are set forth most vividly in two texts, one of which reflects a futurist conception of the kingdom ('thy kingdom come,' Matt. 6.10; Luke 11.2), the other a 'realized eschatology' ('the kingdom of God is within you,' Luke 17.21). There can be no doubt about the future reference of the first passage. On the other hand, those who have wished to minimize the present reality of the kingdom have pointed out that the saying found only in Luke is addressed to (hostile?) Pharisees (the kingdom cannot have been within them), and must therefore mean 'in your midst'; furthermore, the hypothetical Aramaic original would not use the verb 'to be' and therefore can be interpreted as future in meaning. There are other passages, however, in which the kingdom is regarded as actually present. For instance, 'if I by the finger of

God cast out demons, then the kingdom of God has come upon you' (Luke 11.19; cf. Matt. 12.28). (We cannot use Matthew 5.3, 'theirs is the kingdom,' because of the ambiguity of whatever the original saying may have been.) Other passages can easily be collected on both sides.

Several attempts have been made to resolve this dilemma by doing justice to both aspects. (1) It can be argued that God's kingdom is eternal. It is 'an everlasting dominion, which shall not pass away, and his kingdom that which shall not be destroyed' (Dan. 7.14). But this kingdom is eternal in the sense that it will continually last once it has been given 'to the people of the saints of the Most High' (Dan. 7.27); the reference remains future. A reference to an eternal reign in past, present and future can be found in Ps. 145.13, however; if this psalm is related to the expectations of Daniel it places far less emphasis on the future. 'Thy kingdom is an everlasting kingdom, and thy dominion endureth throughout all generations.' If the kingdom is understood in this way, it means that God is king; his throne is established of old; he is 'from everlasting' (Ps. 93.2). But men have revolted against him, and he is now about to put down their rebellion by calling them once more to obey him. On this supposition, the present nature of the kingdom is based on the perpetuity of God's rule; the future aspect is concerned with his act to reinforce it. (2) It may also be claimed that the two emphases arose because Jesus spoke with such intensity and immediacy of the future that some could regard the kingdom as already present. To say this means that the futurist view is correct, while the 'realized' view is wrong. (3) It has been held that he not only regarded the kingdom as future but also believed that to a considerable extent he was inaugurating it. The kingdom was present as the mustard seed of Mark. 4.30–2 was present before it became a great plant.

It appears that the most adequate solution will be one which accounts for both the presence and the future fulfilment of the kingdom. In providing a solution of this kind we can use such terms as potentiality and realization – provided that we do not limit the range of potentiality by overstressing the difference between it and the realization still to come. In the mission of Jesus, in his words and in his deeds, the kingdom had been inaugurated. Its fullness was still to come, but the 'shape', so to speak of the kingdom 'with power' (Mark 9.1) would not be essentially different from what had already arrived.

There is a considerable measure of ambiguity in the gospel tradition, as in later Christian theology, as regards the way in which the kingdom is finally to be realized. Sometimes its coming is described as sudden and catastrophic; sometimes it is viewed as a process of growth, whether gradual or not (Mark 4.26–32). Again, some sayings point towards a kingdom regarded almost entirely as this-worldly; others point towards a more 'spiritual' conception. Finally, some sayings indicate that the precise time of its coming cannot be predicted. It comes like a thief in the night, and no one but the Father knows when it will arrive (Mark 13.32).

To be sure, the sayings to which we refer can be regarded as possessing varying degrees of authenticity; but taken as a whole they point in the same direction. They suggest that Jesus was concerned almost exclusively with the reign of God, present and future, and with calling men to assume its yoke. He was not concerned with telling them whether it would come catastrophically or not, or with whether it would be this-worldly or not, or when it would come. Because he was not concerned with these matters he left his disciples free to consider them in various ways, and they did so. Perhaps they should not have considered them, but they did. In this sense the view that he intended simply to call men to follow him is correct; it must be added, however, that he told men in what ways to follow him.

We now come to the question of the way or ways in which he intended his statements about God's moral demands to be taken. Various views of this matter have been advocated. (1) Was his teaching, for example in Matthew's sermon on the mount, intended chiefly to convict disobedient men of sin? Certainly this aspect of it cannot be neglected; in order to repent, his disciples must have been or become aware of their sinfulness. But this cannot have been the sole purpose of his teaching, for he came to call sinners to repentance, to heal the sick, to cast out demons, to bring men to a new life. (2) Was his teaching intended to provide norms for behaviour in the very short period before the coming of the reign of God? Were the disciples expected to lead lives of perfection – a perfection which could not have been required if he had believed that the world would go on? This theory of an 'interim ethic' is based on two postulates: (*a*) Jesus expected nothing but the imminent end of the world, and (*b*) his teaching is in fact impracticable. The first postulate is historically incorrect, and the second cannot be assessed by means of any historical method. (3) Did Jesus set forth the pure will of God, apart from any historical circumstances, just as it for ever is? On this view, he was giving a new law to guide his disciples to a 'righteousness' which would exceed that of scribes and Pharisees (Matt. 5.20). He expected his disciples to obey its commandments (cf. Gal. 5.14; Rom. 12.2; 13.8–10).

We should incline to accept the third view, while recognizing that his message was historically conditioned and that under different circumstances the supreme principles of love of God and neighbour might be differently worked out in practice. In other words, later theological and historical considerations should not influence our recognition that Jesus expected his disciples to 'do what he said' (Luke 6.46; cf. Matt. 7.21). The problem of the ways in which his expectation was to be fulfilled belongs to the study of church history or of systematic theology.

WHAT JESUS TAUGHT ABOUT HIMSELF

In the New Testament the title 'Christ' or 'anointed one' is so frequently used of Jesus that in the Pauline epistles and elsewhere it has become a proper name. It is therefore something of a surprise when we observe that in the famous 'recognition scene' at Caesarea Philippi (Mark 8.27–33) Peter says to Jesus, 'You are the Anointed One,' but is immediately instructed to say nothing about him to anyone. Jesus proceeds, instead, to discuss the suffering through which the Son of Man must pass before his triumph. Luke's version (9.18–23) is much the same. Only in Matthew (16.13–23) do we find Peter's confession amplified, given the approval of Jesus, and separated from the prediction about suffering. Peter gives a more complete Christological statement: 'You are the Anointed One, the Son of the living God,' and Jesus answers, 'You are blessed, Simon Bar Jona, for flesh and blood did not reveal this to you, but my Father who is in heaven.'

The only point in Mark at which Jesus is represented as declaring that he is the Anointed One is in the investigation before the high priest, who asked him, 'Are you the Anointed One, the Son of the Blessed?' According to Alexandrian and 'Western' manuscripts, Jesus said, 'I am,' and went on to predict the coming of the Son of Man on the clouds of heaven (14.61–2). Several questions arise here. (1) Caesarean manuscripts agree with Origen that the answer was less direct; they read, 'You have said that I am.' Do they preserve Mark's original reading, reflected in different ways in Matthew 26.64 and Luke 26.67–71? Or has the text of Mark been influenced by the later gospels? (2) How did the evangelists know precisely what went on during the investigations? Are their statements about the charge due to reliable information or to inferences drawn from the title on the cross, 'the king of the Jews' (Mark 15.26)?

Perhaps these questions can only be answered by considering what the title 'the Anointed One' may have meant in first-century Palestine. There the expression was commonly employed with reference to an anointed king of Davidic descent, who with God's help would restore independence to Israel, freeing it from foreign domination. In this sense it is obvious that Jesus cannot have accepted the title for himself, though it is, of course, possible that he used the term and gave it a new meaning.

There is a strange passage in Mark 12.35–7 which may cast some light on the question. Jesus was teaching in the temple and he asked this question: 'How do the scribes say that the Anointed One is David's son? David himself, inspired by the Holy Spirit, said, "The Lord said to my Lord, Sit at my right hand until I set your enemies under your feet." David himself calls him Lord, and how can he be his son?' In this saying it is assumed that (1) Psalm 110.1 was written or spoken by David, (2) it has a direct reference to the Anointed One, who is called 'my Lord', and (3) a man's son cannot be his master. Therefore the Anointed One is not of Davidic descent. If this is so, the word of address, 'Son of David', used by blind Bartimaeus (Mark 10.48–9) is due to a blindness more than physical, and the cry of the crowd at the 'triumphal entry' (Mark 11.10), 'Blessed be the coming kingdom of our father David,' is a symptom of their misunderstanding of the mission of Jesus. Such errors are not surprising, for Mark often speaks of the disciples' failure to comprehend what Jesus said or did (see page 122).

We conclude that the representation of Jesus as the Anointed One was a view which, though probably current during his ministry, was not accepted by him and became popular among Christians only after the resurrection (cf. Acts 2.36). If he was in fact descended from David (as Paul states in Romans 1.3), he made nothing of this genealogical consideration.

The most significant term found in the gospels is the expression 'Son of Man'.

Professor Bultmann has attempted to bring some order out of the chaos in which we find sayings about the Son of Man by classifying them in relation to (1) his future coming, (2) his suffering, death and resurrection, and (3) his present work. The first class includes the following sayings:

> Whoever is ashamed of me and my words in this adulterous and sinful generation, of him the Son of Man will also be ashamed when he comes in the glory of his Father with the holy angels (Mark 8.38).

> Then they will see the Son of Man coming on the clouds of heaven [cf. Dan. 7.13] with great power and glory. And then he will send his angels and will gather his elect ... (Mark 13.26–7).

> You will see the Son of Man seated at the right hand of the Power and coming with the clouds of heaven (Mark 14.62; cf. Dan. 7.13).

> As the lightning comes forth from the east and shines to the west, so will be the coming of the Son of Man (Matt. 24.27; cf. Luke 17.24).

> As were the days of Noah, so will be the coming of the Son of Man; they ate, they drank, they married, they were married, until the day when Noah entered the ark and the flood came and destroyed them all (Matt. 24.37–9 and Luke 17.26–7; cf. Luke 17.28–9).

> As Jonah was a sign to the men of Nineveh, so will the Son of Man be to this generation (Luke 11.30; different in Matt. 12.40).

Everyone who acknowledges me before men, the Son of Man will acknowledge him before the angels of God (Luke 12.8; different in Matt. 10.32).

According to Bultmann, these sayings must come from very old tradition, since it is impossible to see how early Christians could have dissociated Jesus from the Son of Man. The tradition is obviously close to Jewish apocalyptic thought.

The second class includes these words:

The Son of Man must suffer many things and be rejected by the elders and the high priests and the scribes and be killed and rise after three days (Mark 8.31; similarly 9.31 and, with more detail, 10.33–4).

The Son of Man came not to be served but to serve and to give his life as a ransom for many (Mark 10.45; cf. Isaiah 53.10–12).

The Son of Man goes as it is written of him ... (Mark 14.21).

The Son of Man is betrayed into the hands of sinners (Mark 14.41).

Bultmann points out that none of these sayings refers to the coming of the Son of Man, and he claims that all represent prophecies after the event.

The third class contains sayings directly related to Jesus.

... that you may know that the Son of Man has authority on earth to forgive sins ... (Mark 2.10; cf. Matt. 9.8, referring to 'men').

The Sabbath was made for man, not man for the Sabbath; therefore the Son of Man is lord even of the Sabbath (Mark 2.28; only the conclusion of the sentence is retained in Luke 6.5 and Matt. 12.8).

The foxes have holes and the birds of the heaven have nests, but the Son of Man has nowhere to lay his head (Matt. 8.20; Luke 9.58).

The Son of Man came eating and drinking, and men say, 'Behold, a glutton and a drunkard, a friend of tax-collectors and sinners' (Matt. 11.19; Luke 7.34–5; contrasted with John the Baptist).

Whoever says a word against the Son of Man, it will be forgiven him (Matt. 12.32; Luke 12.10).

Bultmann claims that in all these passages the common Hebrew and Aramaic use of 'son of man' for either 'man' or 'I' is reflected. A more restricted use is suggested by other scholars, who prefer to translate the phrase as 'this man', somewhat like the expression 'thy servant' in Psalm 19.13.

To these materials found in Mark and Matthew-Luke can be added a few found either in Matthew or in Luke alone. For instance, there is an apocalyptic prediction in Matthew 10.23, 'You will not finish the cities of Israel before the Son of Man comes,' and another in Matthew 19.28, 'When the Son of Man sits on the throne of his glory . . .' In Luke 18.8 there is an apocalyptic question: 'When the Son of Man comes, will he find faith on the earth?'

Before we can either agree or disagree with Bultmann we may also consider the Son-of-Man passages in the Gospel of John. There are twelve of them, or eleven if with Wendt and Bultmann we regard the words 'of man' as a gloss in John 5.27 (the context requires this deletion). Eight of them refer to the crucifixion-exaltation of Jesus (1.51, 3.13–14; 6.62; 8.28; 12.23, 34; 13.31); two others refer to the eucharistic flesh and blood of Jesus, and presumably are not authentic (6.27, 53); and one identifies Jesus precisely with the Son of Man (9.35; compare 12.34 with 12.32). This picture shows that in John the synoptic, or rather pre-synoptic, idea of the future coming of the Son of Man is lacking.

Are we then to treat John as late and argue that the only authentic words of Jesus about the Son of Man as a person distinct from himself are to be found in Bultmann's first category? This is one possibility. Another is that Jesus at first spoke of the Son of Man as distinct from himself and later came to identify himself as this person. A third is that Jesus, deeply influenced by the prophecies of Daniel, at first attempted to create 'the Son of

Man' (the kingdom of the saints) by a public appeal; next he found this Son of Man concentrated in his own disciples; finally he stood alone as the individual Son of Man (as in I Enoch 37–71). A fourth is that on different occasions he presented different doctrines, and that no single conception of the Son of Man was really central to his mission.

How is such a question to be settled? The various uses of the term in pre-Christian Judaism may well illuminate its meaning – or rather, the possible range of meanings which it possessed. (We have no idea as to which usage Jesus must or should have accepted.) When we look at the Old Testament and apocalyptic literature, we find four conceptions. (1) In the visions of Ezekiel, he is addressed as 'son of man'; this means 'man' as contrasted with God, though the reference is to an individual man. (2) In the Psalms (e.g., 8.4), 'son of man' means 'man in general'. (3) In Daniel there is a vision of 'one like a son of man', in other words, like a human being as contrasted with animals (7.13 contrasted with 7.3–8). Daniel himself is addressed as 'son of man' in 8.17, as 'man' in 10.11. The figure 'like a son of man' is identified with 'the people of the saints of the Most High' in 7.27. What we learn from Daniel is that for the purposes of his vision the Jewish people, or the saints among them, were depicted as a single human-like being. (4) To be sure, Jewish exegetes often interpreted isolated passages and found special significance in them. Such a process may be reflected in I Enoch 46, where we read that 'this is the Son of Man who has righteousness, with whom dwells righteousness, and who reveals all the treasures of what is hidden.' Enoch is told that 'this Son of Man whom you have seen will put down the kings and the mighty from their seats and will loose the reins of the strong and will break the teeth of sinners.' Did this passage influence Jesus? Unfortunately, among all the fragments of Enoch found at Qumran, chapters 37–71 are not included, and this lack tends to confirm the suspicions of those who have regarded the section (called the 'similitudes' of Enoch) as a Christian or, at any rate, post-Christian interpolation.

From our glance at Jewish ideas of the, or a, Son of Man we conclude that they provide no positive evidence concerning the meaning of the term as used by Jesus. We are therefore left with the data with which we began, the passages in the synoptic gospels. What conclusions can be drawn from them? (1) We may hold that the only authentic passages are those belonging to Bultmann's first and third categories. Jesus spoke of the future coming of the Son of Man; he did not use the phrase to indicate his identity with this personage. (2) We may hold that all three kinds of passages are authentic, and that Jesus spoke explicitly of himself as the Son of Man, more vaguely of his own return in glory. Such a judgement might help to explain the way in which various shades of meaning seem to be expressed in the various sayings. It would also point towards the meanings to be found in the Gospel of John. Nowhere in the synoptic gospels does Jesus speak explicitly of his own return to his disciples. Such statements are, however, to be found in the Gospel of John, where Jesus speaks of his going away and returning (chs. 14 and 16) and he is so completely identified with the Son of Man that he can speak of his own exaltation and his opponents begin to discuss the exaltation of the Son of Man (12.32, 34). Unless John is simply inventing these themes, he presumably relies on traditional materials in which Jesus and the Son of Man were identified. Again, it is difficult to account for the early Christian belief in the return of Jesus unless somehow it is related to what he himself had taught.

Son of Man is the most difficult of Jesus' titles to understand. The reason for the difficulty may possibly lie in the fact that it was the title which Jesus himself chose in order to express the mystery of his person and his mission. He was not explicitly fulfilling Old Testament prophecy or the dreams of the apocalyptic writers. He was unique; in his mission was summed up the destiny of the Hebrew people as the saints of the Most High, as well as the purpose of God for them and for all mankind.

Even in the Gospel of Mark, however, this is not the only title by which Jesus is known. A man possessed by demons addresses him as 'the Holy One of God', and this title may be based on Psalm 16.10 ('thou wilt not suffer thy holy one to see corruption') or Psalm 106.16 (Aaron as the holy one of God). More common titles are 'rabbi' or 'teacher', but they bear no distinctive meanings. Most significant for Mark seems to be the title 'Son of God'. Mark probably uses it in the first verse of his gospel; demons employ it (3.11; 5.7); it is used by the high priest (14.61), a Roman centurion (15.39), and a voice from heaven (1.11; 9.7). In the Old Testament it is used of the king and of the Hebrew people, and its origin need not be ascribed to 'Hellenistic' influence upon early Christianity. It is worth noting, however, that except in the Gospel of John, Jesus never uses it of himself, though the expression 'the Son' in Mark 13.32 implies such use.

Another idea about the ministry of Jesus may be reflected in such verses as Mark 9.12, 10.45, and 14.24, where we find references to suffering, rejection, and dying 'for many'. These are probably allusions to the suffering servant of God portrayed in Isaiah 53. To be sure, in Jewish exegesis of the time this servant was usually regarded as the Jewish people. But there is no reason to suppose that Jesus was incapable of original ideas. The fact, however, that in the gospels he does not explicitly identify himself with the servant suggests that he referred to him only by implication, and that the Church later developed his implications.

We conclude that in general Jesus spoke about himself allusively, and that among the various conceptions he employed, 'Son of Man' was probably primary. In the Gospel of John we find reflections either of private discussions with the disciples or of a process by means of which the implicit was made explicit.

The question which remains after we have looked through the records of the teaching of Jesus is this: are the records 'authentic', or are the sayings 'genuine'? We have already indicated at several points that this question probably cannot be answered on the basis of the materials (and the methods) we possess. (1) Sometimes it is claimed that the 'Semitic' form of certain sayings gives them a guarantee, but it must be remembered that (*a*) most 'retranslations' of sayings into Aramaic are not wholly convincing, and (*b*) they take us to a 'Jewish' stage of tradition but not necessarily to Jesus himself. (2) Sometimes it has been thought that some document or hypothetical source deserves special confidence (Mark or 'Q' or 'L'), but there is usually no ground for absolute faith in one evangelist or one 'source' as against others. In some instances it can be seen that a later evangelist has modified the work of a predecessor; but this fact does not guarantee the predecessor's work. (3) Analysis of the history of tradition, in addition to being rather subjective, leads only to an early stage of tradition, not necessarily to the earliest stage. (4) The idea that one can analyse the purpose for which a saying was transmitted in relation to the *Sitz im Leben* of either (*a*) Jesus or (*b*) the apostolic Church is mistaken, generally speaking, because we do not know exactly how the two *Sitze* were different from each other.[1]

What we suggest is that in the absence of some external control authenticity cannot be established on internal grounds alone. 'Consistency' serves only as a very general criterion, and in view of the inconsistency (logically speaking) found in many of the sayings it does not help us much. All we can say is that the general impression the gospels give is that they come from reliable witnesses.

THE TRANSFIGURATION

The three synoptic evangelists relate that Peter's confession near Caesarea Philippi was followed by a divine confirmation of the identification of Jesus. This scene is omitted by John, who believes that the 'glory' of Jesus was revealed through a number of 'signs' (2.11, etc.), not at one specific moment. To analyse the historical origin of the transfiguration-story is very difficult. Fairly simple solutions have been offered by a number of scholars who have suggested that it is purely mythical or a symbolic apocalyptic scene or a misplaced resurrection-story. Others have held that it represents the coming of the Messiah at the feast of Tabernacles, though Mark misunderstood the nature of his materials.

Certainly it must be said that in the tradition the story was told in relation to the epiphany of Yahweh to Moses on Sinai. In Exodus (24.15–16) we find the six days of Mark 9.2, the mountain, the cloud, and the voice of God. It was also related to the prophecy of Malachi, according to which the messenger of God is like a refiner's fire and like fullers' soap (3.2, cf. Mark 9.3) and before the day of the Lord Elijah would return (4.5; Mark 9.4).

These aspects of the story show that in describing an event of crucial significance those who described it made use of language

---

[1] For part of this analysis I am indebted to a paper by Professor Batdorf read to the Chicago Society of Biblical Research on November 18th, 1961.

derived from the tradition of revelation. They do not show that something did not take place, even though we may not be able to describe that something in some other terminology. It would appear that, just as in the story of Peter's confession, Peter did not adequately understand the meaning of the event. Here he wanted to erect tabernacles for Jesus, Moses, and Elijah. He did not understand that the way of Jesus was to be the way of the cross (Mark 8.31–7). It must remain uncertain whether or not he could have understood this at the time. Many passages in the gospels seem to indicate that there were various ideas about when and how the kingdom would come, even among the closest disciples of Jesus.

THE JERUSALEM MINISTRY

The journey of Jesus to Jerusalem is finally finished, and he arrives there to encounter an atmosphere of intense expectation. Luke (19.11) comments that when he drew near to the city his disciples supposed that the kingdom of God would immediately appear. There is no reason to doubt this statement. The only question is whether or not he shared their hopes.

His actions at the time seem to indicate that he did so, and that like the disciples he regarded his coming to Jerusalem as a fulfilment of the apocalyptic prophecies of Zechariah 9–14. (1) The central point of his Jerusalem ministry was the Mount of Olives (Zech. 14.4). (2) He obtained a colt and rode upon it into the city (Zech. 9.9). (3) The crowds carried branches as at the feast of Tabernacles (Zech. 14.16–19). (4) He went into the temple and drove out traders from it (Zech. 14.21c). (5) He would not allow anyone to carry any vessel through the temple (Zech. 14.20b–21a). In other words, he entered Jerusalem as a king of the kind foretold in Zechariah – 'lowly, and riding upon a colt' – not as the warrior king of popular expectation. His disciples probably did not understand what he was doing, as John 12.16 points out. They remembered what he did, however.

The hope that at this point the kingdom would come was not fulfilled. Either before (Mark 11.13) or after (Matt. 21.19) the cleansing of the temple, Jesus saw a fig-tree in leaf and looked for figs on it. Mark comments that 'it was not the season of figs' before recording Jesus' curse upon the tree. Why should he have expected to find fruit? Because miraculous fruitfulness was to accompany the coming of God's kingdom, as we read in Ezekiel 47.12 and in the Jewish apocalypses. The time foretold in Zechariah 14.11, when there would be 'no more curse', had not arrived.

When Peter spoke to Jesus of the withering of the fig-tree, he was told to 'have faith'.

Whoever says to this mountain, Be torn away and cast into the sea, . . . it shall take place for him.

Once more, a prediction in Zechariah seems to be in view. 'And the Mount of Olives shall be torn asunder towards the east and towards the west' (14.4); the Hebrew word for 'towards the west' is 'to the sea' – the Mediterranean. The saying is transmitted in differing forms and contexts in Matthew 17.20 and Luke 17.6, and something like the Matthaean form is alluded to in I Corinthians 13.2. But the original context, in view of the parallel in Zechariah, is probably to be found in Mark.

The conclusion we ought to draw from the 'Zechariah-pattern' is not altogether clear. (1) Is the pattern due to Christian reflection on the meaning of the entry into Jerusalem? Such an explanation is suggested by the words of John 12.16. After quoting Zechariah 9.9, the evangelist adds, 'His disciples did not know these things at first, but when Jesus had been glorified, then they remembered that these things were written of him and that they did these things to him.' Moreover, in Mark there is no explicit quotation from Zechariah such as we find both in Matthew (21.4–5) and in John. (2) On the other hand, does the pattern go back to Jesus himself? In favour of this view is the fact that while the parallels exist Mark does not make anything of them. The tradition may well contain materials whose precise significance the evangelist did not know. He was certainly not concerned with discussing unfulfilled prophecy. On balance, we should incline to think that Jesus did intend to fulfil the prophecy of Zechariah and that some of it remained unfulfilled. Like his disciples, he had believed that when he went up to Jerusalem the kingdom of God would come.

For some time in Jerusalem – perhaps between Tabernacles and Passover – Jesus was engaged in teaching and in controversies with religious leaders. (Only Matthew 21.14–15 intimates that he performed healings there.) The stories of these controversies reflect the continuing tension between Jesus and the authorities. They ask for his credentials in relation to his cleansing the temple; he counters by asking them what credentials John the Baptist had. He tells them a parable of warning: to reject God's messenger means to be rejected by God. He explains that his mission is not directed against Rome; he argues with Sadducees about the resurrection and summarizes the law for a scribe; he asks how the coming of a Davidic messiah can be expected, when David referred to the messiah as 'Lord'; and he praises a poor widow for her gift to the temple. The impression which this section gives (Mark 11.27–12.44) is one of marking time while waiting for the crucial action which is to come.

Finally the crisis is at hand, and Jesus predicts to a disciple that the temple will be destroyed (Mark 13.1–2). Such predictions had been uttered by some of the Old Testament prophets. Micah denounced the priests and the false prophets who claimed that since Yahweh was in their midst no evil would come upon them; 'therefore for your sake Zion shall be ploughed like a field and Jerusalem shall become heaps, and the mountain of the house as the high places of a forest' (3.11–12). Similarly Jeremiah proclaimed that if the people did not repent and turn from evil, Yahweh would 'make this house like Shiloh' (26.6; the tent of meeting had once been there, Josh. 18.1).

It is clear that some early Christians (like the Essenes of Qumran) believed that the temple would be destroyed and that Jesus had said so (Acts 6.14). On the other hand, Mark 14.57–8 relates that only false witnesses said of Jesus that he would destroy the temple and in three days build another. Perhaps what Mark means is that the witnesses made the prediction too precise and did not understand its reference to Jesus himself (cf. John 2.19–21). We should conclude that Jesus did predict the destruction of the temple.

In Mark there follows a section of eschatological predictions which has been called 'the little apocalypse' (13.3–37). This section is almost certainly a compilation from various kinds of materials and has been worked into a literary composition ('let the reader understand,' 13.14). As it stands, it contains a secret revelation given only to the four disciples first called (1.16–20). Following the tradition of prophets and apocalyptic writers it describes the catastrophes which will precede the end, not only on earth but in the heavens; but it concludes with a statement that the precise day or hour is known to no one – neither to the angels in heaven nor to the Son, but only to the Father (13.32).

This saying may reflect a post-resurrection view of Jesus as the Son; it is equally likely that he regarded himself as God's Son in a special way and that he was expressing his faith in the Father's purpose in spite of his ignorance of a detail. According to Zechariah 14.7 there would be 'one day which is known to Yahweh'. This prophetic statement may lie at the foundation of the word of Jesus.

If we are right in concluding that at this point Jesus was influenced by the predictions found in the prophet Zechariah, we are immediately involved in the question as to whether or not his proclamation was fully consistent. (1) It is possible to argue that different aspects of it were brought out on various occasions, and that a central core of emphasis on both present and future lies underneath the expressions found in the gospels. (2) It is also possible to suggest that, humanly speaking, 'though he was a Son, he learned obedience by the things which he suffered' (Heb. 5.8); his view of the coming of the kingdom was modified in relation to (a) Galilean rejection of his message, (b) his journey to Jerusalem, and (c) his experiences in Jerusalem itself. We should not expect the evangelists to set forth any clear picture of such modifications. Like most ancient writers, they were not interested in psychological (or even in theological) development.

Either of these two solutions, it would appear, is historically possible.

THE LAST SUPPER

The last supper of Jesus with his disciples took place in a private house in Jerusalem on a Thursday evening which was either on the day of Passover (synoptics) or a day earlier (John). The chronological difficulty is important because the meal either did or did not have Paschal overtones. If it did, we see Jesus rein-terpreting the Passover celebration in relation to his own mission; if it did not, some other meaning was presumably intended.

In the book of Exodus the Paschal killing of a lamb and consuming it is described as taking place on the fourteenth day of the month, 'between the two evenings' (Exod. 12.6). 'Evenings' are mentioned because the Jews reckoned the day as beginning at sundown and continuing to the next sunset. The instruction is made more precise in Deuteronomy 16.6: 'Thou shalt sacrifice the Passover at even, at the going down of the sun.' This is the practice described for the first century by Josephus; the sacrifice took place at the beginning of the 14th of the month Nisan (*Ant.* 2, 312); elsewhere (*War* 6, 423f.) he states that it was performed between the ninth and the eleventh hour, presumably between three and five in the afternoon of the 13th. Among the Essènes, according to the Book of Jubilees (49.1), a different schedule was followed: the lamb was killed on the 14th and eaten on the 15th.

In addition, from the 14th to the 21st only unleavened bread was eaten. Mark 14.1 thus refers to the festival as 'the Passover and the Unleavened Bread'. When he speaks in 14.12 of 'the first day of unleavened bread when they sacrificed the Passover' and indicates that this time preceded the eating of the Paschal meal, he is probably following a non-Jewish chronology. According to all three synoptic gospels Jesus ate the Passover with his disciples. Luke (22.15) makes the point most explicit; Jesus says, 'With desire I have desired [a Semitic turn of phrase, meaning "I have strongly desired"] to eat this Passover with you before I suffer.' But in the others it is fairly clear. Though details of the Passover meal are lacking (the lamb, the bitter herbs), the atmosphere is Paschal. Jesus identifies himself, however, not with the lamb but with the bread and with the first of the four cups characteristic of the meal. The bread signifies his body, which is to be given for the disciples; the cup is the seal of the new covenant in his blood, a covenant between God and the disciples. Jesus takes an oath that he will not drink wine again until he drinks it new in the kingdom of God (Mark 14.25). Luke views the scene from the standpoint of the apostolic Church and portrays Jesus as 'covenanting' the kingdom to his disciples as the Father has

Latin version). It has often been thought, therefore, that they reflect the Church's intention to relate the Lord's Supper to the last supper. After the death and resurrection of Jesus, the meaning of the last supper was understood in relation to the continuing life of the Church. Indeed, the account of the last supper was presumably transmitted because it had this significance.

In attempting to defend the historical character of the words of institution, scholars have claimed that the words 'in my remembrance' (or 'for my remembrance') refer not to the community's remembering or recalling Jesus but to their calling upon God to 'remember' him with favour. Old Testament parallels show that this interpretation is possible, but it does not necessarily exclude the more natural meaning of the words. Paul's own statement, 'as often as you eat this bread and drink this cup, you proclaim the Lord's death, until he comes' (I Cor. 11.26), can bear either meaning. The Lord's death is proclaimed to God and to the Church.

Another difference between Mark and Paul lies in Paul's use of the word 'new' in relation to the covenant. Since this word is found neither in Mark nor in Matthew we should assume that it has been added as an interpretation of the significance of the work of Jesus – though presumably the newness was implied in what Jesus did.

The real historical difficulty arises, however, when we compare the synoptics and Paul, on the one hand, with John on the other. (1) In John the last supper is not a Paschal meal. John states that it took place 'before the feast of the Passover' (13.1–2); the next morning the priests are still waiting to 'eat the Passover' (18.28). It may be that John has changed the date in order to bring the crucifixion into synchronization with the killing of the Paschal lamb. According to Mark 15.23 Jesus was crucified at the third hour; according to John he was handed over for crucifixion at the sixth. The synoptics state that Jesus died at the ninth hour; John may be relying on a similar tradition but emphasizing the lateness of the time for the sake of synchronism. Whether this be so or not, Jesus does die about the time when the lambs were killed; and John regards Jesus as 'the lamb of God' (1.29, 36; 19.36 may be a quotation from Exod. 12.46). (2) In John the last supper contains no reference to the Lord's Supper. Even if we should suppose that the allegory of the vine in John 15.1–16 is related to the wine of the last supper, it has nothing to do with blood or a covenant or drinking from a cup. Instead, wine occurs in John only in the story of the wedding at Cana (2.1–11) and bread in the story of the feeding of the five thousand (6.1–15) and in the discourses related to it (6.26–65; an incidental allusion in 21.9). Jesus refers to himself as the bread of life (6.35, 48–51) and states that the only means of obtaining eternal life is to eat his flesh and drink his blood (6.51c–58). This statement is corrected for the disciples, since 'it is the spirit that gives life; the flesh is of no avail' (6.63). Apparently John is speaking of the Lord's Supper and is rejecting interpretations of it which relate it (*a*) to the last supper and (*b*) too closely to the eucharistic elements.

These differences require some kind of explanation. (1) It has been argued that John really treats the last supper as a Passover; his chronology reflects Essene usage, not that of the priesthood in Jerusalem. This argument is wrong, for the Essenes killed the lamb on the 14th, not the 13th. (2) It has been argued that John is right, and that the last supper was really a 'fellowship meal' of a general kind or a special 'Passover-Kiddush' anticipating the Paschal feast. It cannot, however, be proved that this is so. (3) It has been argued that the pre-Pauline Eucharist contained no reference to the death of Jesus and that therefore Paul was responsible for introducing it. (*a*) The disciples broke their bread with gladness (Acts 2.46); therefore they cannot have been thinking about Jesus' death. But this statement does not necessarily refer to the Lord's Supper, and we are not in a position to state that gladness excluded remembrance of the Lord's death. (*b*) The Corinthians were not thinking about the death of Jesus. But this fact does not prove that their practice was primitive. Paul is correcting aberrations, not fidelity to tradition. We conclude that the synoptic account is probably correct and that the last supper was a Passover meal. In John the last supper has been interpreted differently; perhaps it was already interpreted differently when Paul was writing to the Corinthians, for in I Corinthians he says that 'Christ, our Passover, has been killed' (5.7, obviously a reference to the lamb), and dates the last supper 'in the night in which he was betrayed' (11.23), not with reference to the Passover. For Paul and John the sacrificial death of Jesus was more important than his eating the Paschal lamb. Indeed, by the second century only Ebionites and Quartadecimans continued to regard the Jewish Passover as significant.

Leaving the upper room which their friends had provided in Jerusalem, Jesus and his disciples went out of the city to the Mount of Olives. John (18.1-2) specifies that the location was a garden 'across the brook Kidron', and that this spot was known to Judas because the disciples had often met there. Before their departure they had concluded their Passover meal by singing either the whole of Psalms 113 to 117 or, as Rabbi Shammai had required, only Psalm 117. These psalms speak not only of God's acts in the past but also of his continuing care for his own, though in Psalm 116.10-11 we read these words:

> I kept my faith, even when I said,
>   'I am greatly afflicted';
> I said in my consternation,
>   'Men are all a vain hope.'

Something of this motif is reflected in Jesus' prediction that his followers will be scattered and that Peter will deny him (Mark 14.27-31). It is reflected even more strongly in the scene in Gethsemane (apparently in the valley below the Mount of Olives). There he takes aside only Peter, James and John, and tells them that his soul is very sorrowful, even to death (cf. Ps. 42.6, etc.). They are to keep awake or to watch while he prays. His prayer resembles the prayer he had taught his disciples.

Abba (Father), all things are possible to thee;	Father (Luke 11.2),
take this cup from me;	lead us not into testing (Luke 11.4);
nevertheless, not what I will but what thou willest.	thy will be done (Matt. 6.10).

The similarities surely do not suggest that we have here a Christian meditation on an early prayer; instead, it may be supposed that in Gethsemane Jesus prayed in a manner not unlike that to which he and his disciples were accustomed. He expressed his human hope that God would bring in the kingdom without the pangs of the last days; his comment on the sleeping disciples, 'The spirit is ready, but the flesh is weak,' could be applied to his own words as well as to their failure to watch.

The Gethsemane scene ends with the arrival of Judas and emissaries from the high priest carrying swords and clubs; John (18.3) mentions a cohort of soldiers, probably temple police. At the signal given when Judas kisses Jesus, they move in and take Jesus. One of the disciples who is armed with a sword – Peter, according to John – cuts off the ear of the high priest's slave (only Luke says that Jesus healed him). Jesus himself asks his foes why they have come out for him as for a robber. The Greek word '*lēstēs*' is used by Josephus to mean 'revolutionist', and it may bear that meaning here.

Mark alone (14.51–2) speaks of a young man who followed Jesus (was his disciple?) who escaped arrest by leaving his outer robe in the hands of the police. It would appear that this odd episode is recorded because it happened rather than because someone created it as a fulfilment of Amos 2.16: 'He who is stout of heart among the mighty shall flee away naked in that day.' Hoskyns and Davey suggest that the parallel, while perhaps fantastic, is disquieting. Probably it is just fantastic.

There follows an immediate 'grand jury' investigation by the Sanhedrin, the Jewish court of seventy-one members which apparently could recommend the death sentence to the Roman procurator but could not execute it. The fact that the investigation violates many of the rules set forth more than a century later in the Mishnah tractate *Sanhedrin* should not suggest that the account is fundamentally wrong. Rules formulated abstractly in the second century cannot be used to discredit an account of an earlier event. On the other hand, the most difficult item in the passion narrative, the crucifixion on the Passover, is explicitly provided for in *Sanhedrin* xi. 4, and the two meetings of the court, required in capital cases, are to be found in Mark 14.55 and 15.1 (*Sanhedrin* v. 5).

The first charge brought against Jesus was that he had threatened to destroy the temple (Mark 14.58; cf. a revised version in John 2.19–21). According to Mark, Jesus had predicted the destruction of the temple to one of his disciples (13.1–2), but apparently he did not make this statement publicly. To predict such a calamity was dangerous. Micah (6.12) had foretold destruction, but the repentance of King Hezekiah and of all Judah had saved him (Jer. 26.19). Jeremiah too had prophesied against the temple (Jer. 7.14; 26.6) and had escaped death only through the influence of a powerful official (26.24). At the same time a certain Uriah was killed, in spite of his escape to Egypt (26.20–3). But since the witnesses against Jesus did not agree, another charge had to be found.

The high priest therefore asked him a double question. 'Are you the Anointed One, the Son of the Blessed?' (Mark 14.61). The present form of the question may owe something to Christian terminology. But since it is not possible to prove that the high priest (1) could not have spoken of 'the Anointed one' and (2) did not know that Jesus regarded the Anointed One as not the son of David (Mark 12.37), we may well suppose that his question has been correctly reported. Whatever Jesus' answer may have been (the gospels disagree), it must have allowed the high priest to view it as affirmative. He tore his outer garments and stated that Jesus had uttered a blasphemy. Technically, blasphemy consisted only of expressing the secret name of God, YHWH. There was a wider use of the term, however, and it could have covered the claim to a unique relationship to God (cf. John 5.17–18). However this may be, it is evident that the idea of blasphemy was in the mind of the high priest. He said that Jesus had blasphemed; the others agreed. The penalty for blasphemy was death (Lev. 24.16).

Meanwhile Peter had denied being a follower of Jesus. Almost apprehended when a servant girl noticed his Galilean accent, he said that he did not know Jesus. It has, of course, been suggested that the account was invented in order to encourage Christian martyrs not to imitate Peter, but as we have often argued, these suggestions reflect the creativity of those who make them rather than that of early Christians.

Jewish form, as we have said, is preserved when the Sanhedrin meets again at dawn. Evidently some revision of the charges was made in order to present them to Pilate, who could understand insurrection better than blasphemy. According to Luke 23.2 the grounds on which Jesus was brought before the Roman procurator were as follows:

(1) leading the nation astray (cf. Deut. 13.1–5);
(2) forbidding the payment of taxes to Caesar (cf. Mark 12.13–17); and
(3) calling himself an anointed king.

According to all four gospels Pilate found it hard to believe that these charges were genuine. Pilate had no interest in revolutionary movements, but from his other dealings with the Jews (see pages 269ff.) it is evident that he was not impressed favourably by the Jerusalem aristocracy. Luke alone says that upon learning that Jesus was a Galilean he sent him to Herod Antipas, who was in Jerusalem for the Passover (23.4–12). Apparently Herod regarded Jesus as a magician and, upon being denied a performance, sent him back to Pilate.

Pilate then sought for a way to please the high priest and the mob (among which, as he knew, were supporters of Jesus). According to Mark (15.6) it was customary for the procurator to release a prisoner at the feast (so Matt. 15.15; John 19.39); Luke, on the other hand, describes it not as a custom but as the result of a request by the mob on this occasion (23.18). Luke's notion seems more probable. There may or may not have been a custom of releasing a prisoner at Passover; it is certain that the procurator, the direct agent of the Roman emperor, who could even put to death a governor of senatorial rank (Tacitus, *Hist.* i. 7), was able to release a prisoner if he wanted to do so. In any case, a popular revolutionary leader named Barabbas (or Jesus Barabbas, as in the Caesarean text of Matthew 27.16) was released.

Pilate had Jesus scourged, and delivered him to Roman soldiers for crucifixion; this penalty was customarily employed by the Romans in dealing with revolutionists. At this point some of the soldiers mocked and derided Jesus, viewing him as a pretender to the Jewish throne. After the scourging he was so weak that he was unable to carry the heavy wooden beam on which he was to die. The Romans therefore impressed a Jew from Cyrene, apparently on his way to Passover, to carry the beam to a place named Golgotha. As an opiate, wine mixed with myrrh was offered to

Jesus, but he refused it. He was crucified at about nine o'clock in the morning, with the title 'the king of the Jews' placed above his head. After the relatively brief interval of six hours he died.

His words from the cross are given differently by the various evangelists. The simplest version is that presented by Matthew and Mark; according to them he said, 'My God, my God, why have you forsaken me?' They add that bystanders misunderstood what he said and supposed that he was calling for Elijah, in Jewish tradition the forerunner of the Messiah. Such a misunderstanding could arise only from the first words of his statement, in Hebrew 'Eli', in Aramaic 'Eloi'. It is therefore possible, though of course most uncertain, that he actually expressed only these words and that the rest of the sentence – the beginning of Psalm 22 – was filled in as the saying was transmitted.

The centurion in command of the Roman soldiers was standing facing Jesus, and when he saw how he died he was moved to say, 'Truly this man was a son of God' (Mark 15.39). Mark probably intended to provide a gentile testimony for his own belief that Jesus was the Son of God. Luke records the centurion's words in a different way: 'this man was really innocent' (23.47). A striking pagan parallel, however, suggests that something like what Mark reports may really have been said. After a great snake coils itself around the head of the crucified Cleomenes, the Alexandrians regard him as a hero and 'son of the gods' (Plutarch, *Cleomenes* 823e).

After this point the evangelists describe the burial of Jesus, an event also mentioned by Paul in I Corinthians 15.4. Unlike the other evangelists, Mark (15.45) is willing to refer to his dead body as a corpse.

THE REJECTION OF JESUS

The gospel story is concerned not only with prophecy and its fulfilment and with the preaching and teaching of Jesus, but also with the rejection of Jesus. Many were called, but few followed him. In the gospels we find many groups and individuals who turned away from the gospel.

(1) In the first place, his emphasis on the importance of inner motive in obedience to the commandments, and his choice of

certain commandments as more important than others, meant that conflicts arose with scribes and Pharisees who feared that the stress on inner motive would result in neglect of external obedience. They could not believe that Jesus could forgive sins; only God could do so (Mark 2.7). Indeed, Mark's whole collection of controversy-stories (2.1–3.6) clearly illustrates their fears and disagreements. Jesus not only forgives sins but also eats with unclean tax-collectors and sinners; he does not advocate private fasting; he heals on the Sabbath. His disciples desecrate the Sabbath by plucking grain 'to make a path' through a field. In Mark 7.1–23 another controversy is concerned with the disciples' eating with unwashed hands (apparently it was developed in Christian tradition into a discussion of food laws in general). Some Pharisees ask Jesus for a 'sign from heaven' in Mark 8.11–15; he warns his disciples to avoid the 'leaven' (unclean bread?) of the Pharisees and of Herod. We meet the same adversaries in Jerusalem, where the Pharisees try to trap Jesus into making pro- or anti-Roman statements (Mark 12.13–17) and the scribes ask him what the source of his authority is (11.27–33). He denounces the scribes as hypocritical thieves.

The impression of Jesus' hostility towards scribes and Pharisees is heightened by a collection of 'woes' against them which Matthew has collected in his twenty-third chapter (cf. Luke 11.39–52) and by the parable of the Pharisee and the tax-collector (Luke 18.10–14).

It is fairly plain, in spite of some scholars' doubts in the matter, that Jesus and the Pharisees (in general) were locked in conflict. To be sure, some Pharisaic teachers agreed with Jesus in his attitude towards the law (Mark 12.28–34 gives an example of a scribe who did so) and that some invited him to eat with them (Luke 7.36; 11.37; 14.1; cf. 13.31); but the general attitude of the Pharisees cannot be judged from a few 'Christlike' expressions. The fact that at some points they agreed with him, and he with them (cf. Matt. 5.18–19, probably phrased in Jewish Christian terms), does not contradict the fact of their basic opposition. When he forbade divorce on the ground that part of the Mosaic law was a temporary accommodation (Mark 10.5), he implied that the whole law did not come from God. By his attitude towards ritual observances he necessarily separated himself from the religious leaders of Judaism and their basic emphasis on doing the whole law.

(2) Jesus was also rejected by his family. It is quite clear from Mark 3.21 and 31–5 (separated by the inclusion of a controversy over exorcism, 22–30) that 'those from him' (i.e., his family) came to seize him, 'for they said, He is beside himself.' In verse 31 his mother and brothers finally come on the scene and call for him. Surrounded by a crowd of hearers, he is informed that his mother, brothers and sisters are seeking him. 'Who is my mother? Who are my brothers?' He looks about and says, 'See, my mother and brothers; whoever does God's will is my brother, sister, mother.' For this reason we are not surprised to find him promising his disciples that anyone who abandons home or family will receive a hundredfold reward (Mark 10.29–30). In spite of his denunciation of divorce and blessing of children (Mark 10.13–16) and his criticism of making gifts to the temple instead of helping father and mother (7.10–12), the mission of Jesus and his disciples involved separation not only from traditional religion but also from family ties (cf. Luke 12.51–3). The heavenly Father replaces any earthly father (Matt. 23.9). The disciple's new family is the band of disciples itself.

(3) Jesus proclaimed his gospel in his home town of Nazareth and met with sceptical unbelief there. His synagogue sermon was greeted with questions. 'How did he get this way? Isn't this the carpenter, the son of Mary, the brother of James, Joses, Judas and Simon? Aren't his sisters here with us?' Jesus answered with a proverb: 'A prophet is not without honour except in his own city and among his relatives and in his home.' The result was that 'he could do no miracle there, except that by laying his hands on a few sick people he cured them' (Mark 6.1–5).

(4) This attitude of scepticism was evidently shared by many in Capernaum, the centre of Jesus' mission to Galilee, and in the near-by towns of Chorazin and Bethsaida. Matthew (11.20–4) and Luke (10.12–15) agree that he expressed 'woes' upon what Matthew calls 'the cities in which most of his miracles took place'.

Woe to you, Chorazin!

Woe to you, Bethsaida!

For if in Tyre and Sidon the miracles had taken place which took place in you, they would long ago have repented in sackcloth and ashes.

But I say to you, it will be easier for Tyre and Sidon in the day of judgement than for you.

And you, Capernaum, are you exalted to heaven? You shall go down to Hades!

For if in Sodom the miracles had taken place which took place in you, it would have remained to this day.

But I say to you, it will be easier for the land of Sodom in the day of judgement than for you.

The prophets had denounced Tyre and Sidon; Jesus denounces the cities of Galilee.

(5) Jesus antagonized the political ruler of Galilee, Herod Antipas. Doubtless he was already suspect to Herod because of his association with John the Baptist (cf. Mark 6.14–29), but suspicion would have been confirmed had Herod learned of his warning to his disciples to beware of the 'leaven' of Herod (Mark 8.15; Matthew 16.6 substitutes 'Sadducees') or of his referring to him as 'that fox' (Luke 13.32). To be sure, he had freed Herod's steward's wife from demons (Luke 8.3), but his denunciation of divorce could hardly have pleased the divorced tetrarch.

(6) When Jesus came to Jerusalem, he left none of the old opponents placated; instead, he encountered new ones. In Galilee he had said nothing against the temple. Now, however, he entered the city of Jerusalem accompanied by a large crowd and he proceeded to go into the temple and to 'cast out those who sold and bought in the [outer court of the] temple'. He 'overturned the tables of the money-changers and the seats of those who sold doves, and would not let anyone carry a vessel through the temple' (see page 350). In his view the temple had been defiled by its contents. Citing the word of Jeremiah (7.11), he declared that the temple authorities had made it a 'den of robbers' (Mark 11.15–17). He fiercely criticized the scribes, denounced the rich who were making insignificant gifts to the temple (12.38–44), and finally, like Jeremiah (7.14), predicted the destruction of the temple itself (Mark 13.2).

(7) At this point, if not sooner, the high priest and the other temple authorities recognized that they must take action, and they turned towards the collection of evidence which would convince the Romans that Jesus had to be executed. The procurator of Judaea had already experienced many difficulties with seemingly seditious Jews, as we have seen. Since it was his duty to maintain law and order in this troublesome frontier province, he was bound to suppress any activity even potentially revolutionary. He could not bear the semi-official title 'friend of Caesar' if he were to release a self-styled king (cf. John 19.12). In Jerusalem, then, all the powers that existed, political and religious, were arrayed against Jesus. They did not and could not recognize his authority without ceasing to be powers. Had they known him, Paul says (I Cor. 2.8, where the demonic powers are secondarily political), they would not have crucified him. Historically, it should be said that *since* they recognized him, but did not accept him, they crucified him.

(8) 'And Judas Iscariot, one of the Twelve, deserted to the high priests in order to betray him to them. When they had heard him they rejoiced and promised to give him money. And he sought for the right time to deliver him' (Mark 14.10–11). This time was the night of the Passover and the place was the garden of Gethsemane on the Mount of Olives – 'not at the festival, lest there be a public disturbance' (Mark 14.2). Judas had told the Jewish soldiers that he would identify Jesus with a kiss (14.44). But what did he betray? Did he identify Jesus, not known by sight in Jerusalem? This seems unlikely, since Jesus had been teaching there. Did he betray the 'messianic secret' or the prophecy that the temple would be destroyed? Since these questions were brought up before the Sanhedrin, Judas may have been responsible for raising them. A modern theory, resembling that of the Cainite Gnostics of antiquity, suggests that in Judas's view the death of Jesus was necessary so that the kingdom would come; he therefore tried to advance the kingdom's coming. The tradition in the gospels provides scant support for any of these views; it seems to suggest that he gave information about the whereabouts of Jesus. His motive is unclear, and perhaps can never be recovered. Matthew (26.14–15) agrees with John (12.6) in stating that he wanted money. Luke (22.3) and (John 13.2, 27) ascribe his act to the work of Satan.

(9) Did only Judas betray his Lord? Mark tells the story of Peter's impetuous boast that even if everyone else were to deny Jesus, he would not do so (14.29–31), and then goes on to describe how Peter, avoiding detection, was nearly caught by a maidservant of the high priest who noticed his Galilean accent; he escaped only by swearing that he did not know Jesus (14.66–72). Similarly the sons of Zebedee, who had insisted that they would drink his cup and be baptized with his baptism of suffering (10.39), were among the disciples who swore that they would face death with him (14.31). But when Jesus was crucified, at his right and left were two non-Christian revolutionists (15.27), not these disciples who had asked to be at right and left in his glory (10.37). All the disciples fled (14.50). At the crucifixion, only a group of Galilean women watched from a distance (15.40–1), as well as some charitable women of Jerusalem (Luke 23.28). Only in the Gospel of John (19.25–7) do we read the story (perhaps symbolical) of the beloved disciple and the Virgin Mary at the cross.

(10) Abandoned by all men (cf. Isaiah 53.3) Jesus finally may have felt himself abandoned by God, and at the end of his three hours' agony on the cross he cried out, 'My God, my God, why have you abandoned me?' The fact that this is a quotation of the first verse of the 22nd Psalm, which passes from despair to triumph, does not prove that Jesus was thinking of ultimate victory. We do not know that he intended to quote the entire psalm. Indeed, as we have already suggested (page 362), he may really have called upon Elijah. In any case, no matter which form of his words we may accept, the same conclusion is fairly evident. (1) If he quoted from the psalm, he felt himself abandoned by all, but he still addressed God as 'my God'. (2) If he called upon Elijah, he still believed that God would somehow bring his kingdom into earthly existence.

THE RESURRECTION OF JESUS

If the life of Jesus were the life of some saint, prophet or hero, it would end with his crucifixion or perhaps with an account of his burial. His disciples, however, claimed that his life did not end in this way. He died and was buried, but he was raised from the dead. Obviously any historian who presupposes that death marks the final termination of human life will find this claim unacceptable. He will have to explain why the disciples believed that Jesus was risen, but he can still proceed on the assumption that they misinterpreted the evidence they had. In our view such a presupposition does not belong to historical analysis, which must take the evidence as it stands and try to understand the purposes for which it was transmitted, without making a preliminary judgement as to its modern significance or insignificance. Admittedly such a procedure is difficult, but unless it is viewed as a goal historical interpretation becomes nothing but modern propaganda.

In dealing with the resurrection we are fortunate enough to possess a brief statement about it which the apostle Paul set forth for the Corinthians about the year 54. Since he prefaces his remarks by pointing out that he had delivered the statement to them when he first was with them (about 50) and that he had received it, presumably from tradition, it obviously came into existence no later than the forties of the first century or, in other words, little more than a decade after the events took place. In addition, we should note that among the witnesses to the risen Lord whom he lists are Cephas and James, both of whom he had encountered at Jerusalem no later than the years between 33 and 35. Some, at least, of the evidence goes back to the period within five years after the crucifixion.

Paul's statement consists of four parts. First comes a description, almost credal in nature, about the death and resurrection of Jesus:

> Christ died for our sins, in accordance with the scriptures;
> he was buried;
> he was raised on the third day, in accordance with the scriptures.

It might be suggested that this description is the result of theological reflection. If it is, the reflection is easy enough to identify. It consists of 'for our sins, in accordance with the scriptures' and 'on the third day, in accordance with the scriptures'. Both ideas are obviously based on Old Testament passages, the first on Isaiah 53.12 and the second on Hosea 6.2 or II Kings 20.5. At the least, the words 'according to the scriptures' are reflective; at the most, the phrases related to them. If we remove these words we are left with the skeleton of the traditional statement: 'Christ died, he was buried; he was raised.' This skeleton bears no marks of theological reflection – though we should hesitate to hold that it ever existed in this form; surely those who transmitted the skeleton had some reason for doing so, and the reason is expressed in the 'additions' which we have noticed.

In any event, it looks as if the reasons were added in response to the events. Perhaps pre-Christian Jews were looking for someone who would die for their sins; but there is no evidence of such an expectation. It is most unlikely that a resurrection was anticipated because of the words found in Hosea or II Kings. Before the interpretation came the event.

It should be added that the 'third day' is reflected in Christian observance of Sunday, the third day from the Friday on which Jesus was crucified. The statement about resurrection 'after three days' in Mark 8.31 and elsewhere means the same period of time, as passages in Josephus prove (*Antiq.* 7, 280–1; 8, 214 and 218).

It should also be added that the existence of an empty tomb is probably implied in Paul's reference to burial. No ancient opponents of Christianity denied its existence, and the controversy reflected in Matthew 27–8 suggests that Jewish critics found it embarrassing.

After this brief notice of death, burial and resurrection, Paul goes on to provide a list of witnesses to the risen Lord. Some theologians have stated that the list marks a fatal decline from the primitive, existential Easter-faith. Whether this judgement be correct or not, it is a fact that Paul did not so regard it. He was a witness to the risen Lord (cf. I Cor. 9.1); so were other Christians.

The list has been variously analysed by various scholars. If we lay emphasis on the repetition of the word 'he appeared', it consists of four parts.

He appeared to Cephas, then to the Twelve;
then he appeared to more than five hundred brethren at the same time (most of them are still alive, though some have died);
then he appeared to James, then to all the apostles;
last of all, as to an abortion, he appeared to me also.

(Paul varies the word he uses for 'then', but apparently because of style rather than for any other purpose.) It may be that, as some scholars have suggested, the first three appearances took place in Galilee and the fourth and fifth in Jerusalem. This idea is based on the fact that in Mark and Matthew the Twelve (now eleven) see Jesus only in Galilee (Mark 14.28, 16.7; Matthew 26.32, 28.10, 16), while in both Luke (24.13–49; Acts 1.4–12) and John (20.19–29) he appears to them in the vicinity of Jerusalem. In John 21.1–14 there is a Galilean appearance, but this chapter may have been added later. It is uncertain, however, that the appearances of the risen Lord were confined to one locality or the other, and it remains only a speculation that in Paul's list we can trace notions of limitation. The list as he received it presumably came from Jerusalem, where, as we have said, he met both Cephas and James.

In our earliest manuscripts of Mark there is no account of the resurrection appearances, though the empty tomb is mentioned and the appearance of Jesus in Galilee is predicted (16.3–7). In Matthew 28.9 Mary Magdalene and 'the other Mary' ('of James' in Mark) see Jesus near the tomb, but he appears to the eleven disciples in Galilee. One of Matthew's principal aims is to repudiate a Jewish explanation of the empty tomb. His argument can be set forth in dialogue form as follows:

Christians: the tomb was empty.
Jews: the disciples stole the body.
Christians: the tomb was sealed and guarded.
Jews: the guards were asleep.
Christians: the guards were paid to say they were asleep.

It is obvious that apologetic interests have played a part in the formation of both sides of the debate, but this fact does not prove that underneath it lies some fact.

In Luke we find three women discovering the empty tomb. The same day, Cleophas and another disciple are on their way to Emmaus when a mysterious stranger joins them and explains to them that they did not understand the meaning of Jesus' mission in relation to the Old Testament. At sunset he breaks bread with them and they recognize him as the living Lord. When he disappears they return at once to Jerusalem and are told that

'the Lord has truly been raised and has appeared to Simon.'
As they describe their experience, Jesus stands in the midst of the
disciples and says to them, 'Behold my hands and my feet, that
it is I; handle me and see, for a spirit does not have flesh and
bones such as you see I have.' He eats a piece of fish in their
presence and tells them to remain in Jerusalem until they receive
divine power for a mission to all nations. He then takes them
towards Bethany and, after blessing them, departs. It is tempting
to view this narrative as a compilation from three different
stories: (1) the road to Emmaus, (2) the appearance to Simon
(Peter), and (3) a Jerusalem appearance. The first emphasizes
the Christian interpretation of the Old Testament and the presence
of Jesus at the Eucharist (compare 24.30 with 22.19); the second
points towards the primacy of Peter; and the third explains that
the risen Lord had a body of flesh and bone. At the same time,
even though these interests may be present, their existence does
not prove that the stories are late in origin. Jesus himself used the
Old Testament in a 'Christian' way; he chose Peter first and
appeared to him first; and any attempt to describe the action of
the risen Lord in narrative form must indicate how he could be
visible.

In the Gospel of John several concerns are evident. Mary
Magdalene assumes that the tomb is empty, but the anonymous
'disciple whom Jesus loved' is the first to enter it. John points
out that neither he nor Peter was aware of any prediction of the
resurrection. The first witness of the risen Lord is actually Mary
Magdalene. Later on the same day Jesus appears to the disciples,
passing through closed doors, and imparts the Holy Spirit to
them. A week later they are assembled again, this time with
'doubting Thomas'. Jesus appears and says to him, 'Place your
finger here, and behold my hands, and take your hand and place
it on my side, and do not disbelieve but believe.' Thomas does so,
saying, 'My Lord and my God,' and Jesus blesses those who have
believed though they have not seen. These narratives point
towards a body which, though capable of passing through solid
objects, is tangible and visible. (Nothing different is said on the
subject in John 21.)

If we now attempt to correlate what we have found in Paul's
statement with what we have found in the gospels, it is obvious

that the appearance first to Cephas is corroborated by Luke 24.24 but by no explicit statement in any other gospel; indeed, Matthew (28.9) and John (20.14–18) clearly state that Mary Magdalene was the first witness. Presumably the Jerusalem church regarded her as non-apostolic; she could be criticized as unbalanced, since according to Luke 8.2 seven demons had been expelled from her (the anti-Christian writer Celsus refers to her as 'crazy'). Paul's list has a rather 'official' character.

Appearances to the Twelve are mentioned in the three gospels which contain accounts of appearances, but those to the five hundred and to James are not recorded in them. James was an early convert (Acts 1.14), but the only description of a resurrection-appearance to him is given in the Gospel of the Hebrews. The appearance to 'all the apostles' cannot be identified. What this comparison shows is that in our gospels, as in Paul's list, we have selections from a much larger body of testimonies to the appearances of Jesus. We have only the accounts which later Christians, for one reason or another, considered important.

But Paul does not end his statement with appearances to others. 'Last of all . . . he appeared to me also.' In relation to Paul's own life, this appearance was obviously the most important. It changed his whole word-view (compare Gal. 1.13–15; Phil. 3.5–7) and probably made him an apostle (I Cor. 9.1). And in his opinion the experience which he had was the same as that of the other apostles. Their testimony was the same as his (I Cor. 15.11). A difficulty may arise at this point if we compare the nature of his vision on the road to Damascus (Acts 9.1–9, etc.) with the accounts given in the gospels. If we assume that the various narratives in Acts are ultimately derived from Paul, it is singular that in Acts 9.7 his companions see nothing but hear a voice, while in Acts 22.9 they see a light but hear nothing. The point may be that the nature of the phenomena was irrelevant; what mattered was the meaning which Paul understood. With this idea we may compare the word he uses in Galatians 1.16: the revelation took place 'in' him (if this is what '*en*' necessarily means). We may well conclude that his experience was primarily subjective; in Acts 26.19 it is called a 'heavenly vision'. On this ground we are then likely to suppose that since he had a vision the other disciples also had visions.

But this is not what he says. When he is developing his argument about the resurrection of the dead, he relies on the unity of apostolic testimony not about the nature of the resurrection appearances but about the fact that Christ was raised from the dead. To be sure, he regards his own understanding as universally valid. It is almost certain that in his view the risen Lord did not bear a body of 'flesh and blood' but what he calls a 'spiritual body' (I Cor. 15.44, cf. 50). It had been transformed; it had 'put on' imperishability and immortality (15.33). But given agreement as to the fact of the resurrection, different witnesses would naturally lay emphasis upon different aspects of the risen body. We do not know just how Peter viewed it. Presumably Palestinian Jews were likely to emphasize its corporeality, while Paul – because of the nature of his conversion and because of the nature of his converts – emphasized other features. All that can finally be said is that the disciples were convinced that Jesus had been raised because they saw something which they could identify as someone, more precisely as Jesus. To this fact all early Christian evidence testifies. What they saw can be called a vision, but the word means no more than that something was seen. Theologians who have daringly classified it as a 'veridical hallucination' solve no problems. Historical examination of the evidence does not permit us to state either that it was a hallucination or that, if it should be so regarded, it was veridical. Historical examination permits us to say only that they were convinced that they had seen Jesus. The only proof of the correctness of their conviction lies in the existence and the nature of the early Church.

To the resurrection early Christians often added the ascension of Jesus into heaven. It is not altogether clear whether or not all of them regarded 'heaven' as a place in the sky. The only ascension story we possess in the New Testament (Acts 1.9–11) definitely speaks of heaven in this way

He was taken up, and a cloud removed him from their eyes. And as they were gazing at the heaven as he was going away, behold, two men stood by them in white clothing and said, 'Men of Galilee, why do you stand looking at the heaven? This Jesus who has been received up from you into the heaven will come in the way you have seen him going into the heaven.'

373

The conception of 'heaven' has been literalized, perhaps by Luke (cf. Luke 3.22, the Spirit 'in bodily form'). Elsewhere in the New Testament there are allusions to the ascension of Jesus, but no descriptions of it – any more than there are descriptions of the resurrection. For example, in Ephesians 4.8–10 we find exegesis of Psalm 68.19; the words 'having ascended on high' are understood to mean that Christ ascended 'above all the heavens, in order to fill all things'. And the ascended Christ is regarded as the one who created the ministry of apostles, prophets, evangelists, etc. In Ephesians the ascension is treated as an immediate consequence of the resurrection of Christ: God 'raised him from the dead and made him sit at his right hand in the heavenly places' (1.20). The ascension is also mentioned in Hebrews, where we read that Jesus is a great high priest 'who has passed through the heavens' (4.14), that he was 'made higher than the heavens' (7.26), and that he entered 'into heaven itself' and 'sat down at the right hand of God' (9.24; 10.12). The Mosaic law is reinterpreted so that the true Holy Place is heaven and the veil before it is the flesh of Jesus (9.24; 10.20). Finally, in I Timothy 3.16 (perhaps from an early Christian hymn) there is another allusion: 'he was received up in glory.'

In two of these passages, as elsewhere in the New Testament (e.g., Mark 12.36 and 14.62; Acts 2.34; I Cor. 15.25; Col. 3.1), we find quotations from Psalm 110.1, in which Christians found a reference to the triumph of Christ. 'Yahweh says to my Lord, Sit at my right hand until I make your enemies your footstool.' When Jesus asked a question about the Davidic origin of the Messiah, he suggested that David (the supposed author of the psalm) could not have referred to a descendant as 'Lord'. He did not express any doubt that the psalm was speaking about the Messiah (Mark 12.35–7). From the words of Jesus, then, came the belief in his being seated at God's right hand, and this is the belief which is expressed in the doctrine of the ascension.

In the Gospel of John the doctrine is expressed somewhat differently. 'No one has ascended into heaven except the one who has descended from heaven – the Son of Man' (3.13). 'What, then, if you see the Son of Man ascending where he was before?' (6.62). The first passage is a proleptic reference to the future ascension; the second asks a question about its significance. But the ascension is not described by John, except when he refers to the crucifixion as the 'lifting up' of Jesus (3.14; 8.28; 12.32, 34 [in the last verse there is an allusion to Psalm 110]). To Mary Magdalene the risen Jesus says, 'Do not touch me, for I have not yet ascended to the Father' (20.17); on the other hand a week later he tells Thomas to touch him (20.27). Has he ascended during the interval? John's meaning is not clear.

It is evident, however, that (1) Christians took very seriously, some of them 'literally', the belief that Christ was now seated at God's right hand in glory; (2) he had been raised from the dead and had appeared to his early disciples and to James and Stephen and Paul ('last of all,' I Cor. 15.8) but no longer did so; and (3) he would come down from heaven (I Thess. 4.16; Phil. 3.20, etc.) in the future. These three premises permitted only one conclusion: he was in heaven. The degree to which 'heaven' was given a precise location would vary in relation to the world-views of different writers, though it can probably be said that no New Testament writer would have denied that heaven, or the highest heaven (cf. II Cor. 12.2), was 'up'. Given the limitations of language, they could hardly have said that it was down or across. At the same time, we must observe that in most New Testament writings the conception of heaven is given a symbolical interpretation. In Colossians 3.1–4 the mixture of spatial-temporal language with a symbolical meaning is very clear.

> If, then, you have been raised with Christ,
> seek the things that are above,
> where Christ is, seated on the right hand of God.
> Set your mind on the things that are above,
> not on the things that are upon the earth.
> For you died, and your life is hidden with Christ in God.
> When Christ, our life, is manifested,
> then you too with him will be manifested in glory.

The element of mystery is primary, and no attempt either in New Testament times or later can result in removing the mystery. If we wish, we may say that the human life of Jesus ended on the cross. Historically, this is correct. But it is also historically true that his disciples recognized that God had raised him from the dead and that they expected his return from heaven.

The story of their life before his appearing 'a second time' (Heb. 9.28) belongs to the history of the Christian Church.

The resurrection of Jesus is a historical event in at least the following senses: (1) his appearances to his disciples are well attested in documents whose sources are close in time to the event, and (2) the origin of Christianity is almost incomprehensible unless such an event took place. On the other hand, there are certain difficulties in regard to it. (1) The New Testament writers never describe the resurrection itself; they point only to appearances of the risen Lord and to his empty tomb; the resurrection is inferred from these two kinds of evidence. (2) Ancient Jews and Christians believed in the possibility of resurrection in the sense of resuscitation (e.g. Mark 5.35–43; Luke 7.11–17; John 11.1–46; Acts 20.9–12) and could therefore accept the story of Jesus' resurrection as others, ancient and modern alike, could not.

Ultimately it is not possible to provide a cogent historical proof of the resurrection, since the event was, and was regarded as, unique – though accepted in the context of belief in a future general resurrection. The arguments of Paul are based on (1) the testimony of others, (2) his personal experience, and (3) theological inferences ('if Christ has not been raised, your faith is vain; you are still in your sins,' I Cor. 15.17). A similar form of presentation occurs in the Gospel of John (20.29), where Jesus says to Thomas, 'Because you have seen me, you have believed; blessed are those who have not seen and have believed.' The resurrection, in part because of its unique character, is hard to relate to a general world view. According to the gospel accounts, the earliest disciples experienced trembling, astonishment, fear, and doubt.

In antiquity it was sometimes argued (e.g. by Tertullian) that narratives are transmitted because they are either probable/ credible or true. Such narratives as the resurrection stories are, generally speaking, improbable/incredible; therefore they must be true. Put another way, this means that 'it is likely that unlikely things should happen'. The first argument is unsound because the classification scheme is confused. 'Probable/credible' involves a judgement primarily subjective; 'true' implies an objective judgement. As for the second, 'unlikely' things that are 'likely' to happen are not really unlikely. It would appear that there is no way in which the resurrection can be shown, on historical grounds, to be either probable or true. Historical evidence can point towards a decision, and historical evidence could make a positive decision impossible (proof that Jesus was not actually crucified, for example); but the final decision is that which the early Christians called 'faith'.

XX

THE MISSION OF PAUL

More than a third of the New Testament consists of writings ascribed or related to the apostle Paul. It is evident that this 'least of the apostles', as he called himself (I Cor. 15.9), was actually more significant than any of the others, with the possible exception of Peter; as he said, he worked harder than the rest (I Cor. 15.10). It is impossible to understand early Christianity unless his labours are taken into account.

For interpreting his life and his work we possess two kinds of evidence; his own letters, ten in number, written principally to the communities he himself had established, and the account of his conversion and mission provided in about two-thirds of the Acts of the Apostles. Both kinds of evidence need to be considered, for while the letters provide invaluable insights into his mind and the way in which he viewed his ministry they do not set forth so clearly what it was that he did or the ways in which others viewed him. For historical study, both 'inside' and 'outside' approaches are necessary.

Several statements in Acts shed some light on his early life. He was a member of the Jewish dispersion, born in Tarsus of Cilicia (south-eastern Asia Minor). His family belonged to the upper classes of Tarsian society, for Paul was a Roman citizen by birth (Acts 22.27–8) as well as a citizen of Tarsus (21.39). His youth, however, was spent not in Tarsus but in Jerusalem, where he received religious instruction from a famous Pharisaic teacher, Gamaliel (22.3). His sister's son was later in Jerusalem (23.16), but this fact does not show that his sister also lived there. As a rabbinic student, Paul was taught a trade; according to Acts 18.3 it was tent-making or, perhaps, leather-working.

Paul's name was originally Saul; he had been named after the ancient king of Israel who was the most famous member of Paul's tribe (I Sam. 9.1–2). He may well have borne the Roman name Paulus as well (Acts 13.9), perhaps with an etymological allusion to the 'smallness' of the tribe of Benjámin (I Sam. 9.21).

In Acts, Paul first comes on the scene at the death of Stephen; those who were stoning the first martyr laid their garments at Paul's feet (7.58). The martyr's death may well have impressed Paul, though he never mentions it; later converts to Christianity mention the constancy of martyrs as leading them to consider the new faith. For the moment, however, Paul became a persecutor, arresting Christians in Jerusalem and imprisoning them (8.3). Fairly soon he asked the high priest for authority to become an 'apostle' to the synagogues at Damascus, in order to continue his inquisitorial work there. But on the road to Damascus he experienced an encounter with the risen Jesus, and he became a Christian himself.

In his own view this experience was the last of the resurrection appearances which had begun with appearances to the other apostles (I Cor. 15.5–8). In Acts, however, the resurrection appearances are given only to the earliest apostles; both Stephen (7.55) and Paul (26.16) see Jesus, but they see him glorified and at God's right hand. Acts also sets forth two conceptions of the relation of Paul's mission to his conversion: (1) his mission was interpreted to him by a Damascus Christian (9.10–19; 22.10–16) or (2) it was laid upon him by Jesus himself (26.16–18). The latter conception, presented in a speech before King Agrippa, may be no more than an abbreviation of the former; or Luke may intend to show that Christ's work can be described either in relation to human intermediaries or apart from them.

Both Paul's own view and that of Acts represent attempts to understand the meaning of an event which in its actuality and in its effects transcended ordinary categories of explanation. As far as Paul himself was concerned, the crucial moment of his life was his conversion, and he speaks of the event three times. In Galatians 1.13–16 he tells of his former life in Judaism, his progress beyond that of many of his contemporaries, his zeal for his ancestral traditions, and his devastation of the Church of God; this situation was transformed when God revealed his Son 'in' him so that he might proclaim the gospel among the gentiles. In I Corinthians

15.9–10 he says that he is unworthy to be called an apostle because he persecuted the Church of God, but by God's grace he became an apostle and worked harder than any of the others. In Philippians 3.5–7 he states that he was 'circumcized on the eighth day, of the race of Israel, of the tribes of Benjamin, a Hebrew of Hebrew parents, as to the law a Pharisee, as to zeal persecuting the Church, as to legal righteousness blameless.' But what had been gain for him he counted as loss because of Christ.

Whereas formerly he had believed that righteousness was an achievement for which he could work, he now radically rejected this view and insisted on the universality of sin and the power of God alone to effect salvation. God's grace alone could bring about forgiveness, reconciliation, and justification. This is, at any rate, the major emphasis of Paul's thought. It is reflected not only in the definite statements he makes on the subject but also in his style of writing. Over and over we find Paul setting forth antitheses which he can resolve only by mentioning God or God's work. At the same time, he found himself quite unable to abandon completely his previous emphasis on work.

> Circumcision is nothing and uncircumcision is nothing; what counts is keeping God's commandments (I Cor. 7.19).

But the keeping of commandments is to be achieved by divine power.

> In Christ Jesus neither circumcision nor uncircumcision is effective, but faith working through love (Gal. 5.6).

> Neither circumcision nor uncircumcision is anything; what counts is the new creation (Gal. 6.15).

Other antitheses, real or apparent, are resolved in God – especially those between Jews and Greeks (I Cor. 10.32, 12.1–2; Rom. 2.9–10; 9.12; 11.30–2; Col. 3.11), but also those between men and women (I Cor. 11.11–12), good and evil (Rom. 7.15–25), and Paul and Apollos (I Cor. 3.6–8). In Romans 14.6–9 the tension between vegetarians and non-vegetarians is transposed into a tension between life and death and resolved in the Lord. The most complete statement of this resolution is to be found in Romans 8.38–9.

I am convinced that
>   neither death nor life,
>   nor angels nor principalities,
>   nor things present or future,
>   nor powers,
>   nor any created thing
>>   will be able to separate us from
the love of God which is in Christ Jesus our Lord.

'If God is for us, who is against us?' (Rom. 8.31).

A similar idea can be presented not so much in terms of the resolution of antitheses as in pictures of hierarchical structure, in which the antitheses lose their force because of their subordinate rôle.

>   All things are yours:
>>   Paul, Apollos, Cephas,
>>   the world,
>>   life, death,
>>   things present, things future;
>   all things are yours,
>>   and you are Christ's
>>>   and Christ is God's (I Cor. 3.21–3).

The head of every man is Christ, and
the head of every woman is her husband, and
the head of Christ is God (I Cor. 11.3).

If we may venture to interpret such passages in relation to Paul's own life, we should say that he had found that an intense personal conflict was resolved for him by his recognition of the supremacy of God over all divisions, personal and inter-personal alike. Paul had been proud, as some of the rabbis were proud, that he had been born a Jew and a male Jew. To Israelites belonged adoption by God, the glory of God, the covenants, the divine legislation, the true worship, the promises, and the patriarchs (Rom. 9.4–5). To male Israelites belonged the sign of dedication to God given in circumcision; Paul continued to believe that women were inferior to men (cf. I Cor. 14.34–5). Because of his conversion he recognized, or tried to recognize, the unity of mankind; but he could not turn his back on his nation's history or his own. The gospel was 'for the Jew first, and also for the Greek' (Rom. 1.16; cf. 2.9–10); the Jew has 'much advantage in every way' (3.1). At the end 'all Israel will be saved' (11.26).

Again, Paul insists that if election comes from grace it cannot be based upon works (Rom. 11.6; cf. Gal. 2.16). Even the antithesis between grace and works cannot fully be maintained, however. Paul instructs the Philippians to work out their own salvation, with fear and trembling, 'for it is God who effects in you both the will and the energy to do what pleases him' (Phil. 2.12–13). There is a 'work of the Lord' to which all Christians are called (I Cor. 15.58); it can be compared to a race (Phil. 2.17; Gal. 2.2) in which not all receive prizes (I Cor. 9.24–7). There are definite rewards not only for apostolic missionaries (I Cor. 3.8–15) but for all (Rom. 2.6–10); for 'God will repay each in accordance with his works' (Rom. 2.6). Paul himself has not reached his final goal, but he presses forward to the goal of the upward calling of God in Christ Jesus (Phil. 3.14).

The work of the Lord finds expression not only in personal devotion but, for Paul himself, above all in the work of an apostle. To be sure, it is Christ who has worked through him; but it is he who has proclaimed the gospel from Jerusalem as far as Illyricum (Rom. 15.18–19). It is the grace of God which has given him power, but he has worked harder than all the other apostles (I Cor. 15.10). The apostolic churches are his 'work in the Lord' (9.1). Why does he work? A divine necessity has been laid upon him, whether he wants to preach the gospel or not (9.16–17). He refuses to accept payments from some churches, such as that at Corinth, for he is determined to regard his preaching as independent of them.

We must not suppose that the apostle regarded his work as a means of attaining personal satisfaction. He regards it with no enthusiasm whatever. In I Corinthians 9.19 he obviously regards it as equivalent to slavery, and elsewhere he includes his labours, both physical and spiritual, among the sufferings which he has experienced for the sake of the gospel (I Cor. 4.12; II Cor. 6.5. 11.27; cf. Gal. 6.17). Governors of churches should be highly regarded because of their labours (I Thess. 5.13) – as Paul himself, by implication, should be – but there is no joy directly associated with what they do.

Especially to the Thessalonians, who seem to have thought that with the imminent coming of the reign of God they could rest from their labours, Paul insists upon the necessity of work in general. He may have had in mind the command to labour given to Adam in Genesis 3.17–19, but he never refers to it. Instead, he tells the Thessalonians to work with their own hands (I Thess. 4.11); indeed, anyone who does not work is not to eat (II Thess. 3.6–12). According to Colossians 3.22–3, slaves should work wholeheartedly, 'as for the Lord and not for men'. These examples show that while for Paul an emphasis on work was expressed partly in his life as a Christian it was also set forth in relation simply to the daily lives of his converts. The Christian is one who works hard at everything he does (Col. 3.23). Such an attitude is characteristic of Judaism, in which the professional student of the law was expected to learn a trade and practise it. 'Let him who stole steal no more; instead, let him labour, working with his hands what is good, so that he may have something to give him who has need' (Eph. 4.28).

Paul himself worked 'night and day', partly in order not to burden his converts (I Thess. 2.9), partly as an example to them (II Thess. 3.8). Among his sufferings for the gospel he mentions 'working with his own hands' (I Cor. 4.12). These quotations suggest two inferences. (1) Work was not a good in itself, in Paul's view; perhaps, therefore, he did regard it as a consequence of Adam's fall. (2) Sociologically considered, his status in the society of his time cannot have been low. His Roman citizenship from birth (Acts 22.28) involved a fairly high social status which is confirmed by his regarding 'working with his own hands' as extraordinary.

Both as a Jew and as a Roman, Paul laid great emphasis upon order in society. This order was to be reflected in orderly worship (I Cor. 11.17–34; 14.33, 40) and a hierarchical structure present in church order (12.28–31) and in married life (11.3–10). The empirical state is based upon the order given by God (Rom. 13.1–7). Indeed, had the rulers of this age recognized the hidden Wisdom of God they would not have crucified Christ (I Cor. 2.8). And the conditions of being a slave or being a free man are also due to God's provision (I Cor. 7.17–24). This is to say that for Paul the new creation of the Christian is an inward and spiritual work; it involves no social changes. When Paul says that he himself is poor but makes many rich, and has nothing but possesses all things (II Cor. 6.10), he is speaking not sociologically but spiritually; he is comparing himself with 'our Lord Jesus Christ' who 'though he was rich became poor for your sake, so that through his poverty you might become rich' (8.9). The only 'equality' of which Paul speaks is the equality which can result from the voluntary gifts of other churches to 'the poor of the saints who are in Jerusalem' (8.14; cf. Rom. 15.26), and he explicitly states that this gift should not result in the 'tribulation' of the givers (II Cor. 8.13). It should come from the 'prospering' of those who give (I Cor. 16.2).

The points which we have been mentioning are intended to show that in consequence of his conversion Paul did not become someone completely different from the person he was before it. At the same time, he did experience a change. In his view, he had been crucified with Christ; he no longer lived but, instead, Christ lived in him (Gal. 2.19–20). He had come to recognize in the crucified Christ the power and the wisdom of God (I Cor. 1.24). It was this recognition, and the consequent change in Paul's direction, which was the substance of his conversion. Through Christ, God had called him to proclaim the gospel – not among his own kinsmen but among the gentiles whom he had formerly despised, and along with the Christians whom he had formerly persecuted.

This was the inward change, expressed in the outward action of mission. What did the change involve, as far as Paul's relationship to Judaism was concerned? Before we can answer this question we must ask why he persecuted the Church. The contexts in which he mentions his activities as persecutor plainly suggest that he was opposed to Christianity because of his zeal for the Torah and for the traditions of his ancestors (Gal. 1.13; Phil. 3.6). It is not clear why this zeal would necessarily make him a persecutor. Perhaps the zeal was more defensive than Paul is willing to state. According to Acts 8.1 he was present when Stephen was stoned and approved of his condemnation; and Stephen had rejected the temple cultus, maintaining that the Jewish people had killed the prophets and 'the righteous one' (Acts 7.52). In I Thessalonians 2.15 Paul himself makes the same charge against the Jews. In the same verse he shows how far he has departed from Judaism, for he claims that the Jews have persecuted him and (picking up common Graeco-Roman complaints against them) states that they do not please God and are hostile towards all. Paul's relation to Judaism lacks equilibrium, as one might expect. In Philippians 3.4–6 he describes his life as a Jew not without some pride but then says that he counts it all as loss. On the other hand, in II Corinthians 11.22 and Romans 11.1 he makes no apology for being, and remaining, a Hebrew and an Israelite. And the whole of Romans 9–11 is devoted to trying to understand God's plan for the salvation of Israel.

The clearest explanation of his ambivalent attitude seems to lie in I Corinthians 9.19–23.

> Being free from all, I enslaved myself to all,
>   so that I might win more of them.
> To the Jews I became like a Jew,
>   so that I might win Jews;
> to those under the law, like one under the law
>   (though I am not under the law),
>   so that I might win those under the law;
> to those without the law, like one without the law
>   (though not without the law, but under Christ's law),
>   so that I might win those without the law;
> to the weak I became weak,
>   so that I might win the weak;
> I became everything to everyone,
>   so that I might be sure of winning some.

On the basis of this statement one might infer that ambivalence, at least externally, lies at the heart of Paul's mission activity. Many of his difficulties with the Corinthian and Galatian churches seem to have arisen because his converts could not understand his attitude. Their confusion is not surprising when we find Paul stating to the Corinthians that he pleases all men in every respect (I Cor. 10.33) and to the Galatians that if he pleased men he would not be a slave of Christ (Gal. 1.10).

This is to say that the key to understanding Paul is not to be found by seeking for consistency in his life or in his thought. It is to be found only where he himself found it, in his new relationship to Christ. One must take seriously his words about his experiencing an extreme tension between willing the good and doing the good (Gal. 5.17; Rom. 7.13–25), whether or not he is explicitly referring to himself. The only solution for this tension ('who will deliver me?', Rom. 7.24) he found in the work and the person of Jesus Christ (Rom. 7.25) and in the gift of the Spirit. Paul did 'everything on account of the gospel, in order to become a sharer in it' (I Cor. 9.23); he was strong enough to do everything because of the one who gave him power (Phil. 4.13).

To put it very simply, Paul's conversion gave his life a meaning and a direction it had not possessed before. In this sense it was a new life, a new creation. 'What was gain for me I count as loss because of Christ. I count everything as loss because of the profit of the knowledge of Christ Jesus our Lord, for whom I lost everything; and I count it as refuse so that I may gain Christ and be found in him – not having a righteousness of my own based on the law but the righteousness which is through faith in Christ, righteousness which comes from God and is based on faith – to know him and the power of his resurrection and participation in his sufferings . . .' (Phil. 3.7–10). This is Paul's final statement about the meaning of his conversion.

After Paul's conversion, he says, he did not take counsel with anyone; instead, he went away to Arabia, presumably south-west of the Dead Sea, and later returned to Damascus (Gal. 1.16–17). Presumably he spent this time in prayer and meditation, trying to determine what God's plan for him was. Only after three years had passed did he go up to Jerusalem, where he stayed for a fortnight with Peter and also encountered James, the Lord's brother (1.18–19). It is significant that these two men are the only ones whose names Paul mentions as witnesses to the resurrection in I Corinthians 15.5–7 (cf. also 9.5). They can hardly have failed to discuss the significance of this event. But they were undoubtedly aware of the difficulties which Paul would create in Judaea were he to preach the gospel there, and for this reason he remained apart from the local churches. They heard of his conversion and thanked God for it, but they did not see him in person (1.22–4). At that point he went away to 'the regions of Syria and Cilicia'. According to Acts (9.27–30) he was introduced to the apostles by Barnabas; after disputations with the 'Hellenists' (presumably Greek-speaking Jews) he was taken to Cilicia so that he would not be put to death.

Of these early years of Paul's Christian work we know very little. There is no reason to suppose that when he mentioned Arabia he meant Qumran. A little information about Damascus does not tell us much, but it does show that there Paul was creating such a disturbance that the 'ethnarch' of Aretas, king of Nabataea, tried to arrest him; he escaped by being let down through the city wall in a basket (II Cor. 11.32–3; cf. Acts 9.23–5).

Apparently it was not until a gentile mission was under way at Antioch that Barnabas brought Paul from Tarsus to participate in it (Acts 11.19–26). The rather vague chronology of Acts suggests that this event occurred about the year 46, but it could be somewhat earlier. By the end of a year's preaching, Paul had become one of five leading 'prophets and teachers' at Antioch (13.1). With Barnabas he was sent to visit Jerusalem; with Barnabas he was sent on a mission to the north-west.

The sermon which Luke records as coming from this mission (Acts 13.16–41) is presumably typical of the approach made by Christian to non-Christian Jews. Beginning with the Exodus, it briefly sketches Israel's history through judges and kings and passes from David to the Saviour descended from David. After a brief summary of the work of Jesus, the preacher quotes Old Testament texts in proof of the truth of his message. In consequence, he arouses the interest of 'many of the Jews and of the devout proselytes'.

Another encounter, however, resulted in bitter argument, and Paul and Barnabas concluded that, while the word of God had to be spoken first to Jews, they should now turn to the gentiles (13.44–7). This picture of the gradual development of a gentile mission may not seem to be in harmony with Paul's picture of himself as called to be an apostle to gentiles. But it agrees with the view he presents in Romans; the gospel was for the Jew first, then to the Greek (1.16; 2.9–10). Moreover, in the theological statements he provides in his letters there is practically no mention of 'secondary causes' or occasional circumstances. There is no reason to assume that one must accept either Paul or Acts alone.

The correlation of Acts with Paul's letters becomes especially important when we investigate the nature of his preaching to the gentiles. The book of Acts contains two samples of Paul's preaching in the gentile world. The first is Paul's address to the Lycaonians, just after his healing of a lame man resulted in the crowd's acclamation of him and Barnabas as the gods Hermes and Zeus. Paul explains to these people that the apostles are men like them, but men with a mission. He calls upon them to turn from their 'vain gods' to the living God, the creator. In previous generations God has left the gentiles without revelation, only intimating his power by his gift of rain and of the seasons which produce food and consequent gladness for men (Acts 14.15–17). Unfortunately we do not know how this sermon would have ended; at this point it was interrupted by the arrival of Jews from neighbouring cities. The second sermon we have is Paul's longer address to philosophers and others at Athens. Here too he stresses the work of God as creator and preserver of the world and of mankind, and attacks idolatry, but concludes with the proclamation of the coming judgement of the world by a man whom he has raised from the dead. Paul's mention of resurrection divides his audience. Some ridicule the notion while others express the desire to hear about it some other time (Acts 17.22–32).

The general outline of these two sermons is confirmed by Paul's own statement describing the conversion of the Christians at Thessalonica (I Thess. 1.9–10). Paul reminds his readers 'how you turned to God from idols, to serve the living and real God, and to wait for his Son from the heavens, whom he raised from the dead, Jesus, who delivers us from the coming wrath.' This statement gives us a full and clear picture of early Christian mission preaching, or so it seems at first glance. As in Lycaonia and at Athens, the Christian missionary has first of all to convince his hearers of the meaninglessness and futility of idolatry, idolatry which meant not only the actual worship of images of the gods but also the whole range of pagan religion. Idolatry has been attacked by the Old Testament prophets, especially the Second Isaiah, and it was the chief target of Palestinian and Hellenistic Jewish criticism. For the gods of Greece and Rome and of the orient were essentially human. The myths about them had long been a source of scandal, especially to Greek philosophers, who devoted much time to explaining away their immorality and their weaknesses. The ordinary educated man of Paul's time would be ready to hear that the gods as gods did not exist. He might be inclined to argue that they represented powers of nature, possibly the elements. But he would be unlikely to claim that the stories of mythology were literally true or that the images of the gods were actually in any way divine. Some people, of course, would uphold the old religions; but perhaps these people were not often converted to Christianity.

Paul was not content to attack the old without proclaiming the new. He did not destroy the false without mentioning the true. And in the religious vacuum produced by the demolition of idols, he urged his hearers to turn to 'the living and real God'. Here, of course, he gives us only a summary. We must go on to ask what this 'living and true God' was, or rather *who* he was. In order to convince the Thessalonians of the livingness and reality of God he must have passed beyond philosophy, beyond general revelation, to tell them of the God of the Old Testament, the God who had created the world, who directed human history, who worked in human history. He may have told them something of God's choice of the patriarchs, especially Abraham, and of his saving of the old Israel in the Exodus. He must have pointed to the miraculous breaking in of God's power in human life, perhaps or even probably to God's revelation made to Paul himself. And in dealing with God's work in history he cannot have been silent about God's moral demand. The prophets who speak of human history also denounce human disobedience, and Paul would have to tell his hearers what this disobedience was. We shall return to this point a little later. For the present it is enough to say that the first and primary point of Paul's preaching, the point on which all else depends, is not the Messiahship of Jesus, or his resurrection, or his coming again, but the reality of the living God, the Lord of creation, the governor of history, the saviour of men.

But the second point is closely related to the first. The early gentile Christian is called not only to serve God but to await the coming of his Son. Here the gentile would at first feel that he was on familiar ground. There were many stories in antiquity about 'divine men' who had ascended into the heavens, even though there does not seem to have been any expectation that they would return. And the resurrection of an individual man was not absolutely unheard of, even though stories of resurrection were usually questioned by the educated. The real problem for the gentile convert arose not at this point but in relation to the statement that this particular 'Son of God' saves us from the wrath to come. Philosophical schools were nearly unanimous in holding that wrath was not a characteristic of the divine being. Because they were dealing with ancient myths which depicted the gods as angry in an excessively human way, they tried to interpret this anger away. The result was that educated men would actively resist the notion of divine wrath. It would have to be explained to them, and it would have to be shown that there was just cause for the coming of such wrath upon mankind.

In other words, Paul's proclamation that 'Jesus delivers us from the wrath to come' would be largely meaningless to the audience he addressed unless he gave grounds for belief in such wrath, grounds which could move his hearers to the same belief. Where could he find such grounds? He could find them only in the moral demand, the ethical claim, made by the living God upon all mankind. He could not speak of the Jewish law delivered to Moses, for the apostolic church had already recognized that this law as such was not binding upon the gentiles. He would have to speak of universal moral law and of God's unlimited demand upon all men. And this law, which is what he calls the 'law of Christ' (Gal. 6.2), would have to be set before the gentiles in every possible way. Paul could express it in terms of the Decalogue, already regarded by Hellenistic Jews as the perfect presentation of the whole law of nature. He could use Jesus' own summary of the second table of the Decalogue, the commandment to love one's neighbour as oneself (Gal. 5.14; Rom. 13.9). He could use lists of virtues and vices, invented by the Stoics but long utilized by Hellenistic Jews. He could use tables of household duties, duties of masters and slaves, husbands and wives, children and parents, already common in the Graeco-Roman world. He could use excerpts from the teaching of Jesus or of the prophets. In short, he would speak to the gentiles, as he says in I Thessalonians 4.1, of 'how you must live and please God'. He would speak to them of 'the will of God, your sanctification' (I Thess. 4.3). For, as he goes on to say after speaking of sanctification, 'the Lord is the judge concerning all these things.'

In other words, in order to make Paul's gentile preaching comprehensible we must assume that it was not limited to the 'apostolic preaching'. It must have included a proclamation about God and then about God's moral demand. Paul's gospel was not only 'preaching' but also what he calls 'teaching' (Rom. 16.17). This teaching was probably not very explicit at first. Paul might well have preached to gentiles a sermon in essence like what we find in Romans 1.18–2.16. This sermon deals with the goodness of creation and the revelation of the creator. All men worshipped the creation, however, instead of the creator, and the result was the universality of sin. Whether the teaching was fully worked out or not, such teaching must have been a central part of the proclamation of the gospel to the gentiles. Only if men were convicted of sin could they be convinced of salvation.

This problem can be approached in a different way. What little we know of early Christian baptism shows plainly enough that it involved the confession of sins, washing in water, and the remission of sins, as well as the acknowledgement of Jesus as Lord. But without some previous proclamation of God's moral demand, how could the gentile convert have known what to confess? How could he have known what sins were being remitted? It seems obvious that moral teaching must have been a central part of the mission to the gentile world.

Baptism was never a rite which automatically ensured immortality or automatically produced perfection. The Christian missionary proclaimed God's moral demand before baptism but he continued to proclaim the demand afterwards, since there was nothing automatic about baptism. And it is therefore quite likely that the moral teaching of the Pauline epistles, addressed to Christians, does not differ greatly from what these converts were told before baptism or even before conversion.

On the basis of these sermons in Acts and of Paul's descriptions of the apostolic gospel, we conclude that the 'apostolic preaching' about Jesus does not give an adequate picture of the Christian gospel. And we must add that the four gospels and the epistles, taken together, still leave the gospel imperfectly and inadequately described. If we remind ourselves that the Old Testament was essentially the Bible of the early Church, we still fail to understand how the Old Testament was used. It is a very big book. The Christian preacher must have provided his hearers with excerpts from it or, more probably, summaries of what he considered central. And what he considered central was not simply texts about the Messiah. It must have been teaching about the work of the living and real God and the moral demand which this God made upon all men without exception.

The preaching to gentiles, then, was not precisely identical with that addressed to Jews or to sympathizers with Judaism. To gentiles it was necessary to set forth the oneness and the power – in short, the reality – of God, and the nature of his moral demand, laid upon Jews and gentiles alike. This is not to say that the apostles to gentiles were concerned with philosophical proofs of God's existence, any more than the second-century apologists were. They were proclaiming the gospel, not conducting a philosophical discussion. In so far as their proclamation about God involved novelty, this aspect was to be found in their insistence upon an absolute monotheism. Philosophers might regard the many so-called gods and so-called lords (I Cor. 8.5) of paganism as imperfect symbols of the one god; Paul may even have known the saying of Antisthenes that 'by convention there are many gods, by nature, one' (cf. Gal. 4.8), but for him and for other Christians pagan worship was worship of 'mute idols' (I Cor. 12.2) or demons (10.20).

In making this proclamation, apostles to the gentiles followed lines already laid down in Hellenistic Judaism, as we can see from the works of Philo, Josephus and others. They proclaimed the unity and the power of the one God who was known by his self-revelation in the creation (Rom. 1.20). They reminded the gentiles of God's moral demand 'written in their hearts' (2.15). Philo had already said that the gentiles worshipped the creation instead of the Creator (cf. Rom. 1.25) and had militantly attacked gentile immorality (cf. 1.24–8). What was new in the apostles' message was the proclamation of the crucified Christ (I Cor. 1.18–25); some converts, as at Corinth, could not grasp its meaning.

JEWS AND GREEKS

From the book of Acts it is fairly evident that the admission of gentiles to the early Christian community involved a considerable time and a lengthy discussion. Acts depicts the mission in Samaria as the result of the scattering of Christians because of persecution after the death of Stephen; but no gentiles became converts. Philip baptized an Ethiopian eunuch who was already at least a sympathizer with Judaism. For Luke the crucial encounter was one which took place between Peter and a Roman centurion named Cornelius – though Cornelius too was a sympathizer with Judaism who gave alms and observed regular hours of prayer. Because of a vision, Peter stayed and ate with him and, after recognizing that he had received the Holy Spirit, ordered him to be baptized in the name of Jesus Christ.

At the same time some Jerusalem Christians who were by origin from Cyprus and Cyrene went to Antioch and made converts among the gentiles. Barnabas and other prophets from Jerusalem later joined the mission; but, still later, Christians from Judaea came to Antioch and stated that there was no salvation without circumcision. Paul and Barnabas were sent to Jerusalem to state the gentile case, and there they met Christian Pharisees who argued not only for circumcision but also for observance of the law of Moses.

Under the guidance of Peter and James, a council of apostles and elders reached a compromise solution. Neither circumcision nor observance of the whole law was to be required; instead, gentile converts were to abstain from 'meats offered to idols, blood, things strangled, and fornication' (Acts 15.29). These commandments are probably based on the holiness code in Leviticus and combine minimal dietary regulations with matrimonial injunctions (Lev. 15.19–24; 18.19; 18.6–18). Gentile converts are regarded as equivalent to the 'sojourning strangers' mentioned in Leviticus.

In Galatians 2.1–10 we seem to have an account of the same conference from a rather different point of view. Paul and Barnabas went to Jerusalem chiefly for a private discussion with the 'pillars' of the church there – James and Peter and John. Other 'false brethren' managed to slip in to the conference, but Paul did not yield to them for a moment. The pillars recognized Paul's ministry to the gentiles as analogous to that of Peter to the Jews, and agreed that Paul and Barnabas were to go to the gentiles while the others continued the Jewish mission. In order to bind the churches together they insisted that Paul and Barnabas should 'remember the poor' or, in other words, take up a collection for the Jerusalem church (cf. I Cor. 16.1–3; II Cor. 8–9; Rom. 15.25–6).

The division of mission work into that to gentiles and that to Jews obviously implies some kind of jurisdictional decision, not mentioned in Acts and, in fact, contradicted in Acts 17.1–3, 18.4–5, 19; and 19.8. Paul himself recognizes the existence of various jurisdictions (II Cor. 10.13–16; Rom. 15.20), and he insists that his mission is primarily to gentiles; but he does not believe that Jews can be segregated from gentiles.

In fact, empirical experience has shown how impossible segregation is. After the conference, Peter came to Antioch and at first ate with gentile Christians; then emissaries arrived from James, and Peter and other Jewish Christians (including even Barnabas) withdrew from table fellowship. The situation was intolerable. At a meeting of the whole church, Paul said to Peter, 'If you, as a Jew, live in gentile fashion, not Jewish, how is it that you are forcing the gentiles to keep Jewish customs?' Peter's answer is not recorded (Gal. 2.11–14). The separation of jurisdictions made no sense when one of the primary proclamations of the gospel was that in Christ there was neither Jew nor Greek, and when churches outside Judaea were made up of members who had accepted this doctrine.

If the separation of Jewish and gentile missions proved unworkable, we must also ask what happened to the decree of the apostolic council. According to Acts 15.30–3 the decree was delivered at Antioch not only by Paul and Barnabas but also by the Jerusalem prophets Judas and Silas; Silas accompanied Paul in Syria, into Cilicia, and even into Galatia, where they delivered the decree (15.40–16.4). Delivery in Galatia was a work of supererogation, since the decree was addressed only to gentile brethren in Antioch, Syria and Cilicia (15.23), but according to Acts 21.25 James regarded it as applying to gentiles in general.

Was the decree actually set forth in the Pauline churches? Certainly Paul never refers to it in his letters, but we must remember that they contain only a small part of his teaching. Perhaps we should expect to find it mentioned in Galatians, but the problem there has nothing to do with the decree; it is related to the advocacy of circumcision which the decree was supposed to prevent. Paul's letters have to do with specific problems not always, or indeed often, related to the decree. However, it would appear that his discussion of sanctification as abstention from fornication and from unclean lust (I Thess. 4.3–7) is close to the matrimonial injunctions of the decree, and in I Corinthians 5.1–5 he condemns a man who has violated the regulation of Leviticus 18.8. The lengthy discussion of meats sacrificed to idols in I Corinthians 8–10 is in harmony with the apostolic decree, and Paul says that the Corinthians are to give no offence to Jews (10.32). The same view is expressed in Romans 14.

It looks, then, as if Paul actually continued to teach the commandments of the apostolic decree, though he did so on grounds different from those advocated at Jerusalem. Its injunctions remained effective in Jewish Christianity, as we can see in Revelation 2.14 and 20, as well as in the Clementine literature and elsewhere.

In the West, however, the decree was reinterpreted. By dropping the mention of 'things strangled' and by adding the Golden Rule, the decree assumed a form in which it could be understood as a more general moral command. In this form it is quoted by Irenaeus; without the addition of the Golden Rule it also appears in the writings of Tertullian, Cyprian and Jerome. This alteration reflects the gradual abandonment of the mediating position held by the council; it reflects the altered circumstances of the later Church.

XXI

THE CHURCH IN THE NEW
TESTAMENT

The Church is not mentioned in any of the gospels but that of Matthew, and there it is mentioned only twice. (1) Jesus gives a blessing to Peter, who has acknowledged him as 'the Christ, the Son of the living God'. He blesses him and, with a play on his name (either in Aramaic or in Greek), says that 'on this rock' he will build his Church, against which the gates of Hades will not prevail; this is to say that the Church will be a community of life. It will also be a community of binding and loosing, of retaining and forgiving sins (Matt. 16.16–19; cf. John 20.23). (2) The Church is mentioned in a passage dealing with forgiveness and reconciliation in the community. Difficulties between Christian brothers should be handled first between them alone, next with the assistance of one or two others, and finally – if necessary – in relation to the whole local community. If the principal offender will not hear the Church he is to be treated like a 'gentile' or a tax-collector. The decisions of the community are equivalent to the decisions of God or of the risen Christ; 'wherever two or three are gathered in my name there am I in their midst' (Matt. 18.15–20; cf. I Cor. 5.1–6.11). Evidently in both instances the Church is regarded as incipiently present in the ministry of Jesus but as fully present only in relation to his resurrection. Jesus will build his Church; as risen he will be in its midst.

In the Acts of the Apostles the word 'church' does not occur before a summary which concludes the story of Ananias and Sapphira (a story reflecting the kind of discipline to which Matthew alludes); in it we read that 'great fear came upon the whole Church' (5.11). But while this is the first occurrence of the word, that for which the word stands is obviously present earlier, in nuclear form among the apostolic group and explicitly in the story of the gift of the Spirit at Pentecost (Acts 2).

The existence of the Church is obviously implied by the existence of the oral tradition embodied in the various gospels, as well as by the existence of the gospels themselves. Specifically, when Mark (4.34) writes that Jesus explained everything privately to his disciples, he implies the existence of a community in which the explanations are available; when he writes, as he often does, that the disciples did not understand the meaning of what Jesus said he implies that such understanding is now present. Luke makes this point more explicit when he describes the errors of the earliest disciples, who supposed that the kingdom of God would immediately appear (19.11, etc.); it is in the life of the Church that the kingdom is to be realized (22.28–30). John expresses the idea most clearly. At first the disciples did not understand, but when Jesus was raised from the dead or was glorified they remembered and believed (2.22; 12.16). They remembered under the guidance of the Holy Spirit, who was to teach them and remind them of everything that Jesus had said to them (14.26) and was to remain with the community for ever (14.16), bearing witness to Jesus (15.26) and leading them to the whole truth (16.13). The resurrection story in John 20.19–23 attests the existence of the community and describes its nature. It is a community whose centre is the real Jesus, who 'showed them his hands and his side'. It is a community of mission: 'as the Father sent me, so I send you.' And it is a community of the Spirit and the remission and retention of sins.

Thus far we have neglected the testimony which chronologically comes first – that provided by the Pauline epistles. It is an obvious but important fact that almost all the epistles are addressed to churches, even though the word 'church' occurs in addressing only the Thessalonians and the Galatians. The churches consist of those who have been 'called to be saints'. This is not to say that all the members bear obvious marks of sanctification. Most of the Pauline communities resemble wheat mixed with tares (Matt. 13.24–30) or good fish with bad (Matt. 13.47–50). It is to say, however, that in determining the nature of the Church we cannot consider only the passages in which 'church' is mentioned. 'You' – the members of the various congregations – constitute the Church. In this sense everything in the Pauline epistles, like everything in the gospels, is an expression of the Church's life.

But what is the Church? It is obviously a social group composed of those who have encountered certain things and have done certain things. Its members have heard the gospel and have had Jesus Christ 'placarded' before their eyes (Gal. 3.1); they have turned from idols to serve the real God and to await the return of Jesus (I Thess. 1.9–10). They have received the gift of the Spirit (Gal. 3.2) and have been enabled to call Jesus Lord (I Cor. 12.3); they have been washed, consecrated, and set in a right relationship to God (I Cor. 6.11). They now meet in order to worship God and to eat the Lord's Supper (I Cor. 11–14). And they live in a relationship to God and to Christ which differentiates their behaviour from that of others. We shall later return to this point; here it is enough to say that in finding out what the Church meant to early Christians we need to bear in mind the whole of their life, not just the explicit statements they make about the nature of the community.

Some of the metaphors which Paul uses in speaking of the Church may indicate what he thinks about it. (1) He speaks of Christians collectively (i.e. as the Church) as betrothed to Christ. He has betrothed the Corinthian congregation to Christ and hopes that it is remaining a pure virgin, not led astray as Eve was led astray (II Cor. 11.2–3). Here he combines two ideas: (*a*) the Old Testament and rabbinic picture of Israel as the bride of Yahweh (Yahweh is replaced by Christ, Moses by Paul) and (*b*) Paul's own picture of the new humanity with Christ as the new Adam and the Church as the new Eve. The metaphor is more fully developed in Ephesians 5.22–31, where Christ is the 'head' and husband of the Church which he loves and for which he gives himself (cf. also I Cor. 6.16–17).

(2) In the Ephesians passage Paul also speaks of the Church as Christ's body. This idea is most fully worked out in I Corinthians 12.12–27. And whereas the bridal metaphor seems to be primarily Jewish in origin, that of the body seems to be derived from Graeco-Roman political thought. Indeed, everything Paul says in this passage can be paralleled in Greek and Roman

writers – except for the specifically Christian expressions which are inserted in the description of the co-ordination of the body. Paul has taken over a Graeco-Roman metaphor and has 'baptized' it into Christian service. He uses it again in Romans 12.4–5, in a brief summary of what he had said to the Corinthians (cf. also Col. 1.19).

The metaphor is not, however, strictly political. As is usually the case in Paul's thought, several motifs are bound together in one form of expression. The idea of the 'body' is not only political but also sacramental; it is related to the Church's sharing in the Lord's Supper, in the common cup and in the common loaf of bread.

> The cup of blessing which we bless, is it not sharing in the blood of Christ? The bread which we break, is it not sharing in the body of Christ? For we, though many, are one loaf, one body; for we all participate in the one loaf (I Cor. 10.16–17).

The idea that the Church is Christ's body thus emerges from a level deeper than that of politics alone.

We have already indicated Paul's fondness for combining the terms with which he speaks of the Church. Several more examples occur in I Corinthians. The Church is a farm or garden which the apostles planted and watered, though the growth was given by God; it is also a building erected by the apostles on the foundation which is Jesus Christ (3.6–11). More specifically, it is a temple of God in which God's Spirit dwells (3.16–17; 6.19; cf. II Cor. 6.16).

Once more, we have metaphors drawn partly from the Old Testament, partly from the Hellenistic world, but all used in order to set forth the meaning of the community in relation to God's act in Christ.

Similar images recur in the gospels, especially in John, where we read that Christ is the bridegroom (3.28–30; cf. Rev. 22.17), that he is the Vine of which the disciples are branches (15.1–16), and that his body is the true temple of God (2.19–21; cf. 4.20–4).

In thinking about the New Testament Church it is not enough to consider what early Christians thought; it is also necessary to consider what they did, above all in their life of worship. It is obvious that when they met together they expressed their faith in 'psalms, hymns, and spiritual songs' (Col. 3.16; Eph. 5.19). A hymn of this kind is certainly mentioned by the Roman governor Pliny when he refers to the *carmen Christo quasi deo* used Christians in Asia Minor. Examples are also to be found in the hymns of heavenly worship set forth in the book of Revelation (4.8, 11, etc.), as well as in such fragments as these:

> Awake, O sleeper,
> and rise from the dead,
> and Christ will shine upon thee (Eph. 5.14).

> He was revealed in flesh,
> vindicated in spirit;
> he appeared to angels,
> was proclaimed among nations,
> was believed in the world,
> was lifted up in glory (I Tim. 3.16).

It may also be the case that the prologue to John was originally hymnodic in character. We should not forget the Magnificat, Benedictus and Nunc Dimittis in Luke's opening chapters (1.46–55, 68–79; 2.29–32), or the hymn which *may* underlie Philippians 2.6–11. Other passages can be regarded as liturgical, but it should be remembered that not every instance in which solemn or sonorous language is used necessarily reflects the cultic life of the Church.

In what setting were such hymns and songs employed? We shall presently discuss the rites of baptism and the Lord's Supper; but not every Christian service of worship was 'sacramental'. Presumably the earliest Christians followed the example provided by the synagogue worship to which they were accustomed. But synagogue worship did not follow a rigid pattern, and there is no reason to suppose that Christians introduced rigidity. In the synagogue there were the following items: (1) the Shema ('Hear, O Israel, the Lord thy God is one Lord; and thou shalt love the Lord thy God,' etc.); (2) prayers, including the Eighteen Benedictions; (3) readings from the Old Testament; and (4) a sermon, delivered by anyone invited by the presiding officer. Such a service, at Nazareth, is described in Luke 4.16–21. And presumably it was to this kind of service that ecstatic speech and prophecy were added. Christians at Corinth offered thanksgivings and blessings to God in ways not comprehensible to all (I Cor. 14.16–17). Paul did not deny the inspired character of their speech, but he insisted that it was inferior to more rational prophecy and required that no more than two or three persons speak in this way; their words were to be interpreted or explained. In his view, the principle of order had to prevail (14.33, 40).

In addition to, and perhaps in conjunction with, this kind of worship there was also the Lord's Supper, to which Luke probably refers in Acts 2.42 when he describes the Jerusalem Christians as holding firmly to 'the teaching of the apostles and the fellowship, the breaking of the bread and the prayers'. In Luke's view this 'breaking of bread' was presumably related to the significant bread-breaking at the Last Supper (Luke 22.19) as well as to the disciples' encounter with the risen Lord at Emmaus; there 'their eyes were opened' and 'he was known to them in the breaking of the bread' (24.31, 35).

The Lord's Supper was in part a repetition of the Last Supper and a symbolical re-enactment of Christ's parabolic action. It was also an ordinary meal made extraordinary by the conviction that the risen Lord was present. And it involved the continuing proclamation of his death 'until he come' (I Cor. 11.26). All these meanings were implied, none of them to the exclusion of the others; and there was also the meaning of sacramental sharing in the body and blood of Christ (I Cor. 10.16–17), a meaning more fully expressed in the Johannine doctrine of eating Christ's flesh and drinking his blood (John 6.51–8). It has sometimes been claimed that the Johannine view is based on 'mystery' conceptions of eating the god, but it is more easily interpreted as a natural explanation of the action of the disciples after they had taken the bread which Jesus said was his body.

In the *Didache* (14.2–3) as in the *Adversus haereses* of Irenaeus (4, 17, 5) the Lord's Supper is called a sacrifice, but the sacrifice is probably not a re-enactment of Christ's sacrifice; instead, it is the offering of the first-fruits, of the wine and of the bread.

Another aspect of Christian worship, highly important in a growing Church, is to be found in the rite of baptism. Whatever the origins of baptism may be, it was certainly associated with the risen Lord. Even though John (4.1) says that Jesus baptized, he corrects himself in the next verse: 'Jesus himself did not baptize; his disciples did so.' His correction is undoubtedly related to his view that during Jesus' ministry the Spirit had not yet been given (7.39; cf. 20.22). Similarly in Matthew (28.19) the risen Lord commands the disciples to baptize. Baptism was closely associated with the baptism of John the Baptist – described by all four evangelists as a form of preparation for the judgement and the coming reign of God – and with it was linked the forgiveness of past sins. In Acts it is first mentioned at Pentecost, when Peter urges his hearers, 'Repent and be baptized in the name of Jesus Christ for the remission of your sins, and you will receive the gift of the Holy Spirit' (2.38).

In Luke's view there was nothing automatic about the gift of the Spirit in baptism. The Spirit could accompany baptism (Acts 9.17–18); on the other hand, the gift could be given either before baptism (10.44–8) or through the laying on of hands after it (8.16; 19.1–7).

Paul's view is a little different. He considered baptism as less significant than preaching the gospel (I Cor. 1.13–17); but the preaching led to being baptized 'by [or in] the one Spirit into the one body' (12.13). Baptism was both for the individual, who was baptized into Christ's death and died with him in order to walk in newness of life (Rom. 6.3–4) and for the group as a whole; all Christians 'put on Christ' and became sons of God (Gal. 3.26–7). The idea of baptism into Christ's death has been regarded, like that of emphasis on Christ's death in the Lord's Supper, as Paul's own interpretation, and this explanation of it may well be correct.

The further claim, however, that Paul's ideas were based upon 'pagan sacramentalism' is almost certainly wrong (although it may be suggested that even if it were correct its proponents would simply have pointed towards the catholicity of Paul's thought). On this point we may cite the words of A. D. Nock:[1]

There are fundamental differences in pagan and Christian sacraments. Pagan sacraments turn on the liberating or creating of an immortal element in the individual with a

[1] *Encyclopedia of the Social Sciences* XI 174.

view to the hereafter but with no effective change of the moral self for the purposes of living. Christian sacraments, in their earliest phase, turned entirely on corporate participation in the new order, for which all were alike unfitted by nature.

What Paul apparently did was to take isolated rites of the early communities and relate them more fully to the death and resurrection of Christ. He saw both as prefigured in the events of the Old Testament Exodus (I Cor. 10.1–6); he saw the prefigurations fulfilled in Christ. But neither of them was automatically efficacious (I Cor. 10.6–13; cf. John 3.3–8; 6.63).

As for the practice of baptism, practically nothing is said about it in the New Testament. Probably the earlier baptism in the name of the Lord Jesus was expanded into baptism in the name of Father, Son and Holy Spirit (Matt. 28.19) as the Church turned to the gentile world in which faith in the Father could hardly be taken for granted. The material of baptism is obviously water, ordinarily running water. The mode was immersion. The candidates were normally adults, though infant baptism seems to be implied by the baptism of whole households (e.g. I Cor. 1.16) and perhaps by the holiness of children being brought up in a Christian or semi-Christian family (I Cor. 7.14).

It is obvious that these practices are all based upon the existence of the Church; the Church is not based upon them. Given the existence of the Church, the way was open for extension or modification of the practices, under the guidance of the Spirit. But just as the practices are derived from the Church, so the Church is derived from the action of God in Christ. The freedom which the Church exercised in regard to its rites and other aspects of its life had to be exercised in responsibility towards the purpose of God.

Among the functions which the Church exercised was also that of 'binding and loosing', authority for which was given (according to Matthew 16.19) to Peter and, indeed, to all the disciples (18.18). In rabbinic language this expression was used in regard to making the commandments of the law more or less rigorous. We find this kind of expression employed in Matthew 5.19: 'whoever looses one of the least of these commandments shall be called least in the kingdom of heaven. But this is not the major emphasis involved in the picture of binding and loosing. To Peter, Christ gives the keys of the kingdom of heaven; whatever he binds or looses on earth will be bound or loosed in heaven. The saying in Matthew 18.18 refers to the decisions of the Church concerning the discipline of its members. In John 20.23 a similar statement follows the gift of the Holy Spirit: 'the sins you forgive are forgiven; the sins you retain are retained.' This means that the Church has a disciplinary power which is based either on a word of Christ or on the power of Christ's Spirit. To be sure, this power is not intended for continuous use. The parables of the wheat and the tares (Matt. 13.24–30) and the good and bad fish (13.47–50) show that the final judgement is reserved for the end time. But along the way some judgements were necessary.

The first example of such a judgement we find in the story of Ananias and Sapphira, whose sin is not so much that they have failed to share their possessions with the community as that they have lied against God and the Holy Spirit by keeping back part of their property while claiming to have given all of it (Acts 5.3–4, 9). The result is their sudden death. Another case occurs in I Corinthians 5, where Paul instructs the congregation to meet in Jesus' name, Paul's own spirit being present with them, and to 'deliver to Satan' a man who has been living with his stepmother – in violation of laws both Jewish (Lev. 18.7) and Roman. He regards the judgement as equivalent to the rabbinic 'extirpation', removal from the congregation and therefore from the sphere of God's protection. The offender is to be 'delivered to Satan'; his flesh will be destroyed but his spirit will finally be saved. Probably in consequence of cases like this, Paul goes on in I Corinthians 6 to give instructions for the setting up of Christian judges and Christian courts (following Jewish models). He recognizes that suits brought by Christians against Christians represent a moral failure (6.7–8), but the situation calls for a practical solution.

A different kind of situation is reflected in the letter of James. Here we find counsel of a more 'perfectionist' kind being given to the community, especially in regard to those who are sick and sinful. 'Confess your sins one to another and pray one for another, so that you may be healed' (5.16). In James there is a more literal-minded attempt to maintain the teaching of the Sermon on the Mount, and 'the rich' are regarded as non-Christian (2.1–9; 5.1–6).

We have already seen that Paul could summon the Corinthians to expel an offender from the community. But such a summons did not exhaust the scope of his authority. He had been called by the Lord 'for building up and not for tearing down' (II Cor. 10.8; 13.10). In this expression there is a parallel and a contrast with the call of the prophet Jeremiah, who was set 'over the nations and over the kingdoms, to pluck up and to break down and to destroy and to overthrow, to build and to plant' (Jer. 1.10). Paul's authority was primarily positive; he was given it so that he could build and plant (I Cor. 3.6–15).

Consideration of the authority of the Church and of the apostle Paul leads us to examine the organization of the early communities as a whole. Presumably this organization was not unlike that of the Jewish synagogues; more specifically, the Jerusalem church seems to resemble the community at Qumran. But before making comparisons we should look at the Christian tradition itself in order to see what the organization actually was. Here we find considerable differences between the rather schematic picture in Acts and the situations reflected in the Pauline epistles.

From Acts the following points are clear. (1) There was a group of twelve apostles which was so clearly defined that after the resurrection Matthias had to be chosen to replace Judas Iscariot. These twelve, under the leadership of Peter, governed the church at Jerusalem. When difficulties arose within the community, the twelve chose seven subordinates to deal with the daily distribution of food. When Philip, one of the seven, undertook evangelistic work in Samaria, two of the twelve followed him there in order to supervise his work. After the conversion of Saul, he was brought to the twelve for approval. Finally, Paul and Barnabas visited 'the apostles and the elders' at Jerusalem in order to discuss requirements for gentile converts. (2) The origin of the Jerusalem 'elders' (*presbyteroi*) is not explained, but it can perhaps be inferred from the story of the gentile mission of Barnabas and Saul. The other 'prophets and teachers' at Antioch, under the inspiration of the Holy Spirit, commissioned these two men (13.1–3), now called 'apostles' (14.14), and they appointed elders in each church which they established (14.23). At the end of Paul's ministry in Asia Minor he assembled the 'elders' of the church of Ephesus and addressed them as having been instituted as 'overseers' (*episkopoi*) to 'shepherd the Church of God' (20.17, 28). (3) There were also prophets (11.27–8; 15.32, 21.9–11).

For Luke the Church's ministry thus consists of two groups: (1) at Jerusalem the twelve apostles, the seven appointed by them, the elders (probably also appointed by the apostles), and the prophets; and (2) the prophets and teachers of Antioch, the apostles appointed by them, and the elders appointed by these apostles.

There are certain difficulties in Luke's picture. He does not, and perhaps cannot, explain who James of Jerusalem is, though he mentions him rather abruptly (12.17; 15.13; 21.18). From Paul's letters we learn that James, 'the Lord's brother' (Gal. 1.19) became an apostle (I Cor. 9.15) in the resurrection-experience. Luke does not regard a resurrection-experience as resulting in apostolic commissioning; he therefore treats Paul's Damascus vision as quite different from the resurrection of Christ (contrast I Cor. 15.8; Gal. 1.16; 2.7–8). Moreover, Luke's picture of elders as governing the various Pauline churches is quite out of harmony with what we learn from Paul's authentic letters, in which the word 'elder' never appears. We conclude that Luke has interpreted the ministry of the earliest Church in the light of his own circumstances, not those of earlier times.

In the Pauline epistles we find a situation which looks more like the result of improvisation. At Thessalonica there are leaders of the Church, but Paul gives them no titles; similarly at Corinth, Paul commends the household of Stephanas but does not call Stephanas an elder. 'Overseers' and 'deacons' occur in Philippians 1.1; the 'deaconess' Phoebe is mentioned in Romans 16.1; 'apostles of the churches' are found in II Corinthians 8.23. The Pauline letters suggest, however, that the Pauline churches were administered directly by Paul himself – partly by personal visits, partly by sending emissaries such as Titus or Apollos, partly by correspondence. For this reason we find few references to local ministers.

Instead, there is a list of functional offices in I Corinthians 12.28. 'God set in the Church first apostles, second prophets, third teachers.' Then follows a list of functions which do not involve offices: 'miracle-working, gifts of healing, assistances, governings, various kinds of ecstatic speech'. In Paul's view these functions are different from one another, and his numbering of apostles, prophets and teachers shows that these are distinct offices.

For Paul the apostles were those who were witnesses to the resurrection (I Cor. 15.5–8) and were sent out on the gospel mission. Thus Peter was a witness to the risen Lord and was entrusted with the apostolate to the circumcision (Gal. 2.8). Similarly Paul treated vision and mission as co-ordinate.

> Am I not an apostle? Have I not seen Jesus our Lord? Are you not my work in the Lord? (I Cor. 9.1)
> God was pleased to reveal his Son to me so that I might proclaim him among the gentiles (Gal. 1.16).

This means that for Paul the apostolate was a mark not of status but of mission. His apostolate came not from men or through a man but through Jesus Christ and God the Father who raised him from the dead (Gal. 1.1). It was given him for the proclamation of the gospel (I Cor. 1.17).

To be sure, not everything is clear in Paul's picture. He seems to regard Barnabas as an apostle (I Cor. 9.1–6), whereas Barnabas is differentiated from the apostles in Acts 4.36–7. But we do not know enough about Barnabas to say that he did not see the risen Lord.

As for the prophets, Paul regards their spiritual gift as potentially available to all (I Cor. 14). The prophet speaks intelligibly and produces exhortation, edification and consolation (14.3), but his speech is based upon revelation (14.30). Even though there is a prophetic office (12.28), all Christians can attain to it, for it is the gift of God. Therefore, while from Acts we learn the names of various prophets, in the Pauline epistles no names are given. Prophecy can come through anyone. The

Pauline situation thus differs from that reflected both in Acts and in the *Didache*, where certain men hold the prophetic office; in the *Didache* the local prophets are the principal ministers of the churches.

There are also teachers, but the New Testament says very little about them. The author of Hebrews tells his readers that all of them ought to have become teachers, though they have not reached this level (5.12).

A schematic picture not unlike that in Acts is to be found in the Pastoral Epistles. Here there are (1) an overseer or bishop, apparently an elder who 'rules well' (I Tim. 5.17); (2) elders or presbyters who sometimes meet as a group to lay hands on a man – indicated by prophecy? – and ordain him (I Tim. 4.14), and (3) deacons. Timothy himself, presumably as a 'ruling elder', can ordain (I Tim. 5.22), and Titus has been left in Crete to appoint elders in every city (Tit. 1.5). The origin of the imposition of hands is viewed as apostolic, for Paul himself laid hands on Timothy (II Tim. 1.6). Presumably the picture in the Pastorals reflects church life in Asia Minor and Crete during the last third of the first century.

A somewhat similar picture is set forth in the letter of Clement of Rome to the Corinthians, written in the last decade of the century. He states that the apostles 'appointed their first-fruits, testing them by the Spirit, to be bishops and deacons of those who were to believe' (42.3–4). Later the apostles 'added the codicil that if they should fall asleep other approved men should succeed to their ministry', and these approved men later appointed others (44.2–3). Here there is obviously a succession of office, function and person. It is not, however, a succession in which the Spirit is transmitted from one officer to another; the Spirit remains operative in the Church as a whole.

On the other hand, in the letters of Ignatius of Antioch, early in the second century, there is no trace of a doctrine of apostolic succession. For him the bishop, the presbytery and the deacons reflect the existence of God, Christ and the apostles; but he does not say that the bishop's appointment was apostolic in origin. Indeed, while he says that bishops 'have been appointed throughout the world' (*Eph.* 3.2), he speaks of the Philadelphian bishop as having obtained his ministry 'not from himself or through men' (1.1) – an allusion to Paul's declaration of independence in Galatians 1.1.

The basic elements of the later Catholic view of the ministry were present by the beginning of the second century, but they existed independently; they were not combined until the end of the century, as far as we know.

Were Christian ministers regarded as priests? Luke (Acts 6.7) tells us that many priests at Jerusalem 'were obedient to the faith', but their sacrificial functions presumably terminated when they were converted. Clement of Rome uses the analogy of the priest-hood to interpret the Christian ministry (40–2), but he does not call ministers priests or speak of their offering a sacrifice. Indeed, all Christians constituted a 'royal priesthood' (I Pet. 2.5; cf. Rev. 1.6), offering a constant sacrifice of praise to God (Heb. 13.15). In the new Jerusalem there would be no temple, 'for the Lord God the Almighty and the Lamb are its temple' (Rev. 21.22). Christians, as the body of Christ, are temples of the Holy Spirit. Even in the *Dialogue* (116.3) of the Roman Christian Justin (*c.* 160), Christians as a group are called 'the true high-priestly people'.

The beginning of the description of ministers as priests seems to occur in the *Didache*, where we read that Christian prophets are the high priests of the community; offerings of first-fruits are to be given them (13.3; cf. Deut. 18.4–5; Eccles 7.31–2). This is to say that the priestly motif first recurs in a document which represents the life and thought of Jewish Christianity; it also seems to underlie what Ignatius says about the bishop.[1] Though the testimony of the Apostolic Fathers cannot be neglected, we must admit that Christian priesthood is essentially, for the New Testament, the function both of Christ and of the Church as a whole, not of particular ministers.

THE LIFE OF CHRISTIANS

Life in the Church was different from life in the world, as the apostle Paul stated to the Corinthians. He had written them not to

[1] See my article in *Catholic Biblical Quarterly* (1963).

associate with fornicators, but he had to add that he meant fornicators who were inside the community; otherwise Christians would have to 'go out of the world' (I Cor. 5.9–10). He was concerned not with judging outsiders but with judging those within (5.12). Those within the Church had received from him commandments about how they 'ought to live and please God'; God's will for them required their sanctification (I Thess. 4.1–3).

In principle the Christian had died to the world. 'I have been crucified with Christ,' Paul wrote (Gal. 2.19–20), 'and it is no longer I who live; Christ lives in me. The life which I now live in the flesh, I live in faith in the Son of God who loved me and gave himself for me.' He applies this statement not to himself alone but to others as well. 'Those who belong to Christ Jesus have crucified the flesh with the passions and lusts' (Gal. 5.24). In the Christian's experience there is an 'old man' who has been put to death, a new man in principle already created ('if anyone is in Christ, he is a new creation,' II Cor. 5.17), though actually Christ may not fully have 'taken shape' in him (Gal. 4.19). The Christian lives between death and life, on the borderline between the old age and the new. The 'flesh' has been overcome; the Spirit brings forth its spontaneous fruits such as love, joy and peace (Gal. 5.22–3), and this peace is not only with men but also with God (Rom. 5.1), who has reconciled men to himself (II Cor. 5.18–19).

The Old Testament law pointed towards Christ, but with Christ's coming it is no longer binding upon Christians (Gal. 3.23–5); Christ was the end of the law because he fulfilled it and abrogated it (Rom. 10.4). The law was intended for man's good; it convicted him of sin; but only the power of Christ could deliver him from the frustration of willing one thing and doing another (Rom. 7.1–25; cf. Gal. 5.17). (For Paul's analysis of Old Testament history see the previous chapter.)

Because the law has been abrogated, the Christian has been given the gift of freedom. Is he absolutely free? On the contrary, the positive value of the old law has been summed up for him by Christ in the sentence, 'Thou shalt love thy neighbour as thyself' (Lev. 19.18; Gal. 5.14). 'Bear one another's burdens and so you will fulfil the law of Christ' (Gal. 6.2). This is to say that the old commandments against adultery, murder, theft and covetousness – and any other commandment there may be – are summed up in

the statement about love of neighbour (Rom. 13.8–10). Love of
God brings knowledge of God; love of neighbour corrects the
claims of absolute individual freedom (I Cor. 8.2ff.).

The double commandment to which Paul refers is certainly
based on the synoptic tradition of the saying of Jesus when he was
asked about the primary commandment of the law and he quoted
the *Shema* (Deut. 6.4–5) and the famous words from the holiness
code of Leviticus (19.18). Here he was in agreement with the later
rabbi Akiba, who regarded the Leviticus verse as the most
comprehensive rule in the law.[1]

According to the teaching of Jesus, love of neighbour was to be
all-inclusive, like that of God himself. 'Love your enemies and
pray for those who persecute you, so that you may become sons
of your Father in the heavens, for he makes his sun rise on the
wicked and the good, and makes it rain on the just and the
unjust' (Matt. 5.44; cf. Luke 6.35). Paul too speaks of blessing
persecutors and quotes Old Testament passages about doing good
to enemies (Rom. 12.14, 20; cf. I Cor. 4.12–13). And John also
mentions the new commandment given by Jesus to love one
another as he has loved his disciples. 'By this all will know that you
are my disciples, if you have love towards one another' (John
13.35). Just as Paul says of Jesus that 'he loved me and gave
himself for me,' so John points to the example of Christ: 'greater
love has no one than this, that a man lay down his life for his
friends' (15.13). God's love for the world is shown by his giving
his Son for believers (3.16). But Paul goes farther. God showed his
love for us in that while we were still sinners – his enemies – Christ
died for us (Rom. 5.8).

The love which men are to manifest in their dealings with one
another – love which is the first of the 'fruits of the Spirit'
(Gal. 5.22) – is the love with which God loves the world and his
Son (John 17.26); this love, Jesus prays, will be in believers. It
is the same love with which Christ loved his own to the end
(John 13.36). For those who in turn love God he works
everything for the good (Rom. 8.28). Nothing can separate
Christians from the love of Christ, the love of God which
is in Christ Jesus (Rom. 8.35, 39). This is the love described in
I Corinthians 13.

[1] G. F. Moore, *Judaism* I (Cambridge, 1927), 85.

In expressing this love the Christian must obviously dismiss distinctions based upon nationality or social circumstances. To be sure, the full implications of non-discrimination were only gradually worked out. The mission of Jesus was primarily to Israel; thus Paul calls him 'the minister to the circumcision' (Rom. 15.8) and recalls that he was 'born under the law in order to redeem those under the law' (Gal. 4.4). But already in the ministry of Jesus we see him on the borders of Tyre healing the daughter of a Syrophoenician woman (Mark 7.24–30) or in Capernaum stating to a Roman centurion that he has not found faith equal to his within Israel (Matt. 8.10; Luke 7.9). 'Many will come from the east and the west and will recline with Abraham and Isaac and Jacob in the kingdom' (Matt. 8.11; cf. Luke 13.28–9). The implications of such insights find full expression in the Pauline epistles. 'There is neither Jew nor Greek, neither slave nor free, neither male nor female; for you are all one in Christ Jesus' (Gal. 3.28; cf. Col. 3.11). 'There is no distinction between Jew and Greek, for the same one is Lord of all, enriching all who call upon him' (Rom. 10.12). Christ has broken down the middle wall separating Jew and gentile (Eph. 2.14); by implication he has broken down all similar walls.

As Paul worked out the meaning of the integrative process, he explained that it implied a temporary loss and rejection for the older people of God (Rom. 11.11–15) and a partial 'hardening' until the totality of the gentiles entered in; then all Israel would be saved (11.25–6). The special laws of the old Israel, such as circumcision and dietary regulations, were to be abandoned. On the other hand, as Paul makes clear in I Corinthians 8–10 (cf. Rom. 14.13 – 15.6), the 'emancipated' Christian still has responsibilities towards brethren who are not so emancipated. Freedom is in tension with love and with building up the community; not all rights have to be exercised at all times.

In view of the essentially social nature of the principles of Christian behaviour, we may ask what concrete expressions these principles took in the early Church. There are three areas in which concreteness might be expected: marriage and the family, private property, and the service of the state.

(1) According to the teaching of Jesus, marriage was based on the will of God as expressed in the creation story. Moses

permitted divorce only as a concession to the hard-heartedness of the people; and while separation was possible, remarriage was equivalent to adultery (Mark 10.2–12; in Matthew 19.9, cf. 5.32, the wife's infidelity provides an exception). Paul sets forth the same view in I Corinthians 7, where he deals with various marital situations in considerable detail. He discourages both divorce and marrying, the latter because of the imminence of the end and because of the obstacles which marriage places in the way of serving the Lord. In Ephesians 5.22–33, however, he treats human marriage as analogous to the union of Christ with the Church.

Paul's attitude towards married life involves a combination of traditional attitudes with new insights. From Jewish tradition he retained the view that the husband was the 'head' of his wife; the woman was created for the man, not the man for the woman (I Cor. 11.3, 8–9; cf. Gen. 2.18). Married women were not to speak in church; if they wanted to learn anything, they should ask their husbands at home (I Cor. 14.34–5). They were to be subordinate to their husbands (Col. 3.18; Eph. 5.22–4; cf. I Pet. 3.1–6). Women should wear veils while praying or prophesying (I Cor. 11.5–6, 13–16). At the same time, Paul held that in Christ there was neither male nor female; both were one in Christ Jesus (Gal. 3.28); the wife was not separate from her husband, or the husband from the wife, in the Lord (I Cor. 11.11). Therefore he says of the married couple that the husband is to pay the marital 'due' to his wife and, similarly, the wife to her husband; the wife does not have authority over her body, but her husband does; and the husband does not have authority over his body, but his wife does (I Cor. 7.3–4). This view of mutuality in marriage, which Paul bases on the couple's unity in Christ, is also expressed by Stoic writers of his time. Whatever its source may be, it marks a departure from ordinary Jewish views. Of children, Paul says that they are to obey their parents, but he adds the point that fathers are not to provoke the children (Col. 3.20–1; Eph. 5.1–4).

Like other writers of his time, Paul condemns 'the passion of lust' (I Thess. 4.4–5). Continence is preferable to marriage, while 'it is better to marry than to burn' (I Cor. 7.9). 'Dishonourable passions' are expressed in male and female homosexual acts, which Paul, like contemporary moralists, regards as 'contrary to nature' (Rom. 1.26–7). He could have said that they violate the commandment to 'increase and multiply' (Gen. 1.28), but, probably because of his eschatological situation, he never refers to this injunction.

(2) Jesus stated that one cannot serve both God and Mammon (riches; Matt. 6.24; Luke 16.13), advised against laying up treasures on earth (Matt. 6.19), told a parable about a rich fool (Luke 12.16–21), and urged a rich man to sell his possessions and give the proceeds to the poor so that he might have treasure in heaven (Mark 10.21). It is easier for a camel to go through a needle's eye than for a rich man to enter the kingdom of God (Mark 10.25). In both Luke (6.24) and James (5.1) we find 'woes' against the rich. This emphasis is completely absent both in Paul and in John. To some extent it is replaced in Paul's thought by the idea of bearing one another's burdens (Gal. 6.2), but Paul also says, in the same context, that each is to bear his own (6.5). He mentions giving and sharing only in contexts related to the collection for the Jerusalem church and to gifts made by churches for the support of the mission. In the Jerusalem church, as at Qumran, Christians were expected to give their property to the community (Acts 2.44–5; 4.32–5.11); but Paul says not a word about this practice. Instead, he insists that his converts must follow his example by working night and day; anyone who does not work is not to eat (II Thess. 3.8–10). His emphasis upon the necessity of work is quite remarkable. It may be that, having abolished works in the sphere of faith, he insists on them all the more in the sphere of daily life – though in Philippians he mentions working in regard to salvation and the resurrection of the dead (2.12–13; 3.11–14). The word 'poor' occurs only four times in his epistles, in references to the church of Jerusalem (Gal. 2.10), to the elemental spirits impoverished by Christ's victory (Gal. 4.9), to Christ who, though rich, became poor for us (II Cor. 8.49), and to the apostles who, though poor, make many rich (6.10).

(3) As for the state, Jesus recommended the payment of tribute money to Caesar (Mark 12.15), though he was falsely accused of forbidding it (Luke 23.2). According to Matthew 17.24–7 he even paid the Jewish temple tax. To be sure, his whole proclamation

concerning the kingdom of God implied a measure of insubordination to the state; but as far as the tradition tells us, the implications were not worked out. According to John 19.11 the Roman procurator's authority was given him 'from above'; similarly Paul states in Romans 13 that the existing authorities (political, according to unanimous early Christian exegesis) have been ordained by God; obedience, including the payment of taxes, is due to them.

In the Pastoral Epistles as in I Peter honour is due to the emperor, and prayer is to be offered for him (I Tim. 2.1–2). Christianity, as is made clear in Luke-Acts, is no revolutionary movement in opposition to the state. And according to John 18.36 Jesus' kingdom is 'not of this world'.

But while Christianity was not a revolutionary movement, it was not counter-revolutionary either. In I Peter 4.16 it is clearly possible to suffer persecution from the state as a Christian; in Revelation the possibility is an actuality. For this reason the disciple John violently attacks Rome under the guise of Babylon and exults over her fall, which he can already see beginning. Christians refuse to worship the image of the beast; they can make no compromise with a self-deifying state. All they can hope for is a new heaven and a new earth and the descent of a new Jerusalem from heaven.

The inclusion of both Romans and Revelation in the canon means that the Church could never commit itself wholly to any particular social system or to any state. Under various circumstances the Church could approve a system or denounce it; but the approval could not be final or complete. Revelation relativizes the Church's relation to any state.

If we now return to the cardinal principle of all-inclusive love, we find that its application is presumably relativized by considerations such as those we have just mentioned. A great deal depends upon the circumstances. For instance, though Paul says that in Christ there is neither male nor female (Gal. 3.28), in dealing with the Corinthians he believed it necessary to state that wives were to be subordinate to husbands (I Cor. 11.3, modified in 11.11–12), and that women were not to speak in church (14.34–5). Again, very little is said about justice in the New Testament. Paul rebukes the Corinthians for seeking justice in pagan courts, states that they have already suffered a loss by bringing suits against one another (it would be better to be treated unjustly or defrauded), and recommends the establishment of Church courts (I Cor. 6.1–11). It is doubtful that this kind of counsel was intended for universal application (yet see Matt. 18.15–17).

The relative nature of early Christian ethics seems clearly evident in relation to the institution of slavery. Jesus accepted it without question. Paul used it as a model for the relation of the Christian to Christ and, practically, urged slaves to obey their masters while reminding masters of their obligations to slaves (Col. 3.22–4.1; Eph 6.5–9). It is hard to tell whether or not Paul wanted individual slaves to become freedmen. A verse which could point towards emancipation (I Cor. 7.21) seems, in view of its context, to recommend remaining in slavery; and Paul's hope that Philemon will do 'more' than Paul asks in accepting the runaway Onesimus (Philemon 21) does not necessarily imply freeing him. Slavery is a part of Paul's world (see also I Peter 2.18–20). He has no idea of changing it.

If, then, the heart of early Christian behaviour lies in the motivation given by love, within the community and outside it, we must ask to what extent this love is itself conditioned and perhaps relativized by the eschatological context of early Christian thought. Paul's discussion of love in I Corinthians 13 suggests that he did not regard it as eschatologically conditioned. Prophecies, ecstatic speech and 'knowledge' will be superseded, while faith, hope and love will last; and love is the greatest of the three. Again, since early Christian eschatology is not purely futurist but has its roots in the present, it is the love which already finds expression in action which will continue on. Circumstances vary, but the gospel of love remains the same – end of the world or world without end.

THE HISTORY OF GOD'S ACTS IN PAUL AND JOHN

We have already seen, in dealing with the question of New Testament ethics, that the problem of eschatology arises in a fairly acute form. To what extent are the minds of the New Testament writers conditioned by eschatology? What are their

views of their historical situation in the sequence of God's acts?
In order to determine the extent of the conditioning we must first
ask what their eschatological ideas really were. Now following the
approach which we have previously employed we must continue
to insist that we cannot speak of New Testament eschatology as
purely futurist in direction; we cannot speak of Jesus as one who
simply proclaimed the imminent advent of God's reign. On the
other hand, we cannot say that he announced nothing but the
realization of eschatology, as if the possibilities of God's action
were exhausted in his mission or even in the creation of the
Church. Both aspects, it would appear, were present in his
proclamation. On the one hand, his mission, with all that it
involved, was the inauguration and the incipient realization of
God's reign. On the other, there was still more to come, and this
'more' is expressed in the Lord's prayer, 'Thy kingdom come,'
in the promise of the Spirit, and in the expectation of the future
coming of the Son of Man. The kingdom of God is not fully
made actual in the Church; to quote from the *Didache* once more,
Christians pray to God to gather the Church into the kingdom.

The attitude of Jesus is not fully comparable, then, to that of
his Jewish contemporaries who spoke of 'this age', the present
one, and 'that age', the age to come. In the mission of Jesus the
present age was already giving way to the future age of God; as
he drove out demons the kingdom was incipiently present and
Satan had already fallen like lightning from heaven.

But in the teaching of Jesus there is no fully developed interpretation of the past of Israel in relation to present and future.
At most, we encounter the hint of such an interpretation in his
remarks about the divine plan in creation, where it is stated that
Adam and Eve were to become, and did become, 'one flesh',
and that the divine plan was modified by Moses when he
permitted divorce (Mark 10.1–12). What God has yoked together,
a man must not separate. If we take these words seriously, we
see that the man involved must be Moses; the time of Moses must
be one in which men's hearts were hardened. But this criticism
does not apply to everything Moses said. Some of his words were
obviously expressions of the commandments of God – for example,
'Honour thy father and thy mother' (Mark 7.10) and other
commandments of the decalogue (Mark 10.19), as well as the

Shema and the command to love one's neighbour (Mark 12.29–31). Generally speaking, Jesus criticized the traditions of men (presumably including the words of Moses in Deuteronomy 24.1) as erroneous and misleading additions to the true law of God. On this basis we can probably proceed to say that in Jesus' view there was a pre-traditional period, a traditional period of human corruption, and the age to come, already breaking in – and restoring the authentic plan of God. During the traditional period the prophets (including David, Mark 2.25; 12.35–7) were given insight into what was to come.

Something not unlike this picture is to be found in the Pauline epistles, and it underlies much of what Paul has to say about the human situation. At the beginning and the end of the history of God's people stands God the creator, he who is the source and origin of creative activity (I Cor. 8.6) and of the new creation; both works of creation were and are effected through Christ. Paul refers what is said of 'man' in the first creation story in Genesis to Christ, who is at once the Wisdom-image of God through which creation was made and the created image of God mentioned in Genesis 1.26. But he does not speak of Christ the image of God as man. He goes ahead to the second creation story in order to find there the one whom he calls 'the first man', the man of earth (I Cor. 15.47). He calls Christ, the 'man from heaven', the second because he is thinking of eschatology, not of history or of *Vorgeschichte*. We have borne Adam's image (I Cor. 15.49) because, according to Genesis 5.3, Adam begat sons after his own image.

The most significant observations about Adam are to be found in Romans 5. Adam's sin of disobedience to God was imitated by his descendants, but the penalty of death which was given him affected even those who did not, like him, sin. Because of his transgression all his descendants died.

Even before Adam's sin (and Eve's), the later human situation was depicted in the second creation story. According to I Corinthians 11, man, not woman, is 'the image and glory of God'; apparently Paul has Genesis 5.1 in mind, where the mortal Adam is described as made in God's image. Paul insists that woman is to be subordinate to man, for she was made from man and for man (Gen. 2.18–22). Yet 'in the Lord' woman is not entirely apart from man or man apart from woman, for the human situation points beyond itself to an original and an eschatological mutuality. While woman is from man, man is born 'through the woman' and ultimately all things are from God. With this we may compare Galatians 3.18; in Christ there is . . . neither male nor female. Though at the fall Eve was deceived by the serpent and was no longer a 'pure virgin' (II Cor. 11.2–3), in the restoration effected by Christ husbands are to love their wives as themselves and as Christ loved the Church; thus the prophecy of Adam about the two becoming one flesh will be fulfilled (Eph. 5.25–33).

A somewhat different way of depicting the primeval history is found in Romans 1.19–32, perhaps because the material comes from a homily explaining the wrath of God to gentiles. God made himself known to all 'from the creation of the world'; men were once aware of his eternal power and deity; they knew God. But they turned aside to worship the creation instead of the Creator, and as a penalty God delivered them to 'uncleanness', to 'dishonourable passions', and to 'an unsuitable mind' (1.24, 26, 28). Such men and women are 'worthy of death' (1.32), as are those who look favourably on them. The analogy of this account with that in Romans 5 is obvious; whether man's sin consisted of disobedience or of idolatry, it was an affront to God, the source of his being, and death resulted.

In the midst of the reign of death God did not leave himself without witness. 'Abraham believed God, and it was accounted to him as righteousness' (Gen. 15.6; Gal. 3.6; Rom. 4.4). The story of Abraham shows that God requires faith, not obedience to a legal code, for he was called by God when he was not circumcised. Moreover, a promise was given him, that he would be the father of many nations; the promise was given to him and to his descendants, and his true descendant was the Christ who was to come. Indeed, imaginatively (that is to say, allegorically) one can find even more in the story of Abraham. He had two wives, one slave, one free. The children of the slave girl Hagar correspond to the children of the present Jerusalem; the children of Sarah resemble Isaac, her son, who is like Christ. The promise of God, given to a people yet to come, was not annulled by a law which was added 430 years later as a mere codicil (Gal. 3.17).

Yet the law was given. Why was it given? According to Galatians 3.19 it 'was ordained because of transgressions, until the coming of the seed to which the promise had been given; it was enjoined through angels by the hand of a mediator.' The words we have translated 'because of' are ambiguous and may well mean 'for the sake of'. Romans 4.15 states that 'where there is no law, there is no transgression.' Thus there was a commandment not to covet; the commandment was holy and just and good, but sin seized the opportunity to produce covetousness and other kinds of lawless desire. Sin perverted the good. Therefore, as good, the law presumably was laid down because of transgressions or in order to prevent them; but as the occasion of sin, it was laid down with the result that it multiplied transgressions. 'The law locked up everything under sin so that the promise based on faith in Christ Jesus might be given to believers' (Gal. 3.22). It had a temporary goal, and it was nullified with the death of Christ.

Paul explains this nullification in relation to two passages in Deuteronomy. First, a curse was laid upon everyone who did not perform all the commandments in the legal code (Deut. 27.26). He does not deny the possibility of such legal observance (cf. Phil. 3.6), but he does state that legal observance could not produce righteousness, for righteousness comes from faith (Hab. 2.4). It would appear that for his argument, however, the notion that most people could not observe the law is required, for he assumes that the curse had to be taken away. It was taken away because in Deuteronomy 21.23 a curse was also laid upon anyone who 'was hanged on a tree'. This curse was assumed by Christ (Gal. 3.10–14).

It is obvious that in Paul's view the effect of the Mosaic law was largely bad, whether the law was bad or not. This is the problem to which he devotes much of Galatians and Romans. On the other hand, in II Corinthians he tries to explain that the true meaning of the law was misunderstood by the Jews, and he makes use of a passage in Exodus 34.33–5 according to which Moses placed a veil on his face – a veil taken away whenever a man turned towards the Lord. Christians behold the glory of the Lord with unveiled faces.

Paul's emphasis upon the problem of the law prevents him from making much of the Exodus, but this motif is present in his letters, especially I Corinthians. There he expressly identifies

Christ with the paschal lamb and urges Christians to keep the true, spiritual Passover (5.7–8). Again, he compares the crossing of the sea and the guidance by a pillar of cloud with Christian baptism, and finds prefigurations of the Lord's Supper in the gift of manna and the water from the rock. Indeed, the whole period of wandering in the desert provides a prefigurative warning to Christians who may assume that baptism and the Eucharist work automatically or finally. Some of the Israelites in the desert were idolaters; some committed fornication; some tested the Lord. Such men suffered penalties given by God or his destroying angel (10.1–11). But Paul's emphasis on the Exodus is of minor importance compared with his emphasis upon the promise to Abraham. In part, as we have suggested, this is due to his concern for the rôle of Moses not as leader but as legislator. In part it is also due to the importance of the work of Christ, far superior to that of Moses.

In the period from Moses to Christ, then, men were under a curse, under sin, under death. Sin worked through the flesh, with the result that the law, even though potentially good, was not actually good. As for the gentiles, they were slaves of gods who actually have no existence; they served the elemental spirits (later, through Christ's work, weak and impoverished). Both Jews and gentiles lived by a calendar of days, months, seasons and years (Gal. 4.8–10).

Finally God sent his Son, 'born of a woman, born under the law, in order to redeem those under the law, so that we might receive adoption' (Gal. 4.4–5). Christ took the curse of the law upon himself; he became a 'curse' for us. He 'became sin' for our sake (II Cor. 5.21). He delivers us from the wrath to come (I Thess. 1.10). Christ reconciles us to God (Rom. 5; II Cor. 5); he triumphs over death (I Cor. 15). All have sinned and fallen short of the glory of God, but God has forgiven all because of the sacrifice of Christ, who died for sinners. To be baptized into his death means dying with him and in principle rising with him, though our final resurrection is yet to come. It means receiving a new life in which the Spirit of God becomes the guiding force.

This is to say that Christ undid or reversed the work of Adam by obeying God instead of disobeying him; he fulfilled the promise made to Abraham; and he nullified the evil effects of the law of Moses.

But while Christ's victory has already taken place, there is still more to come. We are children of God and heirs of God, joint heirs with Christ; sufferings in the present age are insignificant when compared with future glory (Rom. 8.17ff.). We live on the borderline between the two ages, and Paul can speak either of what has already been done or of what will be done. Apparently there are more sufferings yet to come, but ultimately Christ will absolutely overcome whatever in the cosmos is hostile to God, and God will be everything to everyone (I Cor. 15.25–8). The end is not yet; something – perhaps the Roman state – is restraining the powers of lawlessness and preventing the final conflict (II Thess. 2.7); but the Christian knows that final victory is certain.

This framework and foundation of Paul's thought can be called eschatological history. In many respects it resembles contemporary Jewish eschatological histories, but the difference between it and them lies simply in the fact that for Paul the Christ has already come and the messianic age has already begun. There is a shift of emphasis from something exclusively or at least largely future to something in which the present already represents and is the future. The new creation has already taken place, though it is still to be fully realized in the future.

But we must avoid limiting the range of Paul's thought simply to the historical or even the eschatological. His thought goes beyond the historical; it has dimensions both cosmic and personal. For example, the personal ('outer man', 'inner man') is combined with the cosmic in II Corinthians 4.16–18, which concludes with the words, 'not looking at what is seen but at what is not seen; for what is seen is temporary, while what is not seen is eternal'. Or again (Col. 3.1–4),

If then you have been raised with Christ, seek things above, where Christ is, seated at the right hand of God; think of things above, not of things on earth. For you have died, and your life is hidden with Christ in God; when Christ is manifested, then you too will be manifested in glory with him.

The various motifs are combined, and the eschatological is blended with the cosmic and the personal.

For this reason it is not a complete surprise when we find a similar blending in the Gospel of John. The eschatological is certainly present in John, and so is the emphasis on the premonitions of eschatology in the Old Testament. Abraham rejoiced to see the day of Christ (John 8.56), presumably because he had been promised that Isaac would be born (Gen. 17.17). The law was given through Moses, but Moses performed symbolic actions pointing towards Christ and actually wrote about him (John 1.17; 3.14; 5.46). Isaiah beheld Christ's glory and spoke of him (12.41). But in John's writing the eschatological is to a considerable extent subordinated to the cosmic and personal. Jesus is the incarnation of the creative Word of God which expressed itself as light and life. He came down from heaven (3.13) or 'from above'. His resurrection was his exaltation; his being 'lifted up' took place so that he might draw all men to himself. Finally he ascended into heaven in order to show men the way and to prepare a place for them. This is to say that the cosmic is emphasized rather more strongly than it is in Paul's writings. Moreover, the emphasis on personal decision and the 'present' nature of decision and its consequences is equally strong. 'He who hears my word and believes him who sent me *has* eternal life and does not come to judgement but *has passed* from death to life' (5.24; cf. 11.25–6). To be sure, the future is not completely dismissed (unless we regard 'futurist' passages as interpolations), but John's stress is laid on the present. To overstate the situation somewhat, the essential Pauline contrast between past and present/future is replaced by emphasis on the present, and while Paul's scheme is primarily historical/eschatological John's is cosmic/personal. This is an overstatement, however, since all these elements are to be found in both writers. For both, what matters is that Christ has come, that the Spirit has been given, and that there is more yet to come. Both understand the past and the future in the light of Christ's crucifixion and resurrection.

Conclusion

Now we have reached the end of our introduction to the New Testament. We have tried to follow a method which, in our opinion, is likely to produce relatively verifiable conclusions in relation to the documents we actually possess. This method is not the only one there is, nor is it the only one which can be applied to the materials. Its principal virtue is that it proceeds from the known to the unknown, beginning with the texts we have and proceeding to a literary analysis of them, then to historical analyses and syntheses. In the last section we come close to New Testament theology, which in our judgement is a branch of historical theology, that study of the historical manifestations of the Church's faith which lies on the borderline between church history and systematic theology. We have dealt only indirectly with New Testament theology because our aim has been primarily historical, and because to deal with the subject would require another volume.

We should perhaps set forth somewhat more fully how we regard our conclusions. This book is incomplete, as already stated, because it does not contain a full treatment of New Testament theology. It is also incomplete because the history to which it has led does not continue into the writings of the Apostolic Fathers and the Apologists and Irenaeus, to mention no others. The Christian tradition looks back to the life, death and resurrection of Jesus – the period of the Incarnation – and to the missionary work of Peter and Paul and the other disciples – the apostolic age. But the tradition, which provides the essential subject matter of church history, does not end with the deaths of the apostles. It continues into the second century, and beyond. For the Christian religion the time of Jesus and his apostles is always primary; it was then that Christianity came into existence; and the records related to this time are therefore also primary. But the records point beyond themselves (1) back to Jesus and his disciples and what they did and said, and (2) forward to the living communities of believers in and for which the records were written and preserved. The records are less important than that which they record and reflect. Of them may be used the Pauline expression, 'We have this treasure in earthen vessels, to show that the transcendent power belongs to God and not to us' (II Cor. 4.7, RSV). By analogy the treasure is the gospel; the earthen vessels are the gospels and the rest of the New Testament literature.

Moreover, if the conclusions of Helmut Koester are correct – that the earlier Apostolic Fathers made use of oral tradition, not of the written gospels – these Fathers are just as reliable witnesses to the early tradition as the synoptic evangelists are. This is to say that the distinction between scripture and tradition is an artificial one. The gospels represent the crystallization of tradition in various forms; the earliest Fathers reflect the same kind of process either at the same time or only a little later. Not only can one not draw too sharp a distinction between scripture and tradition, but also one cannot differentiate too distinctly the writings of the New Testament and the writings of the Fathers, at least the earlier ones. Naturally it is possible for the tradition to become corrupted, but the criteria of corruption are more easily stated than applied. If one supposes that the 'Hellenization' of Christianity involved its corruption, then one must ask what the difference is between corruption and meaningful proclamation, and one must also ask what Paul meant when he said, 'I have become all things to all men, that I might by all means save some' (I Cor. 9.22).

This is to say that we regard New Testament literature as the beginning of Christian literature, New Testament history as the beginning of church history, and New Testament theology as the beginning of Christian theology. The New Testament cannot be separated from the life and thought of the Church. It reflects the beginning of the Church's existence, but this existence is a continuous one which did not come to an end with the apostolic age. It has a classical significance, but there is no reason to suppose that God's revelation is limited to the pages of the Old and New Testament or even to the events therein described. There are New Testament passages, as E. Stauffer has pointed out, which look beyond the time of the New Testament itself and speak of the continuing revelation of and by the Holy Spirit. There is more to write of Jesus than is contained in the gospels; Jesus has more to say to his disciples than they can hear now; and therefore Jesus has entrusted the Spirit to the Church, and he will lead Christians into all the truth of Christ.

Additional Note

THE ESTABLISHMENT OF NEW TESTAMENT CHRONOLOGY

In dealing with historical method we have already insisted upon the importance of chronology as the backbone of historical understanding. But when we try to discover the chronology of the New Testament we encounter considerable difficulties. The New Testament writers were not as much concerned with chronology as we are, or as Christian writers since the middle of the second century have been. Indeed, the only real date provided in the New Testament is that which Luke gives for the coming of the Word of God to John the Baptist (Luke 3.1–2).

> In the fifteenth year of the reign of Tiberius Caesar, when Pontius Pilate was governing Judaea, Herod was tetrarch of Galilee, his brother Philip was tetrarch of the Ituraean and Trachonitic region, and Lysanias was tetrarch of Abilene, under the high priest Annas and Caiaphas. . . .

The reign of Tiberius began at the death of his predecessor Augustus on August 19th, A.D. 14, and his fifteenth year therefore ran from August, A.D. 28, to August, A.D. 29. This year fell in the period when Pontius Pilate was procurator of Judaea (A.D. 26–36), Herod Antipas was tetrarch of Galilee and Peraea (4 B.C.–A.D. 39), and Herod Philip was tetrarch to the northeast (4 B.C.–A.D. 34). The period of Lysanias' rule is not precisely dateable, but it is irrelevant for the chronological scheme. Annas had been high priest from A.D. 6 to 18, when he was succeeded by his son-in-law Caiaphas (18–37); both are mentioned because Annas, whose five sons also held the office of high priest, remained extremely influential (cf. Acts 4.6; John 18.13).

The year 28–29 is therefore probably the year in which John's mission began.

Other dates are less well established. According to Matthew

2.1, Jesus was born 'in the days of king Herod', and Herod's order for the killing of children at Bethlehem who were two years old or less (2.16) suggests that Matthew regards the birth as having taken place at least two years before Herod's death (4 B.C.). Luke too mentions 'the days of king Herod' (1.5) but associates the birth of Jesus with the taking of a census in the Roman empire. 'This census first took place when Quirinius was governing Syria' (2.2), at the time when Judas of Galilee led an insurrection (Acts 5.37). Such a census, as Josephus makes plain, was made necessary when Judaea was placed under Roman procurators in A.D. 6. While Quirinius was in Syria during the period 10–7 B.C., he was not then governor of Syria and there is no record of a census at that time. It is possible that there was an earlier census, but unlikely that Roman tax officials could have taken one in Herod's kingdom. Apparently Luke has combined two traditions, one which, as in Matthew, placed the birth of Jesus before 4 B.C., the other which placed his birth in A.D. 6. His statement that at the beginning of Jesus' ministry he was 'about thirty years old' (3.23), suggests that he favoured the former view.

The precise length of Jesus' ministry cannot be determined from the gospel materials, though the rôle of Pontius Pilate in the crucifixion proves that Jesus was crucified before A.D. 36. Moreover, the chronology of Paul's life (see pages 378 ff.) suggests that the crucifixion took place before A.D. 32. It is remarkable, but true, that we encounter no attempt to give a precise date for the crucifixion before the end of the second century. Justin Martyr, writing about A.D. 150, says that Jesus' ministry took place about 150 years earlier. This date does not give us much help.

One of the most important dates in the first century, and one which we might hope would be of assistance in determining the dates of various New Testament materials, is that of the destruction of the temple, A.D. 70. Unfortunately this date does not provide as much help as we should wish to have. (1) In the past, some gospel materials (and therefore the gospels containing the materials) have been related to the destruction of the temple in the belief that they look back to it. (a) Luke 21.20–4 speaks rather precisely about a siege of Jerusalem, which will be surrounded by troops and captured. The passage seems to be a later development based on Mark 13.14–18, and scholars have therefore sometimes regarded it as a prophecy based on the event. C. H. Dodd, however, has argued that while details of the prediction in Mark are based on the book of Daniel, those in Luke are based on prophetic descriptions of the capture of Jerusalem in 586 B.C.; the differences are due to variations in apocalyptic style, not necessarily to chronological considerations. The passage in Luke, therefore, was not necessarily written after 70. (*b*) In John 4.21 Jesus says to the Samaritan woman, 'The hour is coming when neither on this mountain nor in Jerusalem will you worship the Father.' It has been supposed that this prediction is based upon the destruction of the temple; but the point of the statement is not that the temple will be destroyed but that true worship is not a matter of location. True worship is that conducted 'in spirit and truth' (4.23). Therefore this passage does not necessarily have anything to do with the events of A.D. 70. The considerations involved are theological, not chronological.

(2) An effort has also been made to show that the Epistle to the Hebrews must have been written while the temple was still standing, for its author speaks of the work of the earthly high priest as still being performed (e.g. 5.1; 8.3; especially 10.1–2). This argument too encounters difficulties. (*a*) Writers discussing the temple and its rites use the present tense even though they are writing long after A.D. 70. As examples we may cite (1) Josephus, (2) the author of I Clement, and (3) the collectors of the traditions contained in the Mishnah. (*b*) It is not absolutely certain that the temple was completely destroyed or that the rites came to an end. K. W. Clark has assembled evidence to show that the ceremonies continued to be performed well after A.D. 70. Therefore the use of the present tense in references to the existence of the temple or to its rites does not prove that the document in which such references occur was written either before or after 70.

On the other hand, there *are* some chronological anchors in the apostolic age, three of which may be mentioned here. (1) According to Josephus, Herod Agrippa I was made ruler of all Palestine by Claudius early in A.D. 41, and reigned for three more years.

His death, described in Acts, therefore took place in 44. (2) The famine in Claudius's reign mentioned in Acts 11.28 took place when Tiberius Alexander was procurator of Judaea, towards the end of the period 44–48; Egyptian papyri showing that the price of wheat was very high suggest that the famine began in 46 (K. S. Gapp in *Harvard Theological Review*, 1935). (3) An inscription found at Delphi gives a date for Gallio, proconsul of Achaea when Paul was at Corinth. It mentions his proconsulship and correlates it with 'Claudius being Imperator for the twenty-sixth time'. Claudius was hailed as Imperator for the twenty-third and twenty-fourth times in the year 51 and for the twenty-seventh time not later than August 1st, 52. The twenty-sixth time, and Gallio's term of office (probably a year), are therefore to be dated either in 51 or in 52.

INDEX

Index

Index

Index

Index

Also in the Fontana Theology and Philosophy Series

Luther

GERHARD EBELING

'On reading this book one recovers a sense that theology is about what really matters . . . Although it is a deeply serious book it is very readable and deserves a wide public.'
A. D. Galloway, Glasgow Herald

Erasmus of Christendom

ROLAND H. BAINTON

'In this book, which carries lightly and easily the massive Erasmian scholarship of the last half-century, Erasmus comes to life. He speaks for himself and, speaking, reveals himself.'
Hugh Trevor-Roper, Sunday Times

Calvin

FRANCOIS WENDEL

'This is the best introduction to Calvin and his theology that has been written, and it is a work of scholarship which one salutes and admires.'
Professor Gordon Rupp

The Religious Experience of Mankind

NINIAN SMART

In this study of great world religions the author shows that religions grow and change and affect each other just as living organisms do. He points out that one cannot understand human history without knowing something about man's religion.